A HISTORY OF
ANCIENT GREECE
IN ITS MEDITERRANEAN CONTEXT

A HISTORY OF ANCIENT GREECE
IN ITS MEDITERRANEAN CONTEXT

Nancy Demand
Indiana University

2006
SLOAN PUBLISHING
Cornwall-on-Hudson, NY 12520

Library of Congress Control Number: 2005938215

Demand, Nancy
    A History of Ancient Greece in its Mediterranean Context / Nancy Demand.
        p.   cm.
    Includes index.
    ISBN 1-59738-003-2

Cover designer: Amy Rosen

© 2006
Sloan Publishing, LLC
220 Maple Road
Cornwall-on-Hudson, NY 12520

First edition published in 1996 by McGraw-Hill under
the title A HISTORY OF ANCIENT GREECE

Printed in Canada
10 9 8 7 6 5 4 3 2 1

ISBN 1-59738-003-2

For Erhart

ABOUT THE AUTHOR

Nancy Demand is an emeritus professor of Greek history at Indiana University, Bloomington, Indiana. She received a Ph.D. in Philosophy from the University of Pennsylvania in 1965, an M.A. in Greek from the University of Vermont in 1973, and a Ph.D. in Greek from Bryn Mawr in 1978. She has taught at Trenton State College, Ohio State University, and from 1979 to 2002, in the Department of History at Indiana, where she was a full professor. She has published numerous articles and reviews, and three books: *Thebes in the Fifth Century, Urban Relocation in Archaic and Classical Greece,* and *Birth, Death and Motherhood in Classical Greece,* for which she received a Fellowship from the National Endowment for the Humanities in 1990-1991. She is currently writing a book on the Mediterranean context of the rise of the Greek city-state.

TABLE OF CONTENTS

LIST OF MAPS

PREFACE

A NEW VIEW OF GREEK HISTORY: GREECE IN ITS MEDITERRANEAN CONTEXT

Since the publication of the first edition of this book in 1996, a paradigm shift has taken place in the field of ancient Greek history. New evidence, much of it archaeological, coming not only from Greece, but from Greece's contemporary neighbors in the Mediterranean, has shown that Greek civilization was not an isolated miracle that sprang up to shed its influence on other, lesser cultures, as was once thought. Rather, it was one of a number of very similar Mediterranean societies that developed as a result of mutual interactions within a shared world of maritime interconnections.

The conception of Greek history as essentially a part of the Mediterranean cultural context has made necessary a substantial revision in the second edition of this book. This is especially the case in the discussion of the so-called "Dark Age" of the first centuries of the Common Era, which is now recognized to have been a very active period and far from dark. During this formative period, which saw the origin and early development of the Greek city-state (*polis*), Greek culture was shaped by interactions in a common cultural matrix that also involved the Cypriots, Phoenicians, Sardinians, and Italians. The ramifications of the new Mediterranean perspective extend, however, to all periods of Greek history, and led me to the second major change in the new edition–the addition of a chapter on Hellenistic history. The result is essentially a new book that presents the history of Greece in its Mediterranean context.

PEDAGOGICAL FEATURES, OLD AND NEW

The new edition continues the focus of the first edition on primary source material, both archaeological and literary-historical, with heavy reliance on the works of Herodotus,

Thucydides, Aristophanes, and Arrian for the Classical period. The Source Analyses assume that students have their own copies of these texts, but provide the texts for other sources. The book covers social and cultural issues, as well as political and military events, and follows the first edition in making suggestions for map study. Four new maps are included: a map of both Greek and Phoenician overseas settlements that portrays the situation more accurately than the earlier map of Greek Colonization, a new map of Sparta and the Peloponnesus, and two maps of the Hellenistic period. Blank maps are still included at the back of the book, and map identifications are suggested at the end of each chapter.

Each chapter contains numerous endnotes that will lead students to supporting materials or to discussions of underlying historical issues that can serve as a basis of student research papers. In addition, an important new pedagogical feature is the inclusion of many references and study suggestions that make use of websites. Such sites offer a wealth of visual and other information to students in an easily accessed form, and they often provide interactive features impossible to obtain in textbook illustrations—examples are sites that let the student "walk around" the sculptures of the Parthenon frieze and investigate the Ulu Burun shipwreck. The websites are chosen for their academic merit, and they will be kept up to date on the Course Web Site maintained by Sloan Publishing at http://www.sloanpublishing.com/demand.

A note on the spelling of Greek names is necessary in any book dealing with Greek history. The problem arises from the need to transliterate Greek words. For a long period of time this was done by scholars who adopted Latinized forms, and many names became quite familiar in that form (Greek kappas became c's, ai became æ, final -oς became -us, etc.). More recently, however, it has become popular to transliterate directly from the Greek original. Often, however, this results in familiar names taking on a new and (to us) odd-looking form—for example, "Aeschylus" becomes "Aischylos," "Pericles" becomes "Perikles." How much of this any given scholar is willing to engage in varies widely. There really seems no possibility of reaching complete consistency. As a result, most historians keep some Latinized forms that seem too familiar to change, and adopt Greek transliteration for the rest. Thus students will find that names vary in their spelling in different books, and at times different spelling even occur within a single book (when quotations are used that employ a different system).

SOME BIBLIOGRAPHY ON THE MEDITERRANEAN CONTEXT OF GREEK HISTORY

Bartoloni, G. (1991), "Populonia: Characteristic Features of a Port Community in Italy During the First Iron Age," pp. 101–116 in *Papers of the Fourth Conference of Italian Archaeology: The Archaeology of Power, Part 2.*, ed. E. Herring, R. Whitehouse, and J. Wilkins.

Bietti Sestieri, A. M. (1997), "Italy in Europe in the Early Iron Age," *Proceedings of the Prehistoric Society* 63:371–402.

Crielaard, J. P. (1998), "Surfing on the Mediterranean Web: Cypriot Long-distance Communications During the Eleventh and Tenth Centuries B.C.," pp. 187–206 in *Eastern Mediterranean: Cy-*

prus-Dodecanese-Crete 16th-6th Century B.C.: Proceedings of the International Symposium, Rethymnon 13–16 May, 1997., ed. V. Karageorghis and N. Stampolidis.

Coldstream, J. N. (1994), "Prospectors and Pioneers: Pithekoussai, Kyme and Central Italy." pp. 47–59 in *The Archaeology of Greek Colonisation*, ed. G. R. Tsetskhladze and F. De Angelis, esp. 47, 49;

De Angelis, Franco. 1994. "The Foundation of Selinous: Overpopulation or Opportunities?" pp. 87–110 in *The Archaeology of Greek Colonisation*, ed. G. R. Tsetskhladze and F. De Angelis.

D'Agostino, B. (1996), "Pithekoussai and the First Western Greeks," *Journal of Roman Archaeology* 9:302–309.

Giardino, Claudio (1992), "Nuragic Sardinia and the Mediterranean Metallurgy and Maritime Traffic," pp. 304-315 in *Sardinia in the Mediterranean : A Footprint in the Sea: Studies in Sardinian Archaeology Presented to Miriam S. Balmuth*, ed. Robert H. Tykot and Tamsey K. Andrews.

Giardino, Claudio. (1995), *Il Mediterraneo Occidentale fra XIV ed VII secolo a.C. : Cerchie minerarie e metallurgiche = The West Mediterranean Between the 14th and 8th Centuries B.C.*

Guidi, Alessandro (1998), ""The Emergence of the State in Central and Northern Italy." *Acta Archaeologica* 69:139–161.

Lo Schiavo, F., E. MacNamara and L. Vagnetti (1985), "Late Cypriot Imports to Italy and Their Influence on Local Bronzework." *Papers of the British School at Rome* 53: 1–71.

Lo Schiavo, F. (1995), "Cyprus and Sardinia in the Mediterranean Trade Routes Toward the West," pp. 45–60 in *Cyprus and the Sea. Proceedings of the International Symposium (Nicosia 1993)*, ed. V. Karageorghis and D. Michaelides.

Lo Schiavo, F. (2001), "Late Cypriot Bronzework and Bronze Workers in Sardinia, Italy and Elsewhere in the World,." pp. 131–152 in *Italy and Cyprus in Antiquity: 1500–450 BC: Proceedings of an International Symposium Held at the Italian Academy for Advanced Studies in America at Columbia University, November 16–18, 2000*, ed. L. Bonfante, and V .Karageorghi.

Mederos Martín, A. (1996), "La Conexión Levantino-Chipriota. Indicios de Comercio Atlántico con el Mediterráneo Oriental durante el Bronce Final (1150–950 AC)." *Trabajos de Prehistoria* 53:95–115.

Morris, Sarah. (1992), " Greece between East and West: Perspectives and Prospects," pp. xiii–xviii in *Greece between East and West: 10th–8th Centuries BC*, ed. G. Kopcke and I. Tokumaru.

Morris, Sarah (1992), *Daidalos and the Origins of Greek Art*.

Osborne, Robin (1996), *Greece in the Making, 1200–479 B.C.*:104–129.

Pacciarelli, Marco (2000), *Dal Villaggio alla Città. La svolta protourbana del 1000 a.C. nell'Italia tirrenica*.

Popham, M. R. and I. S. Lemos (1995), "A Euboean Warrior Trader," *OJA* 14:151–157.

Purcell, Nicholas (1990), "Mobility and the Polis," pp. 29–58 in *The Greek City from Homer to Alexander*, ed. Oswyn Murray and Simon Price.

ACKNOWLEDGEMENTS

I am very much indebted to the many suggestions made by users of the first editiona s well as those made by my colleagues who heard some of these ideas in papers that I presented at a variety of scholarly conferences; some who have been especially helpful have been Walter Donlan, Carol Thomas, Franco De Angelis, and Kurt Raaflaub. Roger Travis provided many helpful ideas as a reviewer of the first edition. I also want to thank the copy editor Serena Hoffman, cover designer Amy Rosen, and, most especially, Bill Webber of Sloan Publishing, who encouraged me to publish this new edition and has provided continuing support and assistance, especially in the often-difficult task of obtaining the many permissions required for the illustrations. The translations are my own. Finally, I want to thank my husband, without whose patience and support the whole project would not have been possible.

I am very grateful to the organizations and individuals named below for providing and/or granting permission to reproduce the illustrations:

The Archaeological Museum of Volos

The American School of Classical Studies at Athens

Archaeological Museum, Herakleion

The British School at Athens

Gerald Duckworth & Co Ltd.

Edizioni dell'Ateneo, Rome

The Institut Français d'Archéologie de Beyrouth

The Archaeological Society of Athens

Cambridge University Press

Elizabeth French

Verlag Philipp von Zabern

Princeton University Press

The American Schools of Oriental Research

Ernst Wasmuth Verlag

Eleusis Museum

The John Max Wulfing Collection, Washinton University, St. Louis

Collezione Banca Intesa, Milan

The British Museum Department of Coins and Medals

Indiana University Art Museum

University of Texas Libraries. The University of Texas at Austin

Jayne Warner

1

GREEK ENVIRONMENT AND PREHISTORY

THE MEDITERRANEAN AND NEAR EASTERN CONTEXT OF GREEK HISTORY

Greece in antiquity was an integral part of the wider Mediterranean world. Seventy-two percent of Greek land is within 25 miles of the sea, and although, like all early economies, the Greek economy was basically agrarian, it was the sea that lay at the heart of the Greek world. Access to the sea was a formative and often crucial element throughout Greek history, although it was also often a bitter and pitiless neighbor.

It was probably the prospect of better fishing that first led the Greeks to venture out upon the sea. Using simple boats they followed fish migrations, and as they did, they reached nearby islands, which in turn served as stepping stones to further investigation. An important discovery, as early as 6000 B.C.E. on the island of Melos was an abundance of **obsidian**, a vulcanic glass that takes a very sharp edge. Obsidian was the best material known for the production of cutting tools; even today it remains the sharpest cutting edge known and is used in heart and cosmetic surgery.[1] An elementary system of exchange in this valuable material quickly developed, bringing contact between various peoples on the islands and coasts of Greece. These connections grew and developed over time, providing wider access to other materials and products unknown at home.

In the third and second millennia B.C.E., a number of imported materials become central to life in Greece. Large timbers from the north made possible the construction of large ships and monumental buildings. Tin, possibly from Afghanistan, traveled even greater distances to be mixed with local copper, or copper was itself imported, perhaps from Cyprus, to make possible the production of bronze, the useful metal that gave its name to the age. Imported

1

luxury objects of gold and ivory and elaborate purple-dyed textiles from the Levant provided a means of expressing social distinctions that were basic to the organization of Greek society. And with the exchange of physical objects came new ideas and new experiences, and often, the impetus for change and development.

The second vital formative element for Greece was its position on the periphery of the much earlier civilizations of the Fertile Crescent, the lands made fertile by the annual floods of the great rivers of the Near East: the Nile in Egypt and the Tigris and Euphrates in Mesopotamia. During the fourth millennium B.C.E., writing, bronze metallurgy, and urban life emerged, first in Mesopotamia, then in Egypt. The people of Uruk were keeping written records ca.3500 B.C.E. The Great Pyramid of Khufu (Cheops) in Egypt was built ca. 2500 B.C.E., and Hamurabi gave written laws to his people ca.1700 B.C.E. Ancient empires rose and fell before the Greeks "invented" their typical state form, the **polis**, or city-state.

Why was Greece so slow to develop? While the Fertile Crescent offered flat and fertile plains with annual flooding that made possible extensive irrigation, Greece is a land of mountains surrounded by, and even created by, the sea. Formed by a mountain range, the Pindos chain, which extends from the European continent toward the southeast until it is submerged in the Aegean sea, Greece has a jagged coastline and numerous islands. Many of the plains enclosed by the mountains are so small that they can support only a single settlement. Much of the land is rocky and poor. Its rivers are small and usually dry up in the summer, making agriculture dependent upon rainfall and offering no prospects for the large-scale irrigation projects made possible by the annual flooding of the rivers of the Fertile Crescent.[2] No large, unified state that commanded large numbers of workers could arise under these conditions.

In contrast to the large states and empires of the Fertile Crescent, the naturally divided landscape of Greece developed into many small, separate, and independent states. Community was divided from community by sometimes formidable mountain barriers. Although the ancient Greeks recognized that they shared a common language (albeit in various dialects) and a common material culture and religion (again, with a wide variety of divinities and practices), they owed their political allegiance to many small independent states operating under a number of different forms of government: palace-centered kingdoms in the Bronze Age; and city-states (*poleis,* sing. *polis*), which took various political forms (aristocracies, oligarchies, and, by the fifth century, democracies) in later times. Other Greeks lived a more decentralized life in tribal states or *ethne* (sing. *ethnos*).

The more prominent mountain barriers also created natural regions, a few of which were extensive enough to be shared by several small independent states, such as the great plain of Thessaly in north central Greece and the plain of Boeotia in central Greece. At the outer fringes of Greek cultural territory, mountains delimited Macedonia to the northeast and Epeiros to the northwest. In the north the three-pronged peninsula called the Chalkidike was a naturally defined region, as was Attica in central coastal Greece. The Peloponnesus was nearly an island, connected by only a narrow isthmus to the northern mainland, with its own well-defined areas:

Lakonia, Messenia, the Argolid, and Arkadia. Sometimes the independent states that shared a region were formally organized in a religious federation or a political league, as for example, the Boeotian League; but for the most part there was no formal organization, as in the case of the Chalkidike before the fifth-century Chalkidic League, and in Arkadia before the fourth-century Arkadian League. Everywhere, independence was the ideal.

The sea and seafaring offered a strategy of survival that had important ramifications for the development of Greek culture and political forms. Excess production could be peddled by boat to nearby settlements. Moreover, when pressed by problems at home, the possibility existed of setting out by boat to find a new, and hopefully better, home elsewhere. The way had been laid for this option when the first boat was built and men began to explore neighboring coasts. By the second millenium B.C.E., the inhabitants of Greece were creating new settlements by emigration, and in the eighth through the sixth centuries, the diaspora became extensive, with Greeks resettling themselves in Sicily, Italy, Spain, the northern shore of the Black Sea, and the coast of North Africa. As they established these new settlements, Greeks gained experience in urban planning and community organization that influenced developments back home; some scholars even attribute the birth of the Greek city-state to a process of feedback from this experience in the creation of new distant settlements. In large part it was this expansion of Greek settlement that made possible the strong influence of Greek ideas and ideals upon later Western civilization.

Variations in access to the sea helped to create some of the political differences between Greek states. Settlements with easy access to the sea developed lifestyles, values, and even political structures that were significantly more outward looking and open to change than were those of inland settlements. We shall see this clearly in fifth-century Greece, when Athenian reliance upon the sea led to the development of a radical form of democracy, while inland Sparta's reliance upon the land fostered a conservative oligarchy. The Athenian philosopher Plato, whose political orientation was decidedly conservative, in fact recommended that the ideal *polis* be far from the sea. He remarked that the sea "is, in very truth, a briny and bitter neighbor. It fills a city with wholesale traffic and retail huckstering, breeds shifty and distrustful habits of soul, and so makes a society distrustful and unfriendly within itself as well as toward mankind at large."[3]

Agriculture and Land Resources

The Mediterranean climate in the classical period, with its hot, dry summers and mild, rainy winters, while not suitable for irrigation agriculture, was generally favorable for the production of the "Mediterranean triad" of cereals, olives, and vines.[4] Wide variations in climate, however, made success difficult. In terms of regional diversity and interannual variability, the climate has not changed appreciably since classical antiquity,[5] and therefore modern data can give us some idea of the situation that the Greek farmer faced. For example, Kavala, on the north coast of the Aegean, had an average annual rainful during the 1960s of 549 millimeters, while rainfall at Athens in the 1950s varied from 216 to 560 millimeters.[6] Barley can be grown with a minimum of 200 millimeters annual rainfall, but the more desirable wheat requires at least 300 millimeters. Thus we can see that on the north Aegean coast wheat could have been grown every year with reasonable expectation of success, but in Athens the farmer faced years in which even barley might be marginal. Modern human intervention has, of course, changed the agricultural picture in many ways. For example, irrigation, which is central to much agricultural production in Greece today and was the mainstay of agriculture in the Fertile Crescent, was rarely practical in ancient Greece. Moreover, many new crops unknown in antiquity now play important roles in the economy, including cotton, tobacco, and citrus fruits.

For the ancient Greek farmer, land suitable for farming was limited and varied in fertility.[7] Much of the land is rocky and mountainous; plains are often small, and even when comparatively expansive, may suffer from drainage problems. Terracing could extend the usable land and allow even fairly steep hillsides to be planted with olives and vines, but making and maintaining terraces is laborious work. Goats and sheep could graze on even more marginal land, and they provided both clothing and food—wool for clothing, milk, cheese, and the rare meal of meat, eaten only when shared with the gods in a sacrifice. Cattle were kept as well, but horses were an expensive luxury raised only by the wealthy few. Fish provided a source of protein in coastal areas, as did legumes everywhere.

An important device that helped the Greeks make the best of these difficult conditions was crop diversification. Since only in extreme cases would every crop fail, it offered some protection against catastrophic loss of the entire harvest. The Greek ideal of self-sufficiency fostered diversity, for each household and each city-state worked to produce a range of products. Another source of diversity was the system of partible inheritance (an equal part to each son) and, at least in some areas and periods, the use of land as dowry for the marriage of daughters. Both practices contributed to the fragmentation of land into small scattered plots. Although it may seem inefficient for the members of a single household to work small plots in scattered locations to which they have to travel, in fact, it was often advantageous, for even small variations in location brought differences in temperature or precipitation that offered insurance against the loss of an entire season's production.

In addition to its agricultural potential, the land of Greece also provided some mineral resources. Greece has a number of copper deposits, many conveniently found in rock formations that also provide the most fertile soil; thus those who settled on good soil were likely to have come upon copper as well. Copper was known and used in Greece from the Late Neolithic, ca. 4800 B.C.E., although there is no direct evidence that local sources of copper were being used on the mainland until ca. 2700 B.C.E. Copper by itself is too soft to be very useful in producing tools, but by alloying it with tin, people were able to produce the much more useful bronze. However, tin was not present in mainland Greece; in fact, its main sources are all far distant (Afghanistan, Britain, Spain). It is not known exactly where the Greeks obtained their tin when they began to produce bronze ca. 3000 B.C.E. Other important metals, silver and lead, were present in significant quantities in two areas of Greece: Laurion in the southern part of Attica, and in the north Aegean, in the area around the Strymon River, and the island of Thasos. Control of Laurion, and eventually of the northern mines, was a determining factor in Athenian predominance among the Greek states in the fifth century. Other important mineral resources, building stone and marble, were available in abundance, although the type of stone desired was not always available locally, and transport of such heavy material was difficult. Timber of a size suitable for the construction of large buildings and large ships was mostly lacking in southern Greece, although it was abundant in northern Greece, especially in Macedonia, and could be transported by water.

These factors—the Mediterranean environment with its focus on the sea, the fragmented mountainous terrain, and a peripheral position with regard to the older, developed states of the Near East—were key elements in the history of ancient Greece. The Greeks in time were able to learn from their more advanced Near Eastern neighbors, but they were also able to develop their own political form: the small, but fiercely independent city-state, or *polis*.

GREEK PREHISTORY: THE EARLY NEOLITHIC BACKGROUND

Evidence for human settlement in Greece goes back to at least the nineteenth millennium B.C.E. The earliest Greeks lived, as did all early peoples, by hunting and gathering. Populations were small and transient. When people learned to cultivate plants—an innovation called the **Neolithic Revolution**, which in Greece is dated ca. 6000 B.C.E.—they began to settle down, creating permanent settlements.

The Franchthi Cave

Perhaps the best known of these very early settlements is the Franchthi Cave, a site in the northeastern Peloponnesus near the Argolid Gulf on the edge of a well-watered coastal plain. The Franchthi Cave was inhabited, at least on a seasonal basis, from around 18,000 until 3,000 B.C.E., and it provides evidence for the transition from hunting and gathering to settled farming (the Neolithic Revolution).[8]

The first human use of the cave was in the Upper Palaeolithic, when small groups of hunters, numbering no more than 25 to 30, visited it on a seasonal basis. For some reason, however, it was abandoned for a few thousand years from around 15,000 B.C.E. From the twelfth through the eighth millennium it again sheltered small bands of hunter–gatherers. These people had begun to exploit the sea by fishing, and it is possible that they remained in the cave year-round. They used obsidian, which shows that they had probably begun to construct boats and explore and exploit the available resources offered by nearby islands.

WEB SITE 1.1: PICTURES OF THE FRANCHTHI CAVE

http://projectsx.dartmouth.edu/classics/history/bronze_age/lessons/img/1img.html

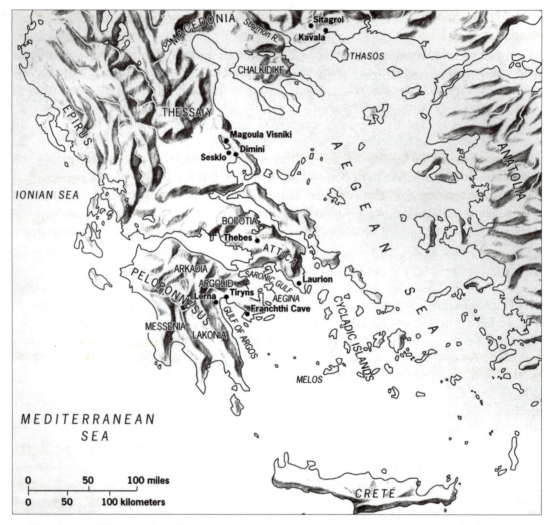

Map 1:   Neolithic and Early Bronze Age Greece

By the seventh millennium the inhabitants of the Franchthi Cave obtained a significant portion of their diet by catching large tuna. They had also begun to experiment with the cultivation of certain plants, especially lentils, which are excellent sources of protein. Such experiments might well have been carried on by the women, who were occupied with gathering plants for food, while the men were hunting or absent on fishing or obsidian-gathering expeditions.

By around 6000 the full-scale Neolithic Revolution had arrived at Franchthi. Both plants and animals (emmer and einkorn wheat, sheep and goats) had been domesticated. Hunting and fishing dropped off drastically with the dramatic shift to food production.

Population may have increased, as suggested by the building of houses outside the cave. The shift from hunting and gathering to settled farming would not necessarily have improved health conditions, however, for the Neolithic diet was less varied than that of hunters and gatherers. People also lived close together and shared their living quarters with their domestic animals, which made them more subject to the spread of disease. However, the number of children that were raised probably increased once it was no longer necessary for women to restrict themselves to raising the one small child at a time that they could carry on gathering trips.

There are no signs that outside contacts were lessened by the demands of farming, however. Obsidian continued to be abundant, and andesite, a stone brought from the Saronic Gulf, was imported for millstones. Marble, another non-local material, also appears. Even the plants and animals that were domesticated must have been imports, for these species were not present earlier on the site. They were brought, possibly from Anatolia, along with the techniques for their cultivation. The confluence of so many imports suggests that we should assume the existence of some sort of network of regional maritime exchange. The Franchthi community seems to have been an egalitarian group, however, for no evidence for social stratification by wealth or status has been discovered. There are a few figurines and objects of personal adornment, but little sense of the development of a sense of personal property.

While the Franchthi Cave people continued to make progress in the transition to the Neolithic, the most intensive development in the new style of life came about not in the Peloponnesus but in the north. In the seventh millennium numerous agricultural villages were established in western Macedonia and especially in Thessaly, and for two to three millennia this area was in the forefront of growth and prosperity. The settlements were in contact with each other, and a fairly uniform culture spread throughout the area.

THE MIDDLE AND LATE NEOLITHIC BACKGROUND

Two of the best-known Neolithic settlements, Sesklo and Dimini, were located in Thessaly.[9] In archaeological terms, Sesklo and Dimini are **type sites**; that is, each is considered to be typical of a number of culturally similar sites, as determined for the most part by shared pottery styles. The name of the type site is applied to all sites with a similar material culture, and it also is used to indicate a relative date.

Sesklo Culture

Sesklo was first occupied during the Middle Neolithic, ca. 5300–4400. Early interpretations of the architectural remains, as reported in Emily Vermeule's widely used book *Greece in the Bronze Age*, portrayed Sesklo as small (30 to 50 dwellings, perhaps a maximum of 250 inhabitants), peaceful (inferred from the site's walls, which were not defensive in type), and with a socially undifferentiated culture (inferred from the similarity of house types). The settlement was destroyed, apparently by a more warlike people who took over the site and also built the nearby settlement of Dimini.[10]

Excavations and reinterpretations of the archaeological evidence since the publication of Vermeule's book in 1964 have, however, considerably modified her picture. They have brought to light the remains of a much larger settlement than her reconstruction postulated at Sesklo. It is now recognized that the settlement covered some 25 to 30 acres, and had an estimated population of 3000 to 4000.[11] In a central location on the **acropolis** (the defensible hill that forms the nucleus of a city or settlement) stood a prominent building with a courtyard. The plan of this building is of a type called a **megaron**: a rectangular building of two rooms having an entrance and porch on the short side. The degree of social differentiation, if any, indicated by this building is unclear. It may have been the meeting place of a group of leaders, but to characterize it as an administrative center seems to go too far. Nevertheless, its presence and the regularity and similar orientation of the houses suggest some degree of community organization. This is also supported by the evidence for craft specialization, attested by the high quality of the pottery. The well-made cream-colored pots were decorated with red geometric designs based on a zig-zag pattern, revealing their derivation from the designs of weaving. The monochrome pots were also innovative, with designs created by scraping, impressing, and varying the color by changes in conditions of firing.

Other products of the clay workers of Sesklo consisted of small figurines of humans and animals, which continued a tradition from the Early Neolithic. Similar prehistoric figurines, which often represent a female, sometimes obese or with sexual features emphasized, have been found over a wide geographical area from western Europe to Russia, and over a time span that extends from Palaeolithic (ca. 25,000 B.C.E.) to the Bronze Age (ca. 2000 B.C.E.). Some scholars believe that these figurines reveal the worship of a "Great Mother-Goddess," but the evidence does not support this.[12] Those who make such claims focus too much on the female figures while ignoring other figures found in the same contexts, which included males, figures without sexual characteristics, and animals. They also overlook the wide variations in the female figures. Modern ethnographic studies of tribal peoples suggest that such figurines could have been put to a variety of uses, not all of which were religious. They could have been used as dolls, as teaching devices in initiation ceremonies or before childbirth, in sympathetic magic rituals aimed at inducing pregnancy, as characters in mythological accounts, or in sorcery and black magic.[13] The fact is that we simply don't know how the early peoples used such figurines.

Aside from these ambiguous figurines, there is little to suggest the religious beliefs of the Neolithic period in Greece. Evidence for cult places, the performance of rituals, or sacrifice is lacking. Nonetheless, we may assume that these people "shared the belief common not only to the religions of the Near Eastern societies but to those of all recorded faming cultures, that there exist supernatural powers that can control the weather, the productivity of the soil and the fertility of living creatures, and that these powers need to be propitiated, if the natural processes are to continue."[14]

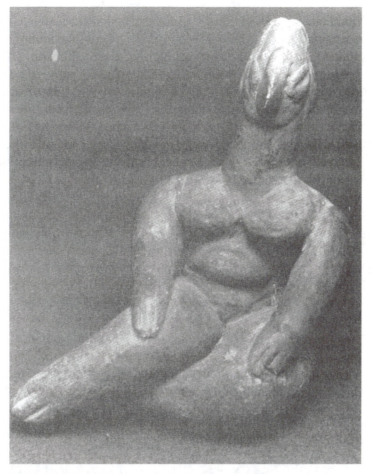

Figure 1.1   "Mother-Goddess" figurine (Volos Museum M168).
Courtesy of the Archaeological Museum of Volos.

Sesklo, by virtue of its size, organization, and evidence for craft specialization, now appears to have been a small town rather than the simple village of the earlier interpretation. Moreover, while the walls at Sesklo were not "fortifications," somewhat more imposing defensive measures have been found at other sites of the Sesklo culture. Reporting on the current state of research on Sesklo, D. Theocharis says, "All this greatly changes the traditional picture of the peaceful rural settlements of the 'Sesklo Culture,' and almost entirely destroys the supposed contrast between them and the 'warlike' disposition of the inhabitants of Dimini."[15]

In about 4400 the settlement at Sesklo was burned and destroyed, and the site remained deserted for 500 years. A few other settlements of the Sesklo culture also show signs of destruction about this same time, but others remained and underwent a gradual cultural transformation. By 4200 there were no traces left of the Sesklo culture; the new culture that

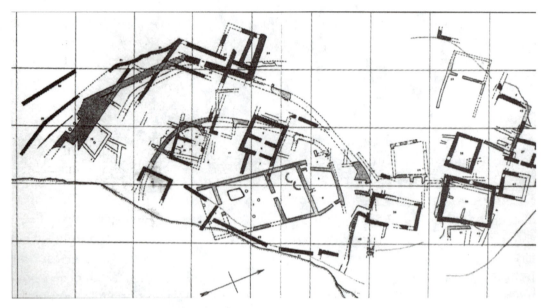

Figure 1.2   Site Plan of Sesklo (Theocharis, Figure 177).

Figure 1.3   Reconstruction of Sesklo (Theocharis, Figure 178).

succeeded it is called simply pre-Dimini. It seems to have been considerably less advanced than the Sesklo culture. A less accomplished dark-colored pottery with incised or linear decoration replaced the attractive red on cream of the Sesklo style, the architecture of the buildings was more irregular, and its people made no figurines.

Dimini Culture

In ca. 3800, still another cultural change occurred at the site of Dimini and gave its name to the succeeding period, the later Late Neolithic (3800–3300). Although this Dimini culture

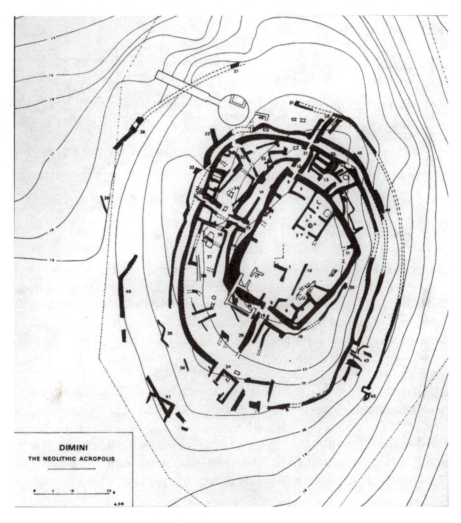

Figure 1.4   Site Plan of Dimini (Theocharis, Figure 185).

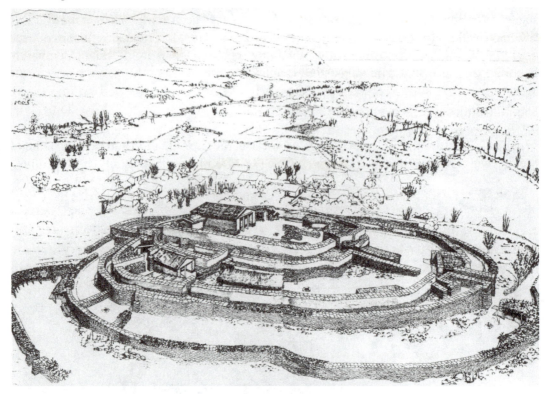

Figure. 1.5   Reconstruction of Dimini (Theocharis, Figure 187).

was earlier seen as representative of the entire Late Neolithic in Thessaly, it is now recognized as somewhat of an aberration, a peak of development reached in only a small area of eastern Thessaly for a relatively short period of time in the middle of the Late Neolithic. In this phase the site of Sesklo was also reoccupied (on the plan of Sesklo in Figure 1.2, the buildings of this later, Dimini phase are indicated). There had been a gap in occupation at Sesklo of ca. 500 years, however, and the Dimini people cannot be held responsible for the destruction of the earlier Sesklo settlement, as Vermeule's earlier interpretation suggested.

The site of Dimini was ringed by six circuits of walls. They were initially thought to have been defensive, but this is now questioned: their size and construction make it more likely that they were retaining walls used to create terraces on which houses could be built, thus maximizing the useful area of the hill. Moreover, since concentric rings of walls are also found at Sesklo, whose acropolis is naturally defensible, the use of a customary or standard plan is suggested.

The central building at Dimini, a megaron in form, occupies a commanding position in the settlement and is much larger than the similar building at Sesklo (in the earlier, Sesklo stage).[16] It is especially large in proportion to the other buildings at Dimini, which suggests social differentiation. This central building may have been a commuity hall or the house of a village leader, but it clearly seems to have been an architectual expression of some sort of authority or power. At another site of the Dimini culture, Magoula Visviki (Velestino), there is a megaron whose length is 30 meters, as long as the "Men's Megaron" found in the Late Bronze Age at the Mycenaean palace of Tiryns (see Chapter 3). Similarly impressive central buildings are not found again in Greece until the settlement at Lerna, some 1500 years later.

The pottery of the Dimini culture was decorated with brown or black geometric designs of meanders, checkerboards, pyramids, or spirals that filled much of the surface. Copper came into use during the Late Neolithic period. Copper axes found at Dimini and at Sitagroi, a site further north, provide evidence for smelting. Local sources do not seem to have been utilized, however; rather, archaeological finds suggest that the sources for both metal and metallurgical skills at that time were the Balkans and perhaps Anatolia.[17] There is, however, no evidence during the Dimini phase for the use of bronze, although in the succeeding period it does appear. While bronze came to be used increasingly, it was not used to a degree that affected the economy or social structure. For this reason, the Late Neolithic is classified as Chalcolithic (copper-stone using) Age rather than Bronze Age.

The notable developments of the Middle and Late Neolithic that we have been considering at the sites of Sesklo and Dimini were much more pronounced in that region of Thessaly and the north of Greece than in the south, which was less fertile and drier, with greater regional fluctuations in rainfall. There settlement was sparse until the late fourth millennium. The people in the Franchthi Cave had few neighbors.

THE EARLY BRONZE AGE

The period called Early Helladic I or Early Bronze I in Greece is marked by a recession, with a decline in the number of known settlements and, most notably, a lack of metal finds. In Early Helladic II Early (2650–2450/2350 B.C.E.), however, a boom occurred in the use of copper, and there was a dramatic rise in settlement numbers in the southern areas. The center of innovation shifted permanently to the south, while settlement in the north declined. Evidence for the production of bronze also appears in this period. Although there were copper resources at Laurion in Attica (later best known for its silver), most of the mainland probably obtained copper from abroad. Sources of tin, which is not found in Greece, may have been Anatolia, the Balkans, Spain, Afghanistan (via Mesopotamia and Syria), or even Britain.[18]

The Early Bronze Age Settlement at Lerna

With the introduction of bronze into the Aegean area in the third millennium B.C.E., settlements increased in number and grew into towns, and some buildings can be called monumental. The best known example of the achievements and vicissitudes of the Early Helladic

Chronology of the Helladic Period, which can only be tentative

Early Helladic (EH)		
EH I	3100/300–2650	Lerna II
EH II Early	2650–2450/2350	Lerna III
EH II Late	2450/2350–2200/2150	Destruction of House of Tiles
EH III	2200/2150–2050/2000	Lerna IV
Middle Helladic (MH)		
MH I	2050/2000–1950/1900	
MH II	1950/1900–1750/1720	Kolonna shaft graves
MH III	1750/1720–1680	
Late Helladic (LH) or Mycenaen		
LH I	1680–1600/1580	
LH IIA	1600/1580–1520/1480	Mycenae shaft graves
LH IIB	1520/1480–1445/1415	

sites is Lerna, which was situated on the Gulf of Argos (the modern Bay of Nauplion).[19] Lerna, which had been settled and then abandoned in the Neolithic (Lerna I), was resettled in EH II by a people who built a row of houses with good-sized square rooms, perhaps along a street or court (Lerna II). They also built a multi-roomed monumental building (**Building BG**) with thick mud walls and a schist roof, and they surrounded the whole settlement with a defensive wall. After some time both Building BG and the wall were destroyed by a violent fire. The destruction was not accompanied by a change of population, however, and the inhabitants gradually recovered, at first building small houses over the site of Building BG (Lerna III). Later they began the construction of another monumental building in the center of the site. This important building is called the **House of Tiles** from its terracotta roof tiles.[20] It measured 25 meters by 12 meters, and consisted of two large rooms and two smaller ones, with exterior corridors accessible from both the inside and outside and used for stairways to an upper floor.

There appear to have been open balconies on the upper floor, and a light well provided light for the interior rooms on the first floor. The interior walls were carefully plastered, and in the largest room the walls were decorated with rectangular panels. Stairs were fitted with clay treads, and doors were set in wooden jambs. The building was also used for storage, for a large number of seals used to seal stores were found, suggesting that the people of Lerna had taken the first steps in the development of writing. Red clay benches were set along the two long exterior walls of the building, providing shelter from sun and rain. The functions of display, storage, and public convenience are apparent, and the building perhaps paralleled the proto-palaces of Crete.

Figure 1.6   The House of Tiles at Lerna, site plan and view of main excavated area.
Courtesy of the American School of Classical Studies at Athens.

Houses of a similar plan, called the **Corridor House**, have been found at a number of different sites in mainland Greece, including Thebes in Boeotia and Kolonna on the island of Aegina.[21] Moreover, not far from Lerna, at Tiryns (a later Mycenaean palace site), the remains of a huge round building have been found, about 28 meters in diameter and more than 26 meters in height. The foundation consisted of three thick concentric ring walls without connecting doors. If it was ever used as a palace, there must have been access to an upper floor by a ramp of some sort. The most likely suggestion, however, is that it was used as a granary.[22]

Historians are divided on the explanation for the rather sudden and widespread appearance of monumental buildings in mainland Greece in the Early Helladic II period. The need to obtain tin for the production of bronze required increasing overseas contacts, for which access to the sea and the seafaring skills that the Greeks living along the coasts of the mainland had developed were vital assets. If, as seems likely, the sources of tin were in Afghanistan and it was transported by way of Mesopotamia and Syria, the contacts with these more advanced cultures may also have been a source of new ideas as well.[23] Influence from Mesopotamia has been suggested,[24] while other scholars prefer to look for evidence of local development.

To call the Corridor buildings palaces is anachronistic, but they do seem to have been built to accommodate large numbers of people and could have provided for differentiation of public and private uses. Vermeule suggested that the best parallel might be with village granges to which all citizens had equal access.[25] Other scholars see these buildings as evidence for the development of a form of social organization called the chiefdom, in which power is concentrated in a single leader who effectively controls the community's resources.[26]

Before the House of Tiles was even completed, it was destroyed by fire, along with the entire settlement, although the inhabitants apparently escaped. The intruders, who appear to have come from somewhere not far away,[27] settled down on the site, constructing small irregular buildings of one or two rooms, some with apsidal (rounded) ends (Lerna IV). Their handmade pottery provides them with a name, the Patterned Ware people. The Patterned Ware people used no seals and had little foreign contact. They did not rebuild the House of Tiles; on the contrary, they heaped up a tumulus over four meters high over the remains of the building and marked off its perimeter with a circle of stones, leaving the area inviolate throughout their occupation of the site. Whether they treated the ruins in this way from fear, or piety, or from some other motivation is a question that cannot be answered. Similar destructions are archaeologically attested at about the same time in a number of other places, yet the once-popular hypothesis of a widescale incursion of new people (the introduction of Greek speakers into Greece?) is now generally rejected, since the destructions did not all occur at exactly the same time, and some of the Corridor houses, such as those at Thebes and Kolonna, appear simply to have been abandoned, with no signs of fire, violent destruction, or special treatment, such as burial under mounds.

MIDDLE HELLADIC—KOLONNA

The period of three or four centuries that followed the destruction of the House of Tiles at Lerna and the other monumental buildings of EH II (Early Helladic III–MH II), was characterized on the mainland by small buildings requiring little skill in construction and showing little evidence for specialized function. Metals were scarce, craft specialization existed at only a few sites, and there was a decline in contacts with the Cycladic islands and a complete break in contact with Crete. Life reverted to a simpler, subsistence level. Asine, a village on the coast of the Argolid, provides a well-published example.[28] Asine had 300 to 500 inhabitants, no fortifications, no evidence of central authority, and no specialized workshops. Its people were less long-lived, shorter, and slighter than Middle Helladic Greeks as a whole. There were some variations in expenditure on burials, but nothing to indicate remarkable wealth. The people were, however, in contact with neighboring settlements and possessed some imports.

One remarkable exception to this rather bleak picture appeared at the settlement of Kolonna on the island of Aegina, in the center of the Saronic Gulf.[29] The settlement of Kolonna had a Corridor house in EH II (town III), called by the German archaeologists the Weisses Haus.[30] In the next phase of the settlement (town IV), however, the Weisses Haus lay in ruins and a smelting furnace was installed in it, suggesting a violent destruction. Unlike the depressed situation at Lerna, however, where the ruins of the House of Tiles were buried in a great tumulus, at Kolonna a well-planned settlement, EH III Kolonna (town V), was built after the destructions. It had impressive fortification walls, and its single-story, three-room houses were set side by side in groups between streets, indicative of planning and of a strong central authority. The walls of town III were destroyed by fire, but they were rebuilt in town IV in a stronger configuration, with two gates flanked by rectangular towers. In the succeeding level (town VII, EH I), hidden walkways and dog-leg gateways were added to the fortifications, and successive rebuildings continued to add to their sophistication. In MH II (town IX) the settlement expanded beyond the fortifications with a fortified suburb; when the suburb was attacked and destroyed at the end of town IX, the inner wall and wall of the suburb were strengthened (town X, MH III). Such impressive fortifications were unique in the Aegean of this period.[31]

Kolonna had numerous maritime contacts, attested by imports of Cycladic and Minoan pottery, as well as by imitations of Minoan Kamares ware. But Kolonna itself was also a producer and exporter of a special pottery, Gold Mica ware, made of volcanic clay containing sparkling bits of gold-colored mica. Gold Mica ware was widely exported, reaching the islands, Attica, and the Argolid. In fact, one of its importers was Asine, where 16 percent of the total sherds of MH III date and 86 percent of all imports were from Aegina.[32] In late MH, Kolonna's pottery business flourished: new shapes and decorations were added, production increased, and distribution was expanded. The organized nature of Kolonna's pottery production is demonstrated by the development of a system of marking the pots before firing, which is thought to indicate the workshop or potter who made the vessel.[33] During LH IIIA-IIIB, however, perhaps because decorated Mycenaean pottery had taken over the market, there was a cutback in production. Kolonna's pottery business was subsequently limited to cooking pots, which continued to be highly desired for their resistance to high heat.

Kolonna's maritime network of pottery distribution was an early forerunner of the later sea routes that brought and kept Greece in contact with the outside world in Mycenaean times and through the so-called "Dark Age," the time of transition following the collapse of the Bronze Age world (Chapter 4).

Perhaps the most striking discovery at Kolonna was a rich **shaft grave** of a male in his early to mid-twenties, buried at the foot of the suburban fortification of town IX. The tomb was first located outside the wall, but later incorporated into a bastion built up against the wall and accessible only from inside the fortifications. It contained a gold diadem, a bronze sword with a gold and ivory hilt, three bronze daggers, one with gold fittings, arrowheads of obsidian, boar's tusks from a helmet, and fine Minoan and Cycladic decorated pottery, including a Melian bowl.[34] This burial at a prominent location in regard to the town's fortifications, with its grave offerings of a golden diadem and a sword—signs of male power and authority—decorated with precious gold and ivory, attests to the existence of clear social distinctions, and perhaps the beginnings of a concept of kingship. It is also important in demonstrating that the rich graves in the famous Shaft Grave Circle at Mycenae (Chapter 3) were not a sudden anomaly, but the product of a mainland tradition of long standing.

CONCLUSION

In the Neolithic and early Bronze Age, the mainland of Greece developed gradually and with recurrent setbacks, from the Franchthi Cave through the village culture of Sesklo and Dimini, and into the beginning of a more complex society such as we see at Lerna. By the middle Helladic, while most of Greece was in a period of recession, as seen at Asine, the settlement of Kolonna on Aegina was an important center of pottery production and distribution that sent its specialized ware to the islands, Attica and the Argolid (including Asine). Moreover, its people lived in a well-fortified and planned city, with signs that suggest the elevation of the ruler to a special status.

Meanwhile, on the island of Crete development through the Neolithic and into the Bronze Age proceeded without the profound interruptions that occurred on much of the mainland. The island's location fostered contacts with the seafaring peoples of the Near East, who probably served as sources of tin and of bronze technology, as well as of ideas about ways to organize the production and distribution of this valuable new resource. By the end of the third millennium a complex, palace-centered, and literate civilization had developed on Crete. This civilization had considerable effects on later Greek culture, as well as being important and interesting in itself, and it is to this that we turn next.

SUGGESTIONS FOR FURTHER READING

An easy-to-read account of the ecology of Greece and its effect on the development of Greek culture and history can be found in Robin Osborne (1987). *Classical Landscape with Figures: The Ancient Greek City and its Countryside*. On the Franchthi Cave, see T. W. Jacobsen (1976). "17,000 Years of Greek Prehistory," *Scientific American* 234: 76–87. For a woman's-eye view of prehistory, see M. Ehrenberg (1989). *Women in Prehistory*. On Lerna, J. Caskey (1960), "The Early Helladic Period in the Argolid," *Hesperia* 29 285–303. J. Caskey and E. T. Blackburn (1997) rev. ed., *Lerna in the Argolid*, Pamphlet of the American School of Classical Studies at Athens. On Kolonna, W.-D. Niemeier (1995), "Aegina—First Aegean 'State' Outside of Crete?" pp. 73–79 in *Politeia: Society and State in the Aegean Bronze Age: Proceedings of the 5th International Aegean Conference/5e Rencontre égéenne internationale, University of Heidelberg, Archäologisches Institut, 10–13 April, 1994*, ed. Robert Laffineur and W.-D. Niemeier. Jeremy Rutter's Dartmouth website on the prehistoric archaeology of the Aegean provides authoritative up-to-date discussions and abundant specialized bibliography: http://projectsx.dartmouth.edu/classics/history/bronze_age/lessons/les/2.html#6.

MAP STUDY

Sites: Sesklo, Dimini, Lerna, Kavala, Franchthi Cave, Thebes, Tiryns
Areas: Macedonia, Thessaly, Boeotia, Chalkidike, Epeiros, Lakonia, Messenia, Argolid, Arkadia, Peloponnesus, Aegean, Melos, Cycladic Islands, Anatolia, Balkans, Gulf of Argos, Aegina, Crete

ENDNOTES

[1] See http://www.ambergriscaye.com/museum/digit1.html

[2] Robin Osborne 1(987.) *Classical Landscape with Figures: The Ancient Greek City and Its Countryside*. More technical books of interest include Thomas W. Gallant (1991). *Risk and Survival in Ancient Greece: Reconstructing the Rural Domestic Economy*; and Peter Garnsey (1988), *Famine and Food Supply in the Graeco-Roman World*.

[3] Plato, *Laws* 705a, tr. A. E. Taylor, in *The Collected Dialogues of Plato*, ed. Edith Hamilton and Huntington Cairns.

[4] The climate in the Neolithic was cooler and wetter; when the triad began to dominate the agricultural scene in Greece is a matter of dispute. See Robert Sallares (1991), *The Ecology of the Ancient Greek World*, 17–18, 32–33.

[5] See Sallares (above, n. 4), 35, 390–394; Peter Garnsey 1988 above, n.2), 8–14.

[6] Osborne (above, n. 2).

[7] A good discussion of the problems of farming can be found in Osborne (above, n. 2) ch. 2.

[8] T. W. Jackson (1976), "17,000 Years of Greek Prehistory," *Scientific American* 234:86–87; T. W. Jacobsen (1981), "The Beginning of Settled Village Life in Greece," *Hesperia* 50: 303–18.

[9]The discussion of these sites by E. Vermeule (1964), *Greece in the Bronze Age*, has been superceded by more recent finds. D. Theocharis (1973), *Neolithic Greece*; and S. Andreou, M. Fotiadis, and K. Kotsakis. (2001). "Review of Aegean Prehistory V: The Neolithic and Bronze Age of Northern Greece," pp. 259–327 in *Aegean Prehistory: A Review*, ed. by Tracy Cullen. An excellent review is available on Jeremy Rutter's Dartmouth website: http://projectsx.dartmouth.edu/classics/history/bronze_age/lessons/les/2.html#6.

[10]Emily Vermeule (above, n. 9).

[11]Estimated populations are based upon the number of occupation units found, the assumed number of occupants in each unit, and the carrying capacity of the territory that is estimated to have been controlled by the settlement. These numbers come from Rutter, Lesson 2 (above, n. 9), revised March 18, 2000.

[12]The work of the archaeologist M. Gimbutas has perhaps done most to further this scenario. See, for example, Gimbutas (1974), *The Goddesses and Gods of Old Europe*; and Gimbutas (1989), *The Language of the Goddess*. Gimbutas's work has appealed to many in the women's movement and has inspired other books, such as Pamela Berger (1985), *The Goddess Obscured*. Arguments against the goddess hypothesis are clearly presented in Lauren E. Talalay (2003), "The Feminist Boomerang: The Great Goddess of Greek Prehistory," pp. 307–318 in Mark Golden and Peter Toohey, eds. (2003), *Sex and Difference in Ancient Greece and Rome*, first published in Mark Golden and Peter Toohey, eds. 2003, *Sex and Difference in Ancient Greece and Rome*. Talalay's article (1994) in its original, unabbreviated publication can be found in *Gender and History* 6:164–183.

[13]The classic article on the interpretation of these figurines is P. J. Ucko (1962), "The Interpretation of Prehistoric Anthropomorphic Figurines," *Journal of the Royal Anthropological Institute of Great Britain and Ireland*, 92:38–54.

[14]Oliver Dickinson (1994), *The Aegean Bronze Age*, 258.

[15]Theocharis (above, n. 9), 66.

[16]The intentional creation of megaron has been questioned, and the form is suggested to have resulted from later modifications of a courtyard area, but there seems to be no evidence for a later date. See Andreou, Fotiadis and Kotsakis (above, n. 9), 266.

[17]On the copper resources of Greece, see V. McGeehan-Liritzis (1983), "The Relationship between Metalwork, Copper Sources and the Evidence for Settlement in the Greek Late Neolithic and Early Bronze Age," *Oxford Journal of Archaeology* 2:147–180.

[18]On the possible sources of tin, see V. McGeehan-Liritzis and J. W. Taylor (1987), "Yugoslavian Tin Deposits and the Early Bronze Age Industries of the Aegean Region," *Oxford Journal of Archaeology* 6: 287–300.

[19]See J. Caskey (1960), "The Early Helladic Period in the Argolid," *Hesperia* 29: 285–303; also J. Caskey and E. T. Blackburn (1997) rev. ed., *Lerna in the Argolid*, Pamphlet of the American School of Classical Studies at Athens.

[20]J. W. Shaw (1987), "The Early Helladic II Corridor House." *American Journal of Archaeology* 91:59–79, esp. 59–65.

[21]See Shaw (above n.20). R. Hägg and D. Konsola (1986), *Early Helladic Architecture and Urbanization*, has a number of articles on the various examples that have been found.

[22]See K. Killian, "The Circular Building at Tiryns," in Hägg and Konsola (above, n. 21).

[23]Colin Renfrew discusses the beginnings of civilization in the Aegean, arguing that no single factor was responsible, but that a number of factors interacted in a complex system of feedback, which he calls the Multiplier Effect. See C. Renfrew (1972), *The Emergence of Civilization: The Cyclades and the Aegean in the Third Millennium*.

[24]See Hiller's article in Hägg and Konsola, (above, n. 21), 85–89.

[25]Vermeule (above, n. 9), 36.

[26]The various views are well represented in Hägg and Konsola (above, n. 21); for an overview, see their conclusion, pp. 95–100.

[27]A number of sites with buildings like the House of Tiles (Corridor houses) were destroyed around the same time, indicating, according to some, perhaps the arrival of new people (see Caskey and Blackburn (above, n. 19), 17. However, the destructions are not now seen as simultaneous nor as evidence for the arrival of a new population group. See Rutter (above, n. 9), 111–116, who suggests that the apparently new pottery style of the new occupants at Lerna may have been developed out of a merging of pottery styles by two groups living nearby. Here the influence upon the interpretation by those who accept versus those who reject "invasionist" hypotheses makes judgment difficult.

[28]G. Nordquist (1987), *A Middle Helladic Village: Asine in the Argolid.*

[29]W.-D. Niemeier (1995), "Aegina—First Aegean 'State' Outside of Crete?" pp. 73–79 in *Politeia: Society and State in the Aegean Bronze Age: Proceedings of the 5th International Aegean Conference/5e, Rencontre égéenne internationale, University of Heidelberg, Archäologisches Institut*, 10–13 April, 1994, ed. Robert Laffineur and W.- D. Niemeier.

[30]J. W. Shaw (above, n. 20).

[31]Niemeier (above, n. 29): 75. The walls of Troy VI were not earlier, and their towers were added in a later phase.

[32]Nordquist (see above, n.28), 41.

[33]Michael Lindblom (2001), *Marks and Makers. Appearance, Distribution and Function of Middle and Late Helladic Manufacturers' Marks on Aeginetan Pottery.*

[34]The diadem is very similar to one in the Aegina Treasure in the British Museum, which was found in a robber's cache at Kolonna. It was formerly thought to have been robbed in modern times from a Cretan burial, but its similarity to the diadem in the shaft grave now establishes it as a tomb-robber's hoard from antiquity, reburied by the robber in a Mycenean tomb in Kolonna. See Reynold Higgins 1987, "A Gold Diadem from Aegina," *Journal of Hellenic Studies* 197: 182.

2

MINOAN CRETE[1]

MYTH AND HISTORY

T he Minoans are among the most colorful characters in archaeology, ranking close to such favorites as the pyramids and mummies of Egypt. In the second millennium they created a palace civilization that rivaled in many ways the older civilizations of Mesopotamia and Egypt. Labyrinthian palatial complexes decorated with brightly colored wall paintings were the site of a bureaucratic economy of collection and redistribution, with written records kept of even apparently minor transactions. The skills of fine workmanship were perfected, and imported luxury items attest to widespread commercial and diplomatic contacts.

The modern world first learned of this highly sophisticated Cretan civilization in the mythological tales of the classical Greeks. Thus the fifth-century Greek historian Thucydides speaks of Crete as the home of King Minos, the first ruler to control the sea (the Greek word for control of the sea is **thalassocracy**). In the fourth century the philosopher Plato knew Minos as a wise legislator, although Greek myth also portrayed him as the possessor of the Minotaur, a terrifying monster that was half man, half bull. The Minotaur was even featured in Athenian history: he lived hidden away in the Labyrinth that the fabulous craftsman Daedalus had constructed for him, and every nine years the Athenians were forced to provide seven boys and seven girls to feed the beast. Relief came for the Athenians only when Theseus, the son of the Athenian king, volunteered to join the sacrificial contingent. Once in Crete Theseus slew the Minotaur with the help of the Minoan princess Ariadne, with whom he then eloped, but whom he later abandoned. But did any historical truth lie behind the myth of Minos, the Labyrinth, and Minoan thalassocracy?

There is always a question whether, and to what extent, actual historical events and situations are reflected and refracted in such traditions, and if they are, how they can be extracted

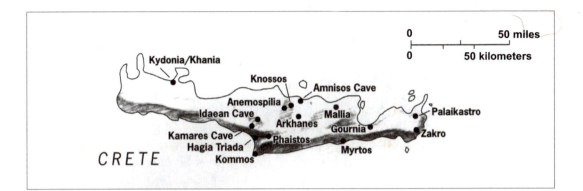

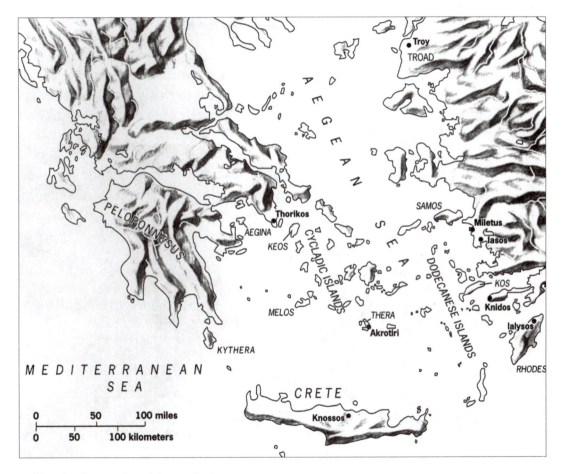

Map 2   Bronze Age: Minoan Crete

from the mythical elements? The first suggestions that there might be a kernel of history in the tales of Minos came in the late nineteenth century when Sir Arthur Evans, a wealthy enthusiast who was investigating hieroglyphic writing on seal stones found in Crete, discovered the remains of a vast labyrinthine courtyard building complex at Knossos, near modern Heraklion. Evans excavated the complex, which he identified as the Palace of King Minos; accordingly, he named the culture Minoan, a name that is still applied to the Bronze Age culture of Crete.[2] The designation of the complex as a palace, the dwelling place of a king, is also still generally applied to similar courtyard complexes that have been found, and continue to be found, throughout the island.[3]

Evans' finds at Knossos in some ways seem to confirm the legend of Minos with startling accuracy. The labyrinthine plan of the building matched the Labyrinth within which the great Minotaur of myth lived, and the bull played a central role in the imagery in the wall paintings and on seals. Two of the most frequently portrayed symbols are the so-called

Figure 2.1 Monumental double axes.
Photo N. Demand

WEBSITE 2.1   HORNS OF CONSECRATION

Notice the possibility that the peak in the background (the site of a Peak Sanctuary) could have been deliberately framed by the horns.

http://ccwf.cc.utexas.edu/~bruceh/cc307/minoan/images/cd.jpg

Horns of Consecration, which Evans interpreted as stylized bull's horns, and a double axe, possibly the sacrificial instrument.

Some sort of bull-leaping game or ritual is portrayed on frescoes and seals. The acrobatic performers in the "game" appear to have grasped the bull's horns as it charged, and somersaulted between the horns and over the back of the bull. Evans suggested that the large crowds shown watching some sort of spectacle in another fresco were watching bull-leaping. It is not known whether the bull-leaper or the bull (if either) was sacrificed in the ritual, but the mythical story of the sacrifice of Athenian youths to the Minotaur suggests that the leapers did not enjoy a long life.

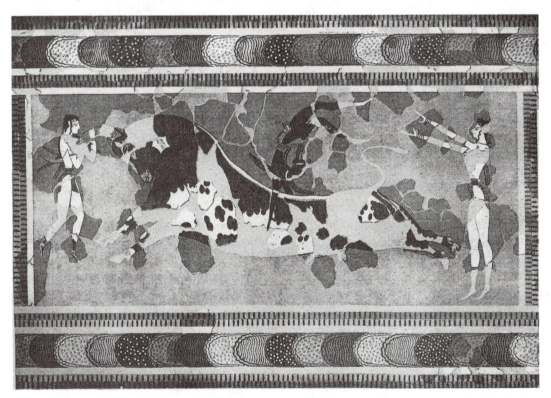

Figure 2.2   Bull-leaping fresco, Knossos.
Archaeological Museum, Herakleion.

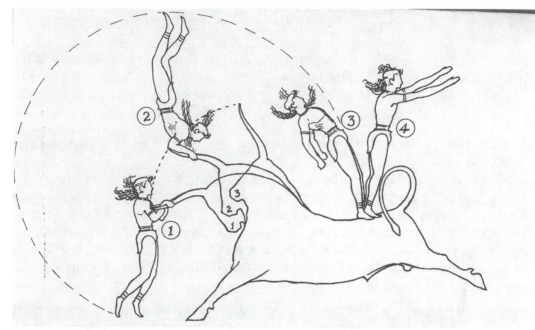

Figure 2.3   Bull-leaping diagram.
From Sir Arthur Evans (1964). *The Palace of Minos: A Comparative Account of the Successive Stages of the Early Cretan Civilization as Illustrated by the Discovereies of Knossos*, vol. III, p. 223. Courtesy Biblio and Tannen.

The palace at Knossos was the first of a number of similar building complexes on Crete that have since been found and excavated. These include palaces at Phaistos in the south, near the port of Kommos on the south coast; at Zakros, on the eastern end of the island; and on the northeast coast at Mallia.[4] In addition, numerous smaller complexes with some palatial features have been found. Excavation of these various sites, the study of the written records found in them, and archaeological surveys that document settlement patterns are slowly yielding a still-fragmented and shifting picture of Bronze Age Crete. In the meantime, the colorfully restored ruins of Knossos have become a major tourist attraction, and the spectacular discoveries of a Minoan-Cycladic town buried essentially intact by a volcanic eruption on the nearby island of Thera have contributed to the popular fascination with Minoan Crete. But before we look more closely at King Minos and his subjects, it will be helpful to consider what is known about how this great palace system came into being.

WEBSITE 2.2   NUMEROUS PHOTOS OF MINOAN SUBJECTS

See especially the bull-leaping fresco and the bull-leaping diagram. In what other forms does the bull appear?

http://ccwf.cc.utexas.edu/~bruceh/cc307/minoan/index.html

PRE-PALATIAL CRETE (EM II - III B)

At the time when the House of Tiles at Lerna and other large buildings were built on the mainland—in the mid-third millennium, Early Minoan II—similar developments were taking place in Crete. In fact, several building complexes have been discovered that have been interpreted as proto-palaces, forerunners of the well-known later palaces at Knossos, Mallia, Phaistos, and Zakros. The best-known of these early complexes is Myrtos,[5] where a cellular building complex of about 100 rooms included an unpaved court, living rooms, kitchens, store rooms with giant **pithoi** (large clay storage pots), workshops, and a shrine. The economy was one of mixed farming and crafts, including apparent specialized production of wine, olive oil, pottery, and textiles. The inhabitants had mastered the arts of making stone vases and cutting seals in stone and ivory. At about the same time, the first Minoan "colony" was also established when a group of Cretans made a settlement on the island of Kythera off the southern coast of the Peloponnesus. It may, however, have been only a seasonal fishing camp at first.

Peter Warren interpreted the site of Myrtos as a miniature prototype of the later Minoan palaces, a nucleus from which the later palace-form developed.[6] And, in fact, the complex at

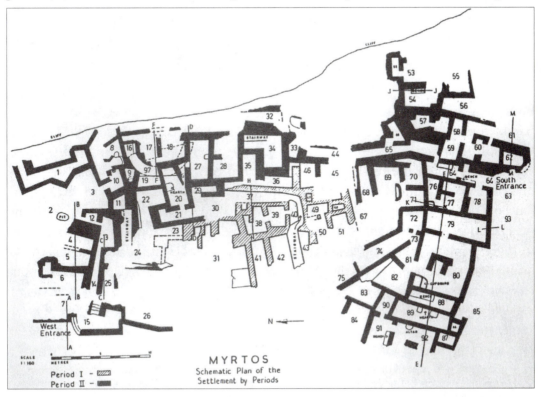

Figure 2.4   Site plan of Myrtos (after Warren), "Schematic Plan of the Settlement by Periods." Reproduced with permission of the British School at Athens.

Myrtos did have some noteworthy architectural features that were characteristic of the later palaces: light wells, use of wall timbers, narrow corridors, storage rooms, central courts, painted walls, wide paved staircases, and intramural wells.

Interpretation of the archaeological remains at Myrtos, however, provides a good illustration of some of the difficulties involved in the interpretation of archaeological evidence. While Warren saw the settlement as a proto-palace with areas devoted to specialized production and storage, another archaeologist, Tod Whitelaw, interpreted the evidence quite differently. He differentiated periods of occupation, identified the uses of the various rooms, and defined individual houses.[7] As a result, he concluded that only five or six households lived in Myrtos at any one time, and that production was on a subsistence level, with each household providing for all of its own needs. Therefore Whitelaw argued that Myrtos could not be seen as a proto-palace.

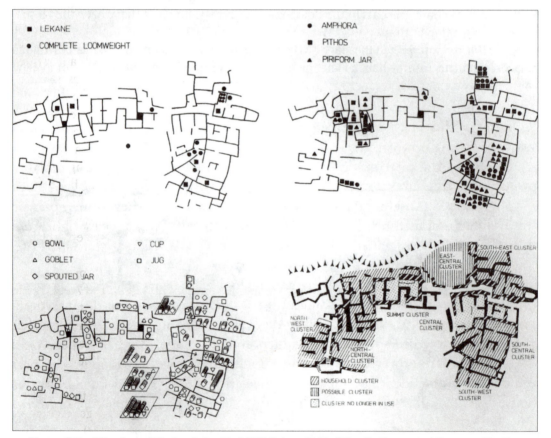

Figure 2.5   Site plan of Myrtos (after Todd Whitelaw 1983, "The Settlement at Fournou Korifi Myrtos and Aspects of Early Minoan Social Organization" in *Minoan Society*, ed. O. Krzyszkowska and L. Nixon. By permission of Gerald Duckworth & Company, Ltd.)

Whitelaw's interpretation is widely accepted.[8] Important evidence in its support has been found in the fact that the gradual growth of the complex can be traced by an analysis of wall joints and abutments. Moreover, analysis of the movable finds such as loom weights, cooking pots, and storage pithoi within their contexts attests to multiple kitchens, weaving work spaces, washtubs, and storerooms—strong evidence that there were a number of individual family units.

OLD PALACE PERIOD (MMIA–MMII, 2000–1750)

At the end of the Early Minoan period, ca. 2000, there were extensive destructions throughout the island of Crete, and many settlements were abandoned, although there is no evidence to suggest foreign intruders. In the subsequent MMIA period, order was gradually restored, overseas contacts were developed, population increased significantly, and the economy reached new levels of organization. Building complexes that can fairly be called proto-palaces were constructed using the techniques of monumental ashlar masonry (construction using square-cut and dressed blocks of stone). The earliest and largest of these was at Knossos; other major complexes were subsequently built at sites throughout the island: Phaistos, Mallia, and Zakros. These complexes combined residential, economic, administrative, and religious uses. One of their basic functions was the collection, storage, and redistribution of foodstuffs, which often formed the basis of large, probably ritualized communal meals. Seals were used to keep records, and writing began in a hieroglyphic script and a script, called **Linear A**, that consisted of signs representing syllables (consonant and vowel combinations). The idea of hieroglyphic writing may have originated in Egypt; however, the forms of the Cretan signs show little dependence on Egyptian hieroglyphics. The handling and distribution of large amounts of stored goods necessitated some form of record keeping, which may have led to the independent development of writing.

Imports from the Aegean, Anatolia, Cyprus, the Levant, and Egypt, and the appearance of Cretan products in these areas, all attest to Cretan involvement in widespread Aegean and Mediterranean trade networks, an important aspect of which was access to metals: copper, silver, tin, and lead. A number of new vase shapes reflect these contacts with the Near East and the influence they had on Minoan cultural conceptions; in particular, animal-shaped libation vessels and bowls with miniature interior figures appear to have been adopted from Near Eastern cults.

Although control by these proto-palaces over various aspects of life appears to have escalated rapidly during this period, it was not total. Large underground storage enclosures (*kouloures*), perhaps used for the communal storage of grain or water, were still located outside the complexes, and evidence for the production of Kamares ware, an eggshell-thin elite pottery that was widely exported, shows that it rested in the hands of families living outside the proto-palaces.

THE NEW PALACE PERIOD (MM III-LM I B, CA. 1750–1490)

The MM II period ended with widespread destructions that have been attributed to earthquakes. After the destructions, the palaces were rebuilt in MM III on the same sites but in many instances with less daring plans, suggesting that care was taken to protect against future earthquake damage. For example, unsupported spans that had served monumental entry ways were cut back to increase stability. Access to the central court was also tightened, apparently reflecting concern about intrusions by hostile outsiders. Colorful frescoes were widely used throughout the palace, many designed for public viewing, and the use of multi-colored building materials added to the vivid polychromatic effect.

Characteristics of the Minoan Palaces

The essential element of all palaces was the central courtyard. Although the courtyards varied in size, most had roughly the same proportions and a similar north-south orientation. At Knossos, a throne room opened off of the central court with an adjacent **lustral basin**, in which a few steps led down to what has been interpreted as a ritual pool. This "throne room," or at least the throne itself, may, however, date only from the later period of Mycenaean control. All the palaces appear to have been built outward from the central courtyard in a style that has been called agglutinative, as if elements were added as needed to the basic core feature of the court. The resulting plan was labyrinthine, as myth would lead us to expect. The complex character of the building layout would have enhanced its defensive potential in case of attack; only a few external defensive walls have been found (at Mallia, Gournia, and Petras), and none of them formed a complete circuit.[9]

To the east of the central court at Knossos were apartments that Evans identified as the private living quarters of the ruler. They featured light wells, often built in conjunction with stairways, and **pillar-and-door partitions** (walls made up of a series of pillars with inset doors that could be opened or closed as the weather dictated, which provided light and air to the internal rooms of the palace). There were also bathrooms and flushable toilets connected to the extensive drainage system of the palace.[10] In keeping with Evans' nineteenth-century assumptions, since there were two similar sets of rooms, one, the larger, has been designated the king's quarters, while the smaller set has been identified as the queen's. However, the absence of a number of features that would suggest kingship—such as portrayals of rulers,[11] and the presence of cult scenes involving not one dominant male individual but several people of apparently similar status—has led a number of archaeologists to reject Evans' assumptions and to interpret the political structure not as a kingship but as a communal organization centered on religious rituals focused on the courtyards.[12]

Another feature that characterized the palaces was large storage areas, which by the New Palace period had been moved within the palace. The most typical form of storage was the long narrow room, or **magazine**, lined with rows of large storage jars (*pithoi*), some as tall as five feet, which were used for the storage of grain, oil, wine, and olives.

Later cists were cut in the floor and lined with waterproof material for the storage of fine textiles and other perishables.

In addition to the central court, all the palaces had **west courts**, paved areas adjacent to the west facade that were open to the surrounding town, providing a place of interaction between palace and people.[13] They were places of large-scale storage; in the Old Palaces they had been the sites of *kouloures* (monumental circular walled underground pits, probably for grain storage), and the west wings of the New Palaces contained extensive storage rooms. Storage areas appear to have had religious connections, for the symbol of a double axe is frequently found cut into the pillars and walls of the storerooms, and the storerooms communicate directly with rooms identified as shrines (basement rooms, or crypts, with a central pillar whose religious significance is suggested by incised figures of double axes or adjacent offering tables). The west wings were also the sites of rooms that are viewed as having had more formal ceremonial or religious uses. These apparent religious associations of the storerooms suggest that the divinity was considered to be the recipient and owner of their contents. Here Cyprus provides a parallel, although from the Late Bronze Age period. Cypriot workshops for the production of copper were often located adjacent to shrines, and figures of divinities standing on miniature copper ingots have been identified as images of an Ingot God.[14] In Cyprus the vital activity of copper production was thus brought under divine protection, and a similar situation may be reflected in the conjunction of storage and workshop facilities and shrines in the Minoan palaces. In three of the west courts raised walkways were provided, perhaps used by the people of the town to bring offerings to be stored in the palace during a harvest or other religious celebration.

The picture supports the position of Halstead and others who see social storage and community involvement as key factors in the development of the palaces. Halstead reasoned that people in Crete, which is characterized by a high degree of localized climatic variation, had adopted the strategy of communal food storage and exchange to protect against localized crop failures. If everyone put his harvest into storage, then everyone could share in the common

Source Analysis

E xamine the plans for the palaces at Knossos, Phaistos, Mallia and Zako. What are the similarities and differences between the plans, keeping in mind the scale according to which each was drawn? In particular, compare the orientation of each palace and the dimensions and proportions of the central courts. Find storage areas and locate stairways and pillar-and-door construction, which may indicate living quarters. Is similarity in layout good evidence for the exercise of central control over all the palaces?

WEBSITE 2.3   THE PALACE AT KNOSSOS
http://www.athenapub.com/11knoss.htm

This website by one of the noted excavators of Knossos offers plans and a summary of the stages of development of the palace. Compare these plans for the palace at Knossos with those for Phaistos and Mallia.

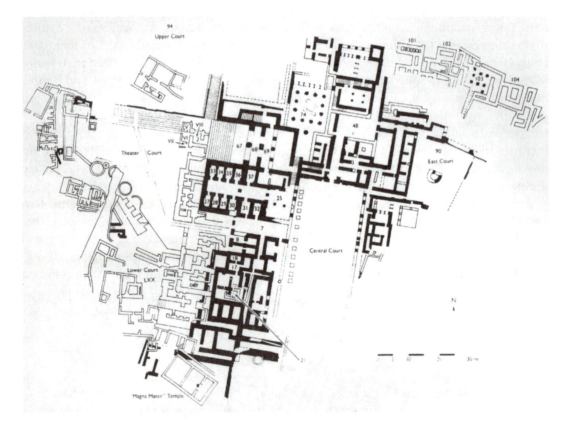

Figure 2.6   The Palace of Phaistos.
Reprinted with permission of Edzioni dell'Ateneo.

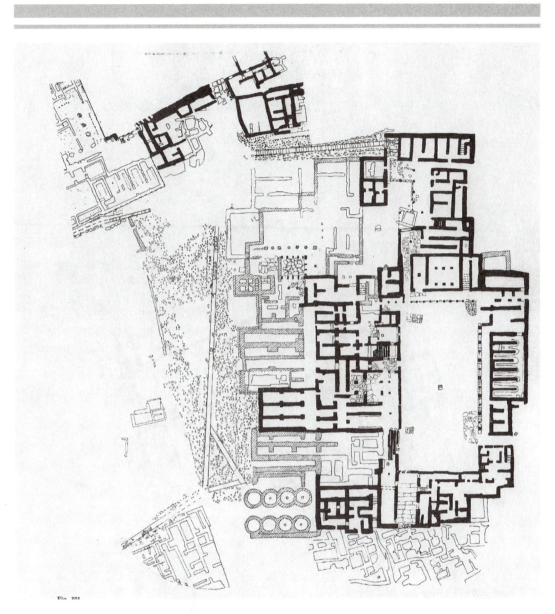

Figure 2.7   The Palace of Mallia.
Reprinted with permission of Edzioni dell'Ateneo.

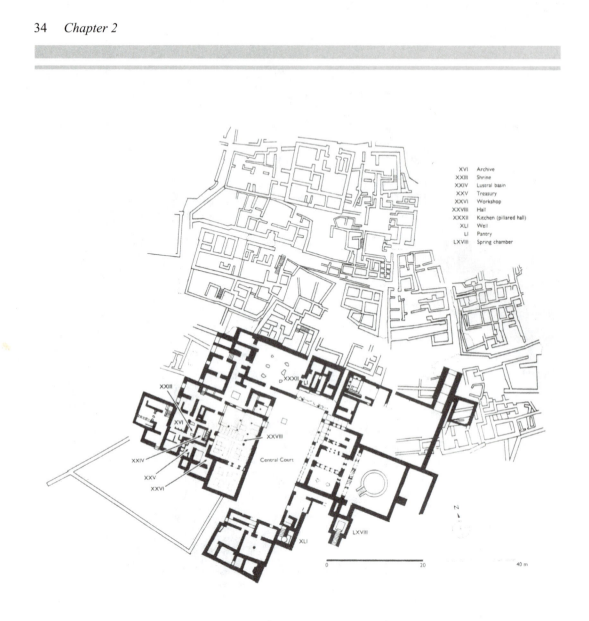

Figure 2.8   The Palace of Zakros.
Reprinted with the permission of Scribner, an imprint of Simon & Schuster Adult Publishing
Group, from *Zakros: The Discovery of a Lost Palace of Ancient Crete* by Nicholas Platon.
Copyright © 1971 by Nicholas Platon.

resources, even those unlucky individuals whose crops had failed that season. Exchanges with neighboring communities would have extended the safety network. An added advantage was that some of the harvest of good years could be stored against the possibility of a more generalized bad year for the community. Surplus could also be stored "on the hoof," by being fed to sheep. The animals could be eaten if necessary, but under normal conditions they would provide wool to make cloth, a desirable item for trade. The large storage facilities of the palaces, including the communal granaries outside the Old Palaces, and the large numbers of sheep in the records of the last stage of the palaces' existence (about 100,000), provide evidence that the Minoans did make use of such survival strategies.

Linear A Script

Our understanding of the Minoan palaces is based not only upon evidence of architecture and frescoes, but also upon written records in **Linear A** script. Linear A was a syllabic writing system in which somewhat fewer than 100 symbols represented syllables rather than individual sounds, as in an alphabetic system. The texts were inscribed on small clay tablets while the clay was still wet; they were also impressed on seals and other small bits of clay whose purpose is unclear. Occasionally inscriptions have been found on portable objects as well. Even though Linear A has not yet been deciphered, much is being teased out of it by detailed study.[15] Many tablets clearly contain accounts of products, for they make use of ideograms recognizable as indicators for grain, wine, olive oil, and figs. Inscriptions found on storage jars may identify or characterize the contents or indicate the owner or producer.

Linear A script was used for a variety of purposes in addition to the keeping of economic records. One such use appears to have been religious, as attested by inscriptions found on portable objects that are similar to later Greek libation vessels and other cultic equipment. Although these inscriptions cannot be read, the repetition of certain groups of signs on various objects, and the resemblance of these objects to later Greek cult equipment, suggests their ritual character.

No evidence exists for the literary use of Linear A, but it is likely that the tablets that have survived were merely temporary; only their accidental baking in the fires that destroyed the palaces preserved them. Other records, and perhaps even literary or religious texts, may have been kept on more valuable substances, such as papyrus or parchment that turned out to be less lasting than the clay tablets. In fact, some seals contain imprints that seem to attest their use for such documents.

Linear A inscriptions have been found not only in palaces, but also in villa and town sites. The use of the script in so many different locations and for differing purposes implies that some level of literacy was relatively widespread, at least in comparison with later Mycenaean syllabic script, **Linear B.** Since Linear A contains fewer than 100 signs, in contrast to the approximately 600 signs used in the cuneiform writing of Mesopotamia and the thousand or so signs out of a repertory of several thousand that were in common use in Egyptian hieroglyphics, its use need not have been limited to professional scribes.

WEBSITE 2.4   LINEAR A SCRIPT
http://www.ancientscripts.com/lineara.html

This is a site by a software engineer whose hobby is ancient scripts.

Functions of the Palaces

From the extensive storage areas and the finds of Linear A records in the palaces and administrative centers, such as the villa of **Hagia Triada**, it is clear that these centers served for the collection, storage, and redistribution of the basic necessities of life, as well as centers of craft production. Grain, oil, wine, wool, flax, metals, and precious materials such as ivory and gold were brought under the control of the administration to be stored; from these stores, food rations went to workers and officials, and raw materials to craft workers who produced both utilitarian objects, such as weapons and military equipment, and luxury items. All materials entering or being distributed were carefully documented, as were workers, officials, animal herds, land holdings, and offerings to the gods. A primary function of the Minoan system was thus the collection and redistribution of resources, although the redistribution may have been mainly to the privileged few.

Another important function of the palaces was their role in centralized administration. Linking the hierarchy of architectural forms with the evidence that sealings found at various locations were made by the same seal, historians have suggested that Crete in the New Palace period was organized in a widespread hierarchical network in which local rulers or governors functioned under the central control of the palace at Knossos. This is in contrast with the Old Palace period, when the existence of fortified sites, and the evidence for burnt destructions of palaces and other buildings, may reflect the presence of several independent and warring states on the island. If these readings of the archaeological evidence are correct, it may have been these unsettled conditions that helped give rise to the overlordship of Knossos and to the development of an organized system of control in a hierarchy of palaces, villas, and town sites.

In their role as hubs of a palace economy, the Minoan palaces resembled the palaces of the Near East, although the typical Near Eastern institution of a powerful temple paralleling and possibly rivaling the palace is not similarly prominent in Crete. One free-standing temple has been found, with what has been interpreted as dramatic evidence of a human sacrifice interrupted by an earthquake that destroyed the building, killing the three officients who were carrying out the sacrifice.[16] But this temple was destroyed in about 1700, probably in an earthquake that also played a role in the destruction of the Old Palaces, and subsequently the temple function appears incorporated into the New Palaces. Thus, at least in the period of the New Palaces, Cretan cult activities seem to have been embedded in the palace itself and, as we shall see, in outlying sacred spots with palatial connections, rather than in independent structures and institutions. Shrines, cult equipment, and religious motifs have been identified throughout the palaces, and religious and cult roles seem to have been played by the personnel of the palaces rather than by independent outsiders. In fact, some have even interpreted the Minoan complexes themselves as cult centers, temple-palaces or palace-temples.[17]

Minoan Religion in the Life of the People

The central role played by religion in solidifying the authority of the palace rested upon the successful integration into the palatial system of the religious customs and beliefs of ordinary Cretans. That the rulers were successful in linking the traditions of ordinary people with the developing interests of the palace is suggested by the existence of signs of palatial connections at extra-palatial shrines centered on natural features such as caves, peaks, and trees.[18]

About 45 **peak sanctuaries** have been identified in Crete. They tend to be on heights between 350 and 1000 meters above sea level, on relatively accessible sites, and usually in summer grazing zones. They may have begun as the sacred places of shepherds and farmers, for votive offerings included many miniature terracotta sheep and goats and replicas of creatures helpful to farmers, such as weasels (which eat mice) and beetles (which aerate the soil). That the divinities also served the popular role of healers is also suggested by offerings in the form of human arms, legs, heads, and torsos. Most such sites are close to, and visible from, a settlement. There is evidence that fire played a central role in the cult, and nighttime ceremonies with giant fires would have provided an impressive spectacle viewed from the nearby settlement. Palaces seem to have been established within the sphere of specific peak shrines, and in the New Palace period, relationships between palace and shrine may have been expressed by visual relationships (see Figure 2.1)

Cave sanctuaries were also favored places of devotion that were frequented by both the exalted and the humble. Evidence for worship has been found in at least fifteen caves. A number of different gods, each with a specific function, appear to have been worshipped in these caves. In some, the dedications, such as prestigious weapons and collections of miniature double axes in gold, attest palatial connections. This fits well with the tradition reported by Plato that King Minos sought out Zeus in the Idaean cave every eight years to renew his royal power.[19] In contrast, in one of the more famous cave shrines at Amnisos, only humble pottery figurines were offered to the goddess of childbirth, Eileithyia (her later Greek name).

Another type of extra-palatial cult place was the countryside **tree shrine**. Since the remains of such shrines would usually be slight and isolated, and therefore unlikely to be found by archaeologists, most of our evidence for them comes from portrayals on gold rings and seals. A large tree was the central feature in these sanctuaries. It was usually enclosed by a wall, which often also protected an altar or even a temple building. Ecstatic activity or dancing around the tree are frequently portrayed. Such shrines, despite their rural location, could not have been only places of peasant worship, for the evidence for their existence comes from objects of great value.

The overall picture of Minoan religion is one of local and traditional religious practices that were taken over and institutionalized in support of the power of the palaces. Cult activities were brought into the palaces or, when this was not possible, were associated with them by monumental architecture, ceremonies in which prestigious offerings were made to the divinity, and visual connections.

The Question of Origins

The similarity of the Minoan palaces to palaces in the Near East, and the fact that the Old Palaces appear to have sprung up very suddenly at the turn of the second millennium, have naturally raised the question of Near Eastern influence on their development, and a variety of interpretations of the type and degree of influence have been offered. On the other hand, some scholars argue for independent development. We will consider some of the arguments for each of these views.

Perhaps the strongest case for Near Eastern influence is the sudden appearance in Crete not only of palaces but of a cluster of features associated with the palatial buildings of the Near East, especially Syria: monumental structures built in ashlar masonry, specialized production, writing, and an extensive administrative system of seal usage. A comparison of **the palace at Mari** in Syria with the Cretan palace at Mallia reveals both similarities and differences.

Minoan palaces share many features with the Near Eastern palace exemplified in the palace at Mari, such as courtyards and storage areas. Nevertheless, there are some fundamental differences that rule out a simple cookie-cutter model of influence. The most basic architectural difference is that the palace at Mari was strongly fortified, with defensive outer walls serving as the determining factor for the interior plan of the palace. The palace was built from the outside in. In contrast, Minoan palaces for the most part seem to have relied for defense upon their labyrinthine organization, and they were built from the inside out, with a notable lack of concern for symmetry and formal order, giving the effect of spontaneous growth. Nevertheless, as we saw above, similarities in the various Cretan palaces suggest that the builders did follow at least a general plan,[20] and the existence of fortifications has been identified in the earliest stages of these buildings.[21]

Arguments for the indigenous origin of the palaces include that of Peter Warren, discussed above, who argued that Myrtos was a proto-palace, a form from which later palaces could have been developed. Another explanation for the rise of palaces from indigenous roots involves the model of social storage as argued by P. M. Halstead (see above).[22] Once extensive stores had been created, control over their distribution became a source of power in itself. Those who were able to exercise this control were also able to determine the utilization and distribution of community resources, and they could use these resources to ob-

Source Analysis

C ompare the plans for the palace at Mari with those of the Minoan palaces. What similarities do you see? What differences?

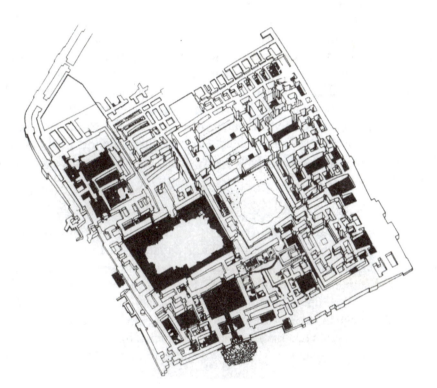

Figure 2.9 The Palace at Mari in Syria.
Reproduced with permission of the Institut Français d'Archéologie de Beyrouth.

tain bronze for weapons and other valuable imports that would enhance their own status. Moreover, as caretakers of the grain and animal resources of the community, they would have appeared as human assistants of the divinities of fertility, a role that sanctioned their control of the resources. We do seem to see such a situation in the New Palaces, where storage was brought into the palace and associated with religious symbols and with the throne room itself.

Most recently, however, attention has shifted back to trade (whether commercial or the gift exchange of prestige items), and the resulting interaction with the palatial centers of the Near East, as the motive factors in the development of the Minoan palaces, an explanation first put forward by Renfrew in 1972.[23] According to this view, improvements in shipbuilding and the use of the sail increased the use of the existing network of maritime trade routes; new craft techniques and materials made possible the production of items desired by a growing class that could afford more luxurious living; and reports of foreign luxuries by travelers and traders stimulated desire on the part of this elite for such luxuries. At the same time, new developments in metallurgy brought an increased market for both metallic raw materials and products, and the conditions of maritime travel led to the development of exchange centers (**emporoi**), at which some traders quickly accumulated wealth. These emporoi eventually became the sites of the first Mediterranean maritime states, in which palaces developed as centers of production and the control of local resources (probably more effectively managed through increased use of ritual than through repression of the local work force), and the sites of luxurious living quarters. The fact that the Minoan palaces are not cookie-cutter replicas of Near Eastern palaces is to be expected, since local building methods and customs were used to implement models whose features were only imperfectly experienced and reported by travelers.

Was There a Minoan Thalassocracy?

The fifth-century Greek historian Thucydides claimed that King Minos was the first to establish a navy, conquer and colonize the Cycladic islands, free the sea from pirates, and exercise a thalassocracy (supreme control of the sea).[24] Sir Arthur Evans accepted this idea. But was Thucydides right? Working in the fifth century, without the evidence revealed by modern archaeology, the ancient Greek historian had little to go on beyond mythological tales. Did the tradition of a Minoan thalassocracy contain a kernel of historical truth, or was it simply a fairy tale, or perhaps even a fifth-century invention to justify Athens' own naval empire?[25]

The widespread distribution of Minoan pottery, which has been found at sites throughout the eastern Mediterranean and as far west as the Lipari islands north of Sicily, seems at first consideration to support the hypothesis of a thalassocracy. But thalassocracy means command of the seas, and given ancient sailing conditions, that means control over landing spots and harbors, which in turn suggests settlement. The remains of Minoan pottery found at archaeological sites need not attest the presence of Minoans either as traders or as settlers, let alone in control of the seas, since they may have been simply items of trade carried by others besides Minoans. Stronger evidence for settlement is provided by finds of the artifacts of daily living that have been found at a number of sites: ordinary kitchen pottery, Minoan techniques of building construction or architectural features, frescoes in the Minoan style, Minoan cult practices and burial customs, or Linear A tablets (not necessarily all at any one site).

Most of the evidence for overseas settlement comes from the palatial periods, and most impressively from the New Palace period. Nevertheless, evidence begins in the pre-palatial period, when archaeological finds on the island of Kythera, off the southern coast of the Peloponnesus, attest that Minoans established themselves, after driving out the original inhabitants. In the New Palace period, this settlement was revived and enlarged. A Minoan presence is also evident on a number of Aegean islands—Kos, Karpathos, Rhodes, Samos, Iasos—and probably at the site of Knidos on the eastern Aegean coast.[26] Another important site of Minoan settlement, beginning in the Old Palace period, is now recognized in Miletus, also on the eastern Aegean coast.[27]

Why would the Minoans have left their fertile land for the relatively infertile Greek islands? One clue may be found on the island of Keos, which lies off the Attic coast opposite the Laurion mines with their deposits of silver, lead, and copper. Evidence confirms that copper was smelted on Keos, and there was also a significant Minoan presence there.[28] In the Bronze Age, large supplies of bronze were essential to national security, just as oil is essential to the running of the modern economy, and Crete lacked both tin and significant sources of copper, the necessary ingredients for its bronze production. There were copper deposits not only at Laurion, but also on some of the Cycladic islands and in the southern Peloponnesus. These deposits may explain the Minoan interest in these places, or rather, in island stepping stones to them, such as Kythera, Kea, Thera, and Melos. Cyprus was, however, perhaps the most important source of large amounts of copper, and there is abundant evidence for contacts between Crete and that island.

To find tin required the Minoans to go further afield. Sources of tin existed in southeastern Anatolia, although it is still unclear whether they were in use at this time. More likely is a source in Elam, supplied via the Syrian state of Mari, and after Mari's destruction by Hammurabi in 1757, via Aleppo. Minoans consequently settled in the chain of the Dodecanese islands and on Rhodes, creating settlements that provided stopping places on the voyage east. The settlers might have been visited by itinerant Syrian merchants carrying tin and copper. The Late Bronze Age shipwreck off the southern coast of Turkey at Ulu Burun, discussed in Chapter 3, provides a later example of such merchants, probably Canaanites, who traveled with supplies of copper and tin and tools for working the metal to order in the ports at which they stopped.[29] In the same area copper was also available on Cyprus. While evidence for Minoan use of Cypriot copper at this period is not strong, there is abundant evidence for Cretan participation in eastern trade in the finds in Cyprus and the Levant of central Cretan transport stirrup jars, many marked with an octopus, the sign of Crete, and some with Cypro-Minoan script. Similar jars also went to Sardinia, South Italy, and Sicily.[30] The interest of Knossos in the Cypriot market is also attested by the appearance of the term for "Cypriot" in the Linear B tablets.[31]

Another metal trading route went up the east Anatolian coast to Troy and the Troad, providing another possible source of copper or bronze.[32] Evidence of Minoan presence has been found at a number of staging points along this route: the Anatolian sites of Knidos, Miletos,

Müskebi, Iasos, and the islands of Kos and Samos. Whether these were full-scale Minoan settlements or small enclaves of traders settled among local people is still not clear.[33]

The evidence for a Minoan presence on the island of Thera is particularly important because of the size and prosperity of the Bronze Age city of Akrotiri and its sudden destruction during the violent volcanic eruption in LM IA that caused the collapse of the island.[34] Thera is the southernmost of the Cycladic islands, lying about 60 miles to the north of Crete. Today, as a result of the eruption, it has the form of a steep rocky semi-circle, part of the rim of the volcanic caldera, or cone. The eruption buried Akrotiri beneath layers of pumice and ash up to 60 meters deep. The absolute date of the eruption is a hotly contested matter among archaeologists (see the discussion of chronology at the end of the chapter). For a long time the eruption was dated ca. 1500, but recent evidence from ice cores in Greenland and tree rings in the United States and Ireland suggests a much earlier date, ca. 1628, and this is now widely accepted.[35]

The Settlement at Thera (Santorini)

Hints of the existence of a Bronze Age settlement at Akrotiri on Thera long existed in sporadic local finds, including masses of ruined building stones that obstructed ploughing. In 1967 the Greek archaeologist Spyridon Marinatos began the excavation of the site, buried many meters under the surface by the volcanic eruption. The excavations were spectacularly successful. Up to this time they have revealed 17 buildings, ten of which have been explored, and the limits of the city have not yet been reached.

Akrotiri lay at a focal point on all of the metal routes, and it must have possessed a south-facing port that was capable of provisioning ships and crews and serving as a base for assembling ships to sail in convoy. The houses that have been excavated are those of a prosperous people. Many of the buildings have two or three stories, and the walls are often decorated with frescoes. Apparently the inhabitants had some warning of the impending disaster and were able to escape, for no signs of bodies or abandoned treasures have been found. However, the remains of a great deal of pottery and stored food, and impressions left by wooden furniture, as well as the frescoes, provide evidence for life in Akrotiri.

Analyses of the architecture, pottery, and wall paintings of Thera have provided a picture of strong Minoan influence upon a basically Cycladic island culture. Typical Minoan features appear in the architecture: a lustral basin, one apparent light well (but since the houses were free standing, the need for light wells might not have been great), pillar-and-door construction, large central pillars, frescoes, the use of timber in wall construction to lessen earthquake damage, and a drainage system. Other evidence of Minoan influence on Thera includes the use of a Minoan system of weights, some inscriptions in Minoan Linear A script on jars (but no tablets), Minoan symbols such as the Horns of Consecration, and more Minoan pottery than at any other site, even on Crete itself, with the exception of Knossos.

The Akrotiri frescoes confirm the picture of Minoan influence on a Cycladic tradition.

WEBSITE 2.5   THERA (SANTORINI) AND THE FRESCOES

This website of the Hellenic Ministry of Culture provides views of the buildings and links to views of most of the most noted frescoes. The Expedition Fresco is called the Flotilla Miniature Frieze.

> http://www.culture.gr/2/21/211/21121a/e211ua08.html

Be sure to view the linked site for Museum of Prehistoric Thera for some important finds made on this site.

Jeremy Rutter's Dartmouth website has a discussion of the eruption and the frescoes, with the linked images providing a number of views of the island and the site.

> http://projectsx.dartmouth.edu/classics/history/bronze_age/lessons/les/17.html

While the style of the paintings is Minoan, it has a Cycladic bent: the approach is more naturalistic and less conventional than the Minoan frescoes. Human figures appear to be in non-ceremonial contexts: fishermen, children boxing (although perhaps this is a puberty rite),[36] and various scenes of activity in and around settlements in the portrayal of a sea-borne expedition.[37] But the differences between Theran and Cretan frescoes may also reflect the fact that the Theran paintings decorated private homes, while most of the Cretan paintings were found on palace sites.

The most interesting of the Theran Fresco in terms of the question of a Minoan thalassocracy is the miniature Expedition Fresco, which decorated the walls of a room in a building called the West House.[38] It depicts a fleet of eight ships, accompanied by many smaller boats, about to arrive at a Minoan (?) town, having passed by a river landscape reminiscent of the Nile, after leaving another town (in Africa?); a raid on still another town is also portrayed. The rowers of the ships are Minoan in dress and appearance, but some scholars identify the soldiers as mainlanders, Mycenaean Greeks.[39] An adjoining room in the same house is decorated with frescoes portraying the cabin of a ship as it appears in the fresco, and the house has therefore been identified as that of the captain.[40] Were the mainland Mycenaeans serving as mercenaries for the people of Thera? If the fresco represents a military-commercial expedition, it might be evidence for a Minoan thalassocracy.

Caution in the interpretation of the Expedition frescoes is suggested, however, by another reading of the scenes. Striking similarities have been pointed out between these scenes and themes familiar from Homeric poetry: the juxtaposition of a city at war and in peace, the cattle raid, the attack on a city, Egypt as a land of fantasy.[41] Evidence that epic poetry began as early as the Mycenaean and Minoan periods is growing, and the Expedition Fresco may reflect this. The events it portrays may not have been a biographical record of the life of the owner of the house, but episodes in a favorite epic poem, recited at banquets of Theran men who gathered in this room to drink and listen to bards sing of far-off adventures.

Figure 2.10   Thera Expedition Fresco (Town)
Reproduced by permission of the Archaeological Society of Athens. Reprinted with the permission of Cambridge University Press.

Figure 2.11   Thera Expedition Fresco (Ships)
Reproduced by permission of the Archaeological Society of Athens. Reprinted with the permission of Cambridge University Press.

The culture of Thera was Cycladic with a strong overlying Minoan veneer. In this it was typical of a number of other, smaller Cycladic communities that also exhibited Minoan features. The question is whether these Cycladic peoples were simply adopting Minoan fashions as a result of frequent contacts with a richer, more sophisticated culture, or whether Minoans were actually living on the sites, and if they were living there, whether they were present unofficially, perhaps as traders, or officially, in order to control a subject people.

Malcolm Wiener has recently made the case for the exercise of Minoan control, arguing that the differences in population, resources, and organization on Crete, as compared with the smaller Cycladic communities, would have made Minoan control likely.[42] Signs of the exercise of central control on Crete itself might be seen in the relative size of the palace at Knossos and its cultural hegemony as expressed in architecture and pottery, and the impressions of sealings made by the same seals at various locations in Crete. There are also signs that peaceful conditions were being maintained by forceful methods: roads guarded by watchtowers, Minoan expertise in the manufacture of bronze weapons, and portrayals of battles on the Expedition Fresco.[43] Moreover, Wiener points to the large number of luxury goods and copper ingots stored at the port site of Zakros as a reflection of the Minoans' dependence upon imports for copper, tin, and bronze, as well as to their interest in Near Eastern luxury items, all of which depended upon the safety of the seas. But was it the Minoans who policed the seas through the exercise of a thalassocracy?

Recent discoveries of Minoan-style frescoes at sites in the Levant and Egypt add new evidence—and new puzzles—to the picture of Minoan overseas contacts. Minoan-type frescoes have been discovered at the Syrian sites of Kabri and Alalakh, and at the palace at Mari. Perhaps the most extensive and well-known of such frescoes, however, are those found at a site in the Egyptian delta called Tell ed-Daba'a, where frescoes portraying Minoan-style scenes of bull-leaping have been discovered. These frescoes have been dated toward the end of the sixteenth century (LM IA), during the period of Hyksos rule in Egypt.[44] It is not yet clear whether itinerant Minoan craftsmen created the paintings, or whether they were imitations of Minoan work, or why they happened to be painted at these sites. At this point there is no other evidence that would indicate the presence of a Minoan settlement at the Egyptian site, but it has been suggested that the scenes were painted for a Minoan princess who had been sent to Egypt in a dynastic marriage. If that were the case, it would show that the Egyptian royal house considered the Minoans of sufficient significance to forge a diplomatic marriage tie with them. Added to passages in Egyptian documents that refer to Crete and the "Islands in the Middle of the Great Green" as a single entity, this would tend to support the hypothesis of a thalassocracy.[45] However, perhaps the greater likelihood is that such paintings were desired mostly for their exotic character, as manifestations of the sophisticated tastes and wealth of those who commissioned them and could command such imported artistry. The question of a thalassocracy remains open; however, we should keep in mind that the suggestion was first made by a fifth-century Athenian historian, and that it may well reflect the interests of Athenian imperialism at that time, rather than the interests and activities of Bronze Age Minoans.

MYCENAEANS AT KNOSSOS (LM II–IIIA: I, 1490–1370)

At the end of LM IB, virtually all the Minoan sites underwent a series of destructions that may have been spread over an extended period of 25 to 40 years. Palaces, villas, small towns, and villages all suffered attack and looting, and many sites were abandoned, including palace sites. The palace at Knossos seems to have been mostly spared, although some of its surrounding houses and buildings suffered. Thus Knossos emerged as the only functioning palace, and it assumed a leading role, dominating the rest of the island.

The destructions were the result of attacks by mainland peoples, the Mycenaeans (see Chapter 3). The precise form of their subsequent control over Crete is not known. Hypotheses include a Mycenaean king, a governor installed by a Mycenaean conqueror, or a Minoan who had seized control with the aid of Mycenaean mercenaries. But a Mycenaean element was definitely present, as attested by burials of non-Minoan type in new cemeteries (Warrior Graves with weapons; single burials in chamber and pit tombs), and grave goods that were not typical of Minoan burials (weapons, bronze vessels, and jewelry that may have indicated military rank). Other evidence of a Mycenaean presence includes the introduction of mainland-style pottery forms and the replacement of the free-flowing, naturalistic motifs characteristic of Minoan pottery by rigid forms—the wildly exuberant Minoan octopus was tamed and organized. There were similar changes in the character of the frescoes, which now reflected militaristic rigidity and heraldic arrangements, with a predilection for formal arrangements such as processionals. While Knossos was predominant stylistically, modern observers see a general decline in the sophistication of architecture and the arts. However, connections with the outer world were maintained, with some exports to the mainland, and imports, especially from Egypt.

There may also have been a shift from the use of Linear A to Linear B in palace records at this time, although it is a contested question whether the Linear B texts found in the palace at Knossos date to this period or to the later period of the palace's final destruction.[46] If the tablets do indeed date to this period, they attest to the continuing role of Knossos in the administration of the economy, with intensified production. They record that large flocks of sheep were pastured and large numbers of women were employed in producing textiles from that wool.

A RETURN TO REGIONALISM (LM IIIA:2 – IIIB, 1370–1320)

In LM III A:2 the political situation shifted again as Knossos suffered destruction while regional centers gained in importance, as evidenced by the spread of habitation throughout the island and by a return to regionalism in pottery styles. Sizable settlements arose again at Kommos, Agia Triada, Tylissos, Khania, and Archanes. At Agia Triada a number of monumental buildings were constructed, including a typical Mycenaean megaron and a **stoa** (a building with an open colonnade on one side). A megaron was also built at Tylissos, as well as a stoa and a large cistern. At Kommos, the largest construction of the period on the island has been identified as a ship shed, and traditional subsistence agriculture seems to have been replaced by production of olive oil for export and metal products such as double-axes, which also were probably not for home use.[47] Minoan pottery continued to be exported to Cyprus, where Karageorghis identifies possible Minoan settlers.[48] Although the palace at Knossos continued to function, Khania appears to have been predominant in the island at this time, at least in terms of in terms of pottery production, export, and import. Its transport stirrup jars (many inscribed) can be traced to the mainland, Sardinia and southern Italy in the west, and to Cyprus and the Levant in the east. Handmade burnished ware of Italian type found in Khania but locally made may point to resident Italians, while Gray ware cups and **kylikes** (drinking cups), similar to material found in in tombs at Müskebi near Halikarnassos, suggest on-going contact with Minoans in that region. [49]

THE FINAL DESTRUCTION OF THE PALACE AT KNOSSOS (1375 B.C.E.)

At the end of LM IIIB, the palace at Knossos suffered a final destruction that brought palatial life to an end. After this, there is no evidence for writing or centralized administration on Crete. In the period of unrest and attacks from the sea that followed, many Cretans took to the hills, establishing refuge settlements in hard to access locations, although some continued to inhabit lowland sites. The most notable of these lowland sites was at Knossos, but the southern port at Kommos continued to function and in future years was visited by passing Phoenician mariners, who built a shrine there. Thus life and international connections continued on Crete through the upheavals of the end of the Bronze Age. But the center of Aegean power had by now shifted northward, to the Mycenaeans, who had begun their own palatial period.

CHRONOLOGY OF THE BRONZE AGE IN CRETE

When Sir Evans excavated the palace at Knossos, he established a tripartite system of chronology that still forms the basis of the island's Bronze Age chronology. It provides a series of relative dates based on pottery sequences; absolute dates are then derived from the correlation of pottery sequences with datable Near Eastern objects and events. The result is a division of Bronze Age Crete into Early Minoan, Middle Minoan, and Late Minoan periods (EM, MM, LM), each of which is in turn subdivided into three, and then further subdivided as needed, which results in designations such as MM II A1. Similar tripartite schemes have been developed for the mainland (Early, Middle, and Late Helladic, EH, MH, LH) and the islands (Early, Middle, and Late Cycladic, EC, MC, LC).

It is important to be familiar with this system of pottery dating, as well as with the absolute dates to which they are pegged, since in many archaeological publications only the relative dates are given. In large part this is because in this early period the connections between the relative series and the absolute dates are few and subject to change with new evidence.

For example, recent debate about the dating of the eruption of the volcanic island of Thera seriously challenges the traditional absolute dates for the pottery series. But whatever happens to the absolute dating, the relative series will remain. Thus it is useful to think in terms of both types of dating.

The chronologies in the table below follow the Revised Aegean high chronology based on Sturt Manning (1995), *The Absolute Chronology of the Aegean Early Bronze Age*, which dates the eruption of Santorini to ca. 1628.[50]

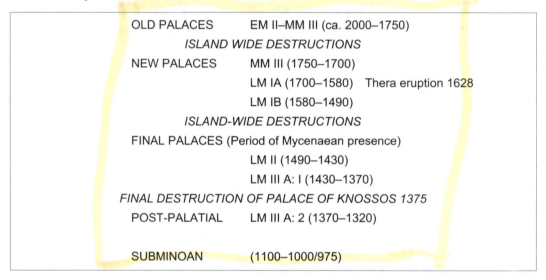

OLD PALACES	EM II–MM III (ca. 2000–1750)	
ISLAND WIDE DESTRUCTIONS		
NEW PALACES	MM III (1750–1700)	
	LM IA (1700–1580)	Thera eruption 1628
	LM IB (1580–1490)	
ISLAND-WIDE DESTRUCTIONS		
FINAL PALACES (Period of Mycenaean presence)		
	LM II (1490–1430)	
	LM III A: I (1430–1370)	
FINAL DESTRUCTION OF PALACE OF KNOSSOS 1375		
POST-PALATIAL	LM III A: 2 (1370–1320)	
SUBMINOAN	(1100–1000/975)	

SUGGESTIONS FOR FURTHER READING

A good, well-illustrated introduction to recent archaeological work on Crete can be found in *Athena Review* 3 (2003), which provides extensive further bibliography. For a more detailed treatment, see Paul and John Younger (2001), "Neopalatial, Final Palatial, and Postpalatial Crete, with Addendum: 1998–1999," pp. 91–173 in *Aegean Prehistory: A Review*, ed. Tracy Cullen. See also O. Krzyszkowska and L. Nixon (1983), *Minoan Society*; R. Hägg and N. Marinatos (1987), *The Function of the Minoan Palaces*; R. Hägg and N. Marinatos (1984), *The Minoan Thalassocracy: Myth and Reality*; and N. Marinatos (1993), *Minoan Religion*.

MAP STUDY

Important Minoan Cretan Sites on Map 2: Crete: Knossos, Phaistos, Kommos, Mallia, Palaikastro, Arkhanes, Anemospilia, Gournia, Myrtos, Zakros, Hagia Triada, Khania, Idaean Cave, Amnisos Cave, Kamares Cave

Sites elsewhere relevant to Minoans: Kythera, Keos, Thorikos, Thera/Akrotiri, Melos, Rhodes, Ialysos, Dodecanese islands, Cycladic islands, Troy, Troad, Knidos, Miletus, Iasos,

Kos, Samos, Mari, Ulu Burun, Cyprus, Mersin, Iskenderum, Tell ed-Daba (Egypt), Lipari islands, Sicily.

ENDNOTES

[1]Thucydides 1.4.

[2]On Evans' excavations, see his *The Palace of Minos at Knossos* (1921–35).

[3]See Michele Miller (2003), "Introduction: Courtyard Complexes and the Labyrinth of Minoan Culture," *Athena Review* 3:16–26, Figure 1. However, a number of archaeologists now object to this terminology, which they feel implies an anachronistic model of a powerful king ruling over a centralized kingdom; they accordingly prefer to use a more neutral term, "courtyard complexes," and to focus on the ritual or ceremonial uses of the courtyard as a key to the significance of the palaces. See Jan Driessen (2003), "The Court Compounds of Minoan Crete: Royal Palaces or Ceremonial Centers." *Athena Review* 3:57–61. In this book, the term "palace" will be used, however, because it is more widely used and familiar than other, probably more accurate, suggested terminologies.

[4]For a discussion of the palaces, see Gerald Cadogan (1976), *Palaces of Minoan Crete*; Hägg and Marinatos (above, n. 1). Aerial photographs of sites and complete bibliographies can be found in J. Wilson, E. E. Myers, and G. Cadogan (1992), *The Aerial Atlas of Ancient Crete*.

[5]Peter Warren (1972), *Myrtos: An Early Bronze Age Settlement in Crete*. For the buildings at Vasiliki and Palaikastro, see Keith Branigan (1988), *Pre-Palatial: The Foundations of Palatial Crete*, 242 and bibliography.

[6]Peter Warren (above, n. 5).

[7]Todd M. Whitelaw (1983), "The Settlement at Fournou Korifi Myrtos and Aspects of Early Minoan Social Organization," in O. Krzyskowska and L. Nixon (1983), *Minoan Society*.

[8]John Cherry, "Evolution, Revolution, and the Origins of Complex Society in Minoan Crete," in Krzyszkowska and Nixon (above, n. 7); also Branigan (above, n. 5), 45–9, 235–236, 242, although he questions a similar interpretation of another of these sites, the House on the Hill at Vasiliki; see the Dartmouth website, "Prehistoric Archaeology of the Aegan," Lesson 5.

[9]Louise Hitchcock (2003), "Understanding the Minoan Palaces," *Athena Review* 3:27–35.

[10]The residential use of these apartments is questioned by some; see, for example, A. C. Nordfeldt (1987), "Residential Quarters and Lustral Basins," in R. Hägg and N. Marinatos (1987), *The Function of the Minoan Palaces*, 187–194.

[11]Evans identified a figure in the frescoes as the "Priest-King," but there is no evidence that the figure was a priest or king, or even, for that matter, a male. For another interpretation, see W. D. Niemeier (1988), "The 'Priest-King' Fresco from Knossos: A New Reconstruction and Interpretation," pp. 235–244 in *Problems in Greek History*, ed. E. B. French and K. A. Wardle.

[12]Ilse Schoep (2002), "The State of the Minoan Palaces or the Minoan Palace-State?" pp. 15–33 in *Monuments of Minos: Rethinking the Minoan Palaces*, ed. Jan Driessen, Ilse Schoep, and Robert Laffineur.

[13]See R. Hägg, "On the Reconstruction of the West Facade of the Palace at Knossos," in Hägg and Marinatos, (above, n. 10), 129–134; and, in the same volume, D. J. I. Begg, "Continuity in the West Wing at Knossos," 178–184.

[14]See L. C. Hulin (1989), "The Identification of Cypriot Cult Figures Through Cross-Cultural Comparison:Some Problems," pp. 127–139, in *Early Society in Cyprus*, ed. E. Peltenburg; Paul Budd and Timothy Taylor (1995), "The Faerie Smith Meets the Bronze Industry: Magic versus Science in the Interpretation of Prehistoric Metal-making," *World Archaeology* 27:133–143.

[15]See John Chadwick (1987), *Linear B and Related Scripts*, Ch. 5; reprinted in J. T. Hooker (1998), *Reading the Past: Ancient Writing from Cuneiform to the Alphabet,* 178–182.

[16]See Y. Sakellarakis and E. Sapouna–Sakellaraki (1981), "Drama of Death in a Minoan Temple," *National Geographic* (Feb.), 205–222. W. A. MacDonald and C. Thomas (1990), *Progress into the Past*, 378–383, identify other free-standing temples on the mainland, on the island of Melos, and at Kition in Cyprus.

[17]Evans first suggested that the Minoan king was a theocratic ruler. More recently, see Marinatos, (1993), *Minoan Religion*; and popularized works by Rodney Castleden (1989), *The Knossos Labyrinth: A New View of the 'Palace of Minos' at Knossos* , and Castleden (1990). *Minoans: Life in Bronze Age Crete*.

[18]On Minoan shrines of various types, see B. Rutkowski (1972), *Cult Places in the Aegean World*. The one free-standing shrine, that at Anemospilia, was destroyed in the earthquake that destroyed the Old Palaces and was not rebuilt in the New Palace period; rather, the shrine form appears to have been incorporated into the New Palaces.

[19]Plato, Laws 624b.

[20]Colin Macdonald (2003), "The Palaces of Minos at Knossos," *Athena Review* 3:36–43, argues that the MMIIIB New Palace at Knossos was "designed as a single coherent structure by one architect, or a group working together."

[21]L. Vance Watrous (1994), "Crete from Earliest Prehistory through the Protopalatial Period," *American Journal of Archaeology* 98: 721–723.

[22]P. M. Halstead (1981), "From Determination to Uncertainty: Social Storage and the Rise of the Minoan Palace," in A. Sheridan and G. F. Bailey (1981), *Economic Archaeology*.

[23]Renfrew, Colin (1972). *The Emergence of Civilisation: The Cyclades and the Aegean in the Third Millennium* B.C. London.

[24]Thuc. 1.4.

[25]This question has inspired enough scholarly debate to produce a symposium on the subject in Hägg and Marinatos (above, n. 10). For an interesting discussion of methods of investigating evidence for colonization, see E. Schofield (1983), "The Minoan Emigrant," in Krzyszkowska and Nixon (above, n. 7), 293–301.

[26]S. Hood, "A Minoan Empire in the Aegean in the 16th and 15th centuries B.C.," in Robin Hägg and Nanno Marinatos, eds. (1984), *The Minoan Thalassocracy, Myth and Reality: Proceedings of the Third International Symposium at the Swedish Institute in Athens* 31 May–5 June, 1982.

[27]W. D. Niemeier and B. Niemeier (1999), "The Minoans of Miletus," pp. 543–554 in *Meletemata: Studies in Aegean Archaeology Presented to Malcolm H. Wiener*, ed. Philip P. Betancourt, V. Karageorghis, R. Laffineur, and W. D. Niemeier.

[28]See M. H. Wiener (1987), "The Tale of the Conical Cups," in Hägg and Marinatos (above, n. 10), 19–20.

[29]G. E. Bass (1987),"Oldest Known Shipwreck Reveals Splendors of the Bronze Age," *National Geographic* 172, 693–733.

[30]H. W. Haskell (2004), "Wanax to Wanax: Regional Trade Patterns in Mycenaean Crete," pp. 151–160 in *CHARIS Essays in Honor of Sara A. Immerwahr*, ed Anne P. Chapin, 157.

[31]Thomas Palaima (1991), "Maritime Matters in the Linear B Tablets," pp. 273–310 in *Thalassa, l'Egée prehistorique et la Mer: Actes de la troisième Rencontre égéenne internationale de l'Université de Liège, Station de Recherches sous-marines et océanographiques (StaReSO), Calvi, Corse*, 23–25 Avril, 1990, ed. Robert Laffineur and Lucien Basch, 280–281, 293–295. John Chadwick (1979), "The Minoan Origin of the Classical Cypriote Script," pp.139–143 in *Acts of the International Archaeological Symposium "The Relations between Cyprus and Crete, ca. 2000–500 B.C.,"* ed. V. Karageorghis.

[32]See Z. A. Stos–Gale (1988), "Lead Isotope Evidence for Trade in Copper from Cyprus During the Late Bronze Age," pp. 265–282 in E. B. French and K. A. Wardle, eds. (1988),*Problems in Greek Prehistory*, esp. p. 275.

[33]See Niemeier and Niemeier, (above, n. 27).

[34]See K. Thorp-Scholes (1978), "Akrotiri: Genesis, Life and Death," p. 439 in *Thera and the Aegean World*, Vol. I, ed. C. Doumas and H. Puchelt, and other articles in that and subsequent volumes of the Thera conferences.

[35]Sturt Manning (1988),"The Bronze Age Eruption of Thera," *Journal of Mediterranean Archaeology* 1: 17–82, esp. table 10 on p.56.

[36]Nanno Marinatos (1989–1990), "A Puberty Rite at Thera: Evidence from New Frescoes," *Journal of Prehistoric Religion*, vol. 3–4: 49–51.

[37] An interpretation of these frescoes as cult scenes has been made by N. Marinatos (1984), *Art and Religion in Thera: Reconstructing a Bronze Age Society* . But convincing arguments against this interpretation are given by Sarah Morris (1989), "A Tale of Two Cities: The Miniature Frescoes from Thera and the Origins of Greek Poetry," *American Journal of Archaeology* 93: 511–535, esp. 512–515 and nn. 9, 15, 27 for other references.

[38]On the Expedition Fresco see P. Warren (1979), "Miniature Frescoes from Thera," *Journal of Hellenic Studies* 79: 115–129; Lyvia Morgan (1988). *The Miniature Wall Paintings of Thera: A Study in Aegean Culture and Iconography.*

[39]See W.–D. Niemeier (1990), "Mycenaean Elements in the Miniature Fresco from Thera?" *Thera and the Aegean World III*, ed. D. A. Hardy, C. G. Doumas, J. A. Sakellarakis, and P. M. Warren, 1:267–284.

[40]But see Morris (above, n. 37).

[41]A. E. Hoekstra (1981), *Epic Verse Before Homer*; Sarah Morrisa (above, n. 37). The existence of epic poetry in the fifteenth century is argued by M. L. West (1988), "The Rise of the Greek Epic," *Journal of Hellenic Studies* 108: 151–172.

[42]Malcolm Wiener (1987), "Trade and Rule in Palatial Crete," pp. 261–266 in Hägg and Marinatos (above, n. 10). Malcolm Wiener (1990), "The Isles of Crete? The Minoan Thalassocracy Revisited," in Hardy et al (above, n. 39), 1:128–155.

[43]Similar scenes are found on the Town Mosaic from Knossos, on Minoan materials from the Mycenaean Shaft Graves (see Chapter 3), on a fragmentary rhyton, and on numerous rings and seals.

[44]The Hyksos were foreign princes, probably from the Levant, who gained control of Egypt and ruled for about a century (1648/37–1540/29) from their capital in the Egyptian Delta.

[45]Y. and E. Sakellarakis (1984), "The Keftiu and the Minoan Thalassocracy," pp. 197–203 in Hägg and Marinatos (above n.10).

[46]This is a complex and technical question; see Rehak, Paul, and John Younger (2001), "Neopalatial, Final Palatial, and Postpalatial Crete, with Addendum: 1998–1999," in *Aegean Prehistory: A Review*, ed. Tracy Cullen, 451–454, for discussion and references.

[47]L. Vance Watrous and Harriet Blitzer (1999), "Central Crete in Late Minoan II–IIIB1: The Archaeological Background of the Knossos Tablets," pp.511–516 in J. Driessen and A. Farnoux, eds. (1997), *La Crète Mycénienne: Actes de la Table Ronde Internationale Organisée par l'École Francaise d'Athènes, 26–28 Mars, 1991 = Bulletin de Correspondance Hellenique* Supplement 30.

[48]V. Karageorghis (1979), "Some Reflections on the Relations Between Cyprus and Crete During the Late Minoan III B Period," pp. 199–203 in *Acts of the International Archaeological Symposium "The Relations Between Cyprus and Crete, ca. 2000–500 B.C.": Nicosia, 16th April–22nd April, 1978*, ed. V. Karageorghis, 199.

[49]W.-D. Niemeier and B. Niemeier (above, n. 27).

[50]On the revised dating for Santorini, see Sturt Manning (1988)."The Bronze Age Eruption of Thera," *Journal of Mediterranean Archaeology* 1: 17–82, esp. table 10 on p. 56.

3

MYCENAEAN GREECE

As the palace civilization of Minoan Crete flourished, a culture was developing on the mainland of Greece that was eventually to produce a palatial civilization of its own, in large part as the heir and conqueror of the Minoans. Yet Mycenaean culture was more than just a development of Minoan antecedents; the Mycenaeans were quite literally the first Greek-speakers to appear in history.[1]

As we saw in Chapter 1, with the introduction of bronze into the Aegean area, settlements on the Greek mainland developed in much the same way as did those in Pre-palatial Crete; settlements increased in number and size, and some buildings could be called monumental. But in around 2350 a series of destructions inaugurated a general cultural setback on the mainland, a situation not paralleled on Crete, where we see the beginnings of proto-palaces. It was not until about 1600, at the time the building of the second palaces on Crete, that signs of wealth and sophistication appeared on the Greek mainland in the form of numerous large scale **tholos** (beehive) tomb burials in Messenia in the southwest Peloponnesus, and even more dramatically, a group of extraordinarily rich shaft grave burials in the Argolid at the site of the later palace of Mycenae.

THE EARLY MYCENAEANS (MH–LH II CA. 1600–1400)

The Shaft Graves at Mycenae, ca. 1600–1500, Middle Helladic to Late Helladic I

The Shaft Graves at Mycenae were monumental in size, and their burials were accompanied by a rich collection of luxury goods that amazed their discoverer, Heinrich Schliemann. The

52

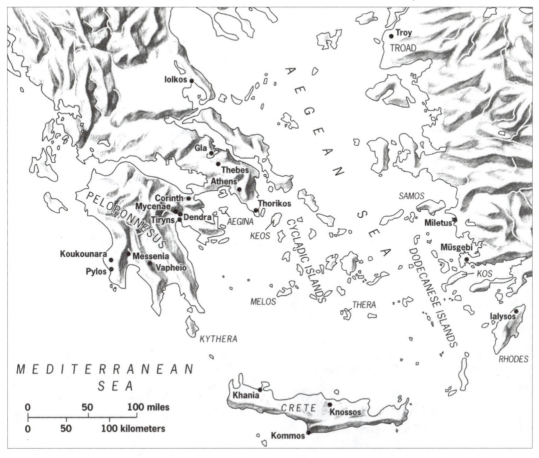

Map 3   Bronze Age: Mycenaen Greece.

burials were made in rectangular shafts as deep as four meters, some large enough to hold as many as five burials. The floors of the shafts were covered with pebbles, and a wall of stones or bricks was built up the sides of the shaft to a height of about a meter and a half. After the body was laid on the pebble floor and surrounded by its grave gifts, log beams were laid down resting on the top of the side walls. They were covered with clay or slate panels to provide a roof for the burial chamber, and then the shaft was filled in with dirt. When the filling reached ground level, a funeral meal was celebrated, and the remains of the meal, including broken wine cups, were scattered on the ground and covered over with a mound of earth. On top of some of the mounds a grave marker, or stele, was placed. The graves were reused; at each new burial, the shaft was dug out again, the previous occupants and their gifts unceremoniously pushed aside and the new occupant installed.

The Shaft Graves at Mycenae are grouped in two circles, one of which, Circle A, was reconstructed and enclosed by a stone circle later in the Mycenaean period. Circle A con-

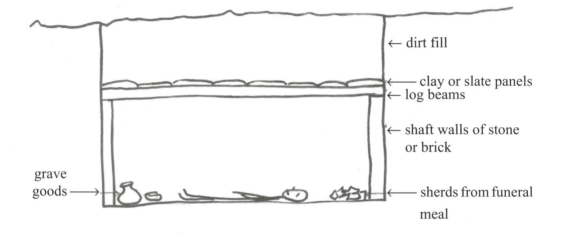

Figure 3.1   Shaft Grave Diagram.
Sketch by N. Demand.

Figure 3.2   Shaft Grave Photo.
Photo by N. Demand.

tained six deep shafts and many humbler burials; Circle B held fourteen true shafts, plus other burials. The two circles are now thought to have been in use in the same time period, from about 1600 to 1500. In Circle A each shaft contained multiple burials of from two to five people; in all there were nine men, eight women, and two children buried in the shafts of Circle A, while Circle B's fourteen shafts held twenty-four bodies. There were rich burials in both circles, but the graves of Circle A were considerably richer than those in Circle B. There are, however, chronological developments in the offerings, which will be considered below.

Objects included among the grave gifts in the Shaft Graves were gold jewelry and clothing ornaments (683 gold disks and ornaments in one grave alone), gold death masks and complete coverings for the bodies of children, and a silver rhyton portraying a siege, probably imported from Crete. There were also swords decorated with inlay, knives, arrowheads, boar's tusks (from boar's tusk helmets), ivory, amethyst and Baltic amber beads, a game board, ostrich eggs, rock crystal, lapis lazuli, alabaster, faience, cobalt blue glass, and bronze and clay vessels, including imports or imitations of Cycladic and Minoan vases.

The question of how such a collection should be analyzed is a fundamental one for the archaeologist, and the answers have changed over time. One approach has been to investigate the origins of the various objects, their materials, and their motifs. The results of this approach have shown that the objects themselves came from a wide geographical range: Egypt, Crete, Syria, Anatolia, the Adriatic area, and central Europe. Many of the objects display mixtures of motifs, materials, and techniques from various areas, and in many objects foreign techniques and materials were used to represent interests quite different from those of their sources. The most striking examples of this are to be found in the famous inlaid daggers. The bronze probably came from Bohemia. The **niello technique** used for the inlay, which has been called "painting in metal," came from the Near East: cut-out figures of gold, silver, electron (a natural mixture of gold and silver), and dark bronze were hammered into cutouts in a bronze blade, details were engraved, and the engraved lines were then filled with black niello (a compound of copper, lead, sulfur, and borax), which was burned in to provide a black outline around the figures. The subject matter varies from a scene reminiscent of the Nile River to a lion hunt that reflects mainland interests.

It is thought that the daggers were produced in Greece, probably by Minoan craftsmen, as were many other objects of Minoan craftsmanship in the graves. The combination of Minoan and Helladic cultures that many of these objects reveal is called "Mycenaean," from the site of these graves, and the name has been extended to the whole culture.

Based on this information about the origins of the grave goods, archaeologists have created various scenarios to explain the Shaft Graves at Mycenae. One suggestion is that the wealth came from raids, especially raids on neighboring Crete, from which much of the workmanship derives. Another possibility, mercenary service for the Minoans, is suggested by the Expedition Fresco from Thera (see Chapter 2). Many close similarities exist between

Figure 3.3   Lion Hunt dagger from the Mycenaean Grave Circles, niello technique. Courtesy of the National Archaeological Museum, Athens.

this miniature fresco scene and the objects found in the Shaft Graves. In particular, there is a similarity between the battle scene and the siege scene portrayed on a silver rhyton in the Shaft Grave collection, while the river scene in the fresco resembles the river scene on one of the niello swords. Mycenaean mercenary service with the Minoans could have provided them with a sudden influx of wealth and knowledge about Minoan and other neighboring cultures. However, analysis of the bones has shown all the burials to be of people in very good physical condition,[2] suggesting that they were members of an elite of longstanding who had had the advantages of good nutrition and a relatively affluent life. They may have been raiders or mercenaries—both probably honorable, even "princely" professions at that time—but they were not poor and deprived.

Nor were the Shaft Graves the abrupt innovation that they were long considered to be. The discovery of earlier shaft graves, especially the rich burial found at Kolonna in Aegina (see Chapter 1), demonstrates that the practice of burial in shaft-graves with rich burial goods was a developing local tradition. Thus the Shaft Graves at Mycenae were not a sudden and unprecedented phenomenon, nor can the Mycenaeans be seen as invading foreign princes who took over power in Mycenae and brought chariot warfare and the Greek language to Greece, as Robert Drews has suggested.[3]

THOLOS TOMBS CA. 1525 TO 1300/1275 (LATE HELLADIC IIA TO EARLY LATE HELLADIC IIIB)

For about 50 years after the last shaft grave burial at Mycenae, there were still no palaces on the mainland, and we can best trace the development of Mycenaean culture in another type of monumental burial: large beehive-shaped tholos tombs. Tholos tombs first appeared in mainland Greece in Messenia at the time of the Shaft Graves of Mycenae, constructed on the principle of a **corbelled** arch. A corbelled arch is not a true arch: each layer is placed slightly farther in, and there is no keystone to support the resultant dome. Support comes from the weight of the earth piled up on the layers of stone. A long entryway, or **dromos**, was also constructed. After the interment (in a side chamber, in a cist grave in the floor, or simply on the floor of the great domed chamber), the whole structure was filled in again. As in the case of the Shaft Graves, multiple burials in one tomb and reuse were the rule.

The tholos tomb now appears to have developed out of a merging of a mainland tradition of burial under or in a tumulus, and a Minoan tradition of large circular tombs with corbelled side walls.[4] A tholos tomb containing rich burial gifts was found at Kolonna (see Chapter 1), and the district of Pylos in Messenia is especially rich in early examples. At one location, Koukounara, 17 tholoi have been found. The earliest are rather small (6 meters in diameter)

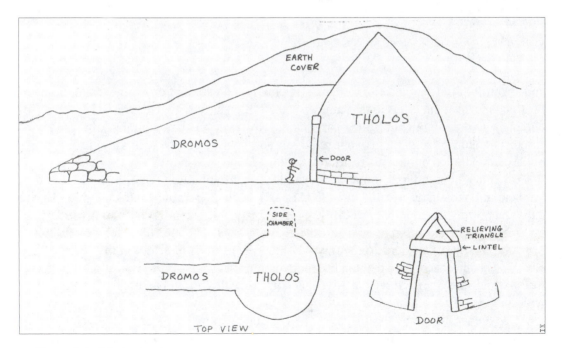

Figure 3.4   Tholos tomb.
Drawing by N. Demand.

Figure 3.5   Tomb of Atreus (tholos tomb).
Photo N. Demand.

and are built of field stones, but they are still clearly indicative of growing wealth. Some of the tombs yielded materials in the same mixed tradition as the Shaft Graves at Mycenae, including a sword inlaid with Minoan argonauts. However, the large number of these tombs associated with one settlement over a relatively short period of time seems to rule out the hypothesis that tholos burial was restricted to "kings."

Two other unplundered tombs also yielded important finds. One, a tholos tomb at Vapheio in Lakonia, discovered in 1888 C.E. and dated after 1500, contained gold Minoan cups that portray the capture of a bull. The second, a chamber tomb at Dendra in the Argolid just east of Mycenae, discovered in the late 1950s and dated about 1400, yielded a full set of Mycenaean armor that fits surprisingly well the descriptions of armor in the Homeric poems. These objects confirm that the interconnections between Mycenaean and Minoan cultures, which the Shaft Graves at Mycenae first revealed to archaeologists, were in fact widespread and continuing.

At Mycenae the nine tholoi have been grouped into three chronological types of increasing size and workmanship. The earliest are probably early fifteenth century (LH IIA), the most advanced date around 1250. Included in the latest group are the so-called "tombs of Atreus and Clytemnestra," which are of truly monumental size (14.6 meters and 13.2 meters in diameter respectively). Unfortunately, all the tholoi at Mycenae were robbed long before modern archaeologists came upon the scene, and none of their contents have been recovered.

The Fall of Knossos

In ca. 1450 there was widespread destruction of the palace sites on Crete. Only Knossos escaped relatively intact, although increasing evidence from the western port site of Khania suggests that a functioning palace may have continued to exist there as well. At the same time, signs of mainland presence on Crete appear: numerous warrior burials; tholos tombs in the mainland tradition; and a new, more stylized and rigid monumental vase type, called *Palace Style*. Somewhat later, a building form typical of the mainland appears, the megaron (a rectangular room with an entry and porch on the short side and a large central hearth). But most important, tablets similar to the Linear A tablets but inscribed in an early form of Greek, called **Linear B**, were reported by Evans in the excavation level of Knossos dated 1450. However, his identification of the level, and hence the date, have been questioned, especially since the script is so similar to that found in the destruction level of Pylos, dated to ca. 1250.[5] It seems to some scholars that the language/script would have been unlikely to have remained unchanged over such a long period of time, and that, therefore, the Knossos tablets may have belonged to the later destruction at Knossos that occurred ca. 1375.

On the traditional view, the archaeological finds show that people from the mainland took over control of Crete after the destruction of 1450. They carried on the administration of the Minoan palace system using a linear style of writing, Linear B, that was based on Linear A, and adopted and adapted Minoan motifs in frescoes and vases of the Palace Style.[6] These Mycenaeans were the first Greeks, judging from their use of Linear B script to write in the Greek language. As for their origins, we can only speculate.

THE MYCENAEAN PALACE PERIOD (LATE HELLADIC IIA–IIIB, CA.1400–1200)

Mycenaean Palaces

The Mycenaeans developed palaces on the mainland only after the final destruction of the Minoan palaces. Mycenaean palaces are known at Mycenae, Tiryns, Pylos, and Thebes, and there was also a fortified center with no palace at Gla in Boeotia. Although at first glance the mainland palaces appear similar to those of the Minoans, in important ways they were quite different. This can be seen by comparing the plans of the three major Mycenaean palaces at Tiryns, Mycenae, and Pylos with those of the Minoan palaces.

The plans of the palaces, with the exception of Pylos, feature very imposing defensive walls. These fortifications, and the tholos tombs as well, were built with huge blocks of stone. For example, the stones in the dromos of the Treasury of Atreus were as large as 18 feet by 14 feet, and the lintel weighed 100 tons. Later Greeks seeing these huge blocks as-

Figure 3.6   Palace at Mycenae. Excavated structures inside the Citadel at Mycenae, prepared by Sibby Postgate for the Mycenae Archive, published E. French "Mycenae, Agamemnon's Capital," Tempus Publishing 2002.

sumed they must have been moved by superhuman forces and attributed them to the giant Cyclops, hence the term, **Cyclopean masonry**. It is now recognized, however, that similar blocks were managed in the building of the Egyptian pyramids by the use of ramps and sledges, and the Mycenaeans must have employed similar methods. In fact, as the building of a tholos tomb proceeded, earth was piled up to cover and support the courses of stone, and this would have created a natural ramp for the next course of stones. This experience would have shown them the method by which fortified walls could be constructed as well. By the end of the effective life of the palaces, the Mycenaeans had equipped the walls with well-developed systems of defensive gates and made provision for safe access to water supplies that were protected from enemy attack by their underground location. Clearly the Mycenaeans, more than the Minoans, felt a great need for physical defense.

The central focus of a Mycenaean palace also differed from that of a Minoan palace. In Minoan architecture, the large central courtyard formed the core of the palace, but the focus of the Mycenaean palace was a monumental building, the *megaron*, or often, a pair of megara, one larger than the other. At its simplest, the megaron was a rectangular room with a porch, but in its fully developed monumental form it usually consisted of a porch with a central column, an anteroom, and an inner room with a large central hearth set within four columns that supported a clerestory and an upper balcony. At Pylos a place for a "throne" and

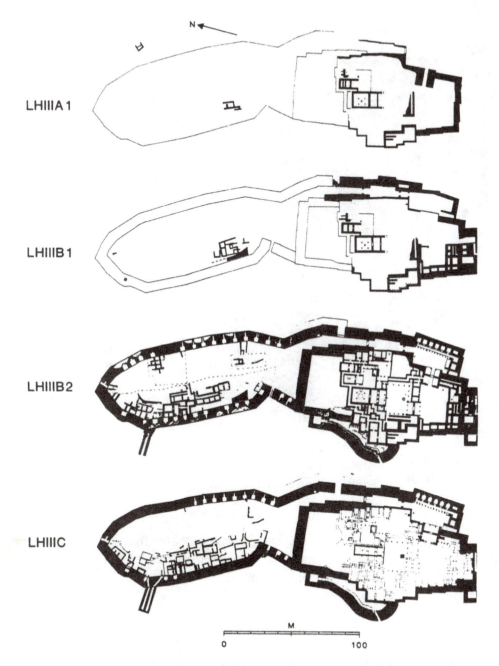

Figure 3.7   Development of the palace at Tiryns. The evidence of survival and rebuilding is presented graphically in these plans of the succeeding phases in the life of Tiryns as revealed by excavation. This example shows how systematic recording of the finds at each level during excavation can provide evidence for the development of a site over time.

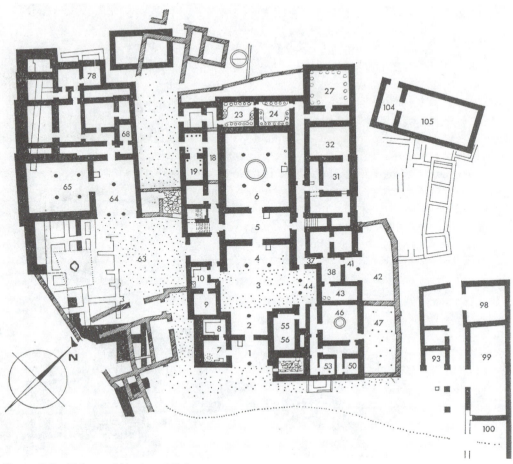

Figure 3.8   Palace of Nestor at Pylos.
Courtesy the University of Cincinnati.

peg holes in the floor connected by sunken channels, probably for pouring libations, have been found in the *megaron*.

Mycenaean palaces lacked the monumental staircases, light wells, and pillar-and-door construction so characteristic of Minoan palaces. Moreover, although Mycenaean palaces had bathrooms and a system of drainage for rainwater, no evidence has been found for the sort of flushable toilet facilities that existed in Minoan palaces. Obviously, comfort, light, and air were not the primary considerations of the Mycenaean rulers.

But despite these fundamental differences, important similarities existed between Minoan and Mycenaean palaces. A major point of likeness is, of course, the very concept of a complex multi-purpose building used as an administrative center, as evidenced by the presence of records, with provision for large-scale storage of commodities, workrooms for the manufacture of various products, ceremonial areas, and residential areas. Like the Minoan palace, the Mycenaean palace was decorated with frescoes, which often feature the same motifs and clearly copy Minoan work. In Mycenaean frescoes, however, hunting and battle scenes are much more popular, and there is more concern for symmetry and order than in the Minoan works.[7] Such similarities and differences suggest that the Minoan palace provided the model, but that in borrowing that model, the Mycenaeans transformed it to suit their own lifestyle and interests.

Evidence does not exist suggesting the political dominance of one Mycenaean palace over the others, as it does for Knossos for a time in Crete. The two palaces at Mycenae and Tiryns, which were very close neighbors and very well-defended, certainly raise questions about palace relationships; but Pylos, Thebes, and a presumed palace at Athens would have dominated well-defined areas, and there is little to suggest that one palace exerted central control over all the others. Perhaps Mycenaean Greece was made up of a number of independent kingdoms sharing a common culture and co-operating sporadically, especially in overseas ventures. This picture would be very similar to that presented in Homer.

In the case of the Mycenaean palaces, we are fortunate to have many Linear B tablets, which provide readable records and a picture of the internal operation of the palaces and their methods of control over people, commodities, and production.

Linear B Tablets[8]

In 1939 C.E. in the initial excavation of the Mycenaean palace at Pylos, conducted by Carl Blegen, the first trial trenches passed through an archive room containing over 600 fragments of tablets inscribed in the same Linear B script already known from the tablets that Evans had found at Knossos. Because the tablets were found in the destruction level of the palace, they are dated to ca. 1250[9]. The sheer number of inscriptions that this discovery made available and the systematic storage of the tablets in the archives at Pylos eventually made possible the decipherment of Linear B. In 1954 Michael Ventris, an architect and amateur linguist, announced to the International Classical Congress at Copenhagen that he had deciphered the language of the tablets and found it to be an early form of Greek. As confirmation, he showed a slide of a tablet containing the recognizable ideogram for a tripod and the Linear B characters to which he had assigned the values *ti-ri-po-de*. Since that time, most scholars have come to accept Linear B as an early form of Greek.

Like Linear A, Linear B is written in a syllabic rather than an alphabetic script. Signs represent combinations of consonants with vowels rather than individual sounds. For example, there are separate signs for the syllables *pa, pe, pi, po*, and *pu*. As Ventris' reading of the tripod tablet showed, ideograms depicting the object described were also employed to aid in reading and perhaps to guide illiterates in handling the tablets.

While Linear B is known to be Greek, the syllabic system of writing has certain intrinsic disadvantages that can make interpretation difficult. For example, Linear B cannot easily express the consonant clusters of Greek; thus to write *tripod* the Mycenaean scribes had to write *ti-ri-po-de*. Certain final consonants that are important elements in Greek words (*-n* and *-s*) were also not written. Another problem that impedes interpretation is the fact that a number of symbols represent more than one sound. For example, the sounds representing *p* and *b*, and those representing *r* and *l*, are not distinguished. Thus the Greek word *basileus* (king) is written *pa-si-re-u*. When several such ambiguous signs are combined, the possibilities are numerous, and in some cases one small group of words may have several dramatically different Greek equivalences. Still another source of difficulty is presented by numerous Linear B words that have no apparent equivalents in later Greek. All of these problems make translation and interpretation difficult, but nonetheless the tablets provide the historian with one of the most valuable sources of evidence about Mycenaean Greece.

Most of the Linear B tablets are simply lists. They record personnel, livestock and agricultural produce, land ownership and use, tribute and ritual offerings, textiles, vessels, furniture, metals, and military equipment (chariots, wheels, weapons, armor). The accounts are often very detailed; some record broken objects, and in one case the name of a cow is recorded (oddly, the name of a king never appears).[10] Religious offerings were also recorded on the tablets, and these provide interesting information about the divinities worshipped by the Mycenaeans, which will be considered in the next section.

The tablets provide especially valuable information about the political and social hierarchy. The highest status, as indicated by land and other allocations, was that of **wanax**, a word applied in Homer to both men and gods and in later Greek only to the gods and often translated "lord." The Mycenaean *wanax* is usually interpreted as the king, but he may have been only one of a number of such men with this rank at Pylos.[11] Lower in status than the *wanax* was the ***lawagetas***, a term that in later Greek had the meaning "Leader of the War-host." The ***basileus***, a word that later Greeks used to designate a king, appears to have been only a comparatively minor local official in Mycenaean times. Priests and priestesses also appear as high-ranking individuals on the tablets; some are listed as holders of parcels of land measured in terms of amounts of grain, and others appear as leasers of land. The ***damos*** (***demos***, or people, in later Greek) also appears as a leaser of land. Military units (***oka***), with their leaders and dispositions, are also detailed. One interesting but enigmatic tablet assigns rowers to watch on the coast; it is tempting to see this as an emergency provision in a time of danger, since the tablet was preserved by the fire that destroyed the palace.

At the bottom of the social pyramid were the workers. Many were skilled specialists: the lists include wheel makers, furniture makers, workers in gold and lapis-colored glass, and smiths. Other workers were listed only as recipients of rations of figs and grain. Some, such as women listed with their working children but without husband or family affiliations, were clearly slaves. Close palatial control over production is attested by allocations of materials; for example, smiths were allocated specific amounts of bronze for the making of items such as arrowheads and spearheads. Inventories of supplies, such as spare parts for chariots, were detailed. Agriculture and animal husbandry were also closely controlled, with numbers and descriptions of animals listed together with the names of their herdsmen.

A good example of the information about the organization of the palatial economy that can be drawn from the tablets is provided by Cynthia Shelmerdine's analysis of the records of the perfumed oil industry at Pylos.[12] Since the Pylos tablets list only finished products and supplementary allotments of ingredients to workers, and not the full list of ingredients used, Shelmerdine studied these records in the context of the architectural evidence at Pylos and information about perfume-making in other ancient societies, such as the portrayal of perfume workers on Egyptian tomb paintings and recipes from Mesopotamian records. Most of the perfume tablets were found not in the archives, but scattered about various other rooms of the palace. By considering their find-spots and the archaeological remains of vessels used for preparing, storing, and shipping perfume, Shelmerdine has been able to identify the perfume workshops in the palace, as well as to draw conclusions about the organization of the palace scribes and their activities.

Because the Linear B tablets appear to have been used almost exclusively for the purposes of palatial administration, it seems unlikely that literacy was widespread in Mycenaean society. This is confirmed by the analysis of scribal handwriting: in the kingdom of Pylos, where a population of about 50,000 has been estimated, only 23 scribal hands have been identified out of an estimated total of 32 scribes.[13]

WEBSITE 3.1   LINEAR B
http://www.ancientscripts.com/linearb.html

This site, which provides a list of the Linear B signs, is run by an engineer whose hobby is ancient scripts. (Michael Ventris, an architect, was also an amateur.)

An academic site provides good photographs of both Linear A and Linear B.
http://ccwf.cc.utexas.edu/~perlman/myth/linb.htm

The web page of Cambridge University offers a detailed history of the process of decipherment, and includes the initial correspondence of Michael Ventris with John Chadwick, a Classical philologist, who became his partner in the further working out of the decipherment at a time when people still wrote letters longhand and on typewriters! It also includes biographies and pictures of both men.
http://www.classics.cam.ac.uk/everyone/linearb/decipherment.html

Jeremy Rutter's Dartmouth website provides a useful discussion of the use of Linear B in Mycenaean society but no pictures.
http://projectsx.dartmouth.edu/classics/history/bronze_age/lessons/les/25.html

---

Mycenaean Religion

In their first contacts, the Mycenaeans were particularly receptive to the much more advanced Minoan culture, and they readily adopted Minoan religious forms and conventions, such as the Great Goddess/Mistress of Animals, snakes, bull rhytons, double axes, and Horns of Consecration. As a result, Mycenaean religion viewed from the archaeological point of view tends to look quite Minoan. When the Linear B tablets could be read, however, it became possible to distinguish a Mycenaean religion under the Minoan façade. For instance, the tablets contain the names of non-Minoan deities familiar in later Greek religion—Hera, Poseidon, Zeus, Artemis, Ares(?), and Dionysus(?)—as well as other unfamiliar but apparently related gods, such as intriguing female forms of Zeus and Poseidon. These divine figures appear on the tablets as recipients of offerings, not only of precious objects but also of men and women, possibly an indication of human sacrifice.

It is, however, in the places of worship that the Mycenaeans differed most clearly from the Minoans. There is no evidence that the Mycenaeans made use of typical Minoan cult sites in the countryside, such as peak, cave, or tree sanctuaries, or that they held ritual celebrations before large groups of people, such as are portrayed on Minoan frescoes. Rather, the Mycenaeans seem to have centered their religious rites within the palace, and in fact, within the *megaron* at its central hearth. There, secluded from general view, they appear to have carried out their most important religious activities. Some shrines have also been found in other buildings within the walls of Mycenae, but no indications that palace and people came together in public rites. There is also no evidence for widespread use of Linear B for dedications by ordinary people. Thus while the Minoan rulers seem to have used religion as an integrative force within the community, for the Mycenaeans official religion appears to have been centered on the elite.

THE MYCENAEANS OVERSEAS

Settlement, Trade, and the Search for Resources

The distribution of Mycenaean pottery, which has been found at sites in the Cyclades, Cyprus, the Levant, Asia Minor, Rhodes, Egypt, Sicily, Italy, and the Balkans, reaching even to central Europe, suggests that the Mycenaeans were the heirs of the Minoans in overseas connections, and prolific exporters of pottery and its contents.[14] A number of Mycenaean swords and daggers also traveled abroad. Other exports are probable—for example, the perfumed oil whose production Shelmerdine has documented at Pylos, and textiles made from flax and from the wool of the large flocks described by the Linear B tablets—but they have left few archaeological traces. Nor do we know what the Mycenaeans received in return, with the exception of a few obvious luxury objects. Other significant imports—metals, slaves, horses—would have left little evidence in the archaeological record.

Evidence for Mycenaean settlement abroad, which might be related to trade and the search for resources, is becoming increasingly evident in many areas. Mycenaean settlement on Rhodes, an important step in the route to the east, is well attested, as well as at the sites of Miletus and Iasos in Asia Minor. At Miletus recent excavations have revealed substantial evidence of the presence, and probably settlement, of Minoans and later Mycenaeans before the end of the Bronze Age.[15]

At Miletus, three building periods have been identified. The first has strong Minoan characteristics and suggests a Minoan presence, although its exact nature—overlordship, commercial enclave, or whatever—is as yet indeterminable. It is separated from the second period by only localized evidence for burning, but rebuilding was carried out on a new orientation and with new building types. Sparse ceramic evidence suggests a Mycenaean occupation, although there was no complete break with Minoan culture. In an early phase of the second period, there is evidence suggesting destruction by earthquake, followed by an attack, probably part of interminable fighting with Hittites over control of the area. The third building period was marked by the construction of a strong defensive circuit wall, and by Mycenaean pottery and figurines, houses of definite Mycenaean type (Corridor house), and finds of Linear B script on locally produced *pithoi*.[16] Seven kilns produced domestic painted pottery, some of which was used in burials at the nearby cemetery at Müsgebi on the Halicarnassus/Bodrum peninsula, where the presence of 48 chamber tombs is now seen as attesting a permanent Mycenaean presence.[17] Mycenaean pottery produced at Miletus was also exported further afield, having been found in both Tiryns and Ugarit.[18] New finds continue to extend the number of known Mycenaean settlement sites on the west coast of Anatolia and on the adjacent islands.[19]

The presence of Mycenaeans on the western coast of Anatolia brought them into contact, and conflict, with the Hittites, whose kingdom was centered at Boðazkale, near the modern Turkish capital of Ankara. The Hittites were one of the "great powers" of the ancient Near East, rivals of the Egyptians in a continuing contest to control the various kingdoms that lay in the Levantine corridor between them. With their power center in central Anatolia, the Hittites depended upon vassal treaties to maintain their often-precarious shifting power in this peripheral region. However, their problems were not confined to this southeastern sphere. They also had to defend themselves against constant threat from the attacks of less civilized enemies to the north, and they also sought to control their neighbors in western Anatolia, as in the east, with vassal treaties. Their interest in the west was always problematic; they could not allow actions there to take too many resources away from the potential of attacks in the north, and in the east Egypt was often ready to encroach. The height of Mycenaean involvement in western Anatolia probably came at one of those moments of impending conflict with the Egyptians: the run-up to the great battle of Kadesh in Syria in 1274. Surviving texts provide a tantalizingly incomplete picture of a situation in which Miletus, for a time independent of the Hittites and under a vassal ruler loyal to the Mycenaeans, seems to have been sponsoring the attacks of a rebel against the Hittites in the region.[20] Some scholars have tried to puzzle out a connection with the legendary Trojan War, but such conjectures are highly speculative. Nonetheless, Mycenaean Greeks seem to have been involved in some way with the shifting political scene in western Anatolia, and this may have left lingering traditions that eventually were woven into a literary conflation hundreds of years in the making—Homer's Trojan War.[21]

A puzzle regarding Mycenaean commercial contacts is that, despite the numerous finds of Mycenaean pottery throughout the Mediterranean, their production of oils and textiles far in excess of their own apparent needs and the evidence for Mycenaean settlement abroad, firm evidence of the Mycenaeans own involvement in trade is lacking in the Linear B tablets.[22] Only one tablet, from Mycenae, even hints at trade by its record of the dispatch of textiles to Greek Thebes; none record overseas transactions. Non-Mycenaeans may have carried Mycenaean objects found on overseas sites along the lively trade routes of the Mediterranean, as the evidence for two Bronze Age shipwrecks off the southern coast of Turkey suggests.

Two Bronze Age Shipwrecks

Archaeological evidence supplied by two recently discovered ancient shipwrecks that bracket the twelfth century and also mark points along the sea route between east and west suggest possible Cypriot involvement in trade with Mycenaean Greece. The oldest of these ships foundered at the turn of the thirteenth century off the southern coast of Turkey at Ulu Burun.[23] The other shipwreck took place about a century later, at the beginning of the twelfth century, at Cape Gelidonya, also on the southern Turkish coast.

The earliest of these wrecks, the Ulu Burun ship, a 15 to 16 meter vessel, was discovered in 1982.[24] The ship's main cargo included at least 354 copper oxhide ingots and about 120 copper bun-shaped ingots, all probably of Cypriot origin; about a ton of tin ingots, whose origin is still uncertain; one ton of terebinth resin, identical to resin from Amarna in Egypt; and glass ingots, probably from the Syro-Palestinian coast. The largest group of manufactured items was pottery: three of the ten giant storage pithoi contained Cypriot pottery (lamps, juglets, nested bowls); the other seven pithoi contained pomegranates and possibly olive oil. Also on board were luxury items: logs of Egyptian ebony, ostrich eggshells, elephant tusks, hippopotamus teeth, tortoise shells, scrap gold and silver, and thousands of beads, including some of amber. Several items seem likely to have been guest gifts to be used in diplomatic trade: a gold chalice, four faience drinking cups in animal and woman's head shapes, and two pairs of glass pendant or relief beads. Possible personal items belonging to the crew or passengers included a scarab of Queen Nefertiti (a good-luck amulet?),[25] bronze tools, spearheads, arrowheads, daggers, swords and stone maceheads, two hinged wooden writing tablets,[26] and fishing gear. The mixture of materials and sources make it unclear whether the ship was Cypriot, Levantine, or Mycenaean. Even the personal possessions and shipboard items were mixed Canaanite and Cypriot, although the presence of two Aegean swords and other Mycenaean items make it likely that at least two Mycenaeans were on board. The size and nature of the cargo suggest that this was an official shipment intended for a specific destination, rather than the diverse collection of items that one would expect on a tramping ship.

WEBSITE 3.2   INVESTIGATE THE ULU BURUN SHIPWRECK
YOURSELF—AN INTERACTIVE WEBSITE
http://www.theellisschool.org/%7eshipwreck/ulusplash.html

Explore the wreck. Study the artifacts. Compare what you find with information you glean from other ancient sites. What do you conclude and why? Do you agree with the suggestions in the text?

1. Where was the ship built?
2. What was the home port of the ship?
3. Where was the ship going?
4. Who was on board the ship? What were their occupations and where were they from?
5. Where did the trade items on the ship come from?
6. What type of trade was taking place? Was this a royal cargo or individual merchants trading?
7. What can this ship and the commodities on it tell us about Mediterranean trade?
8. Was this an established trade route?
9. When did the ship sink?
10. What do the items on this ship tell us about the cultures around the Mediterranean at this time?

Nonetheless, the conditions of sea travel at the time meant that the ship would have made port numerous times before it reached its ultimate destination, and casual trading by the crew was certainly to be expected. The contents of the ship suggest a situation of relative economic and political stability among the "great powers" of the Mediterranean at the end of the fourteenth century.

A century later, the picture appears quite different, although the random nature of shipwreck finds means that they can only illustrate, but not prove, the trend of general conditions. At that time, in the same general area off the south coast of Turkey that had brought the Ulu Burun ship to grief, another ship went down at Cape Gelidonya.[27] The Cape Gelidonya wreck, excavated in 1960, carried a cargo of 34 oxhide and bun-shaped ingots of Cypriot copper; tin ingots, and about a ton of scrap bronze, mostly of Cypriot origin, as well as metal-working tools and a large stone that could have served as an anvil. One passenger may have been a petty trader, for a variety of weights were found, that would have allowed their owner to carry on trade at any of the stops along the route. An eighteenth-century Syrian cylinder seal was found in the cabin area; it along with five scarabs were probably used as talismans. The wreck contained relatively little pottery and it was of mixed origins—Cypriot, Levantine, Mycenaean—typical of what might have been found in any port along the sea routes. In contrast to the

Ulu Burun ship, this ship was small, somewhat over 10 meters, to the 15 to 16 meters of the earlier ship.[28] It carried a modest cargo, while the earlier ship may have been on an official mission from some great power, sent to a specific destination with a cargo that included many rare valuables useful as diplomatic gifts and large shipments of metals.[29]

The metal worker aboard the Cape Gelidonya ship may well have been headed for Sardinia, for there is considerable evidence linking Cyprus with that island, which itself had a long tradition of metal-working.[30] Numerous fragments of copper oxhide ingots and five complete ingots have been found at 26 sites scattered across Sardinia, with new finds continually being added.[31] Mining and metallurgical tools with Cypriot characteristics have been found at a number of other Sardinian sites as well, and the evidence suggests that Cypriot metal workers were working on the island in the period from ca.1200–1150.[32]

There is no agreement about the "nationality" of the Cape Gelidonya ship, with its mixed cargo; but the Syrian or Canaanite character of the personal possessions (weights, scarabs, and the cylinder seal), as well as the discovery in 1994 of the ship's Syro-Canaanite or Cypriot stone anchor, have caused the excavator, George Bass to lean to a Canaanite or early Phoenician identity for the ship.[33] Notably, there is nothing to suggest that the ship was Mycenaean. The stray Mycenaean pottery aboard probably represented small consignments or even casual acquisitions made en route by the non-Mycenaean crew, rather than items involved in large-scale trade. This is in keeping with the spread of Mycenaean pottery in Mediterranean coastal settlements, which often appears in company with Cypriot pots, and can easily be explained as the result of the transport of mixed cargoes by Levantines or Cypriots. Moreover, it is likely that Mycenaean trade was only an occasional affair; the Cape Gelidonya shipwreck was carrying about a ton of copper, which would have provided perhaps a year's supply for a Bronze Age kingdom (one of the Pylos tablets records a ton of bronze).[34] And, of course, given the type of ships employed, all maritime activity was at best seasonal, which might explain the lack of Linear B records attesting overseas trade. Shipments to and from Mycenaean kingdoms were sporadic, and the Linear B records, which were temporary and covered only a portion of a year, may not have had occasion to report any transactions.

We do know that Mycenaeans were settled at Miletus and other lesser sites on the west coast of Anatolia, and pottery produced in Miletus did find its way to these satellite sites and even to sites as far away as Ugarit. Additional indirect evidence for Mycenaean involvement in Mediterranean trade, as suppliers and recipients if not as traveling merchants, exists in the fact that the Mycenaean palatial economy shared in the general collapse of Mediterranean palatial states that occurred in the twelfth century. To be as thoroughly affected as they were by the resulting state of confusion, much of it caused by sea raiders who disrupted normal shipping routes, the Mycenaeans must have been dependent upon this sea traffic and the trade it involved. But this general collapse, and the end which it brought to Mycenaean civilization, is another topic, and one that we must now consider in some detail.

SUGGESTIONS FOR FURTHER READING

John Chadwick (1976), *The Mycenaean World*; O. T. P. K. Dickinson (1994), *The Aegean Bronze Age*; G. Bass (1987), "Oldest Known Shipwreck Reveals Splendors of the Bronze Age," *National Geographic* 172: 693–733; John Chadwick (1987), *Linear B and Related Scripts*.

MAP STUDY

Important sites on chapter map: Mycenae, Tiryns, Pylos. Thebes, Iolkos, Aegina, Corinth, Koukounara (in Pylos district), Gla, Athens, Thorikos, Messenia, Vapheio, Dendra, Rhodes, Ialysos, Miletus, Müsgebi, Knossos, Khania, Kommos

On other maps: Cape Gelidonya, Ulu Burun, Egypt, Nile River, Afghanistan, Cyprus, Babylon, Mittani, Levant

ENDNOTES

[1] See Oliver Dickinson (1994), *The Aegean Bronze Age*.

[2] J. L. Angel (1973), "Human Skeletons From Grave Circles at Mycenae," in G. E. Mylonas (1973), *O Taphikos Kyklos B ton Mykenon*, 379–397.

[3] Robert Drews (1988), *The Coming of the Greeks*. The date on which Greek speakers arrived in Greece is a still unanswered question. The widely accepted date of ca. 2000 has suggested to some that they were the Patterned Ware people who were responsible for destroying the House of Tiles and building Lerna IV. But nothing in the archaeological record supports the suggestion that these people came from some far-distant Indo-European homeland. Rather, they appear to have come from nearby Boeotia (see Chapter 1). On the other hand, Colin Renfrew (1987), *Archaeology and Language*, holds that proto-Indo-European, the root language out of which Greek and other modern Indo-European languages developed, probably had its original home in Anatolia, from which it was spread by the first farmers, ca. 6000. Renfrew's argument rests upon the assumption that a new language will prevail over an existing language only if the speakers of the new language have some clear superiority. In the case of Indo-European, the superiority was that of farming techniques, which allowed far more people to be supported on a given amount of land than did hunting and gathering. If the introduction of Greek can be traced back beyond 6000 B.C., it means that the language developed within Greece for a far longer period than the traditional account of its origins assumes. However, there is still no consensus on this question; see reviews of Renfrew in *Current Anthropology* 29, no.3 (1988): 437–468.

[4] J. B. Rutter (1993), "Review of Aegean Prehistory II: The Prepalatial Bronze Age of the Southern and Central Mainland," *American Journal of Archaeology* 97:745–797, 789.

[5] See Chapter 4, n.1 for the dating.

[6] The Mycenaeans remained in control of Crete until the palace at Knossos was destroyed, ca. 1375. After this, the palace at Knossos continued to be used, but in ways that did not respect earlier usage; for example, industrial production was carried on in former ceremonial areas. Cultural artifacts show strong signs of regionalism, suggesting that control of Crete was at this time decentralized, and Knossos seems to have been displaced as the most important center by the northern port of Khania.

[7] On Mycenaean frescoes, see M. Lang (1969), *The Palace of Nestor at Pylos in Western Messenia II: The Frescoes*: S. A. Immerwahr (1990), *Aegean Painting in the Bronze Age.*.

[8]J. Chadwick (1987), *Linear B and Related Scripts*, provides an excellent introduction to the Linear B Tablets. J. Chadwick (1958), *The Decipherment of Linear B*, gives the story of the decipherment. John Chadwick (1976), *The Mycenaean World*, reconstructs Mycenaean society based on information from the tablets. There has been a great deal of subsequent work and analysis by Thomas Palaima; see, for example, T. Palaima (1984), "Scribal Organization and Palatial Activity," pp. 31–39 in C. Shelmerdine and T. Palaima, eds. (1984), *Pylos Comes Alive*, esp. 31; and T. Palaima (1988), "The Development of the Mycenaean Writing System," pp. 269–342 in *Texts, Tablets, and Scribes : Studies in Mycenaean Epigraphy, Offered to Emmett L. Bennett, Jr.*, ed. J.–P Olivier, E. Bennett, and T. G. Palaima.

[9]On the date, see Chapter 4, n.1.

[10]There is some controversy about this. Chadwick (above, n. 8), 71–72, 116–117, 126, reads the word "Enkhalyawen" as the name of a king, but J. T. Hooker (1979), "The Wanax in Linear B Texts," *Kadmos* 18: 100–111, rejects this interpretation.

[11]Chadwick (above, n. 8) calls him a king, Hooker (above, n. 10) disagrees.

[12]Cynthia Shelmerdine (1985), *The Perfume Industry of Mycenaean Pylos*.

[13]T. Palaima (above n.8), esp. 31–32.

[14] The exported pottery consists mainly of storage jars and a type of jar used for oil, but it also includes many fine painted vases and cups that must have been exported for their own sake. Vase painting styles were adaptations of Minoan work, but over time the motifs were often rendered almost unrecognizable by the Mycenaean tendency to stylization.

[15]W.-D. Niemeier and B. Niemeier (1997), "Minoisch-Mycenisches bis Protogeometrisches Milet: Zielsetzung und Grabungen auf dem Stadionhügel und am Athena-Tempel 1994/95," *Archäologischer Anzeiger*,189–248. W.-D. Niemeier (1997), "The Mycenaean Potter's Quarter at Miletus," pp. 347–351 in *Techne: Craftsmen, Craftswomen, and Craftsmanship in the Aegean Bronze Age:. Proceedings of the 6th International Aegean Conference*, Philadelphia, Temple University, 18–21 April, 1996, ed. Robert Laffineur and Ph. P. Betancourt.

[16]Niemeier and Niemeier (above, n. 15), 200.

[17] C. Mee (1978), "Aegean Trade and Settlement in Anatolia," *Anatolian Studies*. 28:121–156. Identification with Sea Peoples was suggested by Y. Boysal (1967), "New Excavations in Caria," *Anadolu* 11:31–56; and seasonal residence by raiders by Y. E. Ersoy (1988), "Finds from Menemen/Panaztepe in the Manissa Museus," *Annual of the British School at Athens* 83:55–82. 81. Contra, W.-D. Niemeier (1998), "The Mycenaeans in Western Anatolia and the Problem of the Origins of the Sea Peoples," pp. 17–65 in *Mediterranean Peoples in Transition: Thirteenth to Early Tenth Centuries BCE*: ed. S. Gitin, Amihay Mazar, and Ephraim Stern, 40.

[18]Niemeier (above, n. 15).

[19]See C. Mee (1988), "A Mycenaean Thalassocracy in the Eastern Aegean?" pp. 301–305 in *Problems in Greek Prehistory*, ed. E. B. French and K. A. Wardle.

[20]See Trevor Bryce (1989), "The Nature of Mycenaean Involvement in Western Anatolia," *Historia* 38:1–21; 1998. Trevor Bryce, *The Kingdom of the Hittites*, 244–248, 256–263, 320–324, 331–344, 392–404 (Trojan War).

[21]Bryce 1998 (above, n. 20), 404.

[22]See J. T. Killen (1985), "The Linear B Tablets and the Mycenaean Economy," pp. 241–305 in *Linear B: A 1984 Survey*, ed. A. Morpurgo Davies and Y. Duhoux.

[23]G. F. Bass (1986), "A Bronze Age Shipwreck at Ulu Burun (Kos): 1984 Campaign," *American Journal of Archaeology* 90:269–296; G. F. Bass, C. Pulak, D. Collon, and J. Weinstein (1989), "The Bronze Age Shipwreck at Ulu Burun (Kas): 1986 Campaign," *American Journal of Archaeology* 93:1–29. The ship is dated by dendrochronology to 1306 B.C.E. or shortly thereafter; for dating and an extensive bibliography of the excavations at Ulu Burun, see the website of the Institute of Nautical Archaeology at the University of Texas, http://ina.tamu.edu/ub_main.htm

[24]Excavated from 1984–1994; G. Bass (1987), "Oldest Known Shipwreck Reveals Splendors of the Bronze Age," *National Geographic* 172: 693–733; Bass et al (above, n. 23).

[25]Bass et al (above, n. 23).

[26]R. Payton (1991), "The Ulu Burun Writing-Board Set," *Anatolian Studies* 41:99–106.

[27]G. F. Bass (1967), *Cape Gelidonya: A Bronze Age Shipwreck*, American Philosophical Society. E. H. Cline and M. J. Cline (1991), "Of Shoes and Ships and Sealing Wax: International Trade and the Late Bronze Age Aegean," *Expedition* 33:146–154; website of the Institute for Nautical Archaeology; http://ina.tamu.edu/capegelidonya.htm.

[28]C. Pulak (1997), "The Ulu Burun Shipwreck," pp. .233–262 in *Res Maritimae: Cyprus and the Mediterranean From Prehistory to Late Antiquity*, ed. S. Swiny, R. L. Hohlfelder, H. W. Swiny, 249.

[29]Eric Cline (1994), *Sailing the Wine-Dark Sea: International Trade and the Late Bronze Age Aegean*, 100–101.

[30]C. Giardino (1992), "Nuragic Sardinia and the Mediterranean Metallurgy and Maritime Traffic," pp. 304–315 in *Sardinia in the Mediterranean : A Footprint in the Sea*, ed. Robert H. Tykot, and Tamsey K. Andrews, 304–307.

[31]Lucia Vagnetti (2000), "Western Mediterranean Overview: Peninsular Italy, Sicily and Sardinia at the Time of the Sea Peoples," pp. 305–326 in *The Sea Peoples and Their World: A Reassessment*, ed. Eliezer D. Oren, 313.

[32]F. Lo Schiavo, E. MacNamara and L. Vagnetti (1985), "Late Cypriot Imports to Italy and Their Influence on Local Bronzework," *Papers of the British School at Rome* 53: 1–71; Giardino (above, n. 30), 306.

[33]G. F. Bass (1997), "Prolegomena to a Study of Maritime Traffic in Raw Materials to the Aegean During the Fourteenth and Thirteenth Centuries B.C." in *TEXNH: Craftsmen, Craftswomen and Craftsmanship in the Aegean Bronze Age*, ed. R. Laffineur and P. P. Betancourt, 168 and n. 223.

[34]J. T. Killen (1985), "The Linear B Tablets and the Mycenaean Economy." pp. 241–305 in Davies and Duhoux (above, n. 22), 266.

4

FROM THE BRONZE AGE TO THE IRON AGE—A DARK AGE?

THE END OF THE BRONZE AGE

At the end of the thirteenth century, the entire eastern Mediterranean was engulfed in turmoil. Egypt, which had for years experienced sea-borne attacks of various groups of "Sea Peoples," was again attacked in 1186 by a large mixed contingent accompanied on land by their families in wagon carts. The Pharaoh Ramesses III claimed a great victory over these forces, and had an illustrated description of his battle carved on the walls of his funerary temple at Medinet Habu.[1] The portrayal of the invaders is so detailed that the various factions of the Sea Peoples have been identified, but translating the portrayals and the names given them by Ramesses into the names of known peoples has been problematic, with the exception of the Peleset, who can be identified as the Philistines, known from the Bible.

WEBSITE 4.1   THE MEDINET HABU INSCRIPTIONS: A GENERAL DISCUSSION AND EXCERPTS
http://www.courses.psu.edu/cams/cams400w_aek11/mhabu.html

Although Ramesses proclaimed an absolute victory, the strength of the invaders may be reflected in the subsequent Egyptian retreat from areas in the Levant that they had formerly controlled. Moreover, although the Sea Peoples did not succeed in gaining a foothold in Egypt, they did move northward up the coast, where they seized a number of Canaanite towns, which were to be their permanent home (Philistia). They rebuilt these towns on a far grander scale than the Canaanite towns they replaced, with large ashlar masonry buildings set in sophisticated town plans.

WEBSITE 4.2   THE INCURSION OF THE SEA PEOPLES:
A DETAILED DISCUSSION OF A COMPLEX PROBLEM
http://nefertiti.iwebland.com/sea_peoples.htm

Describe the Medinet Habinet reliefs and the historical validity of what has been inferred from them, especially the indentification of the various "ethnic" groups by clothing, equipment, and hairstyles. What evidence is there for earlier attacks on Egypt and Libya?

Some archaeologists identify the origins of the Sea Peoples by their production of a distinctive, locally made pottery (Mycenaean IIIC: 1b), which copies a Mycenaean style and which has also been found in Cyprus and the Syrian coast. Many other aspects of the material culture of Philistia and Cyprus also suggest an original connection with the Aegean: the presence of large central hearths in major buildings, bathtubs, and Aegean-type loom weights and cult figurines.[2] Many now identify the makers of this pottery as immigrants from the Aegean area and as Sea People, but the interpretation of this pottery has spawned a huge debate among archaeologists and historians, centered upon the question of whether these pots provide evidence for the Aegean origin of the Sea Peoples.[3]

Meanwhile, throughout the Mediterranean, well-established kingdoms were falling to unknown attackers. In central Anatolia, the Hittite empire, afflicted by famine, unrest, and outright rebellion in border areas, collapsed shortly after 1200, probably as a result of attacks by their ancient enemies to the north, the Kaska. In the northwest corner of Anatolia the city of Troy suffered extensive destructions that may be reflected in poetic fashion in Homer's famous tale of the Trojan War. A number of waves of raiders and refugees attacked Cyprus from around 1200. Raiders attacked and destroyed the ancient city of Ugarit on the Syro-Palestinian coast, which had been a hub of Levantine trade with Cyprus and beyond with the Mycenaeans, but which never recovered. These attacks filled the area with survivors seeking refuge, and many probably joined the Sea Peoples, whoever they originally may have been. Nevertheless, a few cities survived or rapidly revived, such as Ugarit's neighbor, Ras Ibn Hani, which was soon reoccupied and rebuilt.[4] Farther south, the Phoenicians—the inhabitants of the Canaanite city-states along the coast in roughly the area that is today's Lebanon—appear somehow to have escaped serious destruction, and very shortly they formed the nucleus of the resumption of maritime trade that brought recovery to the Mediterranean area.

In Greece, the Mycenaeans had anticipated trouble before it erupted and had bolstered their defenses. Fortification walls were strengthened and extended, and elaborately fortified gates were added, such as the postern gate at Tiryns with its multiple traps to ensnare unwitting intruders. Special effort was expended to assure safe access to water sources, in anticipation of siege. At Mycenae, a long tunnel was constructed to reach an underground spring

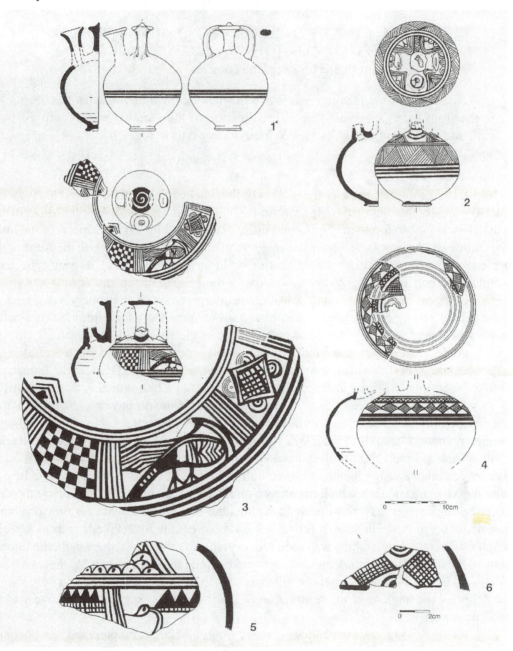

Figure 4.1   Mycenaean IIIC:1b pottery.
From Trude Dothan and Alexander Zukerman, "A Preliminary Study of the Mycenaean IIIC:1 Pottery Assemblages from Tel Miqne-Ekron and Ashdod," *Bulletin of the American Schools of Oriental Research* 333: 19. Courtesy of the American Schools of Oriental Research.

S o u r c e   A n a l y s i s

The Interpretation of Pottery

D oes the fact that very similar pottery (Mycenaean IIIC: 1b) was found in diverse locations (Cyprus, Philistia, the Levant) prove it was made by a single group of people (immigrants from the Aegean)? What other explanations are possible? How likely is each? Does the presence of additional Aegan characteristics at the sites at which this pottery was found make the argument for a single group of Aegean-originating makers more secure? What do we mean by "aegean?" (Mycenaean Greece? Aegean islands? Overseas areas where Mycenaeans had settled?)

beyond the walls. On the acropolis at Athens a shaft 120 feet deep was constructed leading down to a spring; five flights of stone and wooden steps gave access, making the fetching of water possible even if the palace were under attack.

A wall was built at the Isthmus of Corinth, and in Gla in Boeotia, where the Mycenaeans had drained the great Copaic Lake for agricultural use, a fortress stronghold was constructed to provide defense against hostile attempts to flood the plain. Graphic evidence of attack by sea at the palace at Pylos can be read in a tablet whose warning against sea-borne invaders on the eve of the destruction of the palace was broken off in mid-sentence, never to be taken up again. We do not know if the threats that gave rise to these precautions were from external foes or from neighboring Mycenaeans, but a series of palace destructions in the twelfth century shows that they were real. Between approximately 1200 and 1100 B.C.E.[5] both palace buildings and large private houses at numerous sites were attacked and destroyed; in some cases, as at Pylos, a single destruction ended occupation at the site, while other sites suffered repeated destructions and rebuildings.

Troy and the Trojan War

The Greeks may have preserved some memory of this time of troubles in the epic story of the Trojan War attributed to the poet Homer. Although much in the *Iliad* and *Odyssey* reflect the poet's own eighth-century culture, a few elements do go back much earlier and may dimly recall Mycenaean times. In fact, it was belief in the historicity of the Homeric poems by the German businessman and adventurer Heinrich Schliemann that first brought the era of Bronze Age Greece to the eyes of the world. Convinced that Homer's Trojan War had been a

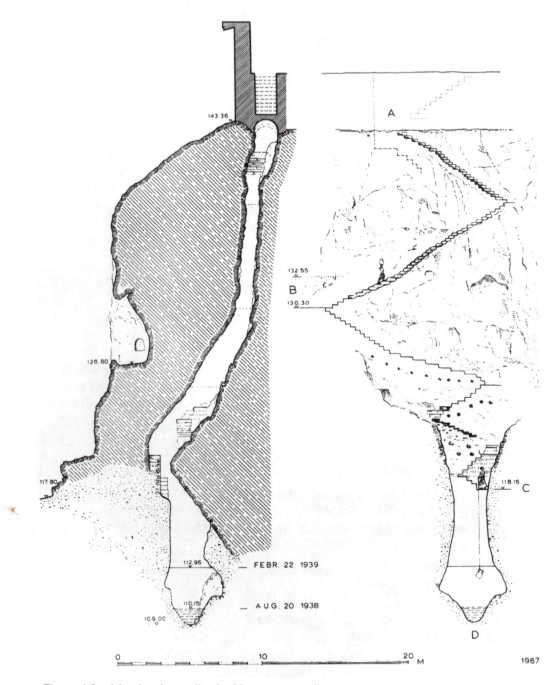

Figure 4.2   Athenian Acropolis, the Mycenaean well.
John Travlos (1971), *The Pictorial Dictionary of Ancient Athens*. Copyright by Ernst Wasmuth
Verlag D- 72072, Tubingen, Germany.

real event, Schliemann used information given in the *Iliad* to identify a site at Hissarlik in Turkey as Troy. Excavating the acropolis mound from 1870 to 1890 C.E., he found the remains of at least seven superimposed cities. In the second level of the site, Schliemann discovered a magnificent treasure, including a copper shield; copper, silver, gold and electrum vessels; copper daggers and lance-heads; two gold diadems; a fillet; four gold ear-drops; 56 gold earrings; and 8,750 gold rings and buttons. He labelled the finds "King Priam's Treasure," and published a picture of his young Greek wife, Sophia, wearing the jewelry, bringing the site to the attention of the world.[6] Later he had similar success at Mycenae, where he discovered the Shaft Graves. Schliemann, however, had no idea that the finds that he identified as Trojan and Mycenaean—the treasure of gold jewelry in the second level at Troy (ca. 2500) and the burial mask of "Agamemnon" at Mycenae—were centuries older than the Trojan War. Nonetheless, his work put an end to the idea that Greek history began only in 776, the date of the first recorded Olympic games.

Further excavation of the site identified by Schliemann as Homer's Troy was carried out by Wilhelm Dorpfeld (1890–1994), Carl Blegen (1932–1938) and Manfred Korfmann (1988–2005). Korfmann verified the existence of a lower settlement that existed from the seventeenth to the early twelfth centuries (Troy levels VI/VIIa) outside and south and east of the citadel, protected by a defensive system consisting of a ditch and palisade with a rampart. The combined upper and lower city is estimated to have covered an area of about 75 acres, with a population of perhaps 5000 to 6000.[7] It was situated at a crucial point for early trade between the Aegean/Mediterranean and the Black Sea area, for ships had to wait for favorable conditions before attempting the trip through the Dardanelles, and Troy offered a handy refuge.[8]

The war over Troy (probably late Troy VI or VIIa) fits well into the time of troubles that engulfed the eastern Mediterranean world in the twelfth century. It also fits well into the intermittent struggles between the Hittites and the Mycenaeans on the Anatolian coast (see Chapter 3). Perhaps the Mycenaeans, driven out of Miletus, turned north to attack the resources of the wealthy city of Troy, with which they had long had commercial contacts, and which was on the peripheries of the Hittite realm and thus less likely to stir Hittite intervention.[9] The city had many attractions, among them possible profits from tolls on ships passing through the straits and the rich fishing grounds of the Hellespont.

If Troy was indeed conquered by the Mycenaeans, it survived their attack and rose again. But at the end of level VIIb, sometime in the eleventh century, and after the collapse of the major Bronze Age civilizations in the Near East, it was destroyed and apparently abandoned.

The Ionian Migration

At this time, large numbers of refugees set out from various sites for new homes. Tradition reports that many moved across the Aegean to sites in Asia Minor. The earliest arrivals there were speakers of the Aeolic dialect from Thessaly and central Greece, who settled sites on the northern Anatolian coast. From the standpoint of later Greek history, however, the best known of these refugees, and those who had the most promising future, were speakers of Ionian Greek who established settlements on the central coast in what would henceforth be known as Ionia.[10] Athens took credit for the leadership of this, the "Ionian Migration."

The Ionian cities that were most probably established in the initial settlement in the eleventh century were Miletus, Ephesus, Myus, Priene, Colophon, Lebedos, Teos, and perhaps Samos. Chios, Phocaea, Klazomenai, and Erythrai were settled a generation later. Halicarnassus was originally Dorian, and Smyrna/Izmir originally Aeolian, although both later became Ionian, either officially (Smyrna) or in culture (Halicarnassus). Some of these sites—Miletus, Halicarnassus (Müsgebi), Ephesus, and Samos—had been occupied by Mycenaeans, and at Miletus both the pottery and the building remains show continuous occupation with no break and only partial destruction and rebuilding, probably due to minor earthquakes.[11] On the other hand, Homer tells us nothing about these sites, which might suggest that the tradition of their Bronze Age existence had been largely lost by the eighth century, or that the poet was careful to avoid anachronisms.

Our information about these early developments in Ionia is heavily dependent upon Greek traditions, but these must be examined carefully for signs of later invention. Tradition gave Athens a key role in the migrations, as a meeting place for refugees and as a provider of assistance and leadership for the trip across the Aegean to Ionia. But suspicion is cast upon this by the fact that the seventh-century poet Mimnermus of Colophon seems unaware of Athenian involvement, for he identified the home of the founders of his city as Pylos. It is only in the sixth century that the Athenian role appears in our sources, and then only indirectly when Solon calls the Athenians the "eldest of the Ionians."[12] By the fifth century, however, Athenian assistance to the Ionian Migration had become a well-established element of Athenian tradition and had entered the "historical record," for Thucydides reported that refugees went first to Athens, and that the Athenians then organized them and sent them on to Ionia (Thuc.1.12).

The tradition of the migration and of Athenian assistance was clearly developed and embroidered over time. A major impetus for this was probably the later formation of an **Ionian League** by the twelve cities established by the Ionian-speaking settlers. The members of this league celebrated their ethnic identity in a common festival, the Panionia, and they also developed foundation legends that celebrated migration settlements, even though some of the cities were, in fact, later foundations. An impetus for the development of the tradition of Athenian assistance can also be found in the later ambitions of Athens. As we shall see, the Athenians in the fifth century created an empire, nominally a league, in which many of these Ionian cities paid tribute and lived under Athenian control. The tradition that these members were originally Athenian settlers would have served to justify the power that Athens then exercised over them. Nevertheless, there are hints that Athens did play some role in the actual migrations, even if not the central and formal role attributed to the city by Athenian tradition. These hints

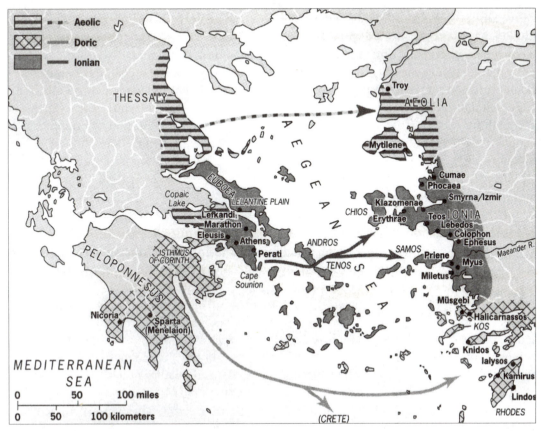

Map 4A   Aegean migrations in the transition from the Bronze Age to the Iron Age.

include the reference in Solon's poems, which predates fifth-century Athenian imperialism and cannot have been affected by it, and the fact that some of the Ionian cities or their Anatolian settlements adopted elements of the Athenian calendar, cults, and tribal system.

Cyprus as a Refuge[13]

Cyprus was well-known to the Mycenaeans as a source of copper and as a point of access to the markets of the Syro-Palestinian coast, although they had never established settlements on the island. Thus it is not surprising that the island attracted Mycenaean settlers in the turmoil of the destruction of the Bronze Age palaces. The choice was not a bad one, for although Cyprus suffered numerous attacks and destructions, it did not experience a general collapse of culture: neither writing nor outside contacts were lost. Major centers recovered rapidly, even from the widespread destructions apparently caused by an earthquake, which brought an end to the Bronze Age on the island.

A number of waves of raiders and refugees reached Cyprus from around 1200; they included Mycenaean Greeks, mixed groups of Sea Peoples, and refugees from the Syro-Palestinian coast, especially Ugarit, which had been destroyed. They introduced locally made Mycenaean-style pottery (LM IIIC:1b pottery). These repeated waves of newcomers created a mixed population in which Mycenaean Greeks played a central role, with the result that in time the island became Hellenized. Those Cypriots who chose to maintain their ethnic identity (the Eteocypriots, or Old Cypriots) concentrated at Amathus, although in some communities, such as Lapethos, Greeks and Cypriots continued to live side by side.[14]

The Cause(s) of the Troubles?

Numerous explanations have been given for the collapse of Bronze Age civilization. The Greeks, looking at it from a much later standpoint and from their own perspective, attributed the destructions in Greece to the "Dorian Invasion." The invasion was seen as the violent return of the Sons of Herakles, or Heraklids, a group that spoke the Dorian dialect and had been driven out of the Peloponnesus a century before. The most convincing argument for this is the distribution of the Greek dialects in the Classical period: while East Greek dialects, such as Aeolic, Attic, and Ionic, were spread across the mid-Aegean region (carried by refugee Mycenaeans), Dorian dialects predominated in the Peloponnesus, the region to which the Greeks claimed that the Dorians "returned," and in areas to which they later migrated (the southern Aegean, Crete).

Although the Greeks themselves, and for some time modern historians as well, believed the hypothesis of a Dorian invasion, a number of difficulties make it no longer acceptable. The most important problem is that it does not account for the widespread nature of the collapse, which involved the entire eastern Mediterranean. If there were Dorian invaders, they played only a minor role in the overall drama. Moreover, if Dorian invaders existed, they left no archaeological traces. The iron objects, swords, fibulae, and cist grave burials that have at one time or another been attributed to them are now all known to have been present in Greece before the destruction of the palaces. A few "barbarian" pots have been found at a number of sites, but their significance and origin is still unclear. Were they the customary pottery of a few newcomers, or simply the homemade products of impoverished local survivors?[15] If these pots do signal newcomers, they were too few to account for the numerous destructions, and they were soon assimilated into the mainstream Mycenaean culture.

As catalysts in the turmoil, the Sea Peoples seem recently to have replaced the Dorians in popularity.[16] They have the advantage of historical documentation, appearing in Hittite correspondence and in Ramesses' funerary inscription. At least some of them have also left archaeological traces in the form of Philistine settlement sites where locally made, Mycenaean-style LH IIIC:1b pottery has been found in quantity, as well as in Cyprus and Levantine coastal sites. Nonetheless, there is no agreement on such basic questions as the identity of the various groups of Sea People, their origins, or the degree of responsibility that they should bear for the general collapse.

Some scholars have argued for a more area-wide cause, such as climate change,[17] earthquakes (attested in LH IIIB at Tiryns, Mycenae, Sparta, Pylos, and Troy),[18] or the spread of violent epidemics (which might have been a consequence of either climate change or earthquakes). Others offer a more generalized explanation, focusing on catastrophe theory (complex systems are susceptible to collapse as a result of relatively minor dislocations, as instanced by the problems that are being caused in our contemporary world by fluctuations in the price and availability of oil),[19] or a Mediterranean-wide economic shift from large-scale palatially-administered trade to small-scale entrepreneurial activity (a shift that did occur, but that was probably an effect of the unrest, rather than its primary cause).

RECOVERY: THE ELEVENTH AND EARLY TENTH CENTURIES

In Greece itself, the Mycenaean palaces were destroyed, and with them went the practice of writing (probably practiced by only a few scribes who recorded palatial transactions), many skilled crafts, and monumental building projects. But life continued. Recent excavations at Tiryns have shown that after the destruction of the palace a period of occupation amidst the ruins was followed by repairs to the fortifications, new building activities in the lower citadel, and the relocation of people from scattered inland settlements into the protection of the reactivated fortress. These changes imply the exercise of some sort of central authority that focused upon the interests of the general population during the upheaval caused by the destruction of the palace. As a result of such evidence for recovery, it has even been suggested that this period (LHIIIC) should be called "late Mycenaean city life," to contrast it with the earlier palatial period.[20]

Lefkandi: The Burial in the Heroön

Other coastal sites were also occupied at this time, including numerous sites on the Peloponnesus.[21] The most abundant evidence for the continuation or reestablishment of contacts between mainland Greece and the East has been found, however, at Lefkandi, a site on the west coast of the large island of Euboea.[22] The site had been occupied by a Mycenaean settlement in the Bronze Age, and about 1200 it had received a large influx of newcomers, probably refugees from the mainland. By the end of the twelfth century, however, it was abandoned. Since Herodotus says that the Abantes from Euboea took part in the Ionian Migration (Hdt. 1.146), we might identify the people who abandoned Lefkandi as the Abantes.

The site was too attractive to remain vacant for long, however. Its good anchorage and access to the extensive Lelantine Plain soon attracted settlers, and it was reoccupied in the

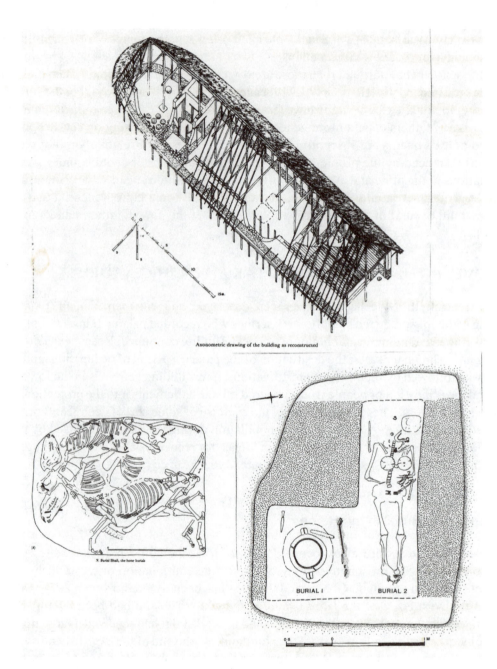

Axonometric drawing of the building as reconstructed

N. Burial Shaft, the horse burial

BURIAL 1   BURIAL 2

Figure 4.3   Site plan of the colonnaded building at Lefkandi, including burial and horse burial. From M. R. Popham, P. G. Calligas, and L. H. Sackett (1993), *Lefkandi II: The Protogeometric Guilding at Toumba,* Plates 5, 13, 22b. Courtesy of the British School at Athens.

eleventh century. The most startling find at Lefkandi was a multiple shaft grave burial of the early tenth century.[23] One compartment of the shaft contained three or four horses, and the second a female inhumation and a male cremation. The male burial was in a bronze amphora of Cypriot origin, decorated with animals and huntsmen with bows. The ashes were wrapped in a remarkably well-preserved cloak made of two lengths of linen, with flokati-type weaving at the top, reminiscent of a modern Greek rug. Placed beside the amphora were an iron sword, spearhead, and whetstone. The female burial was accompanied by rich offerings, including gilt hair coils, a gold pendant decorated with granulation, gold and faience beads, bronze and iron pins (the iron ones covered with gold foil), an iron knife with an ivory handle, and an unusual gold "brassiere." The remains of the cremation site suggest that the male had been given a heroic-style funeral. That he was of high rank is also suggested by the unusual circumstance that the burial site was enclosed within a large apsidal colonnaded building over 45 meters in length, which had apparently never been occupied, and which was dismantled and buried under a huge mound, or tumulus, soon after the burials.

The form of the colonnaded building is suggestive of later Greek temples, and it is by far the earliest building of such size found in Greece up to this time. The excavators suggest that it was not a temple to an Olympian god, but a **heroön**, or hero tomb, where honor would have been paid and sacrifices offered to a deceased mortal; for example, in later times this honor was paid to the founder of an overseas settlement. The hero had been accompanied in death by his horses and his consort, and some have suggested that her burial was a form of *suttee* (wife sacrifice).[24] There are parallels for the sacrifice of slaves in contemporary Cypriot burials and for the sacrifice of horses in eighth- and seventh-century burials in Cyprus.[25]

The Phoenicians

Some of the best evidence for the state of Mediterranean life in the period following the collapse of the palaces involves the Phoenicians, a people who somehow escaped destruction by the Sea Peoples and whose lives were to be intertwined with those of the Greeks from this point forward. The Phoenicians were Canaanites who had lived for centuries in city-states set on the narrow strip of land between the sea and the Lebanon mountains. Limited in arable land, they lived mainly from the resources provided by sea and mountains. The famous cedars of Lebanon were in wide demand for the construction of ships and large buildings, especially by the Egyptians. Excellent natural harbors had led the Phoenicians to become skilled seafarers, and a maritime life provided access to both raw materials and markets for their production of luxury goods, such as ornately decorated bronze and silver bowls, intricate and elaborate gold jewelry, carved ivory used for furniture inlays, faience (a vitreous paste made from ground sand), and finely woven textiles. They excelled in the production of purple dye, so valued in the ancient world that it was considered the color of royalty. In fact, their famed purple-dyed cloth seems to have led the Greeks to call them Phoinikes, Purple Men, from which we get our name for these people, the Phoenicians (they called themselves simply Canaanites).

We have a rare piece of primary evidence about this period in the "Tale of Wenamun," the story of the adventures of an Egyptian envoy sent to obtain timber from the Phoenician city of Byblos ca. 1075. It is known to us from a single incomplete papyrus copy.[26]

Source Analysis

The Tale of Wenamun

Wenamun's story is usually taken to be an official report of an actual journey; it does, however, have some picaresque elements, some of which are omitted in this paraphrase. But even if the account is more a "tale" than an "offical report," it probably portrays fairly accurately the general conditions in this disturbed period. What more specifically can the historian learn from this document?

Wenamun was an Egyptian official sent by the temple of Amun-Re at Thebes to obtain timber from Bybios for renovations on the solar boat of the Delta, and presented his documents to Smendes and Tanetamun, a married couple who were in charge of the Delta (their official status is unclear). Smendes kept the documents and sent Wenamun off as a passenger on a private ship. (Both points were later used by the ruler of Byblos to berate the envoy, pointing out that in the past, those sent on such missions had come on official Egyptian ships with proper documents.) Sailing along the coast, Wenamon suffered many indignities. When he arrived at Dor, which was under the control of one of the Sea Peoples, the Tjekker, someone on his ship stole all his gold and silver, leaving him pennniless. He asked Beder, the ruler of Dor, to repay him for his loss, suggesting that he catch the thief in order to recover the payment, but Deder refused, saying that the thief had been from Wenamun's ship, and was not a Tjekker. He did offer to look for the culprit, but when he had not been successful after nine days, Wenamun left Dor. Continuing on to Byblos, Wenamon took matters into his own hands and somehow seized silver from a Tjekker ship to compensate himself for his loss (a gap in the text makes the situation obscure). On his arrival in Byblos, its ruler, Zakarball, berated and demeaned him, complaining about his lack of credentials and of an official Egyptian naval escort. Zakarball insisted on payment for the timber, presenting detailed accounts of the gifts sent by previous rulers of Egypt in "payment" for timber for the god. He detained Wenamun in the harbor, until finally, by sending Zakarball's scribe to Smendes at Tanis, Wenamun, was able to obtain the necessary payment. But as he was at last preparing to leave byblos, Tjekkers appeared in ships and demanded that he be turned over to them for his theft. Zakarball refused, but said that Tjekker could capture Wenamon once he was out at sea. Thus, as the traveler left the harbor with his timber, his ship was pursued by Tjekker ships. He managed to escape, but then he was blown off course to Cyprus. There the inhabitants threatened to kill him, but he was saved by a princess, who (seductively?) invited him to spend the night (perhaps not unlike Homer's Circe?). Unfortunately, the papyrus breaks off at this point, and we do not know the ultimate fate of Wenamun, although he apparently lived to return to Egypt and tell his tale.

THE GEOMETRIC PERIOD: TENTH AND NINTH CENTURIES

Lefkandi: The Successors of the Hero and Maritime Trading Networks

> "Euboea, famous for its ships."
> Homeric *Hymn to Apollo*, line 219.

At Lefkandi, after the spectacular burials in the heröon, settlement continued through the tenth and ninth centuries. The wealthy associates and successors of the "Hero" almost immediately began a new cemetery, the Toumba cemetery, facing the tumulus. The wealthiest of the six cemeteries so far found at Lefkandi,[27] its burials, rich in gold and imported objects, provide abundant evidence for contacts of upper-class Lefkandians with nearby Athens, Crete, Cyprus, and the Levant in the tenth and ninth centuries. Coldstream suggests that the Lefkandian upper class were wealthy traders. As if to illustrate this suggestion, one of the tombs contained a locally made vessel decorated with one of the earliest Greek portrayals of a ship, dated about 875–850.[28]

The hypothesis that some upper-class Lefkandians were themselves traders is supported by finds from a burial of the early ninth century, which suggest that the grave's occupant was both a warrior and a trader.[29] The burial was unusual in that the cremated remains were placed in a bronze cauldron in a burial similar to that given to the "Hero" in the heroon, but used in no other burials in the cemetery. His warrior identity is established by a "killed" iron sword, a spearhead, two iron knives, about 25 iron arrowheads, and a bronze cheese grater (a similar object was used to prepare a restorative potion in the *Iliad*).[30] His role as trader is suggested by the presence in the grave of 12 stone weights, a number of smaller stone weights, and a possible weighing balance. Other offerings in the grave provide evidence for overseas connections: an antique North Syrian cylinder seal dating to around 1800, parts of two bichrome Phoenician jugs (the earliest known example of this type to reach the Aegean), fragments of three Cypriot jugs, and two Attic Early Geometric II vases. Local Euboean pottery included two monumental standed craters and six pendent-semicircle plates. The plate was a form found chiefly as a Euboean export to the Levant, but little used in Greece, which led Coldstream to suggest that the Lefkandians may have even engaged in market research in their pottery production.[31]

Maritime trade by Euboeans is further attested by evidence of a Euboean trading network (***koine**, marked by a common general style*) in the Aegean, encompassing Lefkandi, Skyros, Boeotia, east Lokris, Thessaly, and some of the Cycladic islands.[32] While identified first by pottery styles, it also involved similarities in housing preferences (apsidal buildings), dress style (the use of fibulae rather than pins), and the use of exotic and valuable objects as funerary gifts (chiefly in Lefkandi and Skyros). In support of the existence of this *koine* were fragments of transport amphorae made in the north Aegean, which were found in the fill of the Heroön at Lefkandi and in the Toumba cemetery.[33] They could have contained wine, oil, grain, or perhaps preserved fish, and they attest that Euboean imports involved basic needs as well as exotic luxuries. It has also been suggested that the Euboeans may have made settlements in the north Aegean, in Chalkidiki, as early as the twelfth or eleventh century, in activity paralleling the Ionian Migration.[34]

There is abundant evidence in the Toumba cemetery for Euboean contacts in the Levant. Among the more striking finds were two Phoenician engraved bronze bowls, one decorated with a procession of Near Eastern figures (gift bearers and musicians, and a tree with antithetic animals), the other with fantastic winged lions with human heads.[35] Such finds of Levantine objects at Lefkandi have their counterparts in abundant finds of characteristic Euboean pendent-semicircle pottery in the east. For example, large numbers of these vessels found at Tyre present a clear picture of intensive trade between that city and Euboea.[36] The settlement area at Lefkandi, about 600 meters from the cemeteries, has provided evidence for the production of these pendent-semicircle cups. Similar Euboean pottery found on Cyprus, especially at Amathus on the southern coast, supports the suggestion that a Tyrian-Euboean trade route had been established in the tenth century, with Amathus serving as a port of call.[38]

Cypriot contacts are also indicated by the sophisticated metal-working techniques employed by the Lefkandians, as evidenced by finds of crucible fragments and fragments of lost-wax moulds for the production of tripod legs of the Cypriot type.[39] The mould makes the presence of Cypriot metalworkers as instructors in Lefkandi seem very likely, since it is not a technique that could be learned simply by observing the finished products. There are also similarities between the mould and a tripod stand found at Knossos,[40] which add to other evidence for links between Lefkandi and Crete. While pottery finds are more abundant because of their near indestructibility in at least fragmentary form, it was probably metals that provided the main impetus for the wide-ranging maritime connections in this period.

Athens

Euboean connections closer to home with Attica are well-attested in the Toumba cemetery. A few burials appear to have been those of Athenian residents in Lefkandi.[41] Two inhumations employed a form of burial not otherwise found in the Toumba cemetery but used in Attica: warrior burials in wooden coffins.[42] Three urn burials were also of Attic type,[43] and one of these was especially significant in providing evidence for further international contacts. In addition to an Attic-type cremation with a "killed sword," it contained a pedestalled krater similar to kraters found at Amathus and Salamis on Cyprus and at the royal capitals of Hama, Tyre, and Samaria.[44]

Many Toumba graves also included Attic imports, some of them noteworthy. Three carefully decorated Attic miniature spouted vessels for the feeding of infants provide evidence, missing in Attica itself, that the Athenians were concerned with the care of small infants. Another grave, probably of an adult woman, contained a doll with incised decoration of a type found otherwise only in Attic graves. Finally, a female grave in the cemetery contained among its 30 vessels an Attic *pyxis* (ceramic chest), an earlier version of a pyxis found in an astonishingly rich grave in the Agora at Athens, ca. 850, usually referred to as the Tomb of the **Rich Athenian Lady**. [45]

The cremated remains of the Rich Athenian Lady at Athens were placed in a very large belly-handled amphora, 71.5 centimeters high. Among the rich grave goods was a miniature *pyxis* that was more elaborate than the Toumba *pyxis*, for it was topped by five small beehive-shaped granaries and decorated with carefully done Geometric-style ornamentation. The five granaries have been connected with the later Solonian wealth classification, in which the highest class, the *penticosiomedimi*, was made up of those whose land produced 500 bushels of grain, who alone were eligible for the offices of archon and treasurer. The burial contained other offerings attesting to the high rank of the woman and to overseas connections: a necklace of over a thousand pale green faïence disk beads with a large central Phoenician bead of variegated glass, six simple gold rings, and a spectacular pair of large gold earrings with pendent pomegranates suspended from massive gold trapezoidal plates that were decorated with granulation and filigree. The funeral banquet was also extremely lavish, estimated to have included some 70 kilograms of meat, enough to feed perhaps 350 people. The woman was probably in her thirties, and in remarkably good condition, with no signs of the stresses of a life spent at the hard labor of farming tasks, carrying water, or grinding grain, thus providing more evidence of her high status.

Recently a reexamination of the cremated remains of the Rich Athenian Lady led to another rather startling discovery. Among the remains were the bones of a fetus within four to eight weeks of a full-term pregnancy.[47] There was no way to know if the fetus had been delivered, although the remarkable preservation of such small bones suggests that they may have been partially protected within the mother's body from the heat of the fire during cremation. Thus the Rich Athenian Lady was probably pregnant or died giving birth.[48]

This find illustrates dramatically the risks that even well-to-do women ran in giving birth in antiquity, before the advent of the procedures of modern medicine.[49] The hazards ran all the way from uncontrollable hemorrhaging, physical impediments to delivery (pelvic deformity, pelvis smaller than the child's head, abnormal presentations such as transverse lies),

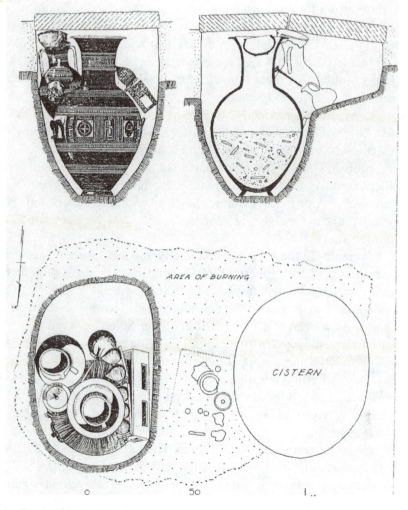

Figure 4.4   Tomb of Rich Athenian Lady.
From Maria Liston and John Papadopoulos (2004), "The 'Rich Athenian Lady' was Pregnant: The Anthropology of a Geometric Tomb Reconsidered,"*Hesperia* 73, figure 4, p. 11. Courtesy of the American School of Classical Studies at Athens.

toxemia, infection (not only the dreaded Puerperal Fever, but also increased susceptibility to fatal outcomes in diseases that affect the general population, such as tuberculosis, pneumonia, and especially malaria, due to the immune suppression of pregnancy).[50]

The evidence for connections between Lefkandi and Athens attest one branch of a complex network of interconnections—some familial, some between elite males, some perhaps commercial—that linked these two centers and cities in Cyprus and further east. These interconnections were part of a wider network that also extended to Crete and the west.

Perati

At Perati, a natural harbor on the east coast of Attica, the discovery of a cemetery used in the period of transition after the fall of the palaces provides evidence for continued mainland overseas contacts in the twelfth and eleventh centuries and the prosperity they generated.[51] No settlement has been discovered, but since the cemetery has been totally excavated, it provides a remarkable picture of family life and outside contacts. Two hundred nineteen tombs were found in an area of over 13 acres; of these, 192 were chamber tombs, cut deep into the rock. Most (150) were family tombs, containing multiple burials made over a period of time, attesting a settled existence. The grave goods in the cemetery provide evidence of considerable prosperity: abundant painted pottery and terracotta figurines; jewelry and clothing ornaments and accessories, some in gold and silver; Egyptian and Near Eastern amulets and seals; and weapons and tools in bronze and iron. The earliest burials were contemporary with the first houses at Lefkandi, and contacts were maintained between the two settlements. The numerous imported items at Perati also attest to continuing contacts with Asine, Crete, Melos, Naxos, Kos, Asia Minor, Cyprus, Syria and Egypt.[52] During the period in which the cemetery was in use, the practice of cremation was introduced from Asia Minor and grew in popularity, showing that contacts were not simply commercial but extended to the adoption of new ideas and customs. At the end of the period, as overseas connections became more difficult, a trickle of imports indicate new connections with central and eastern Europe. Eventually (ca. 1075), however, with the loss of maritime contacts, burials at Perati ceased, and the mainland sank into a depressed and impoverished existence.

Crete

At Knossos over a hundred Attic pots were imported in this period. Of these, over a half were concentrated in only two tombs in the North Cemetery,[53] Tombs J and G, clearly the burial places of elite families. Tomb J, of the late tenth century, contained gold pins, a Minoan sealstone, ornaments in various precious stones, and a bronze bowl inscribed in the Phoenician alphabet.[54]Tomb G, of the late ninth century, contained a large collection of bronze vessels, as well as very large locally made vases, including an imitation of an Attic cremation urn.

Of the vessels found in these two tombs, most were drinking cups, and they appear in the very large sets that were used for the funeral meal (**symposium**). But they also included some 13 very large belly-handled amphoras of the type used for female cremations in Attica, similar to the one used in the burial of the Rich Athenian Lady. However, the Cretans did not follow Athenian practice in using these vases as cremation urns. Some archaeologists suggest that they served as mixing bowls for the wine of the symposium, but the largest and latest of the large amphora found in the North Cemetery is over a meter high, too large to serve as a mixing bowl; in fact, it is too large to have fit in most cremation graves, and Coldstream suggests that the giant vases were used as monuments marking the graves of elite women.[55]

The role of Crete as a way station on the east-west route is attested by the discovery of evidence for a Phoenician presence at Kommos, a port site on the south coast. In ca. 1020 a small Greek temple was built there,[56] and artifacts from the early tenth to the early ninth centuries attest to at least the occasional presence of Phoenicians. Particularly significant is a Phoenician or Cypriot grafiti on the handle of a Levantine storage jar, dated ca. 900–850,[57] which was found among over 200 fragments of Phoenician pottery, mostly transport amphorae. These fragments testify to a lively trade in some Levantine products. That it was probably the Phoenicians who brought them to Kommos is suggested by the presence of a Phoenician tripillar shrine that was constructed at the site of the Greek temple shortly before 800.[58] However, there is no evidence for Phoenician settlement at Kommos, which the excavators consider was used as a resupply station by Phoenicians on the route west.[59]

Other reflections of Crete as a stopping place on a route from the east Mediterranean to points farther west were also found in burials in the cemeteries at Knossos. Some contained symposium sets, often stacked inside a large krater that rested on rod tripod stands, or intricately decorated openwork stands of Cypriot inspiration, and these were accompanied by iron spits with firedogs that served for the roasting of meat.[60]

Two tombs in the Tekke cemetery at Knossos are especially important because of the evidence they provide for eastern contacts.[61] These are the Tekke Treasure, found in a reused Minoan tholos tomb, and the Tekke bowl, found in Tomb J. The Tekke bowl,[62] which has been dated to ca. 900 or slightly earlier, bears an inscription of about 12 Phoenician letters, probably reading "bowl of X, son of Y."[63] It has been interpreted as the possession of a Phoenician resident on Crete;[64] however, the bowl could have come to its owner as loot or a guest gift, and thus need not define him as a Phoenician.[65]

The Tekke Treasure consisted of a rich assortment of jewelry, including two pendants with elaborate filigree work and granulation, one with amber and rock crystal inlays, together with gold bars and unworked gold, silver, and electrum.[66] The jewelry exhibits a high degree of expertise in the use of granulation and filigree, and again, as in the cases of jewelry found at Lefkandi and in the burial of the Rich Lady of Athens, it is argued that these were skills known in the Bronze Age but unattested and believed lost after that time, and that therefore the presence of a master jeweler must be postulated.[67] Again, perhaps this was a craftsman taught by local practitioners of the technique.[68]

The burial that contained the Tekke Treasure also provided evidence for contacts further west on the east-west route that had Crete as a way station. This evidence is in the form of a Sardinian duck vase (*askos*).[69] It is similar to a duck *askos* found at Populonia in Italy, and Vagnetti suggests that Phoenicians probably brought it to Crete from Sardinia.[70] In addition to the *askoi* found at Knossos and at Populonia, numerous other examples are also known from Etruria;[71]. One traveled to a tomb in Sicily, dated by its context to the ninth century,[72] and another to the Lipari islands.[73] This widespread distribution pattern suggests the existence of a localized trading network run by Sardinians in products that were perhaps produced for commercial purposes. Vagnetti suggests that the small vessels may have been known and valued as containers for a specific product, perhaps a cosmetic or medicine.[74]

Although no *askoi* have been found at Pithekoussai, Euboean contacts with Sardinia are attested by finds from the Nuraghic village of Sant' Imbenia, near Alghero in the northwest of the island. The material consists of fragments of Euboean *skyphoi* (cups) together with Phoenician plates and vessels and two hordes of Sardinian copper ingots.[75] One of the metal hoards was found in a Phoenician amphora of a type widely found in the west, at Sardinia, Carthage, Malta, Sicily, Pithekoussai, and Etruria; the other hoard was contained in a local, handmade version of the Phoenician amphora, found at the same level as the Euboean semi-circular pendent skyphos.[76]

Sardinia and the West

Extension of the east-west network farther west, to Iberia and its Atlantic trading sphere, is attested by the widespread appearance in Sardinia, as well as in Sicily and central Italy, of metal objects produced in Iberia. These include swords, daggers, tools, fibulae, razors, and fixed and articulated spits.[77] The Mounte Sa Idda hoard in Sardinia offers an especially rich collection of Iberian objects, including 174 bronzes found together with local Sardinian artifacts and objects of eastern inspiration.[78] Notable among these was a fragment of an articulated spit. While spits were utilitarian objects in wide use for turning meat over an open fire, the articulated type, combining the functions of spit and firedog, is a relatively rare find and clearly a prestige item for use in elite feasting.[79] A similar articulated spit was found in Sardinia, and 18 have been found in locations along the European Atlantic seaboard, where the

Figure 4.5   Sardinia: Nurage.
Photo by N. Demand.

Figure 4.6   Sardinia: Metal-working village outside Nurage.
Photo by N. Demand.

type originated.[80] The most distant example was found in Amathus in Cyprus in a tomb dated to 1000–950.[81] The spit provides evidence that in the eleventh or early tenth centuries, new (or renewed) trade routes stretched from the Levant and Cyprus by way of Sardinia to the Iberian peninsula.[82] Further evidence for this route can be seen in a group of finds in Portugal that includes fibulae inspired by Cypriot models,[83] as well as bronze vessels similar to others found in Spain, Cyprus, and Palestine.

That these metal-working contacts that link the central and the eastern Mediterranean with the Atlantic cultures may have extended as far afield as England, Ireland, and Brittany (a "tin road"?), is suggested by a hoard found in the Sardinian Nuraghe Flumenelongu, which contained tools, bracelets, and copper ingots that were similar to objects found all along the far northern route.[84]

EARLIEST OVERSEAS SETTLEMENTS IN THE WEST

Phoenician Settlements in Cyprus and Beyond

Both Phoenicians and Greeks at this point were poised on the verge of a rather dramatic change: supporting their westward trading ventures by the permanent establishment of overseas settlements. In the late ninth century, the Phoenicians took the first step, establishing a settlement at Kition on the south coast of Cyprus. This gave them a firm link on the route west, as well as access to the rich Cypriot copper deposits. The central focus of the new city was provided by a vast ashlar temple dedicated to the goddess Astarte, with a triple Holy-of-Holies and two covered porticoes. Unparalleled in the Phoenician world, it has been compared to Solomon's Temple at Jerusalem, also built by Phoenician craftsmen.[85]

The expansion of Tyre to the west is often attributed to pressure for tribute from Assyria. At this time, however, Assyria was in decline and more concerned with threats to its north from Urartu and the North Syrian states than with pressuring the Levantine cities, and its tribute demands were relatively modest. It is also possible that relief of overpopulation at Tyre provided some impetus for the settlement, given the stress on food supplies that is suggested by Tyre's relations with Israel.[86] However, Assyrian tribute demands and overpopulation were probably less important motivations than Tyre's basic overall economic strategy of securing new sources of raw material and markets for its production of luxury trading goods, a vital source of its wealth.

Shortly after their foundation of Kition, the Phoenicians founded an even more distant settlement, Kartihadast (Carthage) on the coast of North Africa. The traditional date for that foundation is 814.[87] Legend attributes the city's foundation to a schism within the royal family of Tyre. The young king Pygmalion assassinated his sister Elissa's husband, the high priest of the god Melqart; Elissa then fled the city, accompanied by a group of aristocratic followers, and together they founded the new city of Carthage. The legend, which may or may not have a core of truth, is significant for the ancient historian mainly because the Roman poet Virgil later made use of it. In Virgil's tale, Elissa became Dido, the seductive queen who, failing in her attempt to persuade the hero Aeneas to abandon his quest to found Rome, threw herself upon a burning pyre.

Al Mina: The First Greek Overseas Settlement in the East?

The discovery in the 1930s of large amounts of Euboean pottery dating from the early eighth century at a site on the North Syrian coast called Al Mina (The Port—its ancient name is unknown)[88] immediately prompted speculation about Greek settlement, and even suggestions that Al Mina should be seen as the first Greek overseas settlement.[89] That remained a common view until recently, when finds of even earlier Greek pottery at a number of sites along the Levantine coast, and especially at Phoenician Tyre, made it obvious that the simple presence of Greek pottery could not be taken as evidence for a Greek settlement.[90] Evidence for Euboean presence at Al Mina, aside from the drinking cups, was lacking. No typically Euboean architecture was found (the buildings were rectangular, not apsidal, as in the Euboean *koine*), nor were characteristic Euboean cooking pots or other types of household artifact. Thus most historians now see the Euboean pottery found at Al

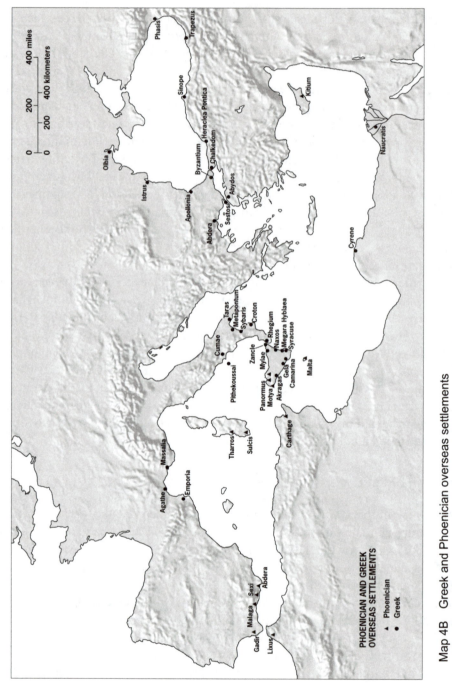

Map 4B   Greek and Phoenician overseas settlements
Adapted from *Historical Atlas* by William R. Shepherd (New York: Henry Holt and Company, 1926), p. 12. Courtesy of the University of Texas Libraries, The University of Texas at Austin.

Mina as goods-in-transit, although some still maintain that a few Greek merchants may have resided there.[91]

Al Mina thus provides an excellent example of the caution necessary in drawing conclusions about people from pots, and a good contrast to the only superficially similar argument that infers the Aegean origins of the attackers called the Sea People from the presence of locally made copies of Mycenaean pottery (Mycenaean IIIC:1b) in Philistia, the Levantine coast, and Cyprus. The significant difference in these two cases lies in the contexts of the pottery finds. Mycenaean IIIC:1b pottery was found along with numerous other indicators of an Aegean origin, such as central hearths, bathtubs, typical Aegean cult figures, and Aegean-type loom weights. In contrast, in the case of Euboean skyphoi at Al Mina, no other evidence of Euboean presence was found: no Euboean-type houses, no household pottery or cooking pots, no cult objects or shrines. These were truly pots out of context.

The Euboean Foundation of Pithekoussai

The Euboeans were not far behind the Phoenicians in the foundation of a settlement in the west. According to ancient sources, people from the Greek cities of Chalcis and Eretria in Euboea founded Pithekoussai on the island of Ischia in the bay of Naples, ca. 750.[92] However, since Eretria itself seems to have been settled at about this same time, and burials at the Toumba cemetery and most habitation at Lefkandi came to an end abruptly in ca. 825, the suggestions that the Lefkandians relocated to establish Eretria, perhaps in order to enhance their strength against neighboring Chalchis,[93] or moved west to establish the settlement of Pithekoussai,[94] or both—first establishing Eretria, and then moving on to found Pithekoussai[95]—have obvious attraction. At any rate, the Euboeans were now embarked on a new venture, the first overseas Greek settlements in the west.

The date for the foundation of Pithehoussai is conventionally given as 750, but it must have been established earlier, for the three known archaeological sites—the cemetery, settlement area, and metal-working center—were all "fully operational" by that time.[96] Moreover, the earliest Pithekoussian pottery, Euboean *skyphoi* of local manufacture, dates from before 750 and has parallels among the earliest Euboean finds from the wider area of Campania and southern Etruruia.[97] Thus it seems, not surprisingly, that some Greeks had been active in the area before the time of the settlement and were aware from personal experience of the possibilities that the area offered. They also would have discovered that they were not the first in the field: Cypriots had been in contact with Sardinia since the eleventh century; the Sardinians had active trading relations with Etruria;[98] and the Phoenicians were in the process of settling in Carthage.[99] Moreover, the indigenous population of Etruria had been engaged in the production of metals from the late tenth century, and by abandoning large numbers of small sites and moving their inhabitants together, had created a few large, well-organized urbanized settlements that were able to control metal resources and circulation routes.[100]

The site of Pithekoussai, the small volcanic island of Ischia, while possessing sufficient agricultural land to support the settlement, nonetheless was poor in comparison with some of the sites that its founders passed as they sailed from Euboea, and most scholars now see the motivation for the settlement as the attraction of metals in central Italy, not as a search for farmland.[101]

The archaeological finds at Pithekoussai have made it clear that, although the Euboeans were predominant, the settlement was a mixed community, with Levantines (probably Phoenicians) present in the settlement throughout its lifetime. Among the earliest burials (750–725), one contains an infant in a Canaanite amphora bearing three Semitic inscriptions, one a religious funeral inscription, suggesting that the infant had at least one Levantine parent.[102] In the cemetery just over a third of the burials contained at least one article identified as Phoenician or North Syrian. Undoubtedly not all burials with Levantine articles were of Phoenicians, but the large number of such finds, as well as the discovery of Semitic inscriptions, nonetheless suggests the stable presence of a number of Phoenicians in Pithekoussai in the second half of the eighth century.[103] In fact, the abundant evidence for Phoenician presence at the settlement has led Ridgway to suggest that "It almost looks as if the Euboeans had Phoenician advice in the selection of a suitable location."[104]

Both Pithekoussai and Carthage played active roles in the central Mediterranean trade network. Finds at Carthage of Pithekoussian/Euboean pottery from the first half of the eighth century[105] have their counterparts in Carthaginian imports discovered in 16 graves in Pithekoussai.[106]

STATE FORMATION AND THE ORIGINS OF THE GREEK POLIS

This period is traditionally called the Dark Age, emphasizing the negative consequences of the collapse of the palatial centers: the ending of large-scale trade and the loss of writing. As we have seen, however, there is abundant evidence that trade and other contacts did not end with the destruction of the palaces. Rather, they changed form as palatial transactions gave way to smaller-scale, entrepreneurial exchange, including the travels of itinerant craftsmen who were carriers of technological expertise.[107] However, the precise role of the various players in this mélange is unclear. Were Phoenicians responsible for the presence of these out-of-context finds? Or the Cypriots? Or was it the Euboeans, famous for their ships?[108] What is clear is that people of various "nationalities" were moving about rather freely over the landscape (or, perhaps better, the seascape), exchanging ideas and knowledge along with material objects.[109]

In this period of ferment of the tenth and ninth centuries, when increased contacts opened up new opportunities for the spread of ideas and technologies, and both the economy and population grew rapidly, there is evidence that the process of state formation was initiated in some locations. Perhaps in some cases traders with experience of the city-states of the Levant carried the idea, but in others, it seems to have resulted from the increased complexity brought by increased production and trade. The process in many cases began with the aban-donment of small villages and the relocation of their population into large central places (**synoikism**).

Thus in central Italy, state development occurred in the tenth/ninth centuries, before the advent of the Greeks,[110] with a radical transformation in settlement pattern involving a con-centration of population in a few major sites, a phenomenon identified by archaeologists as the beginning of the Iron Age and of Villanovan culture. The motive for the consolidation is suggested to have been new demands put upon metalworkers by involvement in a sophisti-cated market.[111] In the twelfth and eleventh centuries, metal work was still fairly simple and sparse, and work had been carried on by individual artisans; but by the tenth century, arti-sans, sometimes working in groups in workshops, had began to produce a wider range of ob-jects, and their work attracted Sardinian and Phoenician traders. As demand increased, the small villages and individual artisans had difficulty coping with the complexities of the situ-ation. The new needs for organization of production, distribution, and exchange were met by a consolidation of small communities, and it was these larger communities that became the urban state.[112]

In Crete, a widespread change in settlement pattern also began in the early tenth century. At that time, more than half of the known refuge sites established at the end of the Bronze Age were abandoned, while surviving sites expanded and a few new, rapidly expanding sites were founded. This process of nucleation was accompanied by the re-use of Bronze Age re-mains, which can be seen as a means of reinforcing community history and identity. It is viewed by some as the first stage in the rise of the *polis*.[113]

Evidence for a number of such settlement changes in various Mediterranean communities suggests that this was a relatively common, and perhaps even typical, feature of the period. Thus, in Israel, Avraham Faust regards the widespread abandonment of villages at the begin-ning of the tenth century, and the movement of their populations together to form towns for added security, as "a state-formation process," which resulted in the Israelite state.[114]

In Greece, the origin of the *polis* is conventionally assigned to the eighth century. Many historians, however, now suggest that it was given impetus by the overseas settlement activi-ties of the Greeks, in a process of feedback whereby the lessons learned in establishing new overseas settlements were applied to the homeland to bring about a new sort of urban entity, the *polis*. These activities began for the Greeks in the west, in Pithekoussai, early in the eighth century, and in the context of a dynamic network of exploration and trading ventures linking Phoenicians, Cypriots, Sardinians, and Italians. The *polis* should be seen as one of the products of this new maritime mélange.

SUGGESTIONS FOR FURTHER READING

E. D. Oren, ed. (2000), *The Sea Peoples and Their World: A Reassessment*; William A. Ward and Martha Joukowsky, eds. (1992), *The Crisis Years: The 12th Century B.C.: From Beyond the Danube to the Tigris*; Louise Steel (2002), *Cyprus Before History: From the Earliest Settlers to the End of the Bronze Age*; M. R. Popham, E. Touloupa, and L. H. Sackett (1982), "The Hero of Lefkandi," *Antiquity* 5: 169–174; M. A. Liston and J. K. Papadopoulos (2004), "The 'Rich Athenian Lady' was Pregnant: The Anthropology of a Geometric Tomb Reconsidered," *Hesperia* 73:7–38; C. Giardino (1992), "Nuragic Sardinia and the Mediterranean Metallurgy and Maritime Traffic," pp. 304–315 in *Sardinia in the Mediterranean: A Footprint in the Sea: Studies in Sardinian Archaeology Presented to Miriam S. Balmuth*, ed. Robert H. Tykot and Tamsey K. Andrews; Lucia Vagnetti and F. Lo Schiavo (1989), "Bronze Age long Distance Trade in the Mediterranean: The Role of the Cypriots," pp. 217–243 in *Early Society in Cyprus*, ed. E. Peltenburg.

MAP STUDY

Euboea, Eretria, Lefkandi, Pithekoussai, Ischia, Carthage, Sardinia, Kommos, Philistia, Cyprus, Troy, Tyre (Phoenicia).

ENDNOTES

[1] Donald B. Redford (2000), "Egypt and Western Asia in the Late New Kingdom: An Overview," pp. 1–20 in *The Sea Peoples and Their World: A Reassessment*, ed. E. D. Oren.

[2] Vasso Karageorghis (2000), "Cultural Innovations in Cyprus Relating to the Sea Peoples," pp. 255–279 in Oren (above, n. 1).

[3] Among those who identify the LH IIIC:1b pottery found in Philistia and also in Cyprus and at sites along the Levantine coast as evidence for an Aegean origin of the Philistines are: Trude Dothan (1981), *The Philistines and Their Material Culture*; A. E. Killebrew (1998), "Mycenaean and Aegean-Style Pottery in Canaan During the 14th–12th Centuries BC," pp. 159–166 in *The Aegean and the Orient in the Second Millenium: Proceedings of the 50th Anniversary Symposium at Cincinnati, 18–20 April, 1997*, ed. Eric H. Cline and Diane Harris-Cline; and Karageorghis, 255–279 in Oren (above, n1). The opposition argument that "pots do not equal people" has been led by Susan Sherratt (1991), "Cypriot Pottery of Aegean Type in LC II–III: Problems of Classification, Chronology and Interpretation," pp. 185–198 in *Cypriot Ceramics: Reading the Prehistoric Record*, ed. J. A. Barlow, D. L. Bolger, and B. Kling; and S. E. Sherratt (1992), "Immigration and Archaeology: Some Indirect Reflections," Part 2, pp. 316–347 in *Acta Cypria: Acts of an International Congress on Cypriote Archaeology Held in Göteborg on 22–24 August, 1991*, ed. P. Aström.

[4] Annie Caubet (1992), "Reoccupation of the Syrian Coast After the Destruction of the 'Crisis Years'," pp. 123–131 in *The Crisis Years: The 12th Century B.C.: From Beyond the Danube to the Tigris*, ed. William A. Ward and Martha Joukowsky: 124–127.

[5] Results from the dating of charred building timbers found at Assiros in Macedonia, Greece by the independent techniques of dendrochronology (tree-ring dating) and radiocarbon dating, with the associated find of a Protogeometric style amphora made soon after the beginning of the Iron Age, now put the period of the destruction of the palaces back 50 years, to 1270/1250 at the latest, and redate the beginning of the Iron Age (Protogeometric) to a ten-year period, 1080–1070 BCE. The new dates "should finally lay to rest the radical proposals of Peter James and others in *Centuries of Darkness* for the removal of over 200 years from "'Dark Age' chronology." See http://artsweb.bham.ac.uk/aha/kaw/oldtreesnewdates.htm. Because of the

newness of this information, which will involve major debate and readjustments of currently accepted chronology and is still subject to debate, the old dating system will be followed in this book.

[6]Schliemann smuggled the treasure out of Turkey and eventually donated it to a museum in Berlin; it disappeared during WWII, then was seized by Russian soldiers, and is now in the Pushkin Museum in Russia.

[7]See the discussion of the site on the website of the Archaeological Institute of America, http://www.archaeology.org/0405/etc/troy.html.

[8]Considerable controversy over the interpretation of the archaeological remains has been engendered by the attacks of Dr. Frank Kolb, Professor of Ancient History at the University of Tübingen, upon Korfmann, his colleague at Tübingen and the director of the Troia-Project. Kolb claims that Troy was not a city and a center of trade, but only a small agricultural village; see Kolb's article (2004) and the response of Korfmann in *American Journal of Archaeology* 108; an earlier report on the controversy is online at http://www.uni-tuebingen.de/troia/eng/kontroverse.html.

[9]Trevor R. Bryce (1989), "The Nature of Mycenaean Involvement in Western Anatolia," *Historia* 38:1–21, 17.

[10]On the Ionian Migration, see J. M. Cook in *Cambridge Ancient History*, 3rd ed.,Vol. II, Part 2, *History of the Middle East and the Aegean Region, c. 1800–1380 B.C.*, ed. I. E. S. Edwards, C. J. Gadd, N. G. L. Hammond, and E. Sollberger, chap. 38.

[11]K. B. Gödecken (1988), "A Contribution to the Early History of Miletus," pp. 307–318 in *Problems in Greek Prehistory: Papers Presented at the Centenary Conference of the British School of Archaeology at Athens, Manchester, April 1986*, ed. E. B. French and K. A. Wardle, 313.

[12] Aristotle, *Constitution of the Athenians* 5.2

[13]A good source on the history of Cyprus is Louise Steel (2002), *Cyprus Before History: From the Earliest Settlers to the End of the Bronze Age*. For more detail on the role played by Cyprus in trading contacts between mainland Greece and the Levant, see J. N. Coldstream (1989), "Early Greek Visitors to Cyprus and the Eastern Mediterranean," in V. Tatton-Brown (1980), *Cyprus and the East Mediterranean in the Iron Age*, 90–94.

[14]Cypriot chronology is expressed in terms of Cypriot pottery, and thus it differs from that used for Greece:

Late Cypriot IIC—thirteenth century

LC IIIA—twelfth century, 1199–1125

LC IIIB 1125–1050

Cypriot Geometric I—1050–950 .

CG II—950–900

CG III—900–850

[15]See H. W. Catling and E. A. Catling (1981), "'Barbarian Pottery from the Mycenaean Settlement at the Menelaion, Sparta," *Annual of the British School at Athens* 76: 71–82; D. B. Small (1990), "'Barbarian Ware' and Prehistoric Aegean Economics: An Argument for Indigenous Appearance," *Journal of Mediterranean Archaeology* 3: 3–25.

[16]For a useful discussion of the Sea Peoples, see N. K. Sandars (1985),*The Sea Peoples*, 2nd ed.

[17]Rhys Carpenter (1966), *Discontinuity in Greek Civilization*.

[18]Klau Kilian (1988), "Mycenaeans Up To Date: Trends and Changes in Recent Research," pp. 115–152 in *Problems in Greek Prehistory*, ed. E. B. French and K. A. Wardle, has collected the evidence for archaeologically proven catastrophic earthquake in this period; see his n. 2 and fig. 10.

[19]Colin Renfrew (1979), "Systems Collapse as Social Transformation," pp. 481–506 in C. Renfrew and K. L. Cooke, eds., *Transformations, Mathematical Approaches to Culture Change*.

[20]Kilian (above, n. 18), 135.

[21]Robert Drews (1993), *The End of the Bronze Age: Changes in Warfare and the Catastrophe ca 1200 B.C.*, 44.

[22]For the excavation reports on Lefkandi, see M. R. Popham, L. H. Sackett, and P. G. Themelis (1980), *Lefkandi I: The Iron Age*, and subsequent Lefkandi volumes.

[23]On this burial, which was discovered after the publication of *Lefkandi* I, see M. R. Popham, E. Touloupa, and L. H. Sackett (1982), "The Hero of Lefkandi," *Antiquity* 5:169–174.

[24]D. Ridgway (1992), *The First Western Greeks*, 7.

[25]Slaves sacrified to serve their masters after death were found in three tombs at Lapethos roughly contemporary with the Lefkandi burials (CG I); Tombs 412, 417, 420; see Gjerstad (1948), in *The Swedish Cyprus Expedition IV*: 2, 431–433. Horses with their chariots were found in the eighth/seventh century necropolis at Salamis in Tombs 1, 2, 3, 10, 47, 50, 79; sacrificed slaves were also found in Tomb 2; asses without vehicles were found in Tombs 19 and 31, which were smaller and less monumental structures than those containing horses and chariots; see V. Karageorghis (1969), *Salamis: Recent Discoveries in Cyprus*.

[26]Various translations, different forms of the name, and interpretations of the text are available: John A. Wilson in James B. Pritchard, ed. (1969), *Ancient Near Eastern Texts Relating to the Old Testament* , 3rd ed., 25–29; M. E. Aubet (2001), *The Phoenicians and the West : Politics, Colonies and Trade*, Appendix I. The translation of Lichtheim (1973–1989), is reprinted in Nels M. Bailkey, ed. (1969), *Readings in Ancient History; From Gilgamesh to Diocletian*, and is available on the Web at http://www.uwm.edu/Course/ egypt/274RH/Texts/ReportWenamun.htm;

[27]See M. R. Popham, P. G. Calligas, L. H. Sackett (1986), "Further Excavation of the Toumba Cemetery at Lefkandi, 1984 and 1986," *Archaeological Reports* 35:117–129; M. R. Popham, E. Touloupa, and L. H. Sackett (1982), "Further Excavations at Lefkandi, 1981," *Annual of the British School at Athens* 77:213–248; I. S. Lemos (2002), *The Protogeometric Aegean: The Archaeology of the Late Eleventh and Tenth Centuries B.C*,164–165. One of the arguments for a special funerary purpose of the monumental building lies in its proximity to the existing cemetery; M. R. Popham, P. G. Calligas, and L. H. Sackett, eds. (1993), *Lefkandi II The Protogeometric Building at Toumba*, 100–101.

[28]Tomb T 61; see M. Popham (1987), "An Early Euboean Ship," *Oxford Journal of Archaeology* 6:353–359.

[29]M. R. Popham and I. S. Lemos (1995), "A Euboean Warrior Trader," *Oxford Journal of Archaeology* 14:151–157.

[30]Homer, *Iliad* 11.639.

[31]J. N. Coldstream (1998), "The First Exchanges Between Euboeans and Phoenicians: Who Took the Initiative?" pp. 353–360 in *Mediterranean Peoples in Transition: Thirteenth to Early Tenth Centuries BCE*, ed. S. Gitin, Amihai Mazar, and Ephraim Stern, 354.

[32]I. S. Lemos (1998). "Euboea and Its Aegean Koine," pp. 45–58 in *Euboica : l'Eubea e la presenza euboica in Calcidica e in Occidente : atti del convegno internazionale di Napoli, 13–16 novembre 1996*, ed. Michel Bats and Bruno D'Agostino; I. S. Lemos (2001), "The Lefkandi Connection: Networking in the Aegean and the Eastern Mediterranean," pp. 215–226 in *Italy and Cyprus in Antiquity, 1500–450 BC: Proceedings of an International Symposium held at the Italian Academy for Advanced Studies in America at Columbia University, November 16–18, 2000*, ed. L. Bonfante and V. Karageorghis; Lemos (above, n. 27) 212–217 and n. 118.

[33]W. V. Catling (1996), "A Tenth-Century Trade Mark from Lefkandi," pp. 126–132 in *Minotaur and Centaur*, ed. R. D. G. Evely, I. S. Lemos, and S. Sherratt.

[34]Antony Snodgrass (1994), "The Euboeans in Macedonia: A New Precedent for Westward Explansion," pp. 87–93 in *I più antichi Insediamenti greci in Occidente: Funzioni*, ed. B. d'Agostino and D. Ridgway. These northern settlements are attested as Euboean in the eighth century, but their projection back into this earlier period is contested by J. K. Papadopoulos (1996), "Euboians in Macedonia? A Closer Look," *Oxford Journal of Archaeology* 14: 103–107.

[35]M. R. Popham, P. G. Calligas, L. H. Sackett (1986), "Further Excavation of the Toumba Cemetery at Lefkandi, 1984 and 1986," *Archaeological Reports* 35:117–129; M. R. Popham, E. Touloupa, and L. H. Sackett (1982), "Further Excavations at Lefkandi, 1981," *Annual of the British School at Athens* 77:213–248, 118 and figure 5; M. Popham (1995), "An Engraved Near Eastern Bronze Bowl From Lefkandi," *Oxford Journal of Archaeology* 14: 1, 3, 7.

[36]J. N. Coldstream and Patricia Bikai (1988), "Early Greek Pottery in Tyre and Cyprus: Some Preliminary Comparisons," *Reports of the Department of Antiquities Cyprus,* Part 2:35–43.

[37]I. S. Lemos and H. Hatcher (1991), "Early Greek Vases in Cyprus: Euboean and Attic," *Oxford Journal of Archaeology* 10:197–208.

[38]Coldstream and Bikai (above, n. 36).

[39]Popham, Sackett, and Themelis (above, n. 22) 93–97.

[40]Catling in Popham, Sackett, and Themelis (above, n. 22), 96. That the production of tripods did not end in 1200, but continued for several centuries, has been demonstrated by H. Matthäus (1988), "Heirloom or Tradition? Bronze Stands of the Second and First Millenium B.C. in Cyprus, Greece, and Italy," pp. 285–300 in *Problems in Greek Prehistory: Papers Presented at the Centenary Conference of the British School of Archaeology at Athens, Manchester, April 1986*, ed. E. B. French and K. A. Wardle.

[41]Fortetsa cemetery, Tomb XI; see H. W. Catling and E. Catling in Popham, Sackett, and Themelis (above, n. 22), 96.

[42]Popham, Sackett,Themelis (above, n. 22), 211.

[43]Popham, Sackett, Themelis (above, n. 22), 160–161 (Palia Perivolia 47), 182–183 (Toumba 26).

[44]Popham, Sackett, Themelis (above, n. 22), 210, Toumba 18; Toumba 14, 1; 14, 2 (two cremation urns, one with killed sword); finds "suggest actual immigrants." Tomb Skoubris 5 also contained an urn burial but in a local urn.

[45]J. N. Coldstream (1995), "Amathous Tomb NW 194: The Greek Pottery Imports." *Report of the Department of Antiquities Cyprus*,189–198. The Amathus tomb contained an Attic MG I or II krater (850–750), an Attic skyphos, EG II–MG I (875–825), and Euboean Subprotogeometric imports.

[46]See also E. L. Smithson, "The Tomb of a Rich Athenian Lady, c.850 B.C.," *Hesperia* 37:77–116; and J. N. Coldstream (1995), "The Rich Lady of the Areopagus and her Contemporaries," *Hesperia* 64:391–403.

[47]M. A. Liston and J. K. Papadopoulos (2004), "The "Rich Athenian Lady" was Pregnant: The Anthropology of a Geometric Tomb Reconsidered," *Hesperia* 73:7–38.

[48]Liston and Papadopoulos (above, n. 48), 28, raise another issue concerning the interpretation of this burial, suggesting that the extraordinarily rich offerings in the tomb, and the large expenditure of resources for the funerary meal, should not be read as an indication of the woman's status, but rather as a response to her death in childbirth, perhaps reflecting some sort of "taboo, or its aversion." However, given the high mortality rate in childbirth at the time, if that were the case, one would expect there to have been a very large number of such rich burials, whereas the burial of the Rich Athenian Lady stands out in the richness of its offerings.

[49]See N. Demand (1994), *Birth, Death, and Motherhood in Classical Greece*, 71–86.

[50]Eugene Weinberg (1984), "Pregnancy-associated Depression of Cell-mediated Immunity," *Reviews of Infectious Diseases* 6:814–831; Eugene Weinberg (1987), "Pregnancy-associated Immune Suppression Risks and Mechanisms," *Macrobial Pathogenesis* 3:393–397.

[51]Spyros Iacovides (1980), *Excavations of the Necropolis at Perati*, Institute of Archaeology, University of California, Los Angeles, Occasional Paper 8; Iacovides (2003), "Late Mycenaean Perati and the Levant," pp. 501–511 in *The Synchronisation of Civilisations in the Eastern Mediterranean in the Second Millennium B.C. II*, ed. Manfred Bietak.

[52]Eric Cline(1994), "Sailing the Wine-Dark Sea: International Trade and the Late Bronze Age Aegean," #23–30.

[53]J. N. Coldstream (1996), "Knossos and Lefkandi: The Attic Connections," pp. 133–145 in *Minotaur and Centaur*, ed. R. D. G. Evely, I. S. Lemos, and S. Sherratt.

[54]M. Sznycer (1979), "L'inscription phénicienne de Tekke, près de Cnossos." *Kadmos* 18:89–93.

[55]Coldstream (above, n. 53), 138.

[56]J. W. Shaw and Maria C. Shaw (1993), "Excavations at Kommos (Crete) During 1986–1992," *Hesperia* 62:129–190, 175; J. W. Shaw (1989),"Phoenicians in Southern Crete." *American Journal of Archaeology* 93: 165–183; J. W. Shaw (2000), "The Phoenician Shrine, ca. 800 B.C. at Kommos in Crete," pp. 1107–1119 in *Actas del 4 Congreso Internacional de Estudios Fenicios y Púnicos, Cádiz, 2 al 6 de octubre de 1995*, ed. María Eugenia et al; Glenn E. Markoe (1998), "The Phoenicians on Crete: Transit Trade and the Search for Ores," pp. 233–240 in *Eastern Mediterranean: Cyprus, Dodecanese, Crete, 16th–6th cent. B.C.*, ed. V. Karageorghis. Nikolaos Stampolidis argues that the Phoenicians were drawn to Crete by the search for iron ore.

[57]E. Csapo, A. W. Johnstone, and D. Geagan (2000), "The Iron Age Inscriptions," pp. 101–134 in *Kommos IV: The Greek Sanctuary*, ed. Joseph W. Shaw and Maria C. Shaw, 101, Graffito 1:108–109 (they note that it was possibly a Bronze Age survivor). Patricia Bikai (2000), "Phoenician ceramics from the Greek sanctuary," pp. 302–312 in the same volume, 310–311, notes that finds of Phoenician pottery at Kommos raise the known date of early Phoenician expansion to Crete to ca. 900.

[58]Shaw (above, note 56); J. W. Shaw and M. C. Shaw(above, n. 57), 1–21 and n. 42 on p. 92.

[59]The existence of this route is confirmed by the find of sherds of a pithos found in Nuraghe Antigori in Sardinia that match pithoi sherds found in south-central Cyprus and are very similar to a Cypriot pithos found at Kommos. See Lucia Vagnetti and F. Lo Schiavo (1989), "Bronze Age Long-distance Trade in the Mediterranean: The Role of the Cypriots," pp. 217–243 in *Early Society in Cyprus*, ed. E. Peltenburg, 221.

[60]J. K. Brock (1957), *Fortetsa: Early Greek Tombs Near Knossos*, 161.

[61]These debates are discussed in full by Gail Hoffman (1997), *Imports and Immigrants: Near Eastern Contacts with Iron Age Crete*. Ann Arbor, who adopts a position of "rational skepticism" about all interpretations.

[62]H. W. Catling (1977), "The Knossos Area, 1974–1976," *Archaeological Reports* 3: 11–14 and Figs. 27–28; Hoffman (above, n. 61) 12, 28, 120–23.

[63]M. Sznycer (above, n. 54); see Hoffman (above, n. 61) 28.

[64]Sznycer (above, n. 54) 89–93; Ora Negbi (1992), "Early Phoenician Presence in the Mediterranean Islands: A Reappraisal," *American Journal of Archaeology* 96:599–615, 608.

[65]Hoffman (above, n. 61) 12, 123.

[66]John Boardman (1967), "The Khaniale Tekke Tombs, II," *Annual of the British School at Athens* 64: 57–75.

[67]Boardman (above, n. 66): 59. Hoffman (above, n. 61): 197–207, objects that the contents do not resemble known deposits of a jeweler's stock-in-trade, which usually include tools as well as scraps of jewelry for reuse.

[68]The presence of a foreign craftsman who either produced the items or taught the technique to local craftsmen appears in three noted instances of jewelry finds: Toumba cemetery at Lefkandi, mid-tenth to early ninth century. See M. R. Popham, E. Touloupa, and L. H. Sackett (1982), "Further Excavations at Lefkandi, 1981," *Annual of the British School at Athens* 77:213–248, 217); E. L. Smithson (1868), "The Tomb of a Rich Athenian Lady, ca. 850 B.C.," *Hesperia* 37: 83; but J. N. Coldstream (1995), "The Rich Lady of the Areopagus and Her Contemporaries," *Hesperia* 64:397–398, noted the discovery of the earlier material at Lefkandi; and the Tekke Treasure, end ninth century, Boardman (above, n. 66); John Boardman (1980), *The Greeks Overseas: Their Early Colonies and Trade*, 56–58 and nn. 72–76. Hoffman (above, n. 62), 189, 240–245, has suggested that the hypothesis that foreign craftsmen were active in these cases might not be fact, but factoid—repeated so often that it is taken for fact.

[69]Hoffman (above, n. 61), 191–245.

[70]Lucia Vagnetti (1989), "A Sardinian Askos from Crete," *Annual of the British School at Athens* 84:355–360.

[71]F. Lo Schiavo (1981), "Osservazioni sul problema dei rapporti fra Sardegna ed Etruria in età nuragica," pp. 299–314 in *L'Etruria mineraria : atti del XII Convegno di studi etruschi e italici.*

[72]Tomb 81: C. Giardino (1992), "Nuragic Sardinia and the Mediterranean Metallurgy and Maritime Traffic," pp. 304–315 in *Sardinia in the Mediterranean : A Footprint in the Sea : Studies in Sardinian Archaeology Presented to Miriam S. Balmuth*, ed. Robert H. Tykot and Tamsey K. Andrews, 308.

[73]Vagnetti (above, n. 70), 357, n. 7.

[74]Vagnetti (above, n. 70), 358.

[75]S. Bafico (1998), "The Nuraghe and Village of Sant'Imbenia, Alghero (Sassari)," pp. 359–360 in *Sardinian and Aegean Chronology: Towards the Resolution of Relative and Absolute Dating in the Mediterranean*, ed. Miriam S. Balmuth and Robert H. Tykot. These finds may "represent a moment preceding the foundation of other colonies on Sardinia," of which Sulcis is now considered the first, dating back only to 750.

[76]David Ridgway (1998), "The Carthaginian Connection: A View from San Montano," pp. 301–318 in *Archäologische Studien in Kontaktzonen der antiken Welt*, ed. Renate Rolle, Karin Schmidt, and Roald F. Docter, 318.

[77]F. Lo Schiavo and R. D'Orieno (1990), "La Sardegna sulle rotte dell-Occidente," pp. 99–161 in *La Magna Grecia e il lontano Occidente*, fig. 1, shows 18 locations throughout Sardinia of such finds; pp. 106–108 lists finds by date of discovery; fig. 6 shows 8 locations of finds in central Italy and 7 in Sicily.

[78]A. Taramelli (1921), "Il ripostiglio dei bronzi nuragici di Monte Sa Idda di Decimoputzu (Gagliari)," *Monumenti Antichi* 27: 6–107; Lo Schiavo and D'Orieno (above, n. 77) 130–131.

[79]Taramelli (above, n. 78) 57–58, fig. 79.

[80]See A. Mederos Martín (1996), "La Conexión Levantino-Chipriota. Indicios de Comercio Atlántico con el Mediterráneo Oriental durante el Bronce Final (1150–950 AC)," *Trabajos de Prehistoria* 53:95–115, fig.2.

[81]Amathus Tomb 523, dated to CG IB; V. Karageorghis and F. Lo Schiavo (1989), "A West Mediterranean Obelos from Amathus," *Rivista di Studi Fenici* 17:15–24; Martín (above, n. 80) 98–99 and table 3.

[82]Karageorghis in Karageorghis and Lo Schiavo (above, n. 81), 16; Martin (above, n. 80),107–112.

[83]A. M. Arruda (1994), "The Lisbon Peninsula Between the Atlantic and the Mediterranean at the Beginning of the 1st Millennium B.C.," pp. 52–57 in *Subterranean Lisbon, Exhibition Catalogue*, 52, 56.

[84]F. Lo Schiavo (1985), *Nuraghic Sardinia in Its Mediterranean Setting: Some Recent Advances.*

[85]J. N. Coldstream (1985), "The Geometric and Archaic Periods," pp. 47–59 in *Archaeology in Cyprus 1960–1985*, ed. by V. Karageorghis, 52.

[86]Patricia Bikai (1987), "Trade Networks in the Early Iron Age: The Phoenicians in Palaepaphos," pp. 125–128 in *Western Cyprus: Connections*, ed. D. Rupp, 126 and note 18; Aubet (above n. 26), 76–79.

[87]Timaeus in Dionysius of Halicarnassus, *Aniquitates Romanae* 1:74, I; and Josephus agree.

[88] L. Woolley (1938), "Excavations at Al Mina, Sueidia," *Journal of Hellenic Studies* 58:1–30. The generally agreed first date of this material is 770/750 BCE Jean-Paul Descœudres (2002), "Al Mina Across the Great Divide," *Mediterranean Archaeology* 15: 51; he offers a table listing the many interpretations of the site by archaeologists from 1936 to 2001.

[89] John Boardman (1980) *The Greeks Overseas: Their Early Colonies and Trade*, 38–54. He has subsequently changed his mind; see John Boardman (1990), "Al Mina and History," *Oxford Journal of Archaeology* 9:169–190.

[90] See Joanna Luke (2003), *Ports of Trade, Al Mina and Geometric Greek Pottery in the Levant.*

[91] See Robin Osborne (1996), *Greece in the Making, 1200–479 BC*, 112–113; J. N. Coldstream (1989), "Early Greek Visitors to Cyprus and the Eastern Mediterranean," pp. 90–96 in *Proceedings of the Seventh British Museum Classical Colloquium: Cyprus and the East Mediterranean in the Iron Age*, ed. V. Tatton-Brown.

[92] Strabo 5.4.9; Livy 9.22.5–6; Ridgway (above, n. 24).

[93] An explanation favored by the excavators, Sackett, Popham and Themelis (above, n. 22), 366.

[94] Ridgway (above, n. 24), 15–16. For a review of the question with bibliography, see Nancy H. Demand (1990), *Urban Relocation in Archaic and Classical Greece : Flight and Consolidation*, 15–19.

[95] The involvement of people from Oropus has also recently been suggested. See A. Mazarakis Ainian (1998), "Oropos in the Early Iron Age," pp. 179–215 in *Euboica: L'Eubea e la presenza euboica in Calcidica e in Occidente*, ed. M. Bats and B. d'Agostino.

[96] Ridgway (above, n. 24), 41.

[97] David Ridgway (2000), "Seals, Scarabs and People in Pithekoussai I," pp. 235–243 in *Periplous: Papers on Classical Art and Archaeology Presented to Sir John Boardman*, ed. Gocha R. Tsetskhladze, A. J. N. W. Prag, and Anthony M. Snodgrass, 237–238.

[98] J. N. Coldstream (1994), "Prospectors and Pioneers: Pithekoussai, Kyme and Central Italy," pp. 47–59 in *The Archaeology of Greek Colonisation*, ed. G. R. Tsetskhladze and F. De Angelis 47, 49; G. Bartoloni (1991), "Populonia: Characteristic Features of a Port Community in Italy During the First Iron Age," pp. 101–116 in *Papers of the Fourth Conference of Italian Archaeology: The Archaeology of Power Part 2*, ed. E. Herring, R. Whitehouse, and J. Wilkins.

[99] Bartoloni (above, n. 95) 112–113.

[100] A. M. Bietti Sestieri (1997), "Italy in Europe in the Early Iron Age," *Proceedings of the Prehistoric Society 63:371–402*; A. Guidi (1998), "The Emergence of the State in Central and Northern Italy," *Acta Archaeologica* 69:139–161.

[101] Jeffery Klein (1972), "A Greek Metalworking Quarter: Eighth Century Excavations on Ischia," *Expedition* 14, 2:34–39; Ridgway (above, n. 24).

[102] Ridgway (above, n. 24), 111–118.

[103] Ridgway (above, n. 24), 114–116. Although both North Syrian and Phoenician artifacts were found, the North Syrians were not actively engaged in maritime trade, which was a specialty of the Phoenicians.

[104] Ridgway (above, n. 24), 111.

[105] Ridgway (above, n. 76).

[106] Ridgway (above, n. 76), 306.

[107] B. D'Agostino (1996), "Pithekoussai and the First Western Greeks," *Journal of Roman Archaeology* 9:302–309; Lucia Vagnetti (2000), "Western Mediterranean Overview: Peninsular Italy, Sicily and Sardinia at the Time of the Sea Peoples," pp. 305–326 in *The Sea Peoples and Their World: A Reassessment*, ed. Eliezer D. Oren, 319.

[108] Wherever exports of Attic pottery are found in the East, they are almost always accompanied by Euboean pottery, suggesting that both types of pottery were exported in Euboean ships, Coldstream (above, n. 53), 142.

[109] Ridgway (above, n. 24), 107–109; Osborne (above, n. 91), 128–129: "opportunistic settlements… a background where mobility was easy, and even normal."

[110] Christopher Smith (1997), "Servius Tullius, Cleisthenes and the Emergence of the Polis in Central Italy," pp. 208–216 in *The Development of the Polis in Archaic Greece*, ed. L. G. and P. J. Rhodes Mitchell; and below, Chapter 5.

[111] A. M. Bietti-Sestieri (1981), "Produzione e scambio nell'Italia protostorico: alcune ipotesi sul ruolo dell'industria metallurgica nell'Etruria mineraria alla fine dell'età," pp. 223–264 in *L'Etruria Mineraria. Atti del XII Convegno di Studi Etruschi e Italici, Firenze 1979*.

[112]Bietti-Sestieri (above, n. 111), 263.

[113]Saro Wallace (2003), "The Perpetuated Past: Re-use or Continuity in Material Culture and the Structuring of Identity in Early Iron Age Crete," *Annual of the British School at Athens* 98:251–277.

[114]Avraham Faust (2003), "Abandonment, Urbanization, Resettlement and the Formation of the Israelite State," *Near Eastern Archaeology* 66:147–161.

5

ARCHAIC GREECE
THE EIGHTH CENTURY RENAISSANCE AND REVOLUTION

The ferment of maritime interchange and activity that increasingly characterized the tenth and ninth centuries accelerated and spread during the Archaic period, from the eighth through the sixth centuries. At this time interconnections between Greece and the Near East reached a peak, and this is reflected throughout Greek culture, from orientalizing motifs in pottery and metalwork to oriental reflections in poetry, mythology, and political forms. The eighth century has been called both the Greek Renaissance, because many of its accomplishments recalled the Mycenaean world as it was then remembered by epic poets, and the Orientalizing Revolution, because Eastern influences are so prominent.[1] It is also the period from which we have our first literary evidence.

LITERARY EVIDENCE: HOMER AND HESIOD

The *Iliad* and the *Odyssey*, epic poems attributed to the unknown singer Homer, are dated conventionally to 750 and 720.[2] They provide a vivid picture of the life of the overseas venturers whose activities we have seen in the archaeological record. The *Iliad* tells the story of the tenth year of the Trojan War and of the coming-of-age of the great hero Achilles, while the *Odyssey* relates the often-fantastic adventures of Odysseus as he returned home from the war to a household barely hanging on to its position of authority.

Homer's poems depicted the Bronze Age for an Iron Age audience through the transforming medium of an oral poetic tradition that preserved only fragments from the Mycenaean past. Homer's heroes knew nothing of the complex bureaucracy of the real Mycenaean palaces of the Linear B tablets; his princess even did the family laundry. No one remembered how the great palaces were constructed, although their ruins were a familiar part of the world in which they lived, and so the labor of moving the great building blocks, some as much as two meters in length, was assigned to the giant Cyclopes. The gods intervened to play a large, and not always admirable, role in the story. Nor do "modern" aspects of life enter into the poems, except in the decorative similes; in fact, the poet seems to have consciously avoided any material that would be anachronistic to the narrative timeframe of his stories. Such care, as well as the elements of fantasy that play such a large role, especially in the *Odyssey*, certainly stand in the way of expecting to find accurate history in the poems. It is very unlikely that Achilles, Hector, Agamemnon, Paris, and Helen as they were portrayed by the poet were actual historical persons. Yet the places described in the poems can be located, and real people may well have borne these names. The problems with the use of Homeric epic as evidence for the reconstruction of history are widely recognized,[3] but archaeology still raises the tantalizing question: Did the Trojan War actually happen? And the answer given by Manfred Korfmann, the archaeologist who is currently carrying on the excavations at Troy, is a very-near "yes." Troy was attacked and destroyed by people from Greece, but by a somewhat different cast of characters than those portrayed by Homer.[4]

The *Odyssey* reflects the increasing Eastern contacts of the Greeks in the eighth century. Odysseus visited Egypt, as did Helen on her way both to and from Troy, and the Phoenicians feature prominently as merchants and pirates in the tales of Odysseus. However, these occupations appear in a decidedly negative light in the *Odyssey*. This negative attitude supports the late-eighth century date as appropriate for the poem's composition, for it was at that time that competition, rather than co-operation, became the predominant feature of the relationship between the two peoples. The result is a one-sided picture of the Phoenicians, shaped by the needs of the narrative and the attitudes of the audience, not by a desire to present an objective picture.[5]

The lasting power of the Homeric poems, and the reason they were so much revered throughout Greek history, was the universality of their basic themes. In the *Iliad*, we see warfare, often less heroic than bloody, and too often with tragic outcome; youthful petulance and rebellion in the face of arbitrary authority; and eventual acceptance of the less-than-perfect human condition. In the *Odyssey*, longing for home competes with the glories of the adventures and perils of the sea.

The Homeric poems were composed orally and sung, probably in nightly installments, to an audience of fellow-drinkers. Our understanding of them has been greatly enhanced by the study of modern poets who employ similar techniques of oral composition.[6] The oral poet's methods depend upon the poetic language with which he works, which in the case of Greek epic was **dactylic hexameter**. The basic line in dactylic hexameter is made up of six metrical units, or feet (hence hexameter, or six-meter); each foot has a pattern of short and long syllables in the form long, short, short (the dactyl); the syllables can be replaced by metrical equivalents, as at the end of the line (long, long). This pattern of long and short syllables, rather than rhyme or accent, is the defining characteristic of Greek epic poetry.

Figure 5.1   Middle Geometric *skyphos* (a type of drinking cup) from Eleusis portrays battles on both land and sea that could well illustrate Odysseus' adventures or those of Greek settlers abroad.
With permission of the Eleusis Museum, Eleusis 741, Hellenic Republic Ministry of Culture.

Because he composed in a well-defined rhythmical form, the poet could use formulaic phrases embodying various parts of the dactylic line as his basic units of composition. These formulae consisted of partial lines of specific metrical pattern, often composed of a name and an epithet, such as "Fleet-footed Achilles" or "Ox-eyed Athena," which could be plugged into a line wherever needed, at the beginning, end, or middle. The poet's formulaic stock also included whole lines, groups of lines, and even entire type scenes (arrivals, departures, meals, sacrifices). He learned all these by years of apprenticeship, and their mastery allowed him to compose his work extemporaneously as he sang. The art of such poets did not lie in original creation, but in the skillful handling and faithful transmission of traditional poetic material.

The poems of Hesiod, who lived around the end of the eighth century, while also in epic form, are quite different in subject matter from those of Homer. Rather than telling stories, they relay information directly. Hesiod's *Theogony* relates the generations and genealogies of the gods and other divine beings, in an account that borrows heavily from Near Eastern sources.[7] The best known example is the Hesiodic story of the castration of Uranos by his son Kronos, which is a version of a succession story that appears in Hittite and Ugaritic mythology in the Near East. Hesiod's *Works and Days* describes the year's work of the farmer, but even here Eastern influence is apparent, for the poet offers advice in the tradition of Near eastern wisdom literature.

As is the case with Homer, we know virtually nothing about the poet Hesiod, beyond what he tells us (which may be a poetic invention). He says that his father moved from Anatolia to Ascra in Boeotia, "miserable Ascra" he calls it. Despite its miseries, he seems not to have been much moved to venture beyond Ascra, yet his admonishments about trading and seafaring suggest a wider experience. While disparaging seafaring and claiming to have been to sea himself only once, to Euboea to attend the funeral games of a king, he admits that at times the farmer must resort to his boat to sell his excess produce, and he has a great deal of advice to offer about the best sailing seasons and the best sort of ship to employ.

The Role of Homer and Hesiod in Religion

Because we lack texts, we know little about religion and the gods in the Bronze Age and the period of transition. For Crete, archaeologists have identified cult places—peaks, caves, and trees. We also have mute portrayals of dancing and processions in what might have been religious rites, and some apparently religious symbols, such as the bull's horns and the double axe. For Mycenae, there is even less: a few familiar names in the Linear B tablets, such as Zeus and Poseidon, and some unfamiliar ones as well; the central hearths in the palace megarons as possible places of sacrifice; an abundance of ambiguous figurines that we call cult figures. But in the epic poets of the eighth century we possess a profusion of evidence. The poets provided the gods with forms and stories, and even with genealogies. The result is something quite different from our modern religion. A few points are important to keep in mind.[8]

As readers of Homer know quite well, the Greeks did not conceive of the gods as transcendent beings. Rather, they saw most of them as human in form, behaving and misbehaving much as humans do, although they were much more powerful than humans. Many embodied elemental forces of nature: Zeus, the storm clouds and bolts of lightening; Poseidon, the sea and earthquakes; Aphrodite, sexual attraction. Like the forces they embodied, the gods were not necessarily good and loving toward men; they could, in fact, be quite capricious. Human life was difficult and at all times subject to catastrophic change, and much of Greek religion centered on ways to placate the gods and thus avoid the worst of life's possible disasters.

Some worship was carried on by individuals, who might offer prayers praising a god and making a request, or making a small sacrifice, but most Greek worship was communal, carried on at sanctuaries or temples. Each family and each city had its own patron divinity or divinities, and each divinity had his or her own expectations. In general, however, they expected honor to be paid to them and sacrifices to be offered, The gods were believed to partake of the burnt offerings of animals through the savory smoke arising from the sacrificial fire, while the worshippers enjoyed a communal meal. The crucial events of human life—birth, reaching adulthood, marriage, childbirth, death—all were occasions that required religious ritual.

The gods were not particularly concerned with what we would consider moral lapses, aside from the breaking of oaths. Their own lives were full enough of such lapses. Rather, certain physical situations were seen as especially dangerous for humans, as literally producing pollution, and they required cleansing rituals. The occasions of pollution were not moral lapses, but physical conditions: contact with dead bodies (both for the innocent families of the dying, and for homicides), engagement in sexual intercourse even within marriage, menstruation, and giving birth.

The gods in their temples and sanctuaries were served by priests and priestesses who oversaw the performance of correct rituals and took care of the sacred objects of the cult, but they were not professional, trained religious specialists, nor did they minister to the cult worshippers. For the most part, priesthoods belonged to certain families, whose members fulfilled the necessary rituals on a part-time basis and were not considered religious experts.

Certain gods were believed to offer assistance to city-states, and occasionally to individuals, in the form of oracles, although the advice offered was almost always riddling and ambiguous. The oracle of Apollo at Delphi, which was especially consulted about overseas settlements, is perhaps the most famous example.

Figure 5.2   The temple of Apollo at Delphi.
Photo by N. Demand.

There were two important exceptions to the public nature of Greek religion. One consisted of the healing cults, especially the cult of Aesclepius, who offered assistance to ailing individuals. His sanctuary at Epidauros was visited by men and women from all over Greece, many of whom, on making a small offering and sleeping overnight in the sanctuary (incubation), received healing directly or by way of prescriptions.

Another type of cult that primarily served individuals was the secret mystery cult, which promised a blessed life after death to its initiates. The most prominent of these was the cult of Demeter, the goddess of the grain, and her daughter Kore, at Eleusis, in the suburbs of Athens. The myth behind the cult was the story of the kidnapping of Kore by the god of the Underworld, Hades. Having lost her daughter, Demeter was consumed with grief and neglected the crops, allowing them to fail. All the world was in danger of dying away. Finally Hades struck a bargain: he would allow Kore to return to the world for a part of each year. It is the annual return of Kore that brings the springtime and the season of fertility. The cult of Eleusis not only focused on individuals, it also allowed even slaves to be initiated. Another important mystery cult was that of Dionysus, the god of wine and holy intoxication, which offered release from the pressures of everyday life, an encounter with the divine, and hope for a life after death.

The Alphabet and Epic

The most long-lasting and significant product of the Greek Renaissance was the adoption by the Greeks of the Phoenician alphabet. From about mid-eighth century (the same date conventionally assigned to Homer's *Iliad*), evidence appears that the Greeks in mainland Greece were once again writing. The new system that they used, the alphabet, was borrowed from the Phoenicians. The Greeks, however, adapted it to their own needs. They revolutionized it by using some of the symbols not needed for Greek in order to express the sounds of the vowels. Unlike the Phoenician and other early alphabetic writing systems that recorded only consonants, with the sporadic use of vowel signs as aids to reading unfamiliar words, the Greek alphabet was based on the principle of a sign for every individual sound (phoneme). Using the alphabet, a person could sound out even unfamiliar words, whereas with consonantal systems the reader depended upon recognizing an already familiar word by the consonant cluster and the context; for example, *ct* could be read as *cat*, *cut*, *cot*, or even *kite*. The addition of symbols for vowels created a highly flexible and easily learned writing system, a true alphabet.

WEBSITE 5.1 ON THE PHOENICIAN ORIGIN OF THE
ALPHABET, WITH HERODOTUS' STORY OF HOW
THIS HAPPENED (HERODOTUS 5: 58–61)
http://phoenicia.org/alphabet.html

The Greek alphabet offered another advantage that may provide a clue to the motive behind its creation. As we saw, epic poetry depended upon the length of vowel sounds in syllables for its rhythms. In contrast to the Phoenician writing system, which did not include vowels, and the Cypriot syllabary, the Greek alphabet was able to record the epic meter in a way that preserved and transmitted this metrical information. Thus, when we ask why the Greeks invented vowels for their alphabet, the answer that suggests itself is that they wanted to record epic verse. It was H. T. Wade-Gery who first suggested this,[9] and recently Barry Powell has argued the hypothesis in detail.[10] Powell attributes the invention of the alphabet to a Euboean, one of those adventurers who traveled the trade route from Lefkandi/Eretria and Chalchis to Cyprus and on to the Levant, and he puts the date at around 800.[11] In keeping with these suggestions, one of the earliest long alphabetic inscriptions was found in Pithekoussai, the first Euboean settlement in the west. The metrical inscription reads, "I am the cup of Nestor, a joy to drink from. Whoever drinks this cup, straightway that man the desire of beautiful-crowned Aphrodite will seize."[12]

Everyone does not agree with Powell's explanation of the invention of the Greek alphabet. An alternative theory is that the alphabet had a commercial origin. Greek traders, most probably in Syria, picked it up to keep records and mark goods. This hypothesis is supported by the fact that the particular form of the Phoenician alphabet that the Greeks adopted was the cursive North Semite version used in commerce. Weighing against this theory, however, is the fact that there are no commercial records among the earliest preserved examples of the use of the alphabet. In fact, many of the early inscriptions are simply graffiti scratched on pots: names indicating ownership, erotic or obscene remarks, abecedaria for learning, and, significantly, snatches of hexameter poetry, such as the verses on Nestor's cup. There are no inventories, contracts, mortgages, or land transfers, such as are common in Near Eastern texts. It is possible, of course, that Greek business records were made on perishable materials, not on clay tablets, as were the Near Eastern records, and for that reason none have survived.

The spread of literacy had far-reaching consequences for Greek civilization. Nevertheless, it must be stressed that, despite the ease with which the new system could be learned, Greek culture remained basically an oral one until the late fifth century,[13] and even Plato in the fourth century decried the use of writing as a pernicious crutch that would destroy memory. Perhaps the most important application of the new literacy by the Greeks came later, in the Archaic period when, in the context of political reforms, the traditional laws were written down in a form accessible to all.[14] After this, the ordinary citizen would no longer be at the mercy of the possibly convenient and self-serving memory of the aristocratic leaders. But this anticipates the full Archaic period. There are no remaining inscriptions or other evidence from the eighth century to suggest that the Greeks immediately began writing down their customary laws and procedures or keeping official records as soon as they learned to write. Nor should we expect them to have done so, for the "way things were done" was still embodied and transmitted through oral tradition.

THE EXPANSION OF OVERSEAS SETTLEMENT

The Phoenician Expansion in the West

The Phoenicians continued their settlement activity in the west with a series of settlements in the eighth century on the Costa del Sol in Andalusia (Spain) that have been characterized by the Phoenician historian and archaeologist Aubet as "one of the most spectacular and ancient archaeological clusters known in the western Mediterranean ... its discovery has given an unexpected turn to the study of the Phoenicians in the west."[15] These settlements, packed in between Malaga and Almeria, appear to have had no clear function in terms of the mining activities at Gadir; nor do they appear to have exploited metal resources in the interior for more than local uses. Rather, their interest in sites at the mouths of rivers seems to have been motivated by access to inland agricultural and pastoral land, the *chora,* and to marketing possibilities among the local population. Specializing to some extent (murex for purple dye, fishing, small-scale metal production), these communities sought self-sufficiency. The discovery of a large warehouse at Toscanos, built around 700 and filled with amphorae and other storage and transport vessels, supports this picture. Evidence from the burials suggests that the settlers came in family groups and were relatively affluent, and that they settled permanently, burying several generations in large, monumental chambered tombs.[16] The settlements, in fact, lasted about 200 years before being abandoned ca. 550. Some were reoccupied in the Punic period, but others did not revive until the Roman period.

A similar concern to exploit the resources of the *chora* can be seen in the numerous settlements made by the Phoenicians in Sardinia. The rich metal resources of that island had been known since the Bronze Age. The Phoenicians concentrated their settlements on the southwestern coast, where they again occupied a series of closely packed harbor sites. Sulcis, the best known archaeologically of these sites, was established probably in mid-eighth century.[17] It followed the typical Phoenician pattern of settlement on small offshore islands; it has since been joined to the mainland by the accumulation of sediment from the River Palmas. Early in its history the settlement built a network of fortifications to secure an inland *chora* that offered fertile land and rich resources in silver and lead.[18]

In Malta, a primary concern of Phoenician settlers with land can also be seen in the fact that the first settlement was made inland. This small island is famous for its strategic location at the crossroads of sea lanes, and it would seem to have been an ideal choice for a Phoenician settlement functioning principally as a staging post, or *emporion*. Yet this is not what the ancient authors or the archaeological record tell us. The earliest Phoenician settlement on Malta dates to the second half of the eighth century. The earliest graves were found inland, associated with the settlement at Rabat, on a hilltop roughly in the center of the island. In contrast, the harbor settlement was founded only towards the fifth century. Similarly, on the Maltese island of Gozo, the first settlement was made in the seventh century at Victoria, again roughly in the center of the island, and on a hilltop.[19] The inhabitants sought the best

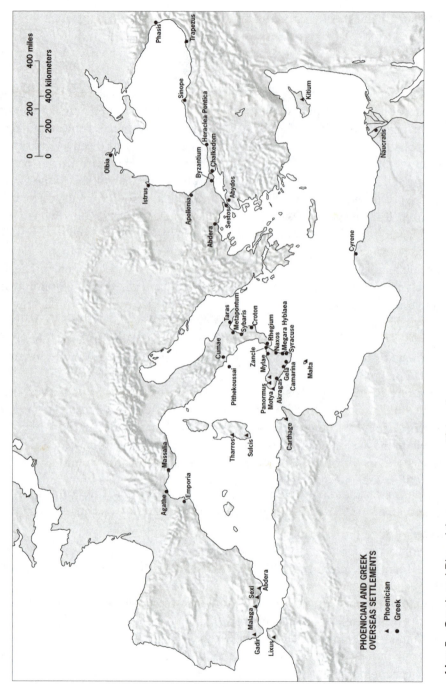

Map 5 Greek and Phoenician overseas settlements.
Adapted from the *Historical Atlas* by William R. Shepherd (New York: Henry Holt and Company, 1926), p. 12. Courtesy of the University of Texas Libraries, The University of Texas at Austin.

living conditions and the best land for cultivation with perennial water sources. It was only at a later date that they developed harbor sites.

Gadir in Spain is the site that best fits the stereotype of a Phoenician settlement established for purely commercial motives, although it later developed into a city with full urban functions. Established in the legendary Tartessos, with its vast resources of silver and other metals, the city also profited from its shipyards and its fishing and allied enterprises (production of salted fish and fish sauces). Founded probably around the beginning of the eighth century,[20] reportedly on the command of an oracle, the construction of a temple of Melqart was an early priority. The temple served to ensure the authority of the god, and hence of the monarchy of Tyre, over the settlement, and to smooth commercial exchanges by guaranteeing the right of asylum and hospitality, and providing security for contracts and commercial exchanges.[21] Despite its origins as an *emporion,* by the Hellenistic and Roman periods Gadir had become a city second only to Rome in population, renowned for its prosperity and luxurious living.

It seems clear, as Aubet pointed out, that there was no one model for Phoenician overseas settlement. She identifies regional clusters that displayed somewhat similar characteristics, such as those in the central Mediterranean, those in the area of Gadir, and the Andalucian settlements, where archaeology has revealed settlements arguably made with a view to the possession and control of fertile land (the *chora*). But even within these groups there was no uniformity. The pure *emporion* model (temporary trading post), traditionally applied to Phoenician settlements, is used in contrast to the *apoikia* model (permanent settlement based on the possession of a *chora*) to differentiate Phoenician from Greek settlements. The *emporion* model applies to only a few Phoenician settlements and usually in their early stages; any that did not develop further have probably escaped modern detection. Most soon adopted a strategy of reliance on the resources of the *chora*. These resources sometimes, but not always, included metals; not surprisingly, however, given the basic need for sustenance, settlements were often agricultural. The Phoenicians in the west were, for the most part, not traveling merchants, but settled family groups that stayed for generations, living off the resources of the land. In all of this, they seem not to have differed in any essential way from the Greeks.

The Greek Expansion in the West

The Greeks also continued settlement activities in the west. Some time between 760 and 735, most of the inhabitants of Pithekoussai moved to the Italian mainland and founded a settlement at Cumae. This site had better agricultural potential than did Pithekoussai, and the settlers were apparently feeling secure enough to take on the risks of the more exposed mainland location. Some people remained on at Pithekoussai, but by 700 the main phase of settlement on the island was over. While Pithekoussai's classification as an *apoikia* is questioned by some, Cumae is generally considered to have been a true *apoikia*. The distinction, which is based upon the possession of *chora*, or agricultural hinterland, is widely used to differentiate between Greek and Phoenician settlements. Already, however, Phoenician settlement in Andalucia brings this distinction into question, and it will be further tested by a consideration of various subsequent settlements, Greek and Phoenician.

The establishment of Cumae was followed in the last third of the eighth century by a great wave of Greek overseas settlement, beginning with the foundation of Naxos in 734 by the people of Chalchis in Euboea. The site was especially favorable to trade, being the first port of call in Sicily for ships traveling from the east. Six years later the Naxians established two other settlements, inland Leontini and Catane on the coast, which gave them control of a rich plain.

The Corinthians soon entered the race to establish overseas settlements, starting in 733 in Corcyra.[22] The motivation of Corinthian overseas expansion is a matter of debate, or perhaps scholarly fashion. The earlier emphasis upon trade (for example, by Dunbabin[23]) was rejected completely by Salmon in favor of the theory of overpopulation and land hunger.[24] Recent analysis of the Corinthian pottery industry by Sarah Morris and John Papadopoulos,[25] however, brings trade back into the picture, and the Phoenicians as well. Morris and Papadopoulos point out that the orientalizing features of Protocorinthian pottery go well beyond the simple adoption of stylized oriental animals to include "the rendering of the ornament in friezes" and "the use of incision for outline and the picking out details," a technique whose origin lies in engraving on metalwork. Such influences, especially those that involve transfer of skills from one medium to another, require not simply objects to copy, but the presence of workers expert in the techniques involved.

At the same time, a "fully-fledged commodity container," the globular *aryballos*, used for perfume and oil, was re-introduced and manufactured in large quantities, and production and export of Corinthian pottery exceeded that of all other contemporary pottery. While Salmon says of this market expansion that it "developed purely by chance,"[26] Morris and Papadopoulos more convincingly resurrect Dunbabin's suggestion that Phoenician craftsmen and traders may have been present at Corinth.[27]

In 733 the Corinthians founded Syracuse on the best harbor on the eastern coast of Sicily, a site that also enjoyed access to good farmland. The Megareans followed immediately after, but found the desirable site already occupied. After brief stops at sites best suited for piracy and an abortive effort to share the site with others, they were invited to found a settlement by the Sikel prince of Hybla, who gave them land on the coast north of Syracuse, which they called Megara Hylaea. It was never prosperous and was later outshown by its daughter city, Selinus.

In the 720s, settlers from Cumae and Chalcis founded Zancle, which commanded one side of the straits giving access to the western Italian coast. Some ancient sources attribute the first settlement to pirates from Cumae. The site was especially suited for preying on ships headed for the west coast of Italy, such as Phoenician ships from Carthage headed towards Etruria. But it lacked adequate agricultural land, and a dependent colony was soon es-

Figure 5.3   Middle Corinthian orientalizing vase (IUAM 77.102.3)
Indiana University Art Museum, Gift of Helena Simkhovitch in memory of her father.
Photograph by Michael Cavanagh, Kevin Montague. Copyright 2005 Indiana University Museum.

tablished on a small plain at Mylae, about 20 miles west of Zancle. Again, trading (or raiding) interests needed to produce their own food supply.

Another early settlement made by Zancle was Rhegion, across the straits on the Italian coast, a site that completed control of the straits. Zancle requested the help of Chalcis in its foundation, but even so, available manpower seems to have run short, for some refugees from the Spartan war against Messenia were also invited to join the new colony.

In 628 Megara Hyblaea established Selinous on the western end of Sicily.[28] It was an advance into territory that was probably regarded as within the sphere of the Phoenicians. The dedication of Temple C to Herakles (the Greek form of Phoenician Melkart), perhaps ameliorated the psychological threat to the Phoenicians, and over time the Greek colony fluctuated between Phoenician, indigenous Elymian, and Greek associations.[29] Franco De Angelis, calculating the carrying capacity of Megara Hyblaea's territory, has found that overpopulation could not have been the reason for the foundation of Selinous. While he did not attribute the foundation *solely* to motives of trade, he pointed out that the colony was in a good position with regard to the Phoenicians and Elymians "for additional economic success." In a more expansive view of trade as that which enhances economic security, he sees "the basic aim of Greek subcolonisation in Sicily as being a 'process of acquisition,' involving the conquest of new lands and all the possibilities embedded in them."[30]

Achaeans from the Peloponnesus sponsored another series of late eighth-century settlements in the west. They selected sites in the rich farmland in the "instep" of Italy, where they established Sybaris (720), Croton (710), and Metapontum (700). While these seem to have been predominantly agricultural communities, the later foundation—perhaps by Sybaris of Posidonia on the west coast of Italy, at the end of an overland route from the instep—allowed the Greek settlers to exploit the commercial as well as the agricultural possibilities of their sites.

At the end of the eighth century, ca. 706, a group of Spartans founded Taras at the heel of Italy. This was the result of an unusual situation. According to Spartan tradition, during the course of a twenty-year war to subjugate their neighbors the Messenians, the Spartans realized that the absence of men at home was causing a drop in the population; they found a solution in sending the younger men home on leave. But the resultant offspring were never fully accepted, and when they became adults they rose up in protest against their inferior status. A solution was found by allowing them to emigrate, and they settled Taras.

Greek Settlements in the Black Sea Area

Starting in the late seventh century, the Ionian cities on the east coast of the Aegean and its adjacent islands, pushed by pressures from their inland neighbors, established a large number of settlements along the shores of Hellespont, Propontus, and Black Sea.[31] Miletus took the lead, reputably responsible for over 90 settlements.[32] These clearly took the form of trading settlements, founded in the Phoenician manner on peninsulas, and without their own *chora*.

The earliest establishment was Berezan. Its original purpose is the subject of debate, but GochaTsetskhladze says that the identification of the settlement as an *emporion* is borne out by the fact that it did not have its own *chora*,[33] an addition that was made "no later than the second quarter of the 6th century."[34] In addition to the Milesian settlements, mainland Greeks established Byzantium—today's Istanbul—as well as other cities. In the late sixth century, as the Persians bore down upon Ionia, many Greeks escaped to found settlements elsewhere, at nearby Teos and Abdera, and even as far away as the southern coast of France, where the Phocaeans founded Ampurias and Massalia, modern Marseilles.

Ampurias and Massalia provide later examples of Ionian settlements founded not for homesteading, but in expectation of profiting from trade.[35] Of Massalia, B. B. Shefton says, "It is presumably in the tow of such an Etruscan trade movement [along the southern coast of France] that the Greek, Phocaean adventurer colonists made their way to that same coast…" to found Massalia, about 600 B.C.E.[36] Of Ampurias, its excavator says that it was certainly in its " first implantation [about 600 B.C.E.] …the establishment of a trading settlement, an *emporion*, on a small island next to the mouth of the Fluvia river rather than the foundation of a colony with planned civic organization…. It was only about a generation or a little later that a bigger settlement was established as a proper *polis* on the mainland a short distance further south. This 'Neapolis' (a modern term) was to be the real emporion."[37] The Phocaean establishment of Elea/Velia ca. 540 on the west coast of Italy was ultimately the result of their resistance to the Persians in Asia Minor; however, the form their resistance took—flight to a location in the center of Phoenician trade activities—reflected their prior experiences in seafaring for trade and in overseas settlement.

Characteristics of Greek Overseas Settlements

Although each case of Greek overseas settlement had its own unique elements, historians have abstracted from the many foundation tales a pattern marked by certain common characteristics that in a sense define that settlement. Recently, however, objections have been raised to the use of this concept, which is seen to focus over much on the "official" aspects of settlement, as well as to the use of the term *colonization*, on the grounds that it is an essentially anachronistic concept defining ancient literary traditions in terms of the activities of Europeans overseas from the sixteenth to the twentieth centuries C.E.[38] The "characteristics" are given here, however, since they are very much a part of the traditional view of Greek history:

1. Settlements were officially sponsored by one or more *poleis*; in the rare cases when they were individual ventures, they were not successful.

2. A founder (*oikistes*) was chosen. He made the detailed plans and led the actual settlement, and usually became the leading citizen of the new *polis* and received heroic honors after his death. Such a man naturally had to have leadership abilities that would inspire confidence in his followers. Probably he also needed wealth, in order to assist with the expenses of the expedition. It is therefore not surprising that the little evidence that we have for such men identifies them as aristocrats.

3. Delphi was consulted, or perhaps the oracle spontaneously suggested the foundation.[39] The approval of the gods was an essential element in overseas settlement. Not only was a new *polis* to be created, but the colony was probably going to take over land that was already occupied by others (non-Greeks, but still people in whom the gods might take an interest). The participants would have wanted to have a clear title to their land, and this could be provided only by the gods. Greek tradition portrays the oracle at Delphi as the primary source of such religious sanction, although only 14 of the 139 settlements known to have been established between 750 and 500 are associated with preserved oracular responses. Sometimes Delphi is portrayed as taking the initiative in ordering a settlement venture, but in most cases the oracle probably merely gave its assent to plans presented to it. Some oracu-

lar responses may even have been invented at a later time by *poleis* tidying up their local histories.

Sites were probably chosen on the basis of information provided by travelers or traders.[40] Such information could have been passed on during the great Panhellenic festivals, when crowds gathered from *poleis* throughout Greece. Since the oracle at Delphi was traditionally consulted about overseas settlement, the priests there may have been especially interested in information about the possibilities and problems of potential sites. According to Herodotus, it was Delphi who directed the Therans to found a colony off the coast of North Africa, an area completely unknown to them. Access to good farming land was a consideration in choosing a site, but locations at strategic points along trade routes were sometimes chosen in apparent disregard of their lack of agricultural potential, as in the case of Pithekoussai, conveniently situated on a rocky island off the Italian coast where it could safely exploit Etruscan interest in metals, and Zancle in Sicily, founded at a controlling site on the straits of Messina, which soon founded Mylae to supply its needs. The potential for native resistance must also have been a factor in choosing a site, but settlers appear to have been willing to fight for their new homes if necessary. Easily defensible sites were naturally favored. Following the Phoenician model, the most desirable were considered to be offshore islands or peninsular sites, from which the initial settlement might spread in later times, or even be relocated, as was Pithekoussai to Cumae.

4. Participants were chosen by a variety of methods. In some cases, as in the case of the foundation of Cyrene described by Herodotus, a lottery was used and force might have been applied to unwilling participants. If voluntary, the individual participants must have had many motivations. Many surely were self-selected: landless men or those with poor or insufficient land; men who were driven to emigrate after taking the losing side in a factional struggle; homocides, or men who had committed some other offense against their kin or the community; traders who saw opportunities to further their professional interests as well as to increase their status by becoming landowners. Often participants were recruited from other cities, or two or more cities joined in organizing a venture.

5. There is some question whether women were included among the settlers. Most of the few who are attested were priestesses whose presence was necessary for ritual purposes, but ordinary women would probably not have been considered worthy of mention. We have seen that the settlers at Pithekoussai took Etruscan wives, and Herodotus relates that the settlers of Miletus in the migration period killed all the local men and took the women as wives. These were pioneering ventures, but even later, when overseas settlement was a more established affair, it seems unlikely that many women were taken along. Most male settlers were probably unmarried. As we shall see, those chosen by lot for the establishment of Cyrene were sons still living at home, and the landless and poor were unlikely to have been able to afford wives. Since marriageable but unmarried girls would have been very unlikely as settlers, the men in most case probably found wives from among the local population.

6. In the actual foundation, after the appropriate offerings had been made to the gods and the cults of the mother city installed (and if no native resistance had to be countered), the first order of business was to lay out the city: setting aside areas for an *agora*, public buildings, and the temples of the gods, and making the individual allotments of land for houses and farming.

The physical planning of the overseas settlements had a great impact upon the development of urban planning. The use of grid plans was adopted for this purpose, and overseas sites offer some of the earliest and best evidence for both city planning and the systematic distribution of farmland.[41] A fifth-century citizen of Miletus, Hippodamos, was credited with the creation of such city planning, and the fact that Miletus is said to have established over 90 overseas settlements may lend some credence to this claim. We now know, however, that similar methods of land distribution were used much earlier in the western settlements; even in the Bronze Age, the city of Enkomi in Cyprus was laid out in a grid pattern. Nevertheless, the fact that Hippodamos wrote a treatise on planning and incorporated it into political theory probably earned him the credit for its "discovery." In later times, such systematic planning was often adopted by older Greek cities as they expanded. For example, Athens is said to have employed Hippodamos to plan the rebuilding of its port, the Piraeus, and an extension of the city of Olynthus was laid out in orderly rectilinear fashion. Such a plan was also widely employed for the many city foundations of the Hellenistic period.

Source Analysis

Herodotus 4.145–158 and a Purported Decree.   On the North African coast, ca. 630, a settlement was established at Cyrene for which Herodotus provides an unusually full account, which gives life to this schematic picture. It also provides a good idea of the type of information about overseas settlement that was available to Herodotus in the fifth century, and the use he made of it, as well as an opportunity to compare the evidence of the historian with that of an inscription purporting to be a copy of the original foundation decree.

Read the evidence of Herodotus 4.145–158. How well does Herodotus' account fit the general pattern of Greek "colonization" outlined in the text? Which is a product of both ancient and modern rationalization? For example, what was the motive for the foundation of Cyrene? What does the story suggest about the role of Delphi? From what sources did the settlers get their practical information about the site?

Consider the inscriptional evidence. The second source for the foundation of Cyrene is an inscription from the fourth century B.C.E. In it a Cyrenian, Demis, seeking to obtain citizenship for recent immigrants from Thera, cites what he claims to be a copy of the original foundation decree for the colony.

It seemed good to the Assembly: Since Apollo on his own initiative told Battos and the Therans to settle Cyrene, it seems right to the Therans to send Battos to Libya as Archegetes and Basileus, and the Therans to sail as his companions. On equal and fair terms they are to sail, according to households, one son from each household …the youths and, of the other Therans, the free-born …[100 in number], to sail. And if they establish the settlement, their kin following later to Libya are to have a share in citizenship, in offices, and in the unowned land. But if they do not succeed in making the settlement, nor are the Therans able to assist them, and they endure suffering for five years, leaving that land without fear they shall return to Thera with their same property and citizenship rights. But if anyone is unwilling to sail and to leave behind the *polis*, he will be liable to the death penalty and his proprety shall be given to the demos. And anyone assisting him or hiding him, a father [his] son, a brother [his] brother, shall pay the same penalty.

(Text from Meiggs, Rissell, and David Lewis, eds. (1988), *A Selection of Greek Historical Inscriptions to the End of the Fifth Century B.C.*; Frag. 5, lines 23–40; tr. N. Demand.)

Since this is a fourth-century inscription purporting to be a copy, it has naturally been questioned; nevertheless, there are good arguments in favor of its authenticity. One is that Demis' source could not have been Herodotus, since the inscription contains information not in the historian's account. A second argument is the fact that the Cyrenians obviously believed that Demis had an authentic source; since foundation documents recorded important rights, they must have been carefully preserved, and the Cyrenians could well have had a copy of the original agreement. In what ways does this document agree with, or conflict with, the account as given by Herodotus?

Even the well-known stories of the foundation of Cyrene related by Herodotus, laden as they are with a double dose of the embellishments to which such traditional stories were prone,[42] can provide clues to Phoenician elements, as John Boardman has shown.[43] Thus in the Theran version, the would-be colonists sent messengers to Crete to find information on the location of Libya. These men came to the city of Itanos, on the east end of the island, where they met a fisher named Corobios seeking shellfish yielding purple dye, a Phoenician specialty. Corobios said that he had been carried away by the winds to Libya and to the offshore island of Platea. Boardman says of Corobios, "[t]he name is not otherwise known to us, but ... I wonder whether the name is a Hellenised version of a Phoenician. One tradition has Itanos founded by a son of Phoinix, and it certainly had eastern associations."[44] The Therans convinced Corobios to lead them to Platea, where they left him with supplies while they went home to Thera to report. Running low on supplies, Corobios was rescued by a Samian named Colaios, who had been carried off course while sailing to Egypt and who left him supplies for another year. Colaios, on leaving Platea, was again carried away by the winds and ended up in Tartessos. Herodotus adds, "Now this trading-place was at that time untouched by any, so that when these returned back home they made profit from their cargo greater than any other Hellenes of whom we have certain knowledge...."[45] What underlay such hints of Phoenician involvement cannot be clearly seen, but they do reinforce the notion that western settlement by the Greeks was made in the context of, and possibly assisted by, Phoenician settlement.

The Greek overseas venture that began in the volatile maritime-centered world of the tenth to eighth centuries (see Chapter 4) lasted well into the sixth century, becoming perhaps more disciplined and institutionalized as settlers and their sponsors gained experience. However, it is hard to see how rigid patterns could have been implemented in the many cases, such as the Black Sea settlements, in which the newcomers were faced with fighting or adapting to local ways. Even in the fifth century, the Athenians sponsored a panhellenic settlement at Thurii in southern Italy, in which Herodotus and Hippodamus, the city-planner participated.[46] It was a re-foundation of the earlier city of Sybaris, which had become famously wealthy before it was destroyed by its neighbor Croton in 510. Greek overseas settlement had far-reaching and long-lasting consequences, spreading Greek culture and language throughout the Mediterranean. It also contributed in vital ways to the development of the *polis* itself, the political form that lay at the heart of Hellenic culture.

THE RISE OF THE PANHELLENIC SHRINES

While many *poleis* developed to the point of recognition in the eighth century, at the same time a number of important cults of panhellenic nature also began their rise to prominence, at first sight seeming to contradict the tendency toward local autonomy that was the ideal of the *polis*.[47] These cults were usually situated in remote regions, far from the strongest of the *poleis*, and it may have been this relative isolation that enabled them to take on a panhellenic role. The best known of these shrines are the oracular cult of Apollo at Delphi and the cult of Zeus at Olympus, whose athletic festival has been revived in modern form in our Olympic games.

Later, panhellenic shrines were organized at Nemea and Isthmia. Other important cult centers included the oracular shrine of Zeus at Dodona in Epiris and the shrine of the twin deities Artemis and Apollo on Delos, which served in particular as a commn cult center for the Ionian Greeks. Other cults that transcended *polis* boundaries but served more limited regions included the Panionion on Mount Mykale in Asia Minor, founded as a communal shrine by the twelve members of the Ionian League in Asia Minor, and the cult of Apollo Ptoion in Boeotia, which served as the center for a league of Boeotian cities. Shrines situated in powerful *poleis* also began to draw clientele from other cities, giving them a panhellenic cast; important among them were the shrines of Athena on the Athenian acropolis, Hera on Samos, and the Perachora in the territory of Corinth.

The development of panhellenic shrines in the eighth century is attested archaeologically by a sudden upsurge in the number of dedications that were made to their patron divinities. No bronze dedications of the eleventh and tenth centuries were found at Delphi or Delos, and only ten terracotta figurines at Olympia; the ninth century saw only one bronze dedication at Delphi, one at Delos, and 21 at Olympia. In contrast, 152 bronze dedications from the eighth century have been found at Delphi, 19 at Delos, and 837 at Olympia.[48]

These panhellenic shrines, while they transcended *polis* boundaries and helped to create a sense of common Greek identity, also played an important role in the definition and enhancement of the individual *poleis*. Great festivals featuring athletic contests were held periodically at these shrines. We are most familiar with the games at Olympia that took place every fourth year, but there also were athletic competitions at the other shrines, as well as literary and musical contests. In these festivals *polis* competed with *polis* for the honors of victory. *Poleis* also competed in giving gifts to the gods, housing the gifts in elaborate and showy treasuries that advertised their civic achievements to all who visited the shrine. The oracular shrines, of which Delphi was the most prominent, offered the god's advice to *poleis*, perhaps even more often than to individuals. Usually this involved the simple ratification of new cult practices or the clarification of ritual questions, but the oracle might involve itself in substantive political decisions as well. For example, the constitution of Sparta was traditionally attributed to the oracle at Delphi, and the Therans established their settlement at Cyrene as a result of Delphic advice and prodding. Thus the rise in the panhellenic shrines not only fostered a sense of common Greek identity among peoples who lived in politically independent *poleis*, but, paradoxically, it also defined and strengthened these *poleis* as independent entities, through the rivalry of competition.

SUGGESTIONS FOR FURTHER READING

Walter Burkert (1992), *The Orientalizing Revolution: Near Eastern Influence on Greek Culture in the Early Archaic Age*. David Ridgway (1992), *The First Western Greeks*. On Greek religion, Walter Burkert (1985). *Greek Religion*. Jan Bremmer (1994), *Greek Religion*, Nanno Marinatos and Robin Hägg, eds. (1993), *Greek Sanctuaries: New Approaches*.

MAP STUDY

Major Greek poleis founding settlements: Corinth, Megara, Sparta, Chalchis, Miletus
   Greek foundations in Italy and Sicily: Cumae, Naxos, Leotini, Catane, Corcyra, Syracuse, Megara Hyblaea, Zancle, Rhegion, Selinous, Sybaris, Croton, Metaponbum, Taras
   Greeks in the Black Sea areas: Hellespont, Propontus, Berezan, Byzantium
   Phoenician settlements: Gadir, Sardinia, Malta, southern Spanish coast

ENDNOTES

[1]See R. Hägg (1983), *The Greek Renaissance of the Eighth Century B.C.*; and Walter Burkert (1992), *The Orientalizing Revolution: Near Eastern Influence on Greek Culture in the Early Archaic Age.*

[2]A useful introduction can be found in Barry Powell (2004), *Homer.*

[3]Kurt Raaflaub (1998), "A Historian's Headache: How to Read 'Homeric Society'", pp. 169–193 in *Archaic Greece : New Approaches and New Evidence*, ed. N. R. E. Fisher. Hans van Wees; Robin Osborne (1998), "Early Greek Colonization? The Nature of Greek Settlement in the West," pp. 251–169 in Fisher and Van Wees. Irene Winter (1995), "Homer's Phoenicians: History, Ethnography, or Literary Trope?" pp. 247–271 in *The Ages of Homer: A Tribute to Emily Townsend Vermeule*, ed. Jane B. Carter and Sarah P. Morris.

[4]Manfred Korfmann (2004), "Was There a Trojan War?" *Archaeology* 57:336–341.

[5]Winter (above, n. 3).

[6]See A. B. Lord (1960), *The Singer of Tales;* A. B. Lord (1991), *Epic Singers and Oral Tradition;* G. S. Kirk (1976), *Homer and the Oral Tradition;* and John M. Foley (1988), *The Theory of Oral Composition: History and Methodology,* who provides a complete bibliography.

[7]See M. L. West (1997), *The East Face of Helicon : West Asiatic Elements in Greek Poetry and Myth*

[8]The most authoritative recent source on Greek religion is Walter Burkert (1985), *Greek Religion.* Jan Bremmer (1994), *Greek Religion,* is a useful short work that deals mainly with developments since Burkert's (1977) German edition, of which the 1985 edition is a translation.

[9]H. T. Wade-Gery (1952), *The Poet of the Iliad,* 11–14.

[10]Barry B. Powell (1991), *Homer and the Origin of the Greek Alphabet.*

[11]Alan Johnston suggests that the contact took place in Cyprus, where a visiting Greek could have become familiar with both the Cypriot use of writing (in a syllabic script similar to Linear B), and the much simpler Phoenician system, Alan Johnston (1983), "The Extent and Use of Literacy; the Archaeological Evidence," pp. 63–68 in Hägg (above n. 1).

[12]Nestor's cup: Homer, *Iliad* 11.632–7. On the inscription, see David Ridgway (1992), *The First Western Greeks,* 55–57; Barry Powell (1991), *Homer and the Origin of the Greek Alphabet,* 163–167.

[13]See especially Rosalind Thomas (1992), *Literacy and Orality in Ancient Greece.*

[14]"Laws" had long been written down for display in the Near East (most famously in "Hammurabi's Code), but the writing system used, cuneiform, was probably unreadable by the majority of the population, in contrast to the easily learned alphabetic writing of Greece.

[15]M. E. Aubet (1993), *The Phoenicians and the West: Politics, Colonies and Trade,* 249.

[16]On Trayamar, see H. Schubart and H. G. Niemeyer (1976), *Trayamar: los hipogeos fenicios y el asentamiento en la desembocadura del río Algarrobo,* 90.

[17]Date according to Aubet (above, n. 15), 205.

[18]F. Barreca (1982), "Nuove scoperte sulla colonizzazione fenicio-punica in Sardegna," pp. 182–184 in H. G. Niemeyer, ed., (1982), *Phönizier im Westen;* S. Bondi (1985), "Monte Sirae nel quadro della cultura fenicio-punica di Sardegna," *Egitto e Vicino Oriente* 8: 73–90.

[19]George A. Said-Zammit (1997), *Population, Land Use and Settlement on Punic Malta : A Contextual Analysis of the Burial Evidence,* 1, 13–16.

[20]The claims of the ancient literary sources of an earlier foundation in connection with the Trojan War are not supported by any archaeological evidence; the first such evidence of Phoenician presence is the finding of Phoenician imports in the interior, dated to 770–760.

[21]Aubet (above, n. 15), 234.

[22]According to Plutarch, *Quaesiones Graecae* 11, they drove Euboeans (Eretrians) out of Corcyra. Although archaeological evidence for an earlier settlement by Eretrians is so far lacking, Irad Malkin argues for the accuracy of the account; see Irad Malkin (1988), *The Returns of Odysseus: Colonization and Ethnicity,* 74–81.

[23]Thomas James Dunbabin (1948a), *The Western Greeks: The History of Sicily and South Italy From the Foundation of the Greek Colonies to 480 B.C.*; Antony Andrewes (1956), *The Greek Tyrants*, 43–44; P. N. Ure (1922), *The Origin of Tyranny.*

[24]J. B. Salmon (1984), *Wealthy Corinth*, esp. 93–100; see also Erik Sjöqvist (1973), *Sicily and the Greeks*, 19.

[25]Sarah Morris and John Papadopoulos (1998), "Phoenicians and the Corinthian Pottery Industry," pp. 251–263 in R. Rolle and K. Schmidt, eds., *Archäologische Studien in Kontaktzonen der antiken Welt.*

[26]Salmon (above, n. 24), 112.

[27]Morris and Papdopoulos (above, n. 25), 257, quoting Dunbabin (1948). *Journal of Hellenic Studies* 68: 66.

[28]Franco De Angelis (2003), *Megara Hyblaia and Selinous: The Development of Two Greek City-States in Archaic Sicily.*

[29]See Irad Malkin (1994), *Myth and Territory in the Spartan Mediterranean*, esp. 211–217.

[30]Franco De Angelis (1994), "The Foundation of Selinous: Overpopulation or Opportunities?" pp. 87–110 in *The Archaeology of Greek Colonisation*, ed. G. R. Tsetskhladze and F. De Angelis, esp. 104–105.

[31]G. R. Tsetskhladze 2002, "Ionians Abroad," pp. 81–96 in *Greek Settlements in the Eastern Mediterranean and the Black Sea*, ed. G. R. Tsetskhladze and A. M. Snodgrass.

[32]Strabo 14.1.6.

[33]Tsetskhladze (above, n. 31), 117.

[34]Tsetskhladze (above, n. 31), 118.

[35]B. B. Shefton (1994), "Massalia and Colonization in the North-Western Mediterranean," pp. 61–86 in G. R. Tsetskhladze and F. De Angelis, eds., *The Archaeology of Greek Colonization.*

[36]Shefton (above, n. 35), 62.

[37]Shefton (above, n. 35), 70–71.

[38]Nicholas Purcell (1997), review of G. R. Tsetskhladze and F. De Angelis (1994). *The Archaeology of Greek Colonization: Essays Dedicated to Sir John Boardman, Antiquity* 71: 501; see also Osborne (above, n. 3). In this book, the term "overseas settlement" is preferred.

[39]P. Londey (1990), "Greek Colonists and Delphi," pp. 117–127, esp. 119, in J.-P. Descoeudres, ed., *Greek Colonists and Native Populations*, provides a useful overview of the debate about the role of Delphi in colonization.

[40]See A. J. Graham (1990), "Pre-colonial Contacts: Questions and Problems," in Descoeudres (above, n. 39), 45–60.

[41]See A. Di Vita (1990), "Town Planning in the Greek Colonies of Sicily from the Time of the Foundations to the Punic Wars," in Descoeudres (above, n. 39), 343–371; J. C. Carter (1990), "Metapontum—Land, Wealth, and Population," pp. 405–441 in the same volume.

[42]Herodotus 4.150–158.

[43]John Boardman (1994), "Settlement for Trade and Land in North Africa," pp. 137–149 in G. R. Tsetskhladze and F. De Angelis, eds., (1994), *The Archaeology of Greek Colonisation*, 142: "The essence of Herodotus' account … is likely to be correct since there would seem to be no particular motivation in anyone inventing it."

[44]Boardman (above, n. 43), 143.

[45]Herodotus. 4.150, tr. G. C. Macaulay.

[46]See *The Cambridge Ancient History*, 2nd ed., Vol. 5. D. M. Lewis, John Boardman, J. K. Davies, eds. (1992), *The Fifth Century B.C*, 141–143.

[47]See Catherine Morgan (1993), "The Origins of Pan-Hellenism," pp. 18–44 in *Greek Sanctuaries: New Approaches*, ed. Nanno Marinatos and Robin Hägg.

[48]Antony Snodgrass (1980), *Archaic Greece: The Age of Experiment*, 53.

6

CRISIS IN THE POLIS
TWO SOLUTIONS

TYRANNY: THE VIEW FROM CORINTH[1]

The growth of formal trade spurred by overseas settlement spread wealth beyond the traditional wealthy landowners in many Greek communities. The stresses of living in these changed conditions under a still very restricted aristocracy brought many cities, especially the small seafaring states around the Isthmus of Corinth, to a state of political crisis that ultimately led to a takeover by a strong-man, or **tyrant**. This is the term used to refer to any ruler who came to power by irregular means, whether he was imposed by an outside authority or seized power for himself as a result of internal political and economic crisis. In its archaic usage, the word does not necessarily imply that the ruler was tyrannical in the modern, oppressive sense, although most tyrannies eventually came to be despotic in the modern sense in the second or third generation. Such men were able to break the grip of the aristocrats and open the way for a reformed and revitalized political structure. In doing so, perhaps inadvertently, they made the *polis*, rather than the aristocratic families, the focus of civic authority, and in the process the people gained a greater share in their own government. However, by giving the people an awareness of their own political potential, the tyrants prepared the way for their own demise, for people brought to civic consciousness often came to throw off their rulers.

The city of Corinth is the best documented of the archaic tyrannies. Its location at the isthmus of the Peloponnesus put it in a position to exact tolls from both land traffic between the Peloponnesus and central Greece, and sea trade, and this, according to Thucydides, was responsible for its great prosperity.[2]

In the eighth century, Corinth was ruled by a closed aristocracy, a group consisting of only 200 members of a single *genos*, or clan, the **Bacchiads**, who intermarried only among them-

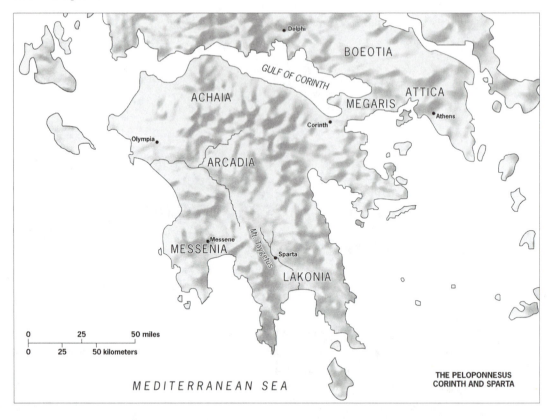

Map 6   Peloponnesus: Corinth and Sparta
Adapted from William R. Shepherd, *Historical Atlas* (New York: Henry Holt and Company, 1926). Courtesy of the University of Texas Libraries, The University of Texas at Austin.

selves. Under their rule, in 734/733, Corinth joined in overseas settlement, founding two western settlements, Corcyra and Syracuse, in a single year.

We know early Corinth best through its pottery, a style that made use of Orientalizing motifs and soon gained great popularity in the Greek settlements in the west, as well as among the Etruscans in Italy. The earliest form of this pottery, called **Protocorinthian**, was characterized by motifs probably borrowed from Near Eastern textiles: stylized flowers and friezes of hybrid animals and exotic beasts such as lions. The vase painters also used a new technique, **Black Figure**, in which the figures were portrayed with black glaze with incised decoration, which was probably derived from Near Eastern metal-working techniques (see Chapter 5).

Many Protocorinthian vases were tiny containers, probably used for scented oil, and their content may have been the principal attraction for buyers. The style developed over time, and in the late seventh century vases show evidence of quantity production, and new Near

Eastern influences become apparent: a new style lion borrowed from Assyria, palm trees, solid rosettes, and figured scenes made their appearance. Archaeologists classify pottery with these characteristics as a new style, Corinthian; they further distinguish between Early, Middle, and Late Corinthian (see Figure 5.1). As Corinthian pottery developed, however, more and more vases were hastily and sloppily painted: lions were stretched out to fill more space, simple motifs that were easily reproduced came to be favored, decorations became stereotyped, and innovations were often bizarre and tasteless (for example, *mastoi*, or breast-shaped vases).

Not all Corinthians, or even most of them, were involved in the pottery business, however. Pottery survives very well, even when broken, unlike other products that the Corinthians may have produced, such as textiles. Moreover, decorated pottery was likely to have been preserved in early excavations because it was highly prized for museum collections. These accidents of preservation and recovery may create a mistaken impression of the significance of decorated pottery. Perhaps as few as 60 painters, and perhaps 200 to 250 workers in all, were active in vase production even at the height of its development. They worked in small workshops and were probably men near the bottom of the social scale, as was generally the case for craftsmen in Greek cities. The fact that Herodotus says that the Corinthians despised craftsmen least of all the Greeks is only a relative statment and does not necessarily imply that such workers were of high social status there.[3] In fact, most of those who were active in the export of pottery and perfumes must have been men of comparatively humble background, and it is unlikely that most pottery makers and dealers became very wealthy by their business. Even elegantly painted vases may not have commanded high prices, although this is a matter of considerable debate.[4] Nevertheless, many of the merchants who dealt in Corinthian pottery seem to have been Corinthian citizens, rather than resident aliens, as suggested by the fact that most merchant marks on the vases are in characteristic Corinthian script. Moreover, the very early date at which trade developed in Corinth, and the probable use of land to secure early loans for ships, makes it likely that many merchants possessed some land. Thus we should not envision the social structure of early Corinth as composed of a few wealthy landowners who oppressed a mass of poor landless peasants and craft workers. It was possible for an enterprising man to reach a middling economic state through his craft skills.

Other Corinthian ceramic products that have left behind evidence for the archaeologist are roof tiles and decorated architectural terracottas. At Delphi over 70 percent of the terracotta roof tiles were Corinthian, and other sites in the area of the Isthmus and the Corinthian Gulf show Corinthian influence. Some of this work may have been done on the spot by travelling Corinthian workmen, but a large tile factory that must have produced for export has been excavated near the center of Corinth.[5] On the other hand, texiles must have provided a large share of exports, for references to the excellence of Corinthian textiles appear in literary sources, and a large dyeing installation has been excavated in the city.[6]

Evidence for Corinthian imports is less ample, and it demonstrates in an interesting way how misleading the survivability of pottery can be. The main archaeological evidence for

---

WEBSITE 6.1   ANALYSIS OF CORINTHIAN POTTERY

An example of a Middle Corinthian vase from the Art Museum at Indiana University, Bloomington (UAM 77.102.3) can be found in Chapter 5, Figure 5.3. Other examples from Indiana and elsewhere are portrayed in the Perseus website, http://www.perseus.tufts.edu. In the Search Box, search for the following. Make sketches of five vases.

Corinthian
>   Bloomington 77.30.4
>   Bloomington 77.30.1
>   Davenport AR 47.33
>   Harvard 1986 370
>   Philadelphia MS548

Protocorinthian
>   London 1889.4–18
>   Boston 03.810
>   Malibu 86.AE 696

Corinthian imports consists in large numbers of Chian and Punic shipping amphorai (undecorated pots used for shipping and storage) that had contained dried and salted fish.[7] Judging from this evidence, one might conclude that salted fish was the main Corinthian import, if that did not seem so inherently unlikely. As it is, archaeologists are left to speculate about other possible products, such as grain, from very meager evidence.

At the end of the eighth century, Corinth took part in the **Lelantine War**, which Herodotus tells us was the first war to involve a number of Greek cities in a widespread general conflict.[8] It was fought between the Euboean cities of Eretria and Chalchis over possession of the rich Lelantine plain that both shared; other participants included the island city of Samos, Corinth and Thessaly helping Chalcis, and Miletus and Megara allied to Eretria. A Corinthian shipbuilder built a new type of warship, the **trireme,** for the Samians for use in this war, and it continued to form the basis for Greek naval fleets through the fifth century. In the end, Chalchis seems to have been the victor in the war, but the conflict exhausted both primary participants. The Euboeans, who had formerly been so active in the east and had founded Pithekoussai in the west, no longer played a major role in trade and settlement. Corinth, on the other hand, appears to have profited by the war, inheriting the predominance in Greek westward trade that the Euboeans had formerly exercised.

In the second quarter of the seventh century, however, Corinth's position was weakened by the growing power of Argos under the tyrant Pheidon. A further indication of the city's growing weakness was its war in 664 with its own settlement Corcyra, in which the first sea battle known to Thucydides took place. These problems undoubtedly contributed to the increased dissatisfaction with Bacchiad rule in Corinth that eventually led to their overthrow and the rule of a tyrant, Cypselus.

Another aspect of the situation is suggested by archaeological finds that reveal a significant surge in the number of bronze weapons, especially helmets and shields, that were dedicated at panhellenic sanctuaries in the seventh century. While this reflects the increasing popularity of such sanctuaries, as well as the development of a fashion of dedicating armor, it also gives good grounds for believing that there was a significant rise in the number of men who could afford to equip themselves with such armor and even to sacrifice it in dedications to the gods, and thus that prosperity had grown more widespread. Since we can assume that aristocrats had long been outfitting themselves with armor, and there is no evidence that these aristocrats had lost their monopoly on power, this means that by the seventh century there must have been a new group of men who were able to afford heavy armor, but who had no say in the aristocratic government of the *polis*. It seems likely that this did indeed provide the setting for revolutionary changes in Corinth and elsewhere.

Herodotus tells the story of the tyrant's rise to power with typical folktale embellishments:

Source Analysis

erodotus 5.92.   In what literary context does the story of Cypselus' rise to power appear, and how might this have affected the account?

Herodotus' story seems to reflect ambivalence in his sources, one stressing popular discontent with the tyranny, the other reflecting elements that favored Cypselus. Another ancient source, the fourth-century Athenian Ephorus, who is known only through later sources, portrays him as a popular ruler.[9] In his version, Cypselus gained popularity when he held office as Polemarch (leader of army) by refusing to imprison those who failed to pay their fines as the office required, but instead accepting security from the debtors or even providing it for them. With backing created by this leniency, he was able to seize power by killing the last Bacchiad king. He then exiled the remaining Bacchiads and confiscated their property, founding settlements in the northwest of Greece to which he sent his opponents. He then ruled mildly without a bodyguard.

The settlements that Cypselus founded, which safeguarded the route to Italy and Sicily and also opened up trade with the interior of Greece, are his best-attested works. In the early sixth century his son and successor Periander built new port installations and the *diolkos*, a stone runway across the isthmus that enabled ships to be pulled across to avoid the dangerous sea voyage around the Peloponnesus (today a canal allows passage). The tyrants also founded, or increased attention to, the popular cult of Demeter and Kore, and may have built fountains and a temple, although the archaeological remains of these cannot be dated precisely.

But if Cypselus was a mild and popular ruler, his son Periander became the archtype of an evil tyrant. The fragments of a lost *Constitution of Corinth* by Aristotle begins with a list of his tyrannical methods, although it ends by saying that he was moderate in other ways and did not tax the people; the state could live from its market and harbor dues.[10] Herodotus elaborates on the vices of the tyranny:

Source Analysis

 erodotus 3.48–53   To what extent might such stories be political invective? Can we take them at face value?

The tyranny in Corinth is only the best attested of a number of tyrannies that arose during this time: the first known of these was Pheidon of Argos, but tyrants are also attested for the cities of Megara, Sicyon, Epidauros, Mytilene, and, somewhat later, Athens. These tyrannies fit a common pattern of dealing with the socioeconomic tensions of the period of growth not by constitutional changes, but by the actions of a strongman. Not surprisingly, given the narrow and arbitrary governments that they displaced, tyrants were often popular rulers, as they seemed to be for a considerable period in Corinth. More than one segment of society had reason to be dissatisfied with the old aristocratic regimes and relieved to see their end. Tyrants also rewarded their supporters by opening citizenship and offices to them, and this gave an opportunity to men with recently acquired wealth who had previously been excluded.[11] They also gained public support by their sponsorship of useful public works, such as the harbor works and *diolkos* of Periander. Water supply and temple building were favorite projects that offered employment and enhanced the quality of life in the city. Tyrants also sponsored elaborate and entertaining festivals and games that celebrated the gods of the whole *polis* rather than the private cults of the aristocratic families, thus encouraging civic consciousness, as the Cypselids did with the cult of Demeter and Kore. And by their patronage of poets, they advertised their own fame and the glory of their *polis*, further increasing civic pride.

The tyrants' emphasis on the *polis* often led them to conduct their rule within the framework of customary laws and institutions, a course made possible by the widespread popularity that they enjoyed, at least in the early years of their regimes. In most cases, it was only in the second or third generation of a hereditary tyranny that personal rule became arbitrary and oppressive, again, as happened in Corinth.

Most of the written evidence about the archaic tyrants dates from times when the oppressive conclusion of tyrannical rule was remembered more vividly than its earlier accomplishments. Moreover, the authors of many of our sources were members of the upper class and thus tended to reflect aristocratic viewpoints. Yet despite this general bias in our sources, tyranny appears in the sources as a generally beneficial episode in the development of the Greek *polis*. It tended to foster the values of the *polis* against aristocratic privilege and to expand the circle of political participation beyond the narrow limits of the aristocratic families.

But not all cities resolved the socioeconomic problems of the period by resort to tyranny. The notable exception was Sparta.

THE SPARTAN SOLUTION

In the classical period, Sparta was universally acknowledged by the Greeks to be the preeminent military power in Greece.[12] Even today, the name "Sparta" calls up images of military strength and prowess, of a way of life devoted single-mindedly to patriotic duty. The image, in fact, has become part of our everyday vocabulary: Webster's defines "spartan" as "warlike, brave, hardy, stoical, severe, frugal, highly disciplined."[13]

The Spartans left no written records of what they thought and why they chose the course they did, and they were a closed society to their contemporary neighbors. As a result, historians have been left to create a picture of Spartan society from the reports of non-Spartans that date at best only to the fourth century (Plato, Aristotle, Xenophon), and for the most part, to the biographer Plutarch. Plutarch's aim was not to record history but to shape the moral character of his readers, and moreover, he wrote almost a millennium after the events he relates. Many scholars thus call the resulting picture the Spartan mirage—an illusion, not a reality. In fact, the Spartan mirage mostly reflects the public image of Spartan austerity and military prowess that the Spartans created to intimidate their enemies, but with the help of those writers who are our ancient sources it has gained a life of its own as an ideal of authoritarian government that has persisted even until modern times.[14] Yet, even though we cannot write a Spartan history in the same way that we can an Athenian history, relying on contemporary records and historical and literary works, the "Spartan mirage" has become part of our own culture and therefore merits a place in the history of Greece.

Some things can be said with certainty about Sparta. Like the people of many other communities in the southern parts of Greece and in Crete, such as Corinth, Argos, and Knossos, its people were Dorians; that is, they spoke a Dorian dialect of Greek. The city lay inland, 46 kilometers from the nearest port of Gytheion, but with a commanding position over the best land in the valley of the Eurotas River and in the center of a naturally defined region, Lakonia, or Lakedaimonia. The position was one of natural security and relative isolation: It was protected from its nearest neighbors to the east by mountains that hemmed in the valley, and towards the west by the peaks of Taygetus, which separated Spartan territory from the much more extensive fertile plains of Messenia. To the north, hill country and sheer distance provided a natural boundary with Tegea, although not an impassable or even difficult barrier. The most valuable land in Lakonia lay in the plain of the Eurotas River, but other habitable niches existed in outlying areas, some occupying plains as small as one square kilometer, some with small harbors, most isolated by natural barriers that made travel to and from the center difficult. Nonetheless, Sparta was not at first as cut off from the rest of the world as might appear from its location, and its later isolation appears to have been the result of deliberate choices that determined that its development would be quite different from that of its Dorian neighbor, Corinth.

In the Bronze Age Lakonia was well populated, the site of roughly 50 settlements. The most important of these was Sparta, the mythical home of King Menelaus, who led the Greeks in the Trojan War, and his wife Helen, whose abduction by the Trojan prince Paris was the legendary cause of that war. Although no palace has been located at Sparta, a large megaron complex found at the nearby site of the shrine of Menelaus was perhaps a forerunner of such a palace.[15] At the end of the Bronze Age there is a gap of about a century in the archaeological evidence for habitation in Lakonia. Nevertheless, there is good reason to suspect that some people survived, probably leading a simple life that has left no archaeological traces, for some cults in the area seem to date back to the Bronze Age era.

According to Spartan tradition, however, in the mid-tenth century a group of Dorian-speakers, who had been expelled from their homeland a hundred years earlier, returned to reclaim their heritage. Known in legend as the **Hereklids (Sons of Herakles)**, they were considered to be the ancestors of the Spartans. They were a simple but aggressive and warlike people who reduced the existing non-Dorian inhabitants of the area to a subservient status, as **helots**. In history, however, they have become most famous as the instigators of the "Dorian Invasion," which was traditionally believed to have been responsible for the destruction of the Bronze Age Mycenaean palatial civilization (see Chapter 3).

Over time the servile status of the helots became more formalized. By the Classical period, which is the earliest time for which we have evidence, helots were in a situation somewhere between slave and free. They were tied to the land and could not be sold, but they were not chattel slaves (slaves who were the property of individuals), but rather were considered to be the property of the state. Because they were tied to the land, not to individual owners, they were able to form stable families without fear that family members would be sold away. Their main function in the Spartan state was as agricultural laborers; they lived and worked allotments of land that were assigned to Spartan citizen-warriors, for whom they provided a livelihood. Evidence from surface surveys suggests that, while helot establishments close to Sparta consisted of individual, relatively isolated house-holds, easily visited by their Spartan lords, as distance from Sparta increased, helots were settled in larger groups in villages, and contact with their Spartan masters was more limited. It was probably the need for control that led the Spartans to institute the **Krypteia**, or Secret Service, probably developed from traditional male initiation rites. They periodically selected the strongest of their young men under the age of 30 for this service. These men, taking only knives and a supply of food, were sent out into the countryside, hiding by day and attacking and killing by night any helots whom they observed to be particularly strong or who otherwise showed dangerous leadership potential. Another element in control-by-terror consisted in an annual declaration of formal war on the helots; as a consequence, during this period any Spartan could kill helots with impunity, for the declaration of war absolved him from legal penalties and even from the religious pollution that normally resulted from the shedding of blood.

Male helots also accompanied Spartan **hoplites** (infantrymen) in battle as servers, and on occasion helots were even freed to be drafted into the hoplite corps; after this they held the still inferior status of **Neodamodes**. The large numbers of helot workers, Sparta's absolute dependence upon them, and the fear of rebellion led to extremely harsh measures being employed in their control, including a perpetual state of war that allowed them to be killed during certain periods without penalty. Such a status was not unique in the Greek world; similar subjected peoples are known in other areas, such as Thessaly and the Black Sea settlements, but none seem to have lived under as brutal conditions as the Spartan helots did in the fully developed Spartan state.

The question is, who were these helots? They were non-Dorian speakers, but they left no records behind to clarify their situation. Nor is there evidence from the early Spartans about the development of their condition. As a result, historians can only speculate, based on evidence from the Classical period.

Another group also held inferior status, the **perioikoi**, or "those living round about." Again, the origins of this status are unclear, just as are those of the helots. Most *perioikoi* towns seem to have dated back to an original Dorian settlement. Perhaps the Spartans were originally simply a particularly aggressive group whose hold on the rich Eurotas valley allowed them to gain control over their neighbors working less productive land over time. Some groups may have voluntarily subjected themselves because they were too small to maintain an independent existence, others may have been coerced, and a few seem to have been purposely settled on the land by Sparta. The type and degree of control may have been dictated in part by the geographical isolation of many of the *perioikoi* settlements, which would have made their active participation in government, and hence a truly unified political system like that in Attica, difficult if not impossible to achieve.[16] However, there are reasons to believe that more was involved than geographical determinism. For instance, the inequality inherent in the *perioikoi* system was marked even in nomenclature. Unlike most *poleis*, Sparta did not share its name with the outlying territory: its citizens were called Spartiates or Spartans, but its territory was called Lakonia or Lakedaimonia. Moreover, the rigid system of control that the Spartans exerted over the helots and even over their own citizens suggests that a system of shared rule with neighboring towns would have had little intrinsic appeal to them.

In the Classical period, although the *perioikoi* settlements occupied only small patches of marginal land, many commanded important non-agricultural resources, and they played a vital role in the Spartan economy. In particular, some *perioikoi* towns had access to iron ore, and it appears to have been *perioikoi* who manufactured and repaired the arms and equipment of the Spartan army. Lead was another *perioikoi* mineral resource that found a ready use: small lead votive figurines, the product of *perioikoi* craft skills, have been found in the thousands at Spartan shrines as well as abroad. *Perioikoi* harbor settlements produced fish and murex shells, the source of the purple dye so valued in antiquity. Among the Greeks, it was the Lakonians and the Spartan colony of Taras in southern Italy who were the primary producers of this dye, which was used to color the famous crimson cloaks worn by Spartan hoplite warriors. *Perioikoi* harbors also provided for whatever foreign imports were necessary: Lakonia was relatively self-sufficient in supplying the needs of the simple Spartan lifestyle, but tin and copper were essential imports for the production of bronze military equipment. Craft production in general, as well as trade, were probably relegated to *perioikoi*, at least by the Classical period, since in Sparta, as in most of the Greek world, neither brought high status.[17]

The Greek tradition of a Dorian Invasion was the Spartans' way of accounting for the superior rank and privileges of the Dorians in Lakonia. Returning to their ancestral lands, they subjected the small surviving local population as helots. As they developed, the superior position of those Dorians who had occupied the best sites became formalized as Spartan citizenship, while the inhabitants of less favored sites fell into the inferior position of *perioikoi*. But as we have seen in Chapter 4, there is great difficulty with the hypothesis of a Dorian Invasion as the cause of the collapse of Mycenaean civilization. If the Dorians were newcomers or newly returned, they must have infiltrated the area gradually, taking advantage of the vacuum left by the collapse, but leaving no archaeological trace. Or perhaps they were there all along in the form of the lower classes of Mycenaeans who could not manage to emigrate, and their identifying feature, the Dorian dialect of Greek, was only a form of sub-Mycenaean speech. In that case, the non-Dorian helots may have been the remnants of the pre-Mycenaean population that had originally been subjected by the Mycenaeans and simply continued to occupy a servile position as agricultural workers as the Spartan state developed.

Whatever its origin, the Spartan system of land ownership, labor, and semi-alliance that made use of these two subservient populations had radical consequences for the development of the Spartan state when it was extended to meet problems that emerged in the eighth and seventh centuries. At that time, when other Greek *poleis* were establishing overseas settlements that could help to alleviate any pressures caused by population growth at home, and also finding solutions to social and political stresses in tyranny, the Spartans followed the path that they had already developed in these early status relationships.

The Conquest of Messenia and Its Consequences

When the population of Sparta began to press upon its resources, the Spartans did not turn to overseas settlement, but looked instead with envy to the fertile land of the Messenians on the other side of Mount Taygetus. Probably the two peoples shared summer pastures in the mountains, which would have given the Spartans knowledge of the resources of the Messenians and familiarity with routes between the two areas, despite the formidable nature of the mountain barrier. Such contacts could also have engendered longstanding border grievances, providing additional motives for a Spartan attack on Messenia.

The First Messenian War is only faintly visible in the historical sources.[18] It lasted for about 20 years in the mid-eighth century, 740–720 B.C.E., and the Spartans were the ultimate victors. Some of the conquered fled to mountainous areas of Arkadia or to havens overseas, as in the case of those who joined the Cumaeans in Rhegion in southern Italy probably shortly after its establishment in 720 B.C.E. Messenians who failed to escape met mixed fates. Those who lived in outlying towns received *perioikoi* status, while those who lived in the fertile plain were incorporated into the Spartan system as helots. The poet Tyrtaeus, who fought on behalf of Sparta in the war, describes them:[19]

> Like asses strained to the utmost by great loads
> Bearing for their masters under baneful necessity
> Full half of all that the ploughed land bears.

How did the Spartans manage to control and exploit the Messenians in the face of the formidable mountains lying between the two? First of all, the Spartans required the Messenians to deliver their produce, and thus it was they who had to negotiate the mountain passage, while their Spartan masters could remain in Sparta, constantly available for their military duties. But it was still necessary to enforce Spartan demands. One factor that helped the Spartans in this was the fact that they took over existing villages inhabited by established farming communities. The Messenian elite, moreover, for the most part escaped, removing experienced leaders from the communities and making their control easier for their conquerors. However, over time the Messenians did develop the ability to rebel, and in 371 succeeded in gaining their independence. Most important probably was the fact that the Spartans were already practiced in the method of controlling moderately distant settlements in Lakonia through the use of the institutionalized terrorism of the *Krypteia*, which they probably augmented to fit the new, more challenging circumstances.

The conquest of Messenia made Sparta wealthy. The first temple of Artemis Orthia is dated to ca. 700, and to it came a flood of exotic votive offerings from many areas of the Greek world and the Near East, as Sparta entered the Orientalizing world of trade and exchange. The export of Messenian grain was an unlikely source of this wealth since it now

Figure 6.1   Modern Sparta and, in the background, Mount Taygetus, the mountain barrier that separated Sparta from its territories in Messenia.
Photo by N. Demand.

had to feed both the Messenians and their new overlords; a more likely source was booty from the war and a continuing trade in slaves. Certainly the enslavement of Messenians not needed for agricultural labor would have been a practical expedient, and one fully in keeping with Greek traditions of the treatment of defeated enemies at that time.

Among the consequences of the First Messenian War was the founding of the Spartan settlement of Taras in southern Italy, according to tradition established by the men born as a result of a compassionate leave granted during the prolonged war. But the most far-reaching result of the war for the Spartans lay in the extension of the helot system to Messenia, a land that was both distant and difficult of access. Spartans traditionally lived and fought together, taking their identity and status in both war and peace from participation in men's messes or common meals (*sysitia*). There is no evidence that they occupied Messenia in the usual pattern of overseas settlement, establishing homes there for themselves in *poleis*. Rather, like the land of Lakonia, the land of Messenia with its helot workers was allotted to individual Spartans, probably mainly to the wealthiest men, who as overlords exacted half the crops produced by the helots, but themselves lived across the mountains in Sparta. While a number of other Greek *poleis* were able to prosper by a system of absentee land ownership, none of them were so far removed, or separated by such difficult terrain, from the land and the workers who provided their sustenance. Problems of transport and of control were inevitable. The former seems to have been solved by requiring the helots to undertake the hardships of the delivery of the produce themselves. Control of such a subject population was another matter, however. The new helots lived in constant hope of regaining their lost freedom, and constant Spartan vigilence was needed to maintain control over them.[20]

After the conquest of Messenia, the Spartans continued their aggressive expansion, aiming next at their northern neighbors. In 669, however, they met a signal defeat at the hands of the tyrant Pheidon of Argos in the battle of Hysiae. Such a defeat could set a small archaic state back for a generation while it made up its manpower losses. Pheidon, in fact, was able to seize control of the Olympic festival of 668 and was for a time effectively master of the northwest Peloponnesus.[21] The Messenians seized the opportunity provided by Spartan weakness and rose in revolt. The result was a second, even longer war, the Second Messenian War, 650–620, which brought Sparta very close to defeat. The perilous situation caused an even greater hardening of attitude and a more rigorous pursuit of security and control on the part of the Spartans, which became an essential element in their culture.

The last line of defense in the event of an open rebellion was the Spartan army. This possibility was never far from the minds of the Spartans, and they devoted themselves to military readiness with a single-mindedness that became proverbial. The result was the creation of the fabled Spartan way of life that eventually made them the strongest hoplite power in Greece.

Internal Problems and Reforms

The Second Messenian War not only extended Sparta's territory and brought it wealth, it also aroused internal discord. According to Aristotle, the poet Tyrtaeus, a veteran of the war, spoke of demands for the redistribution of land on the part of men ruined by the war.[22] If as seems likely, the land acquired in the first Messenian War had gone mainly to the wealthiest men, the expectation that this second long war was also being fought for the benefit of the few, while ordinary men's farms lay neglected in their long absence, would have been an explosive issue. This is the same period—the second half of the seventh century—when tyrants were seizing power in other Peloponnesian cities in response to similar dissatisfactions over the aristocratic monopoly of land and civic status. But just as the helot system had led the Spartans in a different direction than overseas settlement in solving the problem of population pressure, so too it prodded them to solve the problems of internal discord without the open split between citizen factions that was involved in tyranny. Any division in their ranks would have created an opening for helot revolt, and this was their greatest fear.

It seems that the Spartans did bow to the demands for redistribution of land, using the newly acquired territory in Messenia. This at least is a likely origin for the tradition that each male Spartan was allotted a parcel of land at birth, a practice that provided the basis for their considering themselves ***homoioi*** (equals, peers, or similars). Since we know that there were great inequalities of wealth in Sparta,[23] there can be no question of their attaining absolute equality of land holdings by this reform. But the provision of a basic minimum allotment, which would allow the individual to make the required contributions to his mess, may well have been the reform that satisfied the discontented in the seventh century and gave rise both to the tradition of an ancestral allotment and to the political concept of *homoioi*.[24]

But land was only half the issue. Lack of political rights also seems to have rankled many who had fought and suffered in the war, as reflected in constitutional reforms that appear to be dated to this period. These reforms are outlined in an enigmatic document, the **Great Rhetra**, purportedly an oracle of Apollo that tradition held had been given to the reformer Lykurgus. Thucydides (1.82) dates Lykurgus to the ninth century, and Herodotus (1.66) dates him to the sixth. In fact, it was unclear even in antiquity whether the reformer was a real historical figure, and the reforms attributed to him seem to have been enacted at various times.

There is great dispute over the dating of both the Rhetra and the amendment. The Rhetra clearly existed at least in the time of the poet Tyrtaeus, since he refers to it. It is possible that it instituted procedures and institutions to resolve the unrest at that time; but whenever the procedures in the Rhetra were established, the amendment suggests that the experiment in broadening the sphere of political power was soon judged to have gone too far and was curtailed to reassert oligarchic control. Whether Tyrtaeus knew of the amendment is unclear but seems probable.

Source Analysis

he great Rhetra is reported in two ancient sources. Plutarch and Tyrtaeus. Plutarch appears to quote the exact wording; unfortunately, the ending of the passage is corrupt in the manuscript of Plutarch's work.[25]

> Having established the cults of Zeus Syllanios and Athena Syllania,
> and created tribes and divided the people into *obai*,
> and chosen 30 elders [the *Gerusia*], who with the kings were to sit
> season after season in assembly between Babyka and Knakion,
> to introduce and to remove [proposals],
> and the Damos, contradicting it, is to have power.

Translation of the Rhetra reported by Plutarch is difficult not only because of the manuscript corruption, but also because its language is archaic. The "tribing and obing" refer to organizing the citizens in political groups; the tribes were perhaps like the tribes of Kleisthenes in Athens (see Chapter 7), and the obai perhaps like the Attic phratries (a term not well understood, perhaps fictive brotherhoods). The document establishes the meeting place of the assembly and lays down procedures for decision-making: the *Gerousia* together with the kings are to introduce measures to the *damos* (Doric form of *demos*, people, probably the assembled army), who have power over these measures. Later, however, when the people used their power to distort the sense of the motions, Plutarch tells us that the kings introduced an amendment:

> If the damos choose a crooked proposal
> The elders and the kings shall stand aloof [adjourn the proceedings].

They were able to persuade the city that the gods had ordered this, as Plutarch says the poet confirmed with the following words:[26]

> Heeding Phoebus they brought home from Pytho
> Oracles of the god and words that were fulfilled:
> The god-honoring kings [*basileis*] were to rule the council [*boule, gerousia*],
> Eldest-born elders, to whom the beloved city of Sparta is a care,
> And in turn the Damos were to obey their straight sayings.

Although Plutarch lived centuries after these events, the poet Tyrtaeus was a near contemporary, for he seems to have lived during, and perhaps participated in, the second Messenian War in the seventh century. Much of his surviving poetry is in the form of exhortations to battle and marching songs; the risks of wartime are likely to have inspired the amendment that reined in the powers of the demos.

The Spartan Constitution in the Classical Period

The primitive and somewhat enigmatic Great Rhetra formed the essential basis for the Spartan constitution. By the Classical period the Spartans had developed a sophisticated political system that combined elements of both democracy and oligarchy in a "mixed constitution" that was considered by many, including Plato and Aristotle, to be a model for other *poleis*.

The Spartan constitution in its developed form had three parts that were common to most *poleis*: the kingship (Sparta's was unique in being dual); the council of elders, or *Gerousia*;

and the Assembly. Unlike other states, it also had the *Ephorate*, an annually elected body of five that was apparently instituted after the Great Rhetra.

The two hereditary kings came from two separate lines, the Agiad and Eurypontid families; they had equal powers and held office for life. Unlike most Greek kings, those in Sparta did not develop over time into merely ceremonial figures, but retained a significant role into the Classical period, both in the government and as active commanders of the army. As army commanders they had the right to make war upon whatever country they chose, and in the field they exercised unlimited right of life and death. They had a bodyguard of one hundred men. Their powers were, however, restricted by a reform that allowed only one of them, chosen by the people, to lead the army in a given campaign, and held him responsible to the community for his conduct of the campaign.[27] The kings held certain important priesthoods, but they did not have judicial power over criminal cases. They were given perquisites at public sacrifices, but their main source of income was from royal land that they held in the territory of the *perioikoi*. They were ceremonially honored with the first seat at banquets, were served first, and received a double portion.

The power of the kings was intrinsically limited by its dual nature, but as time went on it was further limited by a number of reforms. Perhaps the most important of these reforms was the creation of the annually elected board of five **ephors**, an institution unique to Sparta. Although a variety of duties came to be assigned to the *ephors* in Classical times, the most basic of their duties reveals the primary function of the office—the monthly exchange of oaths between the *ephors* and the kings. The *ephors* swore to uphold the rule of the kings as long as the kings kept their oath, while the kings swore to govern in accordance with the laws. Thus they provided a check on the power of the two kings. We have no sure date for this reform, although the failure of the Great Rhetra to mention the *ephorate* suggests that it was instituted after that time, probably at some time in the century after Tyrtaeus.

The **Gerousia** consisted of 30 members, including the two kings. The other 28 members had to be over 60 years of age, and thus they constituted a true council of elders, such as we see in Homer. They were elected by acclamation by the Assembly and held their office for life, but only men from noble families were eligible for election. The *Gerousia* thus constituted an oligarchic element in the constitution. They served as a court of justice for criminal cases, and as the Rhetra indicates, they prepared measures for consideration by the Assembly. If the decision of the Assembly was "crooked," the *Gerousia* had the power to overturn it.

The Assembly was made up of Spartan male citizens over the age of 30, essentially the Spartan army. Citizenship depended upon successful completion of the course of training and education called the *agoge*, which was provided by the state, and upon election to, and continuing membership in, a mess, in which those who fought together ate together, each providing a contribution. (We will discuss these institutions in detail below). The Assembly elected the *Gerousia*, the *ephors*, and the other magistrates, decided disputed successions to the kingships, and determined matters of war and peace and foreign policy. It was not allowed to debate, but was able only to assent or dissent by acclamation to measures put before it by the *Gerousia*. Thus theoretically Sparta was a democracy, but the power of the people in the Assembly was strictly limited, and their decisions were subject to overturn by an oligarchic body, the *Gerousia*.

By the Classical period, these constitutional reforms had resulted in a mixed constitution that combined both democracy and oligarchy. The ability to compromise and to bring into harmony the interests of competing groups had enabled the Spartans to avoid the tyranny through which many other Greek *poleis* passed in order to achieve similar reforms. Sparta became proverbial for its orderly conduct of government (*eunomia*), as well as for its disciplined military might. But the final key to Spartan *eunomia*, as well as to its military success, lay in the Spartan way of life.

The Spartan Way of Life: *Agoge*, Common Meals, Austerity

With the conquest of Messenia and its incorporation into the helot system, the Spartans committed themselves to a life of constant vigilance in the task of keeping the helot population under control. Over time, the need for this vigilance shaped Spartan lives into an extreme form of militarism focused entirely on the maintenance of an effective fighting force. Because of the nature of our sources, we see the results of this only in their final form, as later admirers and critics portrayed them.

In the Spartan system, the *polis* and its welfare was supreme. Individual and family interests and ambitions were to be put aside to create a society focused on the common good. To this end, the *polis* oversaw the upbringing of children from infancy. At birth, it was the *Gerousia*, not the child's father, as in most Greek *poleis*, who decided whether or not the infant was to be raised. Boys from the age of seven lived in herds in a system of training called the *agoge*. The Greek word comes from the verb *ago*, to lead, and denoted a system of training and also a way of life. The *agoge* was carefully planned to weaken ties to family and to strengthen collective identity; the boys were taking the first steps in becoming *homoioi*. All adults were responsible for the behavior of all children, with the right (and obligation) to discipline not only their own offspring, but any Spartan child.

When they entered the *agoge*, boys were divided into age groups and lived under the immediate supervision of older boys. Although they were taught the rudiments of reading and writing, the focus of the *agoge* was on rigorous physical training to develop hardiness and endurance and on music. Music and the recitation of patriotic choral poetry enculcated Spartan traditions and values, and dancing developed the disciplined control of the body necessary for military maneuvers. When boys reached the age of 12, the *agoge* became increasingly focused on military activities and more demanding. According to Plutarch, the boys were allowed only a single cloak for winter and summer, were required to sleep in beds that they made themselves from rushes picked from the Eurotas River, and were fed meager rations that they were expected to supplement by stealing (if caught, they were whipped for their failure to escape detection). On occasion they attended the men's messes, perhaps in a form of "rushing" in preparation for their later election to one of these groups. To further their acculturation, they were expected to develop homosexual mentor relationships with one of the **hebontes**, men between the ages of 20 and 30 who played a quasi-parental role in socializing their young charges.[28]

For those who successfully completed the *agoge*, the next step was to gain acceptance in the fundamental institution of adult Spartan male life, the mess, or *sysitia*. A mess consisted of a group of about 15 men of mixed ages who ate and fought together throughout their lives, even living together until the age of 30, when they were allowed to set up their own household. Entry into a mess required a unanimous vote by its members. It was a crucial vote, for full citizenship depended upon membership. Those who failed to be elected were relegated to an inferior status, possibly to be identified with the **Hypomeiones**, literally "Inferiors."[29] Continuing membership in the mess (and so, citizenship) was dependent upon a continuing contribution of food and wine, which was supplied by the allotment of land worked by helots. Should a man fail to provide his contribution, he would be expelled from the mess and from full citizenship. Thus he had a strong incentive to keep his helots working efficiently.

Upon election to a mess the young men, now classed as *hebontes*, were still not in possession of full citizenship rights. While they could probably attend the Assembly and vote, they remained under the close supervision and control of the *paidonomos* (the official in charge of all males between the ages of 7 and 30). The *hebontes* were encouraged to marry, but they were not permitted to live with their wives until they reached the age of 30. As a result, they spent far more time and developed a closer emotional tie with their young male charges, whose every stage of development and behavior they were expected to oversee, than with their wives, whom they visited only surreptitiously. This was the period in which they were most active in military service, and as we saw above, they were also subject to serve in the *Krypteia*, keeping watch for and brutally suppressing any signs of helot insubordination or revolt.

At the age of 30, the Spartan male became a full citizen and was expected to move out of the barracks and set up his own household. He also became eligible to hold office. But he continued to take his main meal in his mess, and his military obligations continued until the age of 60. At that time he became eligible for the *Gerousia*, and no longer had military obligations. He still ate in his mess, however, and was expected to participate actively in the training and disciplining of the younger men and boys.

Spartan Women: Responsible for the Downfall of the Spartan State?

Evidence for the role of women in Sparta society is especially susceptible to distortion, for the Greek tendency to see women as "the Other" augments the problem of the non-Spartan nature of the sources and a heavy reliance upon Plutarch, who provides much of the material.

Figure 6.2   Statue of a Spartan in modern Sparta.
Photo by N. Demand.

Athenian tragedy and comedy of the fifth century often express the animosity of Athenians to Spartans in gender terms: Spartan women were seen as unusually liberated, powerful, and sexually promiscuous.[30] Thus the Spartan origins of Helen provided the prototype of a loose Spartan woman in many of Euripides' plays, and the athletic prowess of Spartan women was mocked by Aristophanes' Lampito, whose ability to throttle a bull with her bare hands somewhat detracted from the feminine appeal of Spartan female fitness.[31]

The picture of Spartan women in our sources portrays them as products of the Spartan system. The Spartan bride, like her groom, had been raised with the needs of the *polis* for citizen warriors as her paramount concern. With the aim of developing a healthy and strong body that would produce vigorous offspring, Spartan girls received formal exercise and physical training, often unencumbered by clothing. They were allowed to move freely about the city, rather than being secluded in the home, and regularly took part in religious festivals and processions where they were seen by, and saw, young boys and men. As children, they were fed as much as boys. Nor did the Spartans follow the customary practice of most *poleis* of marrying girls at puberty: in Sparta marriage and childbearing was put off until girls reached physical maturity (18 to 20), again in order to ensure the best reproductive outcome.

Marriage was by "capture": the girl was carried off, her hair was cut, and she was dressed as a boy by her "bridesmaids"; she was then left in a dark room where her husband-to-be would visit her. If pregnancy resulted, the marriage was complete, but the husband continued to live in his mess until he reached the age of 30, visiting his wife only by night and by stealth. The ancient sources report that this regime was adopted to heighten sexual attraction and increase the vigor of any resulting infants. Another view is that it would ensure that the couple would see each other primarily as sexual partners, and that the husband would not invest himself emotionally in the welfare of his wife and family to the detriment of his military duties.[32]

The limitation of affective ties between husband and wife and the strength of such ties between men that resulted from, or were reflected in, Spartan marital customs, can be seen in the openness of Spartan men to the sharing of women. In Spartan law and practice, it was acceptable for a husband to loan his wife to his friends if he wanted no more children himself, or to borrow the wife of another man for reproductive purposes. Old men with young wives were expected to provide a young man as a sexual partner for their wives. Such practices, of course, fostered reproduction; the potential of female fertility was fully exploited, even when the luck of the marriage draw did not favor it. Other Greeks looked askance at these practices and at the reputed freedom allowed to Spartan women, and viewed Spartan women as licentious.[33] But it was not the women who were in control; in each case, it was men who arranged for and sanctioned such extramarital relationships. Spartan marriage practices can thus be looked upon as a logical extension of the general Greek conception of women as property, in the context of the Spartan practice of sharing resources.[34]

Source Analysis

T he philosophers Plato and Aristotle, teacher and pupil in fourth-century Athens, expressed different views of Spartan women. In reading these passages, keep in mind the historical content and also the biases of their authors. Despite these biases, what is it still possible to learn from these passages about the life of Spartan women?

Plato, who grew up during the final years of the Peloponnesian War, which Athens lost to Sparta, contrasted Spartan practices with regard to women to those of Athenians, who "bring together all our belongings …into one household, and give over to the women management of all the possessions and control of the shuttle and of all wool-spinning"(Plato, *Laws* 805e). Plato saw the Spartans' treatment of women as different and perhaps better in some ways, but, in fact, he complains that the Spartans did not go far enough (Plato, *Laws* 806a-c, tr. N. Demand).

Your girls share in gymnastics and musical training, and the women are free from wool spinning, but weave together an industrious life that is in no way trivial nor petty. Tending the sick, managing the house and caring for the children, they arrive at some sort of mean, but they do not share in warfare. The result is that if chance ever forced them to fight on behalf of polis and children, they would not be able to use either a bow, as some Amazons do, nor to throw missiles with skill, nor to take up a shield and spear in imitation of the goddess [Athena], so that, when their country was being attacked, they could resist nobly, inspiring fear, if nothing more, in the enemy as it beheld them arrayed in ranks. …. The legislator ought to be resolved and not content with half-way measures, allowing the female half to live in luxury and expense in an undisciplined way, but disciplining the male half. For in the end in this way he bequeaths half a prosperous life to the city instead of complete prosperity.

Our other source, the philosopher Aristotle, wrote after the Greek world was shocked by the defeat of the Spartan army by the Thebans at the battle of Leuktra in 371, as a consequence of which they lost Messenia. He discusses several reasons for Sparta's downfall, prominent among which is their treatment of women (Aristotle *Pol.* 1269b–1270b6, tr. N. Demand):

Moreover, the laxity concerning women is harmful to the purposes of the constitution and the prosperity of the polis. For just as a man and a woman have a share in an oikos, it is clear that one must also consider the state as divided nearly in two, one body of men and one of women. Thus in constitutions that are lax as regards the regulation of women, one must conclude that half the polis is unregulated, which indeed happened here [in Sparta]. For the lawgiver wishes the whole state to be enduring, and in regard to the men it is obvious that such is the case, but in regard to the women, he is utterly careless. For they live intemperately, indulging in every sort of excess and luxury. As a result, in such a polis, wealth is highly valued, both otherwise and if it happens to be controlled by women, as in the majority of military and warlike races, except the Kelts and any others who honor homosexual male relationships. For it seems that the mythologer first, not without reason, linked Ares with Aphrodite, for all such warlike people appear to be capable of attraction to either men or women.

Among the Spartans, this is the case, and women managed many things during their period of empire. Why does it matter whether women rule or the rulers are controlled by women? For the result is the same.

Although overboldness is useful for none of the activities of normal daily life, but, if for any-thing, for war, that of the Spartan women was most harmful for war. They showed this during the Theban invasion, for they were not useful in any way, as women have been in some other wars [by throwing things from the roofs, for example], but they caused more uproar and trouble than the enemy....

The lack or regulation of the women arose logically in the beginning, for the men were away from home much of the time because of army deployments, fighting the Arkadians and Messenians. But when they the leisure of peace, they handed themselves over to the lawgiver for regulation, being prepared for it by military life (for this has many elements of virtue); they say that Lykourgos also tried to bring the women under the laws, but as they resisted, he gave up. The women themselves are thus the cause of this situation, and it is also clear that they are to blame for it.

Moreover, as was said earlier, not only does the lack of regulation of women cause a certain unseemliness in the constitution itself, but it contributes toward greed. For one might find fault with the inequality of possessions in Sparta, for some Spartans have turned out to possess very much too much property, and others a very little. As a consequence, land comes to be concen-trated in the hands of a few.... And two-fifths of the land is in the hands of women, both because there are many heiresses and because of the practice of giving large dowries.... It is possible for a father to give the heiress to whomever he wishes, and if he dies without having chosen, his heir can give her to whomever he wishes. As a result, the country that can support 1500 horses and 30,000 hoplites has not even a thousand. And as a result of their taking lightly the regulation of these things [women, inheritance by women], the polis did not survive a single blow, but per-ished through a lack of population.

Factors Contributing to Sparta's Demographic Problems

In addition to the problems cited by Aristotle, a number of other factors may have contrib-uted to Sparta's demographic difficulties. Intermarriage within a closed group and a pref-erence for first-cousin marriages, which was exercised more frequently in the closed society of Sparta than in other more open *poleis*, would have resulted in an increased inci-dence of birth defects and raised infant mortality rates even higher than that normal in an-tiquity.[35] Even the effects of a severe earthquake in the mid-fifth century must have contributed to the problem; although demographic losses from natural disasters are nor-mally made up fairly quickly, the Spartan population was already at risk from other fac-tors. One should also consider whether the Spartan system in general might have favored the survival rate of females in contrast to males. Exercise and sufficient nourishment in childhood and delayed childbearing worked to the advantage of females, while males were subjected to a continuous process of testing and culling that began at birth, as the midwife administered a wine bath intended to weed out weaklings—a procedure that would have eliminated more males than females. During childhood the rigorous Spartan *agoge* must have had its male victims as well as its successful graduates. In adulthood war took its toll of males, even though the Spartans were very conservative in exposing their men to the risks of battle. Moreover, the warrior was always subject to loss of citizenship status if he failed to meet community norms of behavior in battle or if he failed to make the required contributions to the common mess. On the other hand, the main threat to women's lives once they reached adulthood was, of course, childbearing.[36] In antiquity all childbearing was hazardous, but Spartan interest in successful reproduction, and the measures they consequently took in the upbringing of girls, probably gave Spartan women some slight edge over other Greek women in surviving childbirth. On the other hand, as we saw above, Aristotle reports that the Spartans favored large families and offered military and political exemptions to fathers of three or four sons. In order to produce three male infants, women on average would have had to bear six children, and in order to produce three grown sons for the Spartan army in an age in which only half the infants born survived to adulthood, they would have had to bear twelve infants. Since each successive pregnancy after the third even in favorable conditions increases likelihood of maternal death, any edge that the Spartan woman had as a result of her upbringing would probably have been overbalanced by the risks of frequent childbearing.

Many Spartan practices appear to have been forms of primitive customs known elsewhere, both in the Greek world and among modern third-world peoples. The races in the nude by prepubescent girls that formed part of initiatory rites at the Athenian festival at Brauron provide a parallel to the alleged nudity of Spartan young women in religious processions. Men's messes and a less rigorous *agoge* were institutions found also in Dorian Crete, while a parallel to the messes can be found in the Men's Houses of some American Indian tribes. Homosexuality as a factor in upper-class male acculturation was also practiced in Athens, and the Thebans had an elite corps of warriors made up of pairs of lovers. Transvestitism that was somewhat similar to Spartan marriage rituals also marked marriage in Dorian Argos, where the girls wore false beards. The sharing of women in polyandry is well known from a number of cultures and has a pale reflection in the relative ease of divorce (by men) in Athens, where a husband might also arrange for the remarriage of his wife, as did Pericles. The *Krypteia* was very similar to widely practiced initiation rites noted by modern anthropologists, in which the young men withdraw from the community to the wilderness and are often expected to prove their manhood by killing an enemy.[37] But in Sparta our sources portray all these customs as instruments that served the single-minded purpose of maintaining Spartan male prowess and their ability to control their subject populations.

The Cost of Security

In terms of the values of Athens and other, more liberal societies, the Spartans paid a high price for their security. Their way of life was marked by extreme austerity. They were notorious for the simplicity of their meals; mess contributions consisted of barley, cheese, figs, and wine, which were occasionally supplemented by bits of meat provided by one of the wealthier men or a successful hunter. They were prohibited from possessing gold and silver and allowed to use only iron spits for coinage (old fashioned, hard to conceal, inconvenient to carry, and without monetary value outside Sparta). In contrast to the Athenian fascination with the poetry of tragedy and comedy and their love of rhetorical display, the Spartans took pride in a parsimonious style of speaking we call laconic, and confined their literary appreciation to patriotic songs such as those of Tyrtaeus. By the Classical period the earlier achievements in the crafts (probably mostly the work of *perioikoi*) had disappeared; even monumental public building had ceased. Thucydides (1.10) says that no one, on seeing the ruins of Sparta in future days, would realize that it had once been the most powerful city in Greece, for the Spartans lived scattered in five villages that possessed no notable buildings.

The Spartans, however, did not see the austere features of their society as drawbacks but as virtues, and many other Greeks agreed. In antiquity the Spartans were widely admired for their courage and military prowess. Many Greeks, and later Romans even had a romantic fascination with the Spartan way of life. This was especially the case among conservative oligarchs and aristocrats, who often adopted Spartan fashions in dress and the long hair that was Spartan custom. Among these admirerers were some of our most important sources—Xenophon, Plato, Aristotle and Plutarch—and this cannot have failed to affect their descriptions of Spartan life.

There were, however, definite weaknesses in the Spartan way of life, even viewed from the standpoint of their own aims. The *agoge*, with its emphasis on strict control and obedience, did not foster the development of individual judgment, and later Greek history provides many instances of Spartans who were at a loss to handle unusual situations. Nor were the Spartans immune to the temptations of luxury or power when they were away from home and the watchful eyes of their fellow Spartans. Moreover, by the fourth century, Aristotle reports that the Spartans were self-indulgent even at home; a system of external controls did not build self-control. Moreover, although the concept of *homoioi*, and the whole system of the *agoge* were directed toward the weakening or elimination of family ties, this seems not to have been successful, at least in the case of the aristocratic families. Again, as attested by Aristotle, by the fourth century there were great differences in wealth among the Spartans, and much was determined by family and patronage. This meant that the most able were not always those who held positions of authority, even in the army, where ineffectual generals with powerful connections were often reappointed to command again and again. The system of inheritance also tended over time to concentrate wealth into a few hands, and unusually for Greece, these hands seem often to have been those of women. Finally, there was the crucial problem of the declining numbers of Spartans, which no measures seem to have been able to stem.

As we consider the events of the fifth and fourth centuries, we will have an opportunity to see these weaknesses, which will allow us to better judge whether the Spartan alternative was as successful in the long run as many Classical Greeks and some modern admirerers have thought it to be.

SUGGESTIONS FOR FURTHER READING

Corinth and Sparta: J. B. Salmon (1984), *Wealthy Corinth : A History of the City to 338 BC.*; Paul Cartledge (2003), *The Spartans: The World of the Warrior-Heroes of Ancient Greece, From Utopia to Crisis and Collapse*; Stephen Hodkinson and Anton Powell, eds. (1999), *Sparta: New Perspectives*.

On women in Sparta: there is a large bibliography, including: Paul Cartledge (1981), "Spartan Wives: Liberation or Licence?" *Classical Quarterly* 31: 84–109; M. B. Skinner, (1987), "Family Dynamics and Female Power in Ancient Sparta," pp. 31–48 in *Rescuing Creusa: New Methodological Approaches to Women in Antiquity*, ed. M. B. Skinner (= *Helios* n.s. 13, no.2). S. Hodkinson (1986), "Land Tenure and Inheritance in Classical Sparta," *Classical Quarterly* 36: 378–406; S. Hodkinson (1989), "Inheritance, Marriage and Demography: Perspectives Upon the Success and Decline of Classical Sparta," pp. 79–121 in *Classical Sparta: Techniques Behind Her Success*, ed., A. Powell. Sarah B. Pomeroy (2002), *Spartan Women*.

MAP STUDY

On Map 6: *Areas*: Peloponnesus, Achaea, Elis, Argolid, Arkadia, Epidaurus, Isthmus of Corinth

Poleis: Corinth, Argos, Tegea, Epidaurus, Olympia, Hysiae, Mantinea, Sicyon, Lakonia, Messenia, Sparta, Amyclae, Eurotas River, Kythera, Mt. Taygetus, Messenia, Messene, Mt. Ithome.

On Other Maps: Rhegion, Leuktra.

ENDNOTES

[1]On Greek tyranny, see A. Andrewes (1956), *The Greek Tyrants*; on Corinth; J. B. Salmon (1984), *Wealthy Corinth*, especially chs. 5–11 on trade and ch. 15 on the tyranny.

[2]Thucydides 1.13

[3]Herdotus 2.167.

[4]For example, D. W. J. Gill (1991), "Pots and Trade: Spacefillers or Objets d'Art?" *Journal of Hellenic Studies* 111: 29–45, argues that vases had a low value and classifies them as spacefillers, or ballast. Opposed to this is John Boardman (1988), "Trade in Greek Decorated Pottery," *Oxford Journal of Archaeology* 7: 27–33.

[5]Salmon (above, n. 1), 120–121.

[6]C. K. Williams (1968), "Excavations at Corinth," *Archaiologikon Deltion* xxliii.B: 134.

[7]Salmon (above, n. 1), 128.

[8]Herodotus 5.99.1.

[9]Ephorus' information on the tyranny survived only because a later historian cited his work, and it is available today only in Greek; see the fragments of Nicholas of Damascus in F. Jacoby (1923–), *Fragmente der griechschen Historiker* 90 Frags. 57–60.

[10]Aristotle, *Fragmenta*, ed. V. Rose (1886), frag. 611.20.

[11]Although tyrants depended on men whom their opponents called mercenaries, many of them probably came from the previously unenfranchised inhabitants of the city itself rather than from foreign recruits.

[12]On Sparta, see L. F. Fitzhardinge (1980), *The Spartans*. Paul Cartledge (2002), *Sparta and Laconia* , 2nd ed. is a very scholarly work. A more popular treatment can be found in Paul Cartledge (2003), *The Spartans: The World of the Warrior-Heroes of Ancient Greece, From Utopia to Crisis and Collapse*. S. Hodkinson and A. Powell, eds. (1999), *Sparta: New Perspectives*, offers a useful collection of papers on various topics in Spartan history.

[13]Webster's *New World Dictionary* (1955).

[14]The term "mirage" was introduced by P. Ollier (1933–1943), *Le Mirage Spartiate*, 2 vols. For the later development of the Spartan tradition in antiquity, see E. N. Tigerstedt (1965–1974), *The Legend of Sparta in Classical Antiquity*, 2 vols.; and in modern times, Elizabeth Rawson (1969), *The Spartan Tradition in European Thought*.

[15]See R. N. L. Barber (1992), "The Origins of the Mycenaean Palace," pp. 11–23 in *Philolakon*, ed. J. M. Sanders.

[16]Fitzhardinge (above, n. 12), 21.

[17]See Fitzhardinge (above, n. 12), ch. 3, and the distribution map of Lakonian fine pottery in fig. 14. A kiln found in Sparta may suggest that some Spartans were still involved in the production of pottery around 600 B.C.E.

[18]The chronology of the Messenian Wars and the reforms associated with them is very unclear, and various books on Sparta may provide different dates from those given here. In general, I have followed the chronology of Cartledge (above, n. 12).

[19]Tyrtaeus, Frag. 5, tr. N. Demand.

[20]Aristotle, *Pol*. 1269a37–8.

[21]Herodotus 6.127.

[22]Aristotle, *Pol*. 1306b36 (= Tyr. Frag. 1 West).

[23]Aristotle, *Pol*. 1270a15–1270b6.

[24]This is the interpretation of Cartledge (above, n. 12), 160–175.

[25]Plut., *Lykurgus* 6, tr. N. Demand.

[26]Tyrtaeus, Frag 4, tr. N. Demand.

[27]C. G. Thomas (1974), "On the Role of the Spartan Kings," *Historia* 23: 257–270.

[28]Xen. *Constitution of the Lacedaemonian* 2. 12–14 claims that these relationships were "Platonic," but adds, "Who would believe this?" In fact, Aristotle seems to have believed it, as suggested in the passage above, *Pol*. 1269b. Anton Powell (1988), *Athens and Sparta*, 223–224, views the conflicting ancient evidence and says that we must look at the details; he finds that "references to particular homosexual attachments of Spartans are conspicuous even by Greek standards."

[29]This term is only used once of Spartans, by Xenophon, *Hell*. 3.3.6; where it refers to some sort of second-class membership in the Spartan community, but it is not clear exactly what. Other terms denoting less than full Spartiate status were *Neodamodeis*, helots freed for army service, *Tressantes*, or Tremblers, those who exhibited fear in battle (Herodotus 7.231, Plutarch, *Ages*. 30.2–4); and *Mothakes*, boys of unclear but inferior status brought up as companions to the sons of wealthy patrons.

[30]See Ellen G. Millender (1999), "Athenian Ideology and the Empowered Spartan Woman," pp. 355–391 in Hodkinson and Powell, eds. (above, n. 12). On Spartan women, there is a large bibliography: Paul Cartledge (1981), "Spartan Wives; Liberation or Licence?" *Classical Quarterly* 31: 84–109; M. B. Skinner (1987), "Family Dynamics and Female Power in Ancient Sparta," pp. 31–48 in *Rescuing Creusa: New Methodological Approaches to Women in Antiquity*, ed. M. B. Skinner (= *Helios* n.s. 13, no.2). S. Hodkinson (1986), "Land Tenure and Inheritance in Classical Sparta," *Classical Quarterly* 36: 378–406; S. Hodkinson (1989), "Inheritance, Marriage and Demography: Perspectives Upon the Success and Decline

of Classical Sparta," pp. 79–121 in A. Powell, ed. *Classical Sparta: Techniques Behind Her Success*. Sarah B. Pomeroy (2002), *Spartan Women* relies heavily upon Plutarch on the grounds that he provides the most evidence, discounting the probability of development over time and the effects on his different (Roman) cultural context and his different aim.

[31]Pomeroy (above, n. 28), 27, 147, sees Aristophanes' Lampito as a favorable portrayal because she is physically fit and confident.

[32]Powell (above, n. 27), 223–224.

[33]Plato, *Laws* 637c.

[34]Xen. *Constitution of the Lacedaemonians* 6.3.

[35]Athenians and other Greeks favored first-cousin marriages but probably practiced them less often than was the case in the more closed citizen group at Sparta. The deleterious effects of such marriages depend upon the presence of adverse recessive genes in both parents. Thus not all couples would have problems, and not all offspring would necessarily be affected; moreover, a higher than normal *rate* of defect and mortality would probably have escaped notice or been otherwise explained in a society that was not aware of modern statistical analysis.

[36]See N. Demand (1994), *Birth, Death and Motherhood in Classical Greece*.

[37]See the classic article by H. Jeanmaire (1913), "La cryptic lacédémonienne," *Revue des Etudes Grecques* 26: 12–50.s

7

ARCHAIC ATHENS:
CRISIS AND REFORM

EARLIEST ATHENS

For most people, Athens is the city that most exemplifies Classical Greece. It is the capital of the modern nation-state of Greece; entry point for the vast majority of visitors, site of the most famous Greek ruin; the Parthenon; and home of the most famous Greek literature: the plays of the tragedians Aeschylus, Sophocles, Euripides, the comic poet Aristophanes, and the historian Thucydides. The historian Herodotus—who was not an Athenian but a citizen of the Greek city of Halicarnassus in Asia Minor—made Athens the centerpoint of his story of the great conflict between the Greeks and the Persians. Although philosophy began in Miletus in Asia Minor, it soon took root in Athens, which was later the home of Plato; Aristotle, a native of Stagira in the Chalkidike, established his school there in the fourth century. Many laud the city as the birthplace of democracy, but up to this point Athens had played only a small part in that development, and that part was mostly through its connections with other sites that were politically more precocious.

It was only in the late seventh century that Athens began the course that led to its predominance among Greek *poleis* in the fifth century, and eventually to defeat by its rival Sparta at the end of that century. After a brief revival in the fourth century, the city became a famous center of learning, but no longer a political player in the much wider world created by the conquests of Alexander the Great.

The beginning of the remarkable trajectory of Athenian development may have come with the unification of its wider territory, Attica. Attica, which covers approximately one thousand square miles, is divided by mountains into three plains: Pedia, including Athens; the central Mesogeia; and the coastal plains, Thriasia, with Eleusis as its chief town and

156

Paralia with Thorikos and the silver mines of Laurion. Attica was thus even less of a natural unity than were the Boeotian or Arcadian plains, which in the historical period were shared by a number of independent city-states in loose and often contested confederations. Yet by the fifth century Attica was politically unified. All its male citizens, regardless of their place of residence, enjoyed equal status as citizens. Outlying towns were not restive under Athenian control, as were the Plataeans under the leadership of Thebes, nor did they have an inferior status, as did the perioikoi towns of Lakonia. This unity was a remarkable achievement whose story spans the archaic period and is closely interwoven with the transition from aristocratic rule to the self-rule of the Athenian people (democracy).

By Classical times the **synoikism** (unification, either physical or, as in this case, only political) of Attica had become an event of the distant mythical past. It was attributed to the Bronze Age Athenian hero, Theseus, who was also credited with killing the Minoan Minotaur. Thucydides relates the tradition as it was known in his time.

Source Analysis

Thucydides 2.15–16 combines an accurate picture of the effects of the synoikism with its mythical attribution to Theseus. What evidence does Thucydides offer for the synoikism? In many Greek *poleis*, synoikism involved the physical relocation of the people. What evidence does Thucydides offer that this was not the case in Attica?

Few scholars today share Thucydides' belief in a Bronze Age unification that survived into the Dark Age.[1] Many date the unification in the early ninth century,[2] a time when Attic graves reveal a period of prosperity that has been associated with the synoikism. People were turning increasingly from a pastoral life to arable farming. The increase in farming may have laid the basis for a rise in prosperity, as suggested by the miniature granaries buried with the woman who has been dubbed the "Rich Athenian Lady" by the excavators of her tomb (see Chapter 4, Figure 4.5). A turn to arable farming would have put a premium upon land ownership and common action in defense of the fields, both of which were closely associated with the concept of citizenship in Classical times. A ninth-century unification is also early enough to have been thoroughly forgotten by the Classical period, as it must have been to escape even the careful investigations of Thucydides. Yet whether the synoikism of Attica, which was a political union of towns, if not of fully formed *poleis*, could have so far preceded the date at which the formation of the *polis* is usually set—the eighth century—is a problem that lends some weight to arguments for a later date.[3]

With more plausibility, several arguments support the period around 700 for the synoikism. For example, J. N. Coldstream interpreted as evidence for the synoikism a cessation of burials in the *agora*, which occurred around 700.[4] In Colstream's interpretation, this would mark the point at which the area was turned into a formal civic center as a result of the synoikism, in keeping with Thucydides' statement that the city center moved at that time from the Acropolis to the area below (the area of the *agora*).[5] Those who date the Athenian conquest of Eleusis to ca. 675 also favor a date in the early seventh century, viewing the synoikism as the last step in unification; however, the date of the conquest of Eleusis is contested.[6]

Only a little is known about the political structure of Athens in the early days of Attic unification, but nothing suggests that it deviated in any significant way from that of other early *poleis*. At the head of an aristocratic society there was the usual *basileus*, or "king"; at some early time he was joined by, or replaced by, an official called an **archon**. Each of the first 12 archons ruled for life; then a series of archons held office for ten years. Perhaps in 682/681, when the official list of annual archons begins, the office became an annual one. Two more archons were added at a later date, making a total of three: the Archon Basileus, who had mainly ritual functions inherited from the early Basileus; the Chief Archon (**Archon Eponymous**), who gave his name to the year and was the effective head of state; and the **Polemarch**, or army commander. A council, the Council of the Areopagus, had broad but ill-defined powers. Only members of an exclusive group of aristocratic families, called the **Eupatrids** (well-born, sons of good or noble fathers) were eligible for the archonship or the council.

In this early period the Eupatrids were also the repositories of the law, which was unwritten and customary. Somewhat later, six other officials with the status of archon, the ***thesmothetes***, were added; their duty in classical times was to act as recorders of judicial decisions and as court officials. The citizen body was distributed among the four traditional Ionian tribes; ordinary citizens may have had some right to express their opinion in an assembly, but political decisions were essentially in the hands of the Eupatrid families.

THE DEVELOPMENT OF THE ATHENIAN POLIS

The First Attempt at Tyranny: Kylon

The first hint of trouble appeared in the mid-seventh century (some time between 640 and 621), when an Athenian aristocrat and Olympic victor named Kylon made an attempt to usurp power. Kylon was assisted by his father-in-law, the tyrant of nearby Megara, a city that was one of Athens' traditional enemies. The conspirators managed to seize the acropolis, but the Athenian people rose up against them, foiling the attempt. Kylon himself escaped, but a number of his followers were cornered and took refuge in a temple as suppliants of the god. The archons induced them to give themselves up by the promise that as suppliants they would not suffer punishment, but as they left the temple they were cut down. This ruthless killing of suppliants in violation of the most sacred laws suggests that longstanding animosities among the aristocrats themselves played an important role in the events.

Kylon's attempt at tyranny, although unsuccessful, was to shadow Athenian history for a long time to come. During the course of the seventh century, the concept of blood pollution became especially strong. Any shedding of blood was held to pollute and to require purification, even that which was accidental or innocent (as in the purely physiological functions of menstruation and childbirth). Deliberate and unjustified killing incurred the most serious pollution, especially when it was associated with sacrilege, as was the Kylonian incident. For a city, the result could be civic disorder and epidemic; for a family, an inherited stain (*miasma*) that continued to inflict calamities on successive generations.[7] In the case of the Kylonian killings, a trial was held, and the archons—including the Eponymous Archon Megacles and his entire *genos*, or clan, the Alkmaeonids—were adjudged guilty. The bodies of Alkmaeonids who had died were ordered removed from Attica, and the living went into exile. Later, when a plague was viewed as a consequence of the pollution, a special purifier, Epimenides of Crete, was brought in to cleanse the city.[8] The city was saved, but the pollution remained upon the Alkmaeonids and their descendants. As a consequence, members of the family, who often played an important role in Athenian politics, had a checkered career, now suffering exile, now received back into the city. This became especially significant when political exploitation of the curse affected such central figures in Athenian political life as Kleisthenes, Pericles, and Alkibiades—all Alkmaeonids.

The fact that Kylon made his attempt at all suggests that some level of popular discontent existed in Athens at the time; aversion to foreign involvement in the affairs of the *polis* may have been the major factor in Athenian disaffection. After the failure of the coup, it was decided to have the traditional laws set down in writing, but not changed or reformed. A man named Drakon, according to tradition, was given the job. It was a significant step forward, despite the fact that no laws were changed, for publication in writing gave the aristocratic keepers of the law less chance to "remember" the laws to their own advantage. Little is known about the content of Drakon's laws, with the exception of those dealing with homicide, for within a generation they were superseded by the laws of Solon. Tradition held that Drakon's laws were extremely harsh; they were said to have been "written in blood." Nevertheless, the laws dealing with homicide made the important distinction between premeditated and unpremeditated homicide. The right to bring a prosecution lay with the male kinship (to the degree of cousin's son), which also had the right to grant or refuse pardon if the homicide was involuntary. However, it was the **Ephetai** (the Fifty-One) who passed judgment. A convicted killer went into exile and could be killed without penalty by anyone if he ventured back into public territory (the *agora*, the games, or the Amphictyonic rites). If he remained beyond the borders, however, his death would be treated the same as the homicide of an Athenian citizen. Another of Drakon's laws dealing with homicide sanctioned self-help: anyone caught in the act of taking away the property of another by force could be repulsed and killed without penalty.[9]

The Legislation of Solon

The publication of the laws by Drakon did not solve the problems that were afflicting Athens; in fact, it may even have made the situation worse, since people for the first time could see the harshness and injustice of the conditions under which they lived. Unrest reached the point of threatening the city, and in 594/593 it was agreed that a special legislator should be appointed with full powers to restructure the political and economic system as he saw fit. Similar situations had given rise to tyranny in many cities, and the aristocrats probably felt that agreement to what they expected would be a moderate reform might spare them a harsher fate under a tyranny. The man chosen was Solon, a member of an aristocratic family but of middling wealth himself.

Source Analysis

T he best descriptions of the situation that led to Solon's appointment come from his own words, expressed in the traditional form of poetry (Solon, Frag 4, Edmonds, tr. N. Demand):

> Our city will never perish by the disposition of Zeus,
> Or by the will of the blessed immortal gods,
> For a great-hearted guardian, daughter of a mighty father,
> Holds her hands over us, Athena Pallas.
> But our citizens themselves chose to destroy a great city,
>   trusting in thoughtless gain.
> The unjust minds of the leaders of the demos
> Will endure many sufferings from their great hybris,
> For they do not know how to restrain their greed,
> Nor with good cheer to conduct the feast in peace.
> Trusting in unjust deeds they grow wealthy,
> Sparing neither the possessions of the gods nor of the demos,
> They steal and plunder, one from the other,
> Nor do they heed the shrine of holy Justice.
> She, silent, knows the present and the past,
> And in time comes without fail to take retribution.
>
> An inescapable infection afflicts the whole city,
> And quickly evil slavery is upon us;
> Kindred stasis rouses sleeping war,
> Which destroys the youth of many.

For from ill-will the much-loved city is quickly worn away
    by the conspiracies of unjust associates.
These evils are rife in the city; and of the poor
Many leave for foreign lands, sold abroad,
Bound in shameful fetters.

What were the main problems leading up to the crisis, according to this poem? More information comes from Solon's description of his actions (Solon, Frag. 36, Edmonds, tr. N. Demand):

She bears witness to these things in the Court of Time,
Greatest mother of the Olympian gods, best,
Black Earth, whose *horoi* set fast everywhere
I have plucked up.
Before she was enslaved, now she is free.
And I led back many Athenians sold beyond the seas
    to the god-created homeland,
some lawlessly, some lawfully, and some fleeing the necessity of poverty,
No longer speaking the Attic tongue, wandering everywhere;
And some held here in shameful slavery
    trembling under the temper of their masters,
I made free. These things I accomplished by power [kratos],
joining together force and right, and I completed what I promised.
And I wrote laws for both the poor and the rich,
Arranging straightforward justice for each man.

How do these actions fit the picture of the crisis in the first poem?

Aristotle adds that many who were **hektemoroi**, or Sixth-parters working the land of others for a one-sixth rent, fell into slavery when they failed to pay.[10] The status of *hektemoros* was probably itself not a result of debt, but a remnant from the Dark Age, when poor men voluntarily gave themselves over for protection to the more affluent and powerful.[11] Solon's picture of aristocratic greed and oppression, enslavement and civil discord, leaves many questions unanswered. Solon's audience did not need to be told in detail about the conditions that led to the crisis, but the modern historian lacks information about vital aspects of the situation. As a result, the exact mechanisms that brought about the crisis cannot be determined, and the historian is reduced to speculation.[12] Some relevant factors are the following:

Debt   As in much of Greece, farming in Attica was marginal at best; a bad year could bring disaster (see Chapter 1). A century earlier in more fertile Boeotia, Hesiod had warned repeatedly that the least lapse in diligence would result in the farmer being forced to borrow. But in Hesiod's Boeotia the worst consequence seems to have been social stigma and going without. Hesiod never suggests that slavery awaited the debtor, as it did in seventh-century Attica.

Greed   In the late eighth century, Hesiod already complains about the bribe-swallowing *basileis*. By the late seventh century in Athens, the costs of maintaining an aristocratic lifestyle had risen with rising prosperity. New "needs" appeared in the form of imported luxury goods, which the Athenians could see in the possession of their wealthier peers on the nearby island of Aegina, whose economy was based almost entirely on trade.[13] Silver was in use as a medium of exchange, but Athens did not yet mint coins. An important clue to the effects of greed on the aristocracy is the reputed "law of Solon" prohibiting the export of every agricultural product except olive oil; certainly in bad years, and perhaps even in good, selling grain to the highest bidder overseas would have been more profitable than selling it to the poor at home.

Horoi   The term means "border marker." In the fourth century it was applied to stones marking mortgaged land, but it is unlikely that the sophisticated concept of a mortgage is applicable to conditions of land tenure in the late seventh century. Solon's poetry tells us only that the *horoi* marked land that was somehow encumbered. They may have indicated *hektemoros* status, or marked land on which other debts were owed, or perhaps even land seized (legally or illegally) for debt. These issues are complicated by uncertainty about whether land was alienable (could be sold or otherwise transferred from the *oikos*).

As evidenced by his poetry, Solon resolved the immediate crisis by freeing the unjustly enslaved, even seeking out and redeeming those who had been sold abroad, and he abolished debt-slavery for the future. He freed the land from its enslavement by the *horoi*, thus wiping out the debts owed by the poor, and the status of *hektemoros* was abolished. These reforms were called the ***Seisachtheia*** or Shaking-off-of-Burdens.[14] Solon was willing to cancel debt, but rejected the radical step of redistributing the land.

In the cancellation of debts, Solon was following an established tradition in the Near East.[15] Laws and edicts curbing the practice of debt-slavery are found as early as the edict of King Urukagina of the city-state Lagash (ca. 2370 BCE), and perhaps even 50 years earlier under King Entemena.[16] Similar laws "establishing justice" by the freeing of debt-slaves in the land can be found in the Akkadian legal collection of Eshnunna (ca. 1790 BCE), in the legal collection of Hammurabi (ca. 1758 BCE), and in the Middle Assyrian laws (ca. 1450–1250 BCE). In addition to these law collections, various Old Babylonian kings issued edicts during their regnal year and irregularly during their reigns, which cancelled various debts and released encumbered land and debt-slaves. These edicts, said to "establish justice in the land," in effect, were efforts to prevent the economy from collapsing.[17] During the Neo-Assyrian period, several texts mention the declaration of edicts that specified the release of debt-slaves and property.[18] The reforms of Solon should be understood in a similar economic context, and as having been influenced by such ideas, which had long been familiar in the Near East. Chirichigno similarly argues for the influence of the Near Eastern tradition upon the Biblical laws for the release of debts during the Sabbatical and Jubilee years (*Exodus*, *Deuteronomy*, and *Leviticus*).

How might Solon have learned about these Near Eastern economic reforms? He lived in a world that was busily incorporating Near Eastern culture: oriental motifs abounded on pottery, and oriental stories penetrated the realm of the gods. He is reported in the ancient sources to have traveled, either for trade or to gain experience and extend his knowledge,[19] and his commitment to learning is twice repeated by Plutarch (*Solon* 2 and 31, frag. 18). Thus we cannot rule out the possibility of his having personally acquired knowledge of foreign traditional political practices. This is, however, by no means accepted by all ancient historians. In particular, M. I. Finley has drawn a sharp distinction between the Near Eastern ameliorative laws and moratoria and Solon's abolition of debts.[20] Finley interpreted Near Eastern debt bondage as a form of labor procurement, whose abolition involved actions taken "from the top down," while he saw Solon's reforms as a response to popular discontent, operating "from the bottom up," and culminating in the absolute abolishment of debt bondage. The result was the creation of a community of free men, whose need for labor was met by the growing use of chattel slavery.

Solon instituted a number of important constitutional changes in addition to his debt reform that may give clues to the nature of these reforms. The most fundamental was a new classification of the citizens that substituted wealth for birth as the criterion for holding office. This suggests that there were men who had accumulated wealth but lacked political input. Solon divided the citizens into property classes according to the produce of their land in measures of both wet (oil, wine) and dry (grain) produce. It is noteworthy that this classification is still based on landed wealth: any man enriched by trade would have had to acquire land in order to qualify. The four groups were:

Pentecosiomedimi (500-bushel men), who were eligible to be treasurer and archon.

Hippeis (300–500 bushel men), perhaps men who could support horses, were eligible for lesser offices and possibly also for the archonship.

Zeugitae (200–300 bushel men), either those with a yoke of oxen, or hoplites,[21] were possibly eligible for minor offices.

Thetes (all the rest, including those without land), were eligible to attend the Assembly.

One of the most important of Solon's reforms for the later development of democracy was his institution of the right of appeal. Judicial decisions had formerly been made by the archons without any recourse to appeal. Under Solon's reforms they could be appealed to the

Assembly meeting as a court of appeal; in that role it was called the **Heliaea**. Solon also added a second council made up of four hundred men, one hundred from each of the traditional four tribes. The new council perhaps provided a check on the basically unrestricted power of the older **Areopagus Council**.[22]

Solon also rewrote the laws, retaining only the murder provisions from the laws of Drakon. Since the Athenians in later times attributed all their laws to Solon, just as the Spartans attributed theirs to Lycurgus, we cannot tell which of the many laws that were later called "Laws of Solon" were actually his. Some that are often cited by historians as genuinely Solonian are: the right of a third party to take action on behalf of a victim who had been wronged (formerly only the family could take action, as is clear from the rules of kinship outlined in the homicide law of Drakon); the prohibition of all exports except olive oil; the law that required all fathers to teach their sons a craft if they were to claim to be supported by them in old age; and the law allowing and encouraging immigrant families (presumably craftsmen) to settle as citizens in Athens.

Solon's solution was a work of moderation. He rejected a tyrant's role,[23] and favored neither side in the dispute:[24]

> I gave to the demos the rights that sufficed,
> Neither taking away from their esteem nor adding more;
> Those who had power and were outstanding in weatlh,
> Even for these I proposed nothing shameful,
> But I fixed a strong shield round both,
> And allowed neither to prevail unjustly.

But such moderation did not make Solon popular with either side in the conflict:[25]

> Because of these things I am embattled on all sides,
> I turn about like a wolf surrounded by dogs.

When the legislation was complete, tradition says that Solon left Athens for ten years in order to avoid being pressured into revising his work. But moderation and restraint did not succeed. The Athenians continued to act like a pack of dogs, and finally a tyrant did arise. Nevertheless, Solon's work set the institutional framework for the future of the Athenian state, guaranteeing personal freedom and establishing rights that were vital to the later development of democracy, especially the right of appeal. His work also greatly affected the character of the tyranny that was to follow, for our sources agree that it was conducted within the framework of existing laws and institutions.[26]

The Tyranny of Peisistratus

The immediate result of Solon's reforms was a state of chaos. They had brought both financial and political losses to the aristocrats and had left the poor discontented by their moderation. But perhaps the greatest problem was Solon's failure to create effective means by which compliance with his reforms could be enforced. It is therefore not surprising that a period of literal anarchy followed. In some years no archon could be elected, and one archon made an attempt at tyranny, overstaying his term of office by two years until he was forcibly removed. In 580/579 a solution was sought in the appointment of a board of ten to fill the role of archon, including five Eupatrids, three *Agroikoi* (probably farmers of less than noble status), and two *Demiourgoi* (craftsmen; probably the owners of workshops run by slaves, since ownership of land was necessary).

While the board of ten seemed to solve the problem of the archonship at least temporarily, factionalism persisted. The names of the three factions suggest that geographical interests formed the basis of the division, for Aristotle says they took their names from the regions in which their leaders farmed: the Plain, Shore, and Beyond-the-Hills. The Plain refers fairly clearly to Pedia, the central plain of Attica in which the best land was located, and among the men who held land there must have been the wealthiest landowners, many of them Eupatrids, and therefore a force for conservatism. The Shore is also not hard to identify as the coastal regions; the men associated with it were probably traders and fishermen, but the silver mines of Laurion were also located near the coast, and men with interests in them might have formed part of this group. Such men included both the owners of the surface land where the mines were located (the *polis* owned the resources beneath the surface), those who leased the right to work the deposits, and those who rented slaves or equipment to do so. Men able to exploit the mines were probably wealthy; silver was the most important single Athenian resource and its only significant export. Both traders and those with mining interests were probably a revisionary rather than a conservative force, and Aristotle identified the Shore as taking a middle position. Finally, the group called Beyond-the-Hills is the most puzzling of all. It may have referred to the land beyond the Parnes-Pentelikon, Hymettos ring, and it surely included both Marathon and Brauron. Peisistratus, the leader of the faction, was from Brauron, but Herodotus says that many of Peisistratus' supporters came from the city, and Aristotle identified them as made up of three elements: the common people, those who had lost through the cancellation of debts, and those not of pure Attic descent. None of these would have been connected with a specific region, but all stood to gain by change and were ready to support a revolution that would bring in a tyranny. It may be that the names given to the groups refer to the home district of their leading members, and not to the membership at large.

Despite the support of various groups, including the *demos* (which, of course, had no power at this time), Peisistratus' accession was not smooth or rapid. In fact, it was only after many years and on his third attempt that he was finally successful. Herodotus' description of his various attempts is instructive about aristocratic political maneuvers and tyrannical methods of gaining power; the dates of the three attempts are calculated as 561/560, lasting five years; 556, lasting six years; and 546.[27]

Source Analysis

H erodotus 1.59–64. What types of support did Peisistratus rely on in each attempt?

Once established, the tyranny provided Athens with nearly twenty years of peace and order. Peisistratus ruled in accordance with the constitution and laws of Solon, but the archon lists show that he maintained ultimate control by making sure that he himself, or one of his relatives or followers, always held the chief archonship, and he used the other, lesser archonships to reward support from aristocratic families, from whom he also took hostages for good measure. Since the archons at the end of their office passed automatically into the Council of the Areopagus, where they had life tenure, the supporters of Peisistratus gradually filled that powerful body. His strongest enemies, the Alkmeonids, at first went into exile, but later in the tyranny one is recorded as holding an archonship, demonstrating that Peisistratus had successfully co-opted them. Nevertheless, they eventually played a central role in ending the tyranny.

Peisistratus gained the support of the poor by economic and other reforms, all of which also tended to cut back the powers of the local aristocratic families. He instituted a tax of one-twentieth of produce to provide for public works. This was considerably less oppressive than the one-sixth required of the *hektemoroi* before the reforms of Solon, and was probably welcomed as a replacement for the random exactions from local aristocrats to which the farmers had formerly been subject. Loans at good rates for farmers also reduced dependence on the local aristocrats, as did the replacement of local aristocratic judges by travelling judges sent out from Athens. Peisistratus himself also toured the countryside to check on the administration of justice.

Like other tyrants, Peisistratus undertook an extensive building program. While this was self-aggrandizing, it also fostered civic pride and provided many with employment. He rebuilt a temple of the goddess Athena on the Acropolis, using marble for the first time for some of the decorative elements; he enhanced the shrine of Artemis Brauron, also on the Acropolis; and he began a giant temple of Zeus at a site in the lower city, which was completed only by the edict of the Roman emperor Hadrian in the second century CE. He improved the water supply by constructing an aqueduct and an ornamental fountain house; and he enhanced the Agora, regularizing it as a civic center and providing a system of drainage that can be seen to this day.[28]

These building activities, which required the services of architects, engineers, and sculptors, as well as imported marble from the islands, created a situation in which the traditional barter economy was no longer adequate. Another factor operating in this same direction was the tyrant's reliance on mercenary forces. Thus it is not surprising that coinage was first introduced into Athens during the rule of Peisistratus. The tyrant himself may at first have provided the silver from his holdings in the mining area of Thrace, where he had spent much of his time in exile. These earliest Athenian coins are called *Wappenmünzen* (German for "heraldic coins"), because they bear a variety of emblems that were once thought to be heraldic crests. A more recent explanation of the "crests," however, looks to models of coinage from Asia Minor. Refugees from Croesus' conquest of Ionia and from the Persian conquest a few years later were coming to the mainland at about this time, and among them may have been silversmiths who exercised their craft in Athens.[29] The denominations of the *Wappenmünzen* were too large to be used for retail trade, but they were suitable for lump sum payments to mercenaries and for long-term contracts of workers in the building trades.

The promotion of religious festivals that celebrated the gods popular with the people, rather than the cults of the aristocratic families, was another way in which the tyranny fostered the *polis* at the expense of the aristocrats. The most important of these festivals was the Panathenaia, held in honor of Athena, patron goddess of the city, which was celebrated with additional pomp every fourth year as the **Greater Panathenaia**. Peisistratus and his sons endowed this festival with special magnificence, adding the recitation of the Homeric poems to the traditional games. Among the prizes for the athletic contests were large Black Figure vases (called Panathenaic vases) filled with olive oil.[30] As the victors carried them home to their various cities, they spread the reputation of Athenian potters and advertised the high quality of Athenian olive oil. An interesting reflection of these events is provided by a number of Attic Black Figure vases that portray Athena ready to lead Herakles into Athens on a cart. John Boardman has suggested that the figure of Herakles alluded to Peisistratus, and Athena to Phye, and that the tyrant used these scenes as propaganda to associate himself with the popular hero Herakles.[31]

Another traditional festival that was given new life and direction was that of Dionysos. Originally a rural celebration of the fertility of the vine and all wild growing things, it took on a new form in the city as the City Dionysia, and began a gradual process of transformation that culminated in classical Attic tragedy and comedy, among the greatest of the achievements of ancient Greece. According to tradition, in 534/533 the poet Thespis both produced and acted in the first performance, with a goat as prize. A marked increase in scenes of Dionysos on Attic vases also has been noted at this time, reflecting increasing interest in the festival.[32]

Abroad, Peisistratus began to establish a basis for the extension of Athenian (or Peisistratid) power in three areas: the Hellespont, the Aegean, and the Greek mainland. Sigeum, which could provide a port of call near the entrance of the Hellespont, was reconquered (it had been settled 40 years earlier, but had subsequently been lost), and Peisistratus installed Hegisistratos, one of his sons, as governor. The settlement of the Chersonese by Miltiades III, a supporter of Peisistratus, ensured that Athenians favorable to the tyranny occupied both shores of the Hellespont. The area had just been brought under Per-

---

WEBSITE 7.1   DIONYSUS DEPICTED ON VASES
Using the Perseus website:http://www.perseus.tufts.edu

Consider these Dionysian scenes. All but one of the vases are typical shapes used in the symposium (amphora and stamnos for mixing, cups for drinking); the alabastron, however, was used for perfumes or oils. Why might it have been considered a suitable shape for a Dionysiac scene?

Tampa 86.15: Euboean Black Figure alabastron, Dionysos, satyr and maenad, making wine

Philadelphia L-64–248 27: Attic Black Figure amphora, Dionysos on a donkey, maenads, satyrs

Jacksonville AP.66.21: Attic Black Figure amphora, Dionysos, maenads, satyrs

Cleveland 508.15: Attic Black Figure Figure Cup, Dionysos, satyr, party

London E 66: Attic Red Figure Cup attributed to the Clinic Painter, Dionysos reclining, while two satyrs entertain him

Naples 2419: Attic Red Figure stamnos, Dions Painter, depicting a feast of Dionysos, with maenads

Berlin F 2290 26: Attic Red Figure Cup, Dionysos, maenads

---

sian control with the fall of the Lydian King Kroisos to the Persian Cyrus in the 540s. Peisistratus' final, successful attempt at the tyranny is dated 546.

Conquest and settlement of these sites brought the Peisistratid family into association with the Persians. Hippias, the son of Peisistratus who succeeded him as tyrant, sought to further relations with the Persians by marrying his daughter to the son of the tyrant of Lampsakos, whom he believed had influence with the Persian king (Thuc. 6.59.3). The strategy worked, for when Hippias was driven out of Athens in 511/510, he found refuge in Sigeion and then Lampsakos (Hdt. 5.65; Thuc. 6.59.4). Later, when the Persian **satrap** (governor) of the area failed to obtain his return to Athens as a Persian vassal because the Athenian Assembly had resolved to fight his return), Hippias appealed to the Persian king for reinstatement and traveled with the expedition of Datis against Greece in 490. Herodotus reports that he had a dream that he would regain control of his homeland, but with typical oracular ambiguity the dream found fulfillment only for one of his teeth, which he lost in the battle at Marathon.[33]

In the Aegean, Peisistratus conquered the island of Naxos and installed the tyrant Lygdamis, who had himself helped Polycrates to gain tyrannical power on the island of Samos. He purified the island of Delos, site of the pan-Ionian sanctuary of Apollo, by removing all the old burials and forbidding deaths and childbirths on the island in the future; this was a strong statement of Athenian leadership over the Ionians. On the Greek mainland, Peisistratus continued to foster the connections that had been useful to him in gaining power: Thebes (where he made dedications to the shrine of the Ptoion Apollo), Eretria, Argos (from which he had taken a wife), Thessaly (after which he named a son, Thessalos), and Sparta.

Peisistratus' most important contribution to the development of Athens was to enhance the *polis* and to reduce the power of the aristocratic families. He managed this by astute diplomacy and clever manipulation of the archonships, by real reforms in the countryside, by building useful and impressive public monuments in the city, and by providing festivals that celebrated gods popular with the people and fostered civic consciousness and pride. He maintained the framework of Solon's constitution, and both Thucydides and Aristotle called him "democratic." The fact that he died of natural causes attests both to his general popularity and to his success in stabilizing the political situation in Athens.

At his death in 527, Peisistratus was succeeded by his son Hippias. Hippias' policies and methods, at least in the beginning, seem to have been a continuation of those of his father; in fact, it is sometimes difficult to differentiate the activities of the tyrant and those of his sons Hippias and Hipparchus, since the sons participated actively in rule during the lifetime of their father. Tradition, however, attributed to Hipparchus a special interest in the arts and made him responsible for inviting the poets Anacreon and Simonides to Athens, while Hippias' place in history was as the successor in the tyranny.

One interesting and important change that can be dated securely to the rule of Hippias was the introduction, in ca.525, of a new coinage that featured explicitly Athenian symbolism: the head of Athena, her owl, and, to make matters absolutely clear, the abbreviated name of the *polis*. They were soon nicknamed "**Owls**."

Figure 7.1   Athenian "Owl;" coin, tetradrachma, head of Athena and owl (ca. 460–450 BC). Courtesy of the John Max Wulfing Collection, Washington University, St. Louis.

Owls were twice the value of the earlier *Wappenmünzen,* and thus they too were too large for retail trade. Since, unlike the *Wappenmünzen,* Owls are found abroad in large numbers, it is likely that silver was exported as a commodity in this form, and that Athens was by then producing more silver than it needed from the mines of Laurion. The Owl remained the basic Athenian coin until the second century, and it served as the standard coin in the Greek world.[34]

In 514 Hipparchus was assassinated in a plot that Thucydides attributed to a lovers' quarrel.

Source Analysis and Comparison

O n the Assassination of Hipparchus.   Herodotus and Thucydides tell the story: Hdt. 5.55–57, 62–65; Thus. 1.20, 6.53 (last sentence)–59. What was the motivation for each historian in relating the story? How do the accounts differ and in what do they agree? What political significance might these differences have had in their own day?

After the assassination of Hipparchus, the rule of Hippias became increasingly harsh and paranoid, truly tyrannical in the modern sense. Relief from the oppression came by way of the Alkmeonids, still suffering under the curse that arose from their participation in the violation of the sanctity of suppliants. They hoped to renew aristocratic power now that the tyranny had become unpopular. Unable to overthrow the tyranny by force, they undertook to subvert the oracle at Delphi. Gaining the gratitude of the Delphic priests by their generosity in building the temple of Apollo, they convinced them (according to Herodotus, by a bribe) to reply to whatever request the Spartans might make that they should free Athens. After repeated messages to this effect, the Spartans decided to comply, despite their earlier friendship with the Peisistratids.

Hippias defeated the first Spartan attempt to expel the tyranny with the help of Thessaly. In the second attempt, the Spartans arrived with a larger force under their king, but they were successful only when the Peisistratid children fell into their hands. In order to retrieve the children, Hippias agreed to withdraw, taking refuge in Persian territory in Asia Minor. He did not abandon his hope of return, however. During the Persian Wars it was the aged former tyrant who guided the Persians across the Aegean with the expectation that they would reinstate him as ruler of Athens after their victory.

The involvement of the Alkmeonids in the fall of Hippias demonstrates that the power of the aristocratic families and their propensity for factional strife had not died out during the rule of the tyrants, although the difficulty encountered by those trying to overthrow the regime also attests to the strength of the new order in Athens. Yet under the tyranny too much had depended upon the personal management of the Peisistratids, and there were no safeguards to prevent the misuse of power; nor was there any permanent and institutional solution to the regionally based factionalism of aristocratic politics. The need was for constitutional reforms that would eliminate the undue power of these factions and their aristocratic leaders.

The Reforms of Kleisthenes[35]

Among the first measures taken after the expulsion of Hippias were the re-enactment of an old law outlawing any person attempting or aiding in the establishment of a tyranny, and a revision of the citizen rolls to exclude "those of impure descent." These "new citizens" included not only the supporters and mercenaries of the tyrant, but also the descendants of craftsmen admitted to the city by the laws of Solon. To the discontent of those excluded was added a return to political strife between rival aristocratic families. The renewed political struggles focused on two candidates for the Chief Archonship in 508/507: the Alkmaeonid Kleisthenes, who had experienced both exile and service as archon under the Peisistratids and had joined the Spartans in expelling them; and a certain Isagoras, who seems to have come to terms with the tyranny, remaining in Athens throughout its duration. Isagoras at first held the upper hand, winning the election for the Chief Archonship. Kleisthenes then took a revolutionary step that was to lead eventually to the establishment of democracy in Athens; he took the people into partnership as his *hetairoi*, a term traditionally applied to the small circle of aristocratic friends who provided each other with political support. In appealing to the people, Kleisthenes promised a comprehensive program of reform. Isagoras retaliated in aristocratic fashion by calling for assistance from his guest-friend, the Spartan king Kleomenes, who had just recently been instrumental in expelling the tyrants.

Kleomenes helped Isagoras first by calling for the expulsion of the accursed Alkmaeonids; as a result, Kleisthenes at once went into exile. Soon after, Kleomenes arrived with a contingent of Spartan troops to see to the expulsion of other Alkmaeonids (700 in number). He also demanded the dissolution of the Council and entrusted the government to a group of 300 of Isagoras' supporters. But the Council resisted, and the people joined them, besieging Isagoras and the Spartans on the Acropolis. On the third day, the Spartans were allowed to leave Athens; some of Isagoras' followers were arrested and executed, but he escaped, fleeing from Attica.

With the expulsion of the Spartans and the flight of Isagoras, the way was open for the reforms that Kleisthenes had proposed. These reforms created an entirely new political structure in which ten new tribes replaced the traditional four Ionian tribes. The old tribes had

Source Analysis

 erodotus 5.66, 69–76. What were Kleisthenes' motives, according to Herodotus?

been based on the aristocratic *gene* (clans), which had great local influence stemming from their wealth, land ownership, and control of cults. By alliances among themselves, these aristocratic families had been able to control all the highest offices in Athens. But their exclusivity and rivalries had been largely responsible for bringing on the tyranny, and after its fall they again threatened the stability of the Athenian state. In contrast to the old Ionian tribes, the Kleisthenic tribes were constituted not on a basis of ancestry but on residence; membership was determined by the **deme**, or village where a man resided at the time of the reorganization; deme membership thereafter was hereditary. It was probably part of Kleisthenes' appeal to the demos that this served to include those who had been excluded by the recent revision of the citizenship rolls, including the descendants of craftsmen whom Solon had admitted. All citizens, new and old, would start as equals under the new system.

The ten tribes were constructed from the demes in such a way as to break up the regional power blocks of the aristocracy. In order to achieve this, a complex arrangement was set up. The 139(?) demes were arranged in thirty groups, or ***trittyes*** (thirds; singular: *trittys*); there were ten *trittyes* in each of three regions: the city, the coast, and inland. Each tribe was constructed of one *trittys* from each of the three regions (hence a *trittys* was a third of a tribe). The regional divisions and the *trittyes*, insofar as they can be conjectured from the evidence, are shown on Map 7.

The result of Kleisthenes' reform was a system in which no tribe had a regional basis; each tribe had residents from each region (hills, plain, and coast), as well as residents from Athens itself. Thus no tribe could be predominant by virtue of having more members resident in the city, where they could easily attend the Assembly, and men from all parts of Attica would be brought together in the administration of the affairs of the state.

After Kleisthenes' reforms, the basic political units were no longer the aristocratic families, or *gene*, but the *demes*, or villages. These now became the guarantors of citizenship and the official basis of citizen identity. A man could only be a citizen if he was accepted as a member of a *deme*, and his official name designated not the name of his father, as formerly, but the name of his *deme*. Thus the historian Thucydides, formerly identified as Thucydides son of Sophillus, became officially Thucydides of Halimus (although most Athenians continued to refer to themselves informally in the old way).

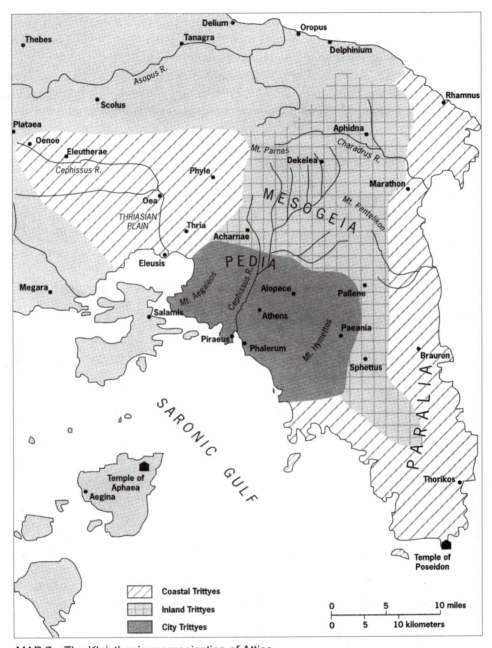

MAP 7 The Kleisthenic reorganization of Attica
Adapted from John S. Trail, 1975. *The Political Organization of Attica: A Study of the demes, Trittyes, and Phylai, and their Representation in the Athenian Council.* Courtesy of the American School of Classical Studies at Athens.

In the decades following the reforms, the ten tribes provided the structural basis for the other organs of government. The army was marshaled by tribes, and from this time on, men from various parts of Attica fought side by side. Each tribal contingent was led by a general, and thus there were ten generals. A new Council of 500, which replaced the Council of 400, was composed of 50 members from each tribe. A *prytany*, or executive body, was created from the Council; each tribe held the *prytany* for one month of the ten-month Attic year. The months themselves were divided into five periods of seven days, and ten men served for a seven-day period; of these, one was chosen each day to be the President. Popular courts were also established on the basis of the tribes: 6,000 jurors were chosen by lot, and from these, 5,000 were selected each day in which the courts were in session. The 5,000 were divided into smaller courts composed of hundreds, and even thousands of jurors. Such large juries were thought to be a safeguard against bribery). Whereas Solon had constituted the Assembly, acting as the Heliaea, as an appeals court, now the people served on primary, independent courts as well, although the Council of the Areopagus continued to judge cases involving religious violations, such as homicide.

A practice known as **ostracism** was probably also introduced as a part of Kleisthenes' reforms, although it was first used only in 487. Ostracism was a sort of reverse popularity contest: the man who received the most votes had to leave Athens for ten years. It was an honorable exile, however, and the ostracized man retained his citizenship and property. Each year a preliminary vote was taken to determine if an ostracism was to be held; if there was a majority in favor, the actual ostracism vote was taken. Voters wrote the name of the person they wanted to banish on broken pieces of pottery, or *ostraca*; hence the term, ostracism. The purpose was to prevent any one man from gaining too much power—in other words, to prevent a return to tyranny—but in time it became a political tool. It was last used in 417, when two "candidates" managed to gang up and throw the vote to a third man.

Kleisthenes' reforms ended the monopoly on political power by the aristocratic families, as well as the regional factionalism that had plagued Athens for so long. They gave every citizen a share in government by membership in a deme; not only could he attend the Assembly, he could also serve in the courts, and in many case he would be judged by his peers if he came before the court himself; he might serve on the Council and on a *prytany*; he might even be president for a day. Thus the reforms gave the people more power and rights than they had had in the past. Nevertheless, the result was not a democracy, for the highest offices were still restricted by law to the upper classes. The name applied to the new system of government seems to have been *isonomia*—equality before the laws. But even though Athens was not yet a democracy, Kleisthenes' reforms laid the basis for it by the creation of a deme-based structure of government and by two new institutions: the board of ten generals and the popular courts. These turned out perhaps unexpectedly to be the key factors in the development of the radical democracy of the fifth century.

SUGGESTIONS FOR FURTHER READING

P. J. Rhodes (1992), "The Athenian Revolution," chap. 4 in D. M. Lewis et al, eds., *The Cambridge Ancient History*, 2nd ed., vol. V.

J. Neils, ed. (1992), *Goddess and Polis: The Panathenaic Festival in Ancient Athens*.

MAP STUDY

Regions of Attica: Paralia, Pedia, Mesogeia
Attic towns: Brauron, Eleusis, Marathon, Salamis, Thorikos
Beyond Attica: Hellespont, Sigeum, Samos, Delos

ENDNOTES

[1]This is argued by R. A. Padgug (1972), "Eleusis and the Union of Attica," *Greek, Roman and Byzantine Studies* 13:135–150.

[2]A. Andrewes (1982), *Cambridge Ancient History*, 2nd ed., vol. III, part 3, 363; S. Diamant (1982), "Theseus and the Unification of Attica," *Hesperia* 19: 38–47; A. Snodgrass (1982), *Cambridge Ancient History* vol III, part 1, 668–669, 676–678. 687.

[3]Or perhaps to an earlier date for the polis, as suggested, mainly on the basis of Homer, by K. Raaflaub (1993), "Homer to Solon: The Rise of the *Polis*, The Written Sources," in M. H. Hansen, ed. (1993), *The Ancient Greek City-State*, 41–105, 75–80.

[4]J. N. Coldstream (1974), *The Formation of the Greek Polis: Aristotle and Archaeology*.

[5]E. T. H. Brann (1962), *The Athenian Agora*, vol. VIII, *Late Geometric and Classical Pottery*, 113. Brann, in the publication of the excavations on the *agora*, suggested that the area ceased to be used for burials because an increasing population needed the space for housing.

[6]See N. J. Richardson (1974), *The Homeric Hymn to Demeter*, 5–11. A still later date, in the sixth century, was suggested by W. R. Connor (1970), "Theseus in Classical Athens," in A. G. Ward (1970), *The Quest for Theseus*, 143–174. Richardson viewed the attribution to Theseus as an invention of political propaganda by the Athenian tyrant Peisistratus, basing his argument on the report of Plutarch (Themistocles, 20) that Peisistratus had a verse dishonoring Theseus deleted from the Homeric Hymns and one favorable to him added to the Odyssey. But it is difficult to see how this revision of the Homeric texts could have been forgotten already in Thucydides' day.

[7]See Robert Parker (1996), *Miasma: Pollution and Purification in Early Greek Religion*.

[8]Aristotle, *Ath. Pol.* 1; Plutarch, *Solon* 12; Diogenes Laertes 1.111.

[9]See R. Stroud (1968), *Drakon's Law on Homicide*, 1–18.

[10]Aristotle. *Ath. Pol.* 2.2.

[11]P. J. Rhodes (1984), *Aristotle. The Athenian Constitution*, Commentary on 2.2. Andrewes (above, n. 2), 180.

[12]For example, Andrewes (above, n. 2), 380–381.

[13]On archaic Aegina, see Thomas J. Figueira (1991), *Athens and Aigina in the Age of Imperial Colonization*.

[14]Aristotle. *Ath. Pol.* 6.1.

[15]Gregory C. Chirichigno (1993), *Debt-Slavery in Israel and the Ancient Near East.*

[16]M. Lambert (1972), "L'Expansion de Lagash au Temps d'Enténéma," *Rivista degli studi orientali* 1–22; Chirichigno (above, n. 15), 56.

[17]Chirichigno (above, n. 15), 85–92.

[18]J. N. Postgate (1976), Fifty Neo-Assyrian Legal Documents, 21–22; N. P. Lemche (1979), "Andurarum and Mešarum: Comments on the Problem of Social Edicts and Their Application in the Ancient Near East," *Journal of Near Eastern Studies* 38: 11–22.

[19]Plutarch, *Solon 2.* This tradition seems to be independent of another report by Plutarch (*Solon*, 25–28), that Solon left Athens for ten years after his reforms in order to keep the Athenians from trying to get him to modify the laws, and that he traveled to Egypt and Cyprus and held (anachronistic) meetings with famous men, including Croesus and Aesopus.

[20]M. L. Finley (1983), "Debt Bondage and Slavery," *Economy and Society in Ancient Greece*, 150–166. See also Raphael Sealey (1994), *The Justice of the Greeks*, chap. 2.

[21]Plutarch, *Pelop*, 23.4 applies the term to hoplites.

[22]Plutarch, *Solon* , 19.2; Andrewes (above, n. 2), 387–388.

[23]Solon, Frag. 32.

[24]Solon, Frag. 5 (West), tr. N. Demand.

[25]Solon, Frag. 36.26–27 (West), tr. N. Demand.

[26]Herodotus 1.59.6; Thucydides 6.54.6.

[27]The evidence for the dates is conflicting; see Andrewes (above, n. 2), 398–401; Sealey (above, n. 20), chap. 2.

[28]See John Travlos (1971), *Pictorial Dictionary of Ancient Athens.*

[29]C. M. Kraay (1976), *Archaic and Classical Greek Coins*, 25–26; Andrewes (above, n. 2), 409.

[30]J. Neils, ed. (1992), *Goddess and Polis: The Panathenaic Festival in Ancient Athens*, gives a full, illustrated discussion of the vases and their use as prizes.

[31]John Boardman (1972), "Herakles, Peisistratos and Sons," *Revue Archéologique*: 57–72. Arguments against this interpretation are offered by J. M. Cook (1987), "Pots and Pisistratan Propaganda," *Journal of Hellenic Studies* 107: 167–169.

[32]Frank Kolb (1977), "Die Bau-, Religions- und Kulturpolitik der Peisistratiden," *Jahrbuch des deutschen archäologischen Instituts* 92: 99–138, 133.

[33]Herdotus 6.107–108. His participation in the expedition is briefly noted by Thucydides, 6.59.

[34]On Athenian coinage, see C. M. Kraay (1976), *Archaic and Classical Greek Coins.*

[35]For the scholarly reconstruction of Kleisthenes' reforms, see D. M. Lewis (1963), "Cleisthenes and Attica," *Historia* 12: 22–40.

8

ARCHAIC IONIA:
GREEKS AND PERSIANS

THE IONIAN ENLIGHTENMENT

Some of the earliest developments in Greek culture took place in the cities of Ionia on the coast of Asia Minor. These cities, according to tradition, had been settled by refugees fleeing the mainland in the Ionian Migration at the close of the Bronze Age (see Chapter 4). By the fifth century, the Athenians laid claim to sponsorship of the Migration and hence to the status of mother city of the Ionians. We do not know to what extent this claim was justified, but the dialect spoken by the Athenians, Attic Greek, was a form of Ionic Greek, and many of their institutions were similar to those of the Ionian cities.

During the Archaic period, the Ionian Greeks also had close ties with their non-Greek neighbors, the Lydians, and later, with the Persians, who were heirs to the ancient civilizations of the Near East. Despite difficulties, especially with the Persians, the expanded horizons that these contacts brought contributed greatly to the flourishing of Greek culture in what has been termed the *Ionian Enlightenment*. Expressions of this cultural and intellectual ferment appeared in the development of geography and history, and especially in the crucial shift from mythological to natural explanations for the cosmos that was made by the Presocratic philosophers. In a political sense, the climax of these interactions was the Persian Wars, in which the Greeks of the mainland successfully defended themselves against attempts by the Persian kings to extend their empire into mainland Greece. However, even after this Greek victory, the Persians remained important factors in Greek history until Alexander the Great conquered the Great King of Persia and took the crown of empire for himself.

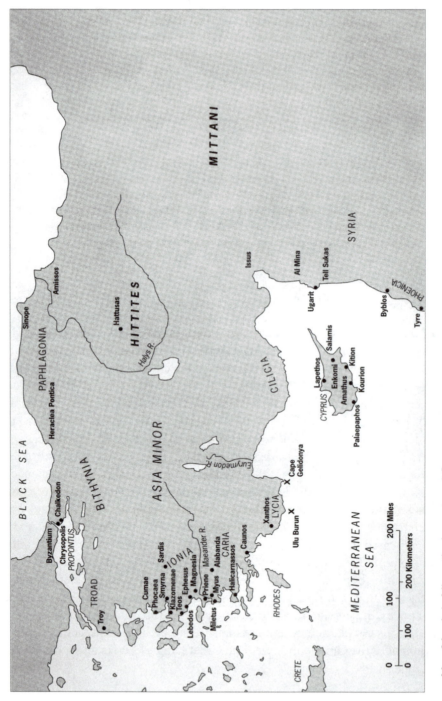

Map 8A   Asia Minor, the Levant, and Cyprus

The Greeks were inclined to frame their ideas in terms of polarities—freedom/slavery, male/female, self-rule/tyranny, ourselves/others—and to use these pairs of opposites to define their concepts. After the Greek victory over the Persians, these non-Greeks came to serve as the "Other" in terms of which the Greeks could better define themselves. Persians were portrayed as slaves fighting under the lash, as feminized, as subjected to tyranny, while the Greeks defined themselves by all the opposites of these qualities: free men who governed themselves. But there were also times when the Persians played a more active role, providing the Greeks with their own version of a Cold War. Just as we cannot understand the history of the United States in the late twentieth and early twenty-first centuries without considering the Soviet Union and the Moslem world, so we cannot understand Greek history of the Archaic and Classical periods without keeping in mind the Persians.

For much of the history of this period, including the history of Persia, the main literary source is the fifth-century Greek historian Herodotus, a citizen of Halicarnassus in Asia Minor and himself a product of the Ionian Enlightenment.[1] Although the subject of Herodotus' history was the Persian Wars of the fifth century, he traced the great confrontation back to the origins of the Persian Empire and investigated in detail many of the peoples encompassed by that empire, from the Scythians to the Egyptians. It is true that Herodotus saw events from a Greek point of view and that his sources were sometimes less than ideal from the standpoint of the modern historian. For example, we do not know to what extent Herodotus could understand the languages of some of the places that he visited, and local guides and interpreters then and now may not always provide the most accurate information. Nonetheless, Herodotus provides the only connected account of these events. Two points are important to keep in mind in evaluating his work as history, however. First, when they exist, we must also consider and compare primary sources, such as inscriptions and official records, even though they are sometimes problematic: official inscriptions tell the official side of the story, and even official records provide only bare-bones facts that require interpretation.[2] Second, we must keep in mind the cultural and intellectual context in which the historian himself worked and how this may have affected his work.

Herodotus as Historian

The historian Herodotus was a native of Halicarnassus in Caria. At the time, Halicarnassus was ruled by the Persians under a local Carian dynast. Some of the historian's relatives bore Carian names, suggesting that the family, like many in Halicarnassus, was a mixed one.[3] Herodotus' family seems to have been active in the political life of Halicarnassus,[4] for they were sent into exile at some point early in the historian's life. The family found refuge on the nearby Greek island of Samos, and the historian recounts at some length, and as a matter of pride, a number of the achievements of the tyrant of Samos.

Herodotus did not live out his life in Samos, however, but spent much of his time traveling, visiting lands ranging from Egypt and Libya to Babylon and Scythia. The ancient evidence that he visited Athens is not strong, but his descriptions of the city, the central role of

Athens in his *Histories*, and his visits to nearby Greek sites, as well as to far more distant and exotic sites, make it most likely. Moreover, in 444 he participated in the Athenian foundation of the panhellenic settlement of Thurii in southern Italy, where he settled, although some believe that he returned to Athens at the end of his life.[5] His work must have been widely known, for he is reported to have given readings at the Olympic games, as he probably also did in Athens.

Herodotus fit well into the expanded world of the Persian Empire, in which travelers' tales were a popular form of entertainment. A reflection of this interest in the wider world had appeared in one of the historian's predecessors, Hecataeus of Miletus, whose work, now mostly preserved in fragments, described the lands and peoples he encountered during his travels in the Mediterranean and the Black Sea area. Herodotus' own interest in foreign peoples led him to devote the second book of his *Histories* to an extended account of his researches in Egypt, and many other passages, such as his descriptions of the Scythians and of the peoples of India, are ethnographic in nature. But he is, of course, best known for his account of the Persian Wars.

In the opening passage of his *Histories*, Herodotus reports his motive in composing the work: so that the great deeds of men, the great and marvelous works produced by both the Greeks and the Barbarians, and the reasons why they fought each other, might not be forgotten. In this he was following in the epic tradition of Homer, and that tradition colors his vision throughout his work. Perhaps most important for us to keep in mind is the oral nature of that tradition, and the fact that the methods by which oral cultures preserve and transmit knowledge are fundamentally different from those of literate cultures.[6] Interesting stories are easier to remember than bare facts, and in the telling of these stories, even more interesting details are often added. We see this in Herodotus, who reports the information as he heard it, relying as much as possible on the reports of eyewitnesses and on what he had himself seen and heard (*autopsy*). He includes many legends and folktales, and at times even offers alternative—and contradictory—accounts. But there is no evidence that he invented tall tales, or lied, as some modern scholars have charged.[7] And some of the reports that scholars have passed off as mere legend or folktale have actually turned out to have a basis in fact. A wonderful example is the historian's tale of the gold-bearing ants.

Source Analysis

R ead Herotodus 3.102–105, his account of the gold-bearing ants.[1] Then check out this website: http://www.marmotburrow.ucls.edu/goldants.html by Marlise Simons: *The New York Times*: Nov. 25, 1996.

While coming from an oral tradition, Herodotus also reflected an emerging literate environment. Although he gave oral performances of his work, it was essentially a written work, and it was a work in prose, not in the traditional form of poetry. Moreover, unlike the poets, Herodotus did not rely on the Muses to reveal the truth about the past, but set out to investigate it for himself. He framed his topic broadly—not simply the war, but everything that came before and contributed to it in some way, among both Greeks and barbarians, going back to "the beginning," which he located in the kidnapping of women by Phoenician traders that was quickly reciprocated by Greeks. In his search for answers, he traveled widely in both Greek and barbarian lands, listening to the stories of merchants, priests, tour guides, veterans of the war—anyone who had a story to tell. Above all, it was this spirit of inquiry (*historie*) that has led to his being called the Father of History.

Ionia and the Origins of Greek Philosophy

Western Anatolia served as a zone of contact between the Greeks and the western Persian Empire.[8] Out of the cultural interactions in this area came not only the world's first written history, but one of the most important intellectual achievements of the Greeks, the development of natural philosophy.[9] The first man to be given the title of philosopher was a Milesian named Thales, who is traditionally dated to ca. 640–546.[10] A number of the practical activities attributed to him reflect experience with the learning of the Near East. Thus Herodotus reports that the common opinion among the Greeks was that Thales enabled Croesus' army to cross the Halys River by diverting its flow (Hdt. 1.75). Manipulation of rivers for irrigation had a long history in the Near East, and awareness of these methods may be reflected in this achievement of Thales, although Herodotus himself skeptically believed that the army used the bridges that were there in his own day. More definitive of intellectual contact is Herodotus' report that Thales predicted the year of the eclipse of May 28, 585, that brought the battle between Lydians and Persians to an end (Hdt. 1.74). Traditionally, the Greeks had viewed eclipses as omens sent to men by the gods. If Thales could have even framed the problem of how to predict an eclipse, he must have considered the phenomenon not as an omen sent by the gods, but as a natural occurrence. To have been successful in his prediction, he must have had access at least to records of previous eclipses, probably Babylonian records accessible in Sardis, and to have been lucky besides, for even these records would not have allowed him to predict that the eclipse would be visible in Ionia.[11]

In cosmology, Thales is said to have held that the earth floats on water, reflecting a Near Eastern concept that contrasts with the traditional Greek mythological picture of an earth that is surrounded by the waters of Ocean.[12] He is also reported by Aristotle to have identified water as the basic substance of the cosmos, that material out of which all other things are created and into which they pass away (Frags. 86, 87 KRS). The idea of a single basic substance was a startling innovation. Thales could have arrived at this idea from reflecting on the various forms that water can take, from airy mist to solid ice, or on the fact that the fetus begins its life in water. Unfortunately, we cannot be sure, for we do not have Thales' own words, and Aristotle tended to read his own ideas in the work of his predecessors.

On the other hand, there is good evidence that Thales' successors took the momentous step of explaining the cosmos in terms of changes in a basic natural substance. Thus the Milesian philosopher Anaximander, by tradition a pupil of Thales and thus dated to 610/609–547/546, postulated that all things arose out of, and passed away into, the *Apeiron* (the Unlimited), a boundless and undefined substance. He described this process in terms of the human values of justice and reparation: "for they pay penalty and retribution to each other for their injustice according to the assessment of Time" (Frag. 143 KRS). He also seems to have held an evolutionary theory about the origin of animals and men: "Living creatures came into being from moisture evaporated by the sun. Man was originally similar to another creature—that is, to a fish" (Frag. 139 KRS). In describing the workings of the heavenly bodies, he postulated not gods but a mechanical system of fiery wheels with apertures through which the fire appeared in the form of stars, the moon, and in the outer ring, the sun (Frag. 125–28 KRS). M. L. West draws attention to the parallel with the heavenly wheels that Ezekiel saw near Babylon in 593–592 BC, and to the fact that the order of the heavenly bodies in Anaximander's theory was the same as that held by the Persians.[13]

The third Milesian philosopher, Anaximenes, by tradition the pupil of Anaximander and thus dated to 585–525, held that the basic substance was *Aer* (something like air), which by a process of rarification, became fire, and by compression, water and then earth (Frag. 143 KRS). This was a theory that proved to have a long life; in the fifth century it was adopted by the philosopher Diogenes of Apollonia on the Black Sea coast, and the comic poet Aristophanes attributed it to Socrates in his play, *Clouds*; it appears in the sophistic treatise *Breaths* in the Hippocratic Corpus of medical texts, and a fourth-century historian of medicine attributed it to Hippocrates himself.

In neighboring Ephesus the philosopher Heraclitus, whose floruit was fixed at 504–501, taught that at the basis of all things was the *Logos* (Word), a term that probably meant measure or proportion. (The same word is, of course, used in the Gospel according to John.) Heraclitus seems to have meant that all things, though apparently plural and discrete, are really part of an ordered arrangement. Heraclitus used a number of metaphors for the cosmic process, and his deliberately obscure and oracular style make consistent interpretation difficult. Prominent among the metaphors was strife: "It is necessary to know that war is common and right is strife and that all things happen by strife and necessity" (Frag. 214 KRS). Another metaphor was fire: "All things are an equal exchange for fire and fire for all things, as goods are for gold and gold for goods" (Frag. 222 KRS). Fire is sometimes identified as Heraclitus' basic stuff, like the *Aer* and *Apeiron* of the Milesians.

In whatever metaphor it was expressed, for Heraclitus the world was in a constant state of flux. This made self-identity a puzzle: "Heraclitus somewhere says that all things are in process and nothing stays still, and likening existing things to the stream of a river, he says that you would not step twice into the same river" (Frag. 217 KRS). A similar insecurity affects human knowledge in general. Heraclitus recognized the joint roles of perception and reason in knowledge, but saw them as problematic: "Evil witnesses are eyes and ears for men, if they have souls that do not understand their language" (Frag. 201 KRS). The result is relativism: "Sea is the most pure and the most polluted water; for fishes it is drinkable and salutary, but for men it is undrinkable and deleterious" (Frag. 202 KRS). Nor was certainty to be found in traditional religion, for Heraclitus was scornful of traditional Greek religious practices: "They vainly purify themselves of blood-guilt by defiling themselves with blood, as though one who had stepped into mud were to wash with mud; he would seem to be mad, if any of men noticed him doing this. Further, they pray to these statues, as if one were to carry on a conversation with houses, not recognizing the true nature of gods or demi-gods" (Frag. 244 KRS).

The possible debt of fire in Heraclitus' system to the role fire plays in the Persian religion of Zoroaster has been noted since antiquity.[14] In the time of Darius, Persian religion was in a state of transition from the early Indo-European and pre-Indo-European polytheistic faith to the religion revealed by the prophet Zoroaster.[15] In its fully developed form, Zoroastrianism is a dualistic religion in which the forces of Justice and Truth, in the person of the god Ahura Mazda, battle against the forces of Evil and the Lie, led by Ahriman. Zoroaster emphasized the purity and value of fire, which he made central to ritual practices. The only altars were fire altars, which were often portrayed on official Persian reliefs. In the time of Darius, however, the religion was still in flux, with some older practices still in effect; thus in some respects Herodotus' description of Persian religious practices and beliefs differs from Zoroastrianism in its fully developed form.[16] It is true that fire plays a central role in both, and Heraclitus may well have been influenced in his choice of the metaphor by his awareness of its role in Zoroastrianism. Nevertheless, the parallel is considered by many to be too general to be very significant, and many of the discussions that suggest a connection are not rigorous enough in their treatment of the sources to proceed beyond speculation and conjecture.

But whether or not we can accept every hypothesis of eastern influence on the Presocratics, it was the interaction of eastern and western traditions in the Ionian border zone between Greece and the East that stimulated the formulation of new ways of understanding the world. By turning away from traditional mythological explanations and toward natural hypotheses, the Ionian thinkers—Thales, Anaximander, Anaximenes, and Heraclitus—prepared the necessary groundwork for the subsequent speculations of Parmenides, Empedocles, Democritus, as well as for the naturalistic medicine of the Hippocratic doctors. Ultimately, these changes provided the basis for the development of today's modern medicine and science.

THE LYDIANS AND THE GREEKS

In the sixth century the kingdom of the Lydians rose to prominence in Anatolia. They were a wealthy and sophisticated people whose capital lay on the two most important trade routes between the Aegean coast and the ancient civilizations of the Near East. Their territory also contained extensive resources of gold, silver, and electrum (a natural mixture of gold and silver). As neighbors to the Greek cities of Ionia, they had frequent trade and even social relations, and they often employed their wealth in seeking the favor of the Greek gods, as the foundation deposit of the temple of Artemis at Ephesus attests. But the Lydians also routinely attacked the Greeks in the coastal cities.

One of these raids—the sack and destruction of the Greek city of Smyrna by the Lydian king Alyattes—is well attested by archaeological evidence, although Herodotus mentions it only briefly.[17] The city of Smyrna was protected by formidable walls, but the Lydians built a huge siege mound that overtopped the walls and allowed them to attack the defenders from above. The remains of the mound today still reach to over 21 meters in height, while the city walls at their highest reached only 10 meters. In constructing the mound, the Lydians used materials from houses that stood outside the walls, and the fill contained construction materials—mud brick, worked stones, and roof timbers—that reveal Lydian construction methods. Household items found in the fill provide clues to daily life, and arrowheads provide information about fighting weapons, suggesting that both sides employed foreign mercenaries.

After the death of King Alyattes, his son Croesus continued intermittent attacks on the Greeks. He also introduced a significant innovation: instead of demanding "gifts" on an arbitrary and irregular basis, he instituted the payment of a regular tribute. While this was an infringement on Greek independence, it had its compensations, for it allowed the Ionians to live in peace and to benefit from economic and cultural interchange with their barbarian neighbors.

The Lydians invented the use of coins, probably initially for the payment of mercenaries rather than for trade or everyday purchases. The Greeks adopted the use of coinage from them, and the first Greek coins, which were found in the foundation deposit of the temple of Artemis that Croesus built in Greek Ephesus, show the evolution of the technique in Greek hands. These earliest Greek coins in Ionia are dated to ca. 600; in comparison, the earliest Athenian coinage, the *Wappenmünzen*, began only in the 550s, and the widely used Athenian Owls, featuring the head of Athena and the owl, date from ca. 525.

Croesus outdid all the earlier Lydian kings in seeking the favor of the gods by his gifts to the oracular shrines of the Greeks. Among the gifts that he sent to Delphi, Herodotus describes the figure of a lion of pure gold that originally weighed ten talents (about 820 pounds); a figure of a woman in gold three cubits (about five feet) high, said to have been a portrayal of the baker of the Persian king Cyrus; and a silver mixing bowl that held 600 amphoras of wine (about 3,600 gallons), said to have been the work of Theodoros of Samos, a Greek from the island where Herodotus lived with his family in exile. The Lydian king also sent a shield and spear of solid gold to the oracular shrine of the god Amphiaraos in Boeotia, which were kept in the shrine of Apollo in Thebes in Herodotus' day. We can assume that the historian himself saw all these treasures on visits to these shrines, and that he learned about Theodoros' accomplishments during his stay in Samos.

Croesus was the primary contributor to the building of the Ionic-style temple of Artemis at Ephesus. Designed by the architect Chersiphron, it was the largest building in the Greek world at that time—377 feet long and 180 feet wide—and the first temple to be built entirely of marble. Pliny relates that the temple had 127 columns, each 60 feet high, and, according to Herodotus, Croesus dedicated most of them (Hdt. I.92). The Roman writer Pliny reports that, since it was constructed on marshy ground, the foundation was laid on a bed of packed charcoal and sheepskins to avoid damage from earthquakes. Today only one restored column stands, the high water table of the marshy site making further restoration difficult.

The temple of Apollo and its oracle at Didyma was built at about the same time (the mid-sixth century) as the temple of Artemis at Ephesus. To rival the temple at Ephesis, the builders employed one of the same architects, and the building had approximately the same dimensions. The temple centered upon an earlier sanctuary, built in the eighth century, at the site of an ancient cult center that consisted of a spring and a sacred grove of laurel trees. The large, unroofed Ionic temple was built to enclose the cult complex, to which a small temple was added. In 494, after the Ionian Revolt, the Persians sacked and laid waste to the temple, as well as to near-by Miletos.

Figure 8.1   The remains of the temple at Artemis at Ephesus.
Photo by N. Demand.

Figure 8.2   The remains of the temple of Apollo at Didyma.
Photo by N. Demand.

For the modern historian, Herodotus' descriptions of the wealth of the Lydian kings provide valuable economic evidence. In the background we can see Greek craftsmen—Theodoros of Samos and other workers skilled in gold and silver work—as well as the countless anonymous workers who helped to build the great temples at Ephesus and Didyma. The period was clearly one of economic prosperity for the Ionian Greeks. In addition to their contacts with the riches of Lydia, the position of their cities on the coast, within easy access to nearby islands, was well-suited to trade by sea. According to Herodotus, it was a ship captain from the island of Samos who was the first Greek to reach the silver-rich land of Tartessos in Spain,[18] and the Ionian cities were prominent among those that the Egyptian pharaoh allowed to establish a trading post at Naukratis in Egypt.

Evidence on a more personal level of Greek prosperity and the close relationships that developed between Lydians and Ionian Greeks is provided by the poet Sappho, who lived on the off-shore island of Lesbos around the end of the seventh century. For her, Lydia was a source of the latest luxury fashions and a place to which her young friends sometimes went as brides. Her poems help to give us some insight into the way in which Greek women (admittedly, the privileged among them) viewed their own lives. Thus they provide a counterbalance to the overwhelmingly male-oriented picture of women that we find in our major sources such as Herodotus. In this fragmentary poem, Sappho consoles a girl whose friend is now a wife in Sardis:[19]

> Sardis . . . .
>   Often thinking of you . . . .
> So that . . . .
>   . . . . regarded . . . .
> thinking you like a well-known goddess ...
> She delighted in your song.
>
> But now in Lydia she is conspicuous among women,
> As, when the sun having set,
> The rosy-fingered moon
> Surpasses all the stars,
> And spreads her light upon the salty sea,
> And upon the meadows rich in flowers,
> And the dew is shed in beauty,
> And roses bloom, and soft flowery clover.
>
> Often she wanders about
> Remembering gentle Atthis with longing,
> Her delicate mind consumed by your fate.

Herodotus tells us that Sappho's brother, Charaxus, bought a well-known prostitute at Naukratis for a large sum of money and freed her, for which the poet strongly criticized him.[20] His presence at Naukratis, a Greek trading post in Egypt, whether on a trading mission or for adventure, reflects the mobility and the foreign connections that formed the basis of Ionian prosperity.

THE COMING OF THE PERSIANS[21]

Meanwhile, farther east, developments were underway that would soon dramatically affect the course of Near Eastern and Greek history. The first step in this process was taken in 612, after the death of the Assyrian emperor Assurbanipal, when the Medes, an Indo-European-speaking tribal people in Iran, joined Babylon in revolt against their Assyrian overlords. The rebels succeeded in sacking the Assyrian capital, Nineveh, and in one of the great mysteries of ancient history, the Assyrian empire suddenly collapsed, apparently weakened by a struggle for the succession. As a result, for more than half a century control of the Near East was fragmented, divided among the Medes, Neo-Babylonians, Egyptians, and Lydians.

From 590 to 585, the Medes, under their king Kyaxares, fought the Lydians in a war that was brought to an unexpected end by the eclipse of 585. The philosopher Thales of Ionian Miletus was said to have predicted the eclipse (the story is told by Herodotus, 1.74). The two

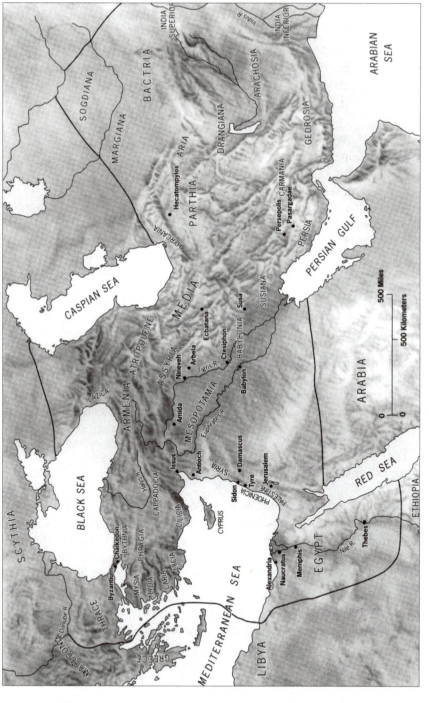

Map 8B   The Persian Empire at its greatest extent

sides concluded a treaty, sealed with the marriage of Astyages, the son of the Median king, to the daughter of the Lydian king, which set the boundary between the kingdoms at the Halys River in central Anatolia.

When Astyages succeeded to the kingship of the Medes, according to Herodotus he had a dream that a child of his daughter would supplant him. To prevent this, he first married her to a Persian, a group subject to the Medes; then when she bore a son, Cyrus, he had the child exposed to die. But Cyrus was miraculously saved and raised by a herdsman; later, when he learned the truth, he vowed to take vengence on Astyages. The Persians accepted him as their leader, with the hope of freeing themselves from subjection to the Medes. Their hopes were fulfilled in 559, when Astyages led an attack against the Persians; Cyrus persuaded the Median army to rebel, and they handed Astyages over to him as a prisoner. Cyrus, who was noted in tradition for his wisdom and clemency, did not kill his captive, but kept him beside him until he died a natural death.[22]

Cyrus, with a legacy from both the Persians and the Medes, forged the two peoples into a single political entity, "the Medes and the Persians," in which positions of responsibility and authority were shared by both peoples. This provides the first illustration of the Persian practice of incorporating conquered peoples into the administration of newly acquired territory. The system proved overwhelmingly successful in the long run, as the Medes and the Persians went on to establish the first effective working empire.

The newly formed coalition of the Medes and Persians and its growing power soon provoked opposition. In 547 Croesus, the son of Alyattes and brother-in-law of Astyages, was king of Lydia (we noted him above as the patron of the great temple at Ephesus). Lydia had been an ally of the Medes since the peace treaty of 585, but Croesus, wishing to avenge the capture and imprisonment of Astyages, and probably concerned about the growing power of the Persians, decided to attack them. As the story is told by Herodotus,[23] Croesus first asked the advice of the oracle of Apollo at Delphi. Yet despite the rich gifts that he had lavished upon the god in the past, he received an ambiguous and essentially deceptive reply: If he crossed the river Halys, a great kingdom would fall. Misled by pride, he interpreted this in the way he wanted to hear it, and confident of victory, he led his army across the river. But the kingdom that fell was his own, for in the war that ensued, the Persians besieged and took Sardis and captured Croesus. Croesus was placed upon a pyre to be burnt, but according to tradition, he was miraculously saved by the god Apollo, and Cyrus, impressed by Croesus' wisdom, made him his friend and advisor.[24]

The victory of the Persian king Cyrus over Croesus had far-reaching consequences for the Greeks in Anatolia. The city of Miletus, which had had the most favorable terms with the Lydians, quickly made terms with the Persians, but the other Greek cities resisted, and one after another they were conquered. Herodotus relates stories of heroic resistance. In Lycia the people of Xanthos committed mass suicide rather than submit (Hdt. 1.176), and two Ionian cities escaped by flight. The people of Phocaea sailed away to the west and eventually founded Elea in southern Italy, and the Teians established a new city, Abdera, on the north shore of the Aegean (Hdt. 1.164–67). The people of Knidos tried to make their land into an island by cutting through the peninsula on which their city stood, but repeated injuries to the workmen finally caused them to seek the advice of Delphi. The god replied that, had Zeus wanted their land to be an island, he would have made it one. And so the Knidians abandoned their efforts and surrendered to the Persians (Hdt. 1.174). In a later chapter, we will see how this resistance against the Persians eventually escalated into a full-scale confrontation between the Persians and the Greeks of the mainland.

After the conquest of Lydia and the Ionian cities, Cyrus continued his imperial expansion, subduing Babylon, Syria, Phoenicia, and Palestine. His conquest of Babylon illustrates one of the reasons for Persian success. The city of Babylon had long been restive under the rule of Narbonidus, a Chaldean from the south who failed to honor the Babylonians' gods and celebrate their principal festivals. When the Persians arrived and began assiduously to revive traditional religious practices, the people welcomed them overwhelmingly. Similarly, in the Bible the Persians are lauded for their religious tolerance in allowing the Hebrews to return from the Babylonian Captivity and rebuild their temple.[25]

With the conquest of Phoenicia, the previously land-locked Persians obtained a fleet and the potential to threaten the Greek islands. But according to Herodotus, Cyrus turned first to Scythia in the north, probably in an effort to secure the land route to Greece and the west. The historian relates that the Persian king died there in 530, fighting against the queen of the nomadic Massagetae, Tomyris. After the Greeks slaughtered her forces and captured her son, the queen offered terms, but Cyrus hubristically ignored her offer. The son committed suicide while captive, and later, when Cyrus fell in battle, the queen wreaked barbarian vengeance upon him, immersing his decapitated head in a skin filled with blood, giving him what he had sought—"his fill of blood" (Hdt. 1.215). The historian notes that there were many accounts of Cyrus' death, but he had chosen the one he thought most likely to be true. Unfortunately, our other ancient sources are silent about the last eight years of Cyrus' reign and the manner of his death. It seems likely that he devoted much of his attention to organizing his conquests, since the traditional tribal organization of the Persians would not have sufficed for the vastly increased territories that they now ruled. We do know that he appointed governors over Sardis and Babylon, thus laying the foundations for a provincial system that was later notable not only for its efficiency, but also for its tolerance of the ethnic, religious, and political identities of its subject peoples. This makes it unlikely that Cyrus acted as Herodotus reports in the account of his death, although he may well have died on a campaign against the Scythians.

Cyrus's son Cambyses succeeded him as king. In the fourth year of his rule, Cambyses set out in a successful campaign to extend Persian rule to Egypt. The main literary source for this is again Herodotus. The historian portrays Cambyses as a madman whose invasion of Egypt was motivated by uncontrolled anger, and who continued on the same dangerous course after the conquest, going so far in his disrespect for Egyptian customs and religious beliefs as to kill the sacred Egyptian Apis bull. In Herodotus' account, the king suffered divine retribution for this grave violation of the divine. In 522 he died from an infection in an accidentally self-inflicted stab wound to his thigh,[26] and Herodotus notes that his wound was just like the one with which he had killed the sacred Apis bull.

In fact, however, other evidence contradicts Herodotus' lurid picture of Cambyses' activities and fate. Inscriptions attest his many actions to propitiate the Egyptian gods and to follow Egyptian royal customs. Moreover, the coffin of the Apis bull bears an inscription that says that Cambyses ordered it made in honor of his father, Apis-Osiris, and a stele represents the king in native costume kneeling before the bull, and records that all due honors for the bull were ordered by him.[27] Such official inscriptions would, of course, have put the best light on the king's activities, portraying them in keeping with traditional Persian policy; if in fact he had been mad, his irrational acts might well not have been recorded in inscriptions. Nevertheless, the inscriptions cast doubt on Herodotus' account.

It seems more likely that Herodotus, in his portrayal of Cambyses, fell victim to the propaganda of Darius, Cambyses' successor. We have two principal sources for the events of his succession: the account of Herodotus and that of Darius himself. Neither is an entirely reliable source. Darius' account, which survives in the form of an inscription on a cliff at Bisitun in Iran, is a primary source, but it is also a piece of propaganda intended to justify his rule, for he was not in the direct line of succession.[28]

Both Herodotus and the Bisitun inscription relate that Cambyses secretly had his full brother Bardiya (called Smerdis by Herodotus) killed, and that a usurper, a Mede posing as Bardiya, then arose. After the death of Cambyses, which both sources agree was somehow by his own hand, Darius, who was a member of a collateral branch of the royal family, took part in a conspiracy in which he killed the false Bardiya. He then succeeded in gaining power, according to his own account, because the Persian god Ahura Mazda chose him. According to Herodotus, he rigged a horse race that the conspirators had agreed would decide the issue. The horse trick may, however, have been a confused reflection of the use of horses in Persian divination;[29] in that case, the two accounts would agree in essence in attributing the choice of Darius to the god. The account in the inscription was widely disseminated in various copies throughout the empire, and the report of one of these by Ionian Greeks may have been the source of Herodotus' fascinating moralizing tale. Thus, while Herodotus and the Bisitun inscription agree on a number of points, they may not be independent and thus cannot be used to confirm each other. Bardiya, whether as impostor, usurper, or legitimate heir,[30] ruled with much support as a popular king for seven months before he was killed by Darius, and the new claimant to the throne was challenged by more than fifteen rebellions in various parts of the empire before his control was finally assured.

In 514, three years after he had become king, Darius turned to plans for the further extension of the empire by an expedition to Scythia. According to Herodotus' version of this expedition,[31] the king took Ionian Greek forces with him, and he left behind a number of Ionian tyrants to guard the bridge over the Danube for the return of his army. The Scythian strategy was to refuse to meet the Persians in pitched battle, withdrawing as the Persians advanced and drawing them further and further into land that they had made useless by choking the springs and destroying the forage. At the same time, they made surprise raids on the Persians as they sought provisions or were encamped for the night. But Herodotus reports that the most effective weapon that the Persians had was an accidental one: their donkeys and mules frightened the Scythian horses and thus hindered the effectiveness of their raids.

As Darius futilely chased the retreating Scythians, Herodotus portrays the Ionian tyrants left behind to secure his return as tempted by the Scythians to break up the bridge and strand the king. Finally, however, the tyrant of Miletus, Histiaeus, persuaded the others to stay at their post, pointing out that their own rule depended upon the continuing power of Darius. As a result, Darius, unlike Cyrus, was at least able to escape with his life from his Scythian adventure. Nevertheless, playing on his audience's emotions, Herodotus reports that the Persian withdrawal was accomplished only at the cost of the heartless abandonment of the injured and sick, as well as of the pack animals, creatures that had done the most to help the Persian cause.

In solidifying his hold over the empire, Darius established the detailed workings of a system of government that would enable him to govern successfully the many peoples who were his subjects. He expanded the provincial system begun by Cyrus, dividing the empire into 20 satrapies. This system provided for the regular collection of taxes and for the rigorous accounting for these taxes as well. A network of roads with way stations for the provisioning of travelers was created to serve both the swift communication of official business (many even minor provincial problems were referred to the king for judgment) and commercial purposes.[32] The king involved himself not only in the collection of taxes, but also in the economic health of his territories through the stimulation of agriculture and trade.[33] Vast water regulation projects are described by Herodotus (Hdt. 3.117), and state involvement in industries such as cloth or rug-making seem to be reflected in the official accounts of rations given to workforces consisting mainly of women, girls, and young boys.[34] Trade was fostered by the development of ports along the Persian Gulf and by the construction of a canal linking the Nile with the Red Sea, although much of the exchange seems to have been carried on using Phoenician and Cypriot ships and traders.[35]

Persians did, however, travel and settle outside the borders of their homeland in other capacities, which provided occasions for interaction with Greeks.[36] In fact, contact was quite frequent, especially in western Anatolia, where Greeks had earlier had frequent contacts (see above, on Lydia and Sappho). To further the expansion of the empire, satrapal capitals were established in Anatolia at Sardis, Daskyleion, and Kelainai; these were staffed, at least at the upper levels, by Persian officials, with minor officials drawn from the subject peoples, some of whom were Greek. Persian governors were also placed in the major East Greek cities to ensure the payment of tribute. Persians were awarded land grants in Lydia and other areas of Anatolia, upon which they built prosperous estates, with large villages for their workers and luxurious homes and Persian enclosed gardens ("paradices") for themselves and their families.[37]

A number of aristocratic Greeks found political refuge in Persian-ruled Anatolia: Gongylos of Eretra (Thuc. 128–9); Damaratos of Sparta (Hdt. 6.67); and from Athens, Themistocles (Thuc. 1.137–8), the Peisistratid Hippias, the Peisistratid soothsayer

Onomakritos (Hdt. 7.6), and an otherwise unknown Dikaios (Hdt. 8.65). Most such Greeks were given land grants within the Persian Empire for the support of their households. Non-elite Greeks also found employment in Persians territories, serving as mercenaries, artisans, laborers, and doctors.[38] Although some of the workers may have traveled under compulsion, being deported for rebellion—such as the Milesians after the battle of Lade (Hdt. 6.19–20) and the Eretrians captured before the battle of Marathon (Hdt. 6.100–101, 119)—most were free men who chose to go. For example, the skilled Greeks from Ionia who helped to build Cyrus' palace complex at Pasargadae included every level from stonemasons to architects engaged in planning, and they are attested to have been paid, working as free laborers attracted by good pay and working conditions.[39] Even those who were deported were sometimes sent as whole communities to locations at the far reaches of the empire where they would cause no trouble; some of these communities were still viable generations later, some even still speaking Greek.[40] Thus Eretrians were settled in Kurdistan, about 25 miles from Susa,[41] where they continued to live in Herodotus' time;[42] Milesians were settled on the Persian Gulf near the mouth of the Tigris (Hdt. 6.20), and Paeonians from Thrace were transported to Phrygia, where they were found and returned to their homes by the Greeks during the Ionian Revolt.[43] In 479, during the Second Ionian Revolt, the priestly family of the Branchidae, who served the temple of Didyma at Miletus, took Xerxes' side, and after his defeat, were resettled in Bactria.[44] Settlements of Boeotians and Carians are also mentioned as living near Susa.[45]

SUGGESTIONS FOR FURTHER READING

For the history of Persia, see Joseph Wiesehöfer (1996), *Ancient Persia from 550 BC to 650 AD*. On Ionia, see Carl Roebuck (1959), *Ionian Trade and Colonization*; and C. J. Emlyn-Jones (1980), *The Ionians and Hellenism*. On Ionian philosophy, G. S. Kirk, J. E. Raven, and Malcolm Schofield (1983), *The Presocratic Philosophers: A Critical History with a Selection of Texts*. M. L. West (1971), *Early Greek Philosophy and the Orient*. In general, relevant sections of *The Cambridge Ancient History IV* (1988): *Persia, Greece and the Western Mediterranean c.525–479*, are useful and provide extensive bibliography.

MAP STUDY

Persian Empire: Bisitun, Pasargadae, Scythia, Egypt, Babylon, Syria, Libya, Phoenicia, Palestine, Danube, Caria, Lydia (Sardis), Lycia (Xanthos), Naukratis, Thurii, Elea, Eretria, Abdera
   Ionian and other Greek cities in Asia Minor: Halicarnassos, Smyrna, Ephesus, Miletus, Samos, Lesbos, Knidos
   Rivers: Halys, Danube

ENDNOTES

[1]On the history of Persia from a wider perspective, see Joseph Wiesehöfer (1996), *Ancient Persia from 550 BC to 650 AD*. Pierre Briant (2002), *From Cyrus to Alexander: A History of the Persian Empire*, sums up the most recent advances in a rapidly moving field.

[2]Scholars disagree on the possibility of reconciling Herodotus' account with the primary sources; most skeptical is P. R. Helm (1981). "Herodotus' Mêdikos Logos and Median History," *Iran* 19: 85–90, who argues that Herodotus' source was non-historic, a "saga of national liberation." For a discussion, see Stuart C. Brown (1988), "The Mêdikos Logos of Herodotus and the Evolution of the Median State," pp. 71–86 in Heleen Sancisi-Weerdenburg and Amélie Kuhrt, eds. (1988), *Method and Theory : Proceedings of the London 1985 Achaemenid History Workshop*.

[3]According the tenth century CE encyclopedia known as the Suda, "Panyassis."

[4]For a discussion of the debate over the exact nature of the contacts between Greeks and Persians at this time, see Margaret C. Miller (1997), *Athens and Persia in the Fifth Century BC*, 105–108.

[5]On the negative side, see A. J. Podlecki (1977), "Herodotus in Athens?" pp. 246–265 in Konrad H. Kinzl and Fritz Schachermeyr, eds. (1977), *Greece and the Eastern Mediterranean in Ancient History and Prehistory.*

[6]The recognition of the basically oral nature of classical Greek culture is fairly recent; some important contributions to the question include Rosalind Thomas (1992), *Literacy and Orality in Ancient Greece*; and Rosalind Thomas (2000), *Herodotus in Context*; W. V. Harris (1989), *Ancient Literacy*. On Herodotus' use of oral sources, see Mabel Lang (1984), *Herodotean Narrative and Discourse*.

[7]W. Kendrick Pritchett (1993), *The Liar School of Herodotos* thoroughly refutes such charges.

[8]The phrase is borrowed from Miller (above, n. 4), 89–108.

[9]The best introduction to early Greek philosophy is G. S. Kirk, J. E. Raven, and Malcolm Schofield (1983), *The Presocratic Philosophers : A Critical History with a selection of texts* (abbreviated as KRS), which also gives the fragments in translation. The Greek texts can be found in H. Diels and W. Kranz, (eds.) (1968), *Fragmente der Vorsokratiker*, 6th ed. Here the fragments are identified by the numbering system used in KRS, and all translations are from that work.

[10]Little is known about the actual dates of these men, with the exception of Thales, who is roughly datable by his prediction of the solar eclipse of 585. In the ancient tradition, men were assumed to have been 40 years old at the peak of their careers (their *floruit*, abbreviated fl.), which is the date often given; without other information, their death was assumed at age 60. The ancient sources also calculate dates for the philosophers after Thales by assuming teacher-pupil relationships, which may or not have been the case. Thus Anaximander is said to have been the pupil of Thales, and Anaximenes the pupil of Anaximander, and both are dated accordingly.

[11]KRS (above, n. 9) 82; A. A. Mosshammer (1981), "Thales' Eclipse," *Transactions and Proceedings of the American Philological Association* 111: 145–255, argues that the prediction and eclipse could not have occurred as Herodotus reports; he suggests that the story was a literary conflation of two outstanding events, on the principle that one marvel deserves another, and that famous men must be connected with famous events that occur in their day.

[12]KRS (above, n. 9), 90–93.

[13]A Biblical reference: Ezekiel 1: 15–19; 3:13, 10:9–22; cited in M. L. West (1971), *Early Greek Philosophy and the Orient*, 88–89.

[14]See West (above, n. 13), chap. 6 for discussion.

[15]For brief discussions of Persian religion, see Briant (above, n. 1), 240–254; Wiesehöfer (above, n. 1), 94–101.

[16]Herodotus, 1.131–132.

[17]Herdotus, 1.16. For the archaeological evidence, see J. M. Cook and R. V. Nicholls 1958/1959, "Old Smyrna," *Annual of the British School at Athens* 53/54: 1–137.

[18]Herdotus 4.152, ca. 650.

[19]Sappho, Frag. 96, tr. N. Demand. The fragmentary nature of the poem renders translation difficult; see the notes in D. A. Campbell (1967), *Greek Lyric Poetry: A Selection of Early Greek Lyric, Elegiac and Lambic Poetry.*

[29]Hdt. 2.135; Sappho, Frag. 5, mentions the brother, but in an affectionate manner.

[21]For a critical analysis of Persian history as presented in Herodotus' text in terms of the Near Eastern sources, see Briant (above, n. 1). A useful shorter account that follows the same approach can be found in Wiesehöfer (above, n. 1).

[22]The Persians were settled in what is today Fars province in Iran; Cyrus was distantly descended from Achaemenes, who was the eponymous founder of the Persian royal family, the Achaemenids.

[23]Herodotus. 1.46–49, 73–91. Thomas Harrison (2000), *Divinity and History: The Religion of Herodotus*, 223–227.

[24]Herodotus. 1.87–91.

[25]A Biblical reference, Isaiah 45: 1–3 and 13.

[26]That the wound was self-inflicted is also stated by Darius' inscription at Bisitun, his own account of his accession to power and unlikely to have been unbiased. See Jack Balcer (1987), *Herodotus and Bisitun*, chap. 1, with illustrations. Whether it was an accident or a suicide, or even whether Darius might have been involved, is not clear.

[27]G. Posener (1936), *La première Domination Perse en Égypte*, #3 and 4, and pp. 171–175.

[28]See Rüdiger Schmitt (1991), *The Bisitun Inscriptions of Darius the Great: Old Persian Text*, vol.1; Wiesehöfer (above, n. 2), 13–21.

[29]Suggested by G. Widengren (1974), "La Royauté de l'Iran Antique," *Acta Iranica* 1: 84–100, 85.

[30]See Mabel Lang (1992), "Prexaspes and Usurper Smerdis," *Journal of Eastern Studies* 51: 201–207.

[31]Herodotus 4.1, 83–98, 102, 118–144.

[32]On the road system, see Briant (above, n. 1), 357–364.

[33]"Letter of Darius to Gadatas," in C. W. Fornara (1983), *Archaic Times to the End of the Peloponnesian War*, no.35), which was a Source Analysis in the previous edition of this book, has been much disputed and is now recognized to be a falsification from the Roman period. See P. Briant (2001), "Histoire et archéologie d'un texte : la Lettre de Darius à Gadatas entre Perses, Grecs et Romains", in M. Salvini and R. Gusmani, eds., *Licia e Lidia prima dell'ellenizzazione* (Convegno Internazionale, Roma, ISMEA, 11–12 ottobre 1999). Briant (above, n. 1) xviii, n. 15, says that it, "should be eliminated from discussions of Achaemenid history."

[34]Richard T. Hallock (1969), *Persepolis fortification tablets*, University of Chicago Press, 919–920.

[35]Miller, (above, n. 4), chap. 3.

[36]Miller (above, n. 26), 91–100.

[37]Herodotus. 6.41; 8.85; 9:107; Athen. 1.20a; Xen. *Hell.* 3.1.10; D. M. Lewis 1977. *Sparta and Persia*, 52; Miller (above, n. 26), 98–100.

[38]Miller (above, n. 26), 100–103.

[39]See Carl Nylander (1970), *Ionians in Pasargadae. Studies in Old Persian Architecture.*

[40]Miller (above, n. 26),100–103; Briant (above, n. 1), 505–507.

[41]And approximately five miles from a well producing asphalt, salt, and oil, which clearly interested Herodotus. Asphalt had many uses in antiquity: waterproofing pottery, matting, and baskets; as a mastic; as mortar for bricks; as pigment; and as a medicine.

[42]Herodotus, 6.119.

[43]Herodotus, 5.15.3, 98.1.

[44]Strabo XI.11.4.

[45]Diodorus XVII.110.4–5.

9

THE PERSIAN WARS

THE FIRST PERSIAN WAR

The Ionian Revolt

The Eastern connections that had been so fruitful for the Ionian Greeks in the Archaic period became problematic as the Persians asserted their imperialistic ambitions more vigorously. The Greeks, who had grown relatively comfortable with tributary status under their Lydian neighbors, at first tolerated the Persian establishment of local rule by Greek collaborators (tyrants). When these tyrants misused their authority, however, resistance grew, culminating in the Ionian Revolt of 499–494. Ionian appeals to mainland Greece for assistance led to the involvement of both the Athenians and the Eretrians of Euboea, and the small contingents sent by these mainland cities took part in a daring attack on Sardis, the seat of the Persian satrap (governor). Sardis was burned, but the revolt as a whole was unsuccessful. Nevertheless, Persian annoyance at Greek intransigence ultimately resulted in a full-scale confrontation between Persians and Greeks, the Persian Wars.[1]

Once the revolt had been put down, even the Persians had second thoughts about the policy of imposing pro-Persian tyrants on the Greeks. A more modern view would posit economic pressures and political unrest as causes for the revolt, causes that the Persians themselves recognized when they later made changes in their relationship with their defeated subjects. After punishing the rebels with various deportations and civic destructions, they turned to constructive efforts to remedy the conditions that had led to the revolt. They abandoned the support of despotic rulers in the subject cities and set up democracies in their stead; they also instituted new and more equitable methods of assessing the tribute.

Historiographical Analysis

erodotus 5.30–38. What can we make of Herodotus' account of the causes of the Ionian Revolt? The story of the secret message sent on the scalp of the slave stands out as a particularly memorable element in the account, and typical of Herodotus' interest in what modern scholars would classify as folktale motifs. Such motifs were useful in keeping alive the oral transmission of stories about the past; their frequent occurrences in Herodotus' work are one mark of his strong reliance upon oral tradition. But even Herodotus' account does not put the whole causal weight upon the scheming of Histiaeus: he recognizes that Aristagoras' own intrigues had brought him to the point of revolt when he received Histiaeus' message. Moreover, other Ionian Greek cities joined in the revolt, as did Greeks as far away as Cyprus.

The Expedition of Mardonius

The Ionian Revolt was the first step in the series of events that led to the great Persian expeditions against Greece itself. As Herodotus saw it, it inspired in Darius a spirit of revenge against the hubristic mainland Greeks who had participated in the burning of Sardis, Athens, and Eretria. But in Herodotus' view, Darius and his successor Xerxes did not act alone; the gods conspired to lead them astray. Modern scholars view the cause in more abstract terms. For example, Peter Green posits economic causes: the Persian king's need for gold to maintain an economy that focused on the stockpiling of wealth, and the pressures put upon the Athenian food supply by Persian control of the Hellespont.[2] He also suggests religious motivations: the Zoroastrian doctrine that "all men must work for the establishment of God's Righteous Order on earth, a clarion-call for would-be imperialists in any age, and especially attractive to Darius."[3]

The first Persian approach to Greece was by sea. In 492 Darius sent his son-in-law Mardonius on an expedition against Macedonia and the Greek island of Thasos. The area, which was rich in both gold and timber for ships, had provided Peisistratus with the resources to establish his tyranny in Athens. Peisistratus' son and successor, Hippias, who had escaped from Athens and found refuge with the Persians, could have provided Darius with specific information about the area, although it is clear from the story of Histiaeus that Darius was already aware of its strategic potential. In fact, the area was probably al-

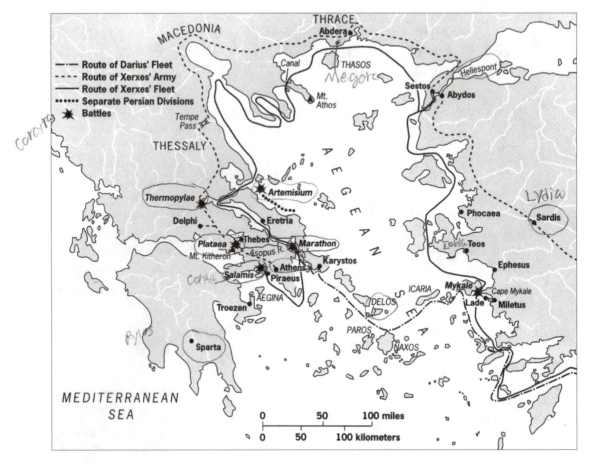

Map 9   The Persian Wars

ready under some degree of Persian control as a result of the Scythian campaign, and Mardonius' expedition was intended to extend and consolidate this control. Mardonius' fleet suffered a spectacular disaster, however, when a violent storm off Mt. Athos destroyed most of the ships.

For Herodotus, the loss of Mardonius' fleet was simply one more factor pushing Darius irrevocably toward an attack on Greece. It was added to the Athenian participation in the burning of Sardis, which his advisors kept continually before his mind; the advice of the Peisistratid Hippias, who was eager to regain his lost position as tyrant in Athens; and the nagging of his queen Atossa, instigated by her Greek doctor, who saw his own role in a reconnaisance trip as a means of getting back to his homeland. This type of multiple motivation embodied the historian's own belief in the inevitability of fate: many factors conspired to goad Darius into his ill-fated attack on Greece.

The Battle of Marathon

In 490 Darius sent a fleet directly across the Aegean, moving from island to island. He thus avoided the dangerous route around the cape of Mt. Athos where Mardonius had lost his fleet, but modern strategists point out that one of his aims was also to gain control of the Cycladic islands. Hippias was on board to lead the way, expecting his supporters at Athens to welcome his return. As planned, the Persians easily subdued the islands as they went. When they reached Eretria, which was betrayed to them after a fierce resistance of six days, they plundered and burned the city and deported its population. But when they reached the Greek mainland, they met unexpected resistance at the hands of the Athenians on the plain of Marathon.

The battle of Marathon is one of the most famous battles of western warfare. From antiquity it has embodied a cluster of ideas central to western culture and western self-definition: the victory of a small contingent of men fighting heroically to defend their homeland and their freedom against a foreign invader whose vastly superior force marched under the lash of political servitude. In brief, Greek freedom stood against Persian slavery.

When the Athenians realized that a Persian attack was imminent, they sent off a long-distance runner to the Spartans for assistance. But the Spartans replied that they were celebrating a religious festival and that sacred law forbid them to leave the city until the full moon, which would occur in six days (Hdt. 6.96–101). Of the other Greek cities, only a contingent of Plataeans, historic allies of the Athenians, joined the Athenian forces.

The Greek forces took up a stand at a strong position commanding the main road into the plain. Herodotus reports that disagreement about the wisdom of resistance arose among the ten generals, each of whom held command for one day at a time. In the debate, the opinion of Miltiades to fight finally won out, but Herodotus says that Miltiades postponed the attack until his day of command. Herodotus was surely mistaken about the rotating command, for at this time the commander-in-chief was the Polemarch[4]. The source of his confusion was perhaps the fact that the Polemarch gave Miltiades a free hand in carrying out the plan that he had advocated. Miltiades' delay is not hard to explain in other terms. The Greeks could only have gained by delay—perhaps the Spartans would arrive—but it was in the Persians' interest to fight as soon as possible. What motivated the Greeks to attack when they did is not known. A report that "the horses are away" seems to have been the deciding factor, but scholars are not agreed whether this meant that the Persians had begun to reembark their horses to head for Athens, or that the horses were away being pastured.[5] Miltiades led the charge in an unusual running attack over the kilometer and a half that separated the two armies. As they fought, the Persians broke through the center of the Greek line, but the Greeks were victorious on the wings and were then able to turn back upon the Persians who had broken through the center. Routed and in confusion, the Persians rushed to the sea and their boats, where many were killed as they tried to reembark. Herodotus put the Greek losses at 192, the Persian at 6,400.

Source Analysis

erodotus 6.102–124. Herodotus' description drew upon the memories of veterans of the battle, aging men who had come to play an almost legendary role in Athenian consciousness. He provides very few details of the battle, and the facts that he did chose to relate differ in many respects from those that a modern historian would choose. Nevertheless, these differences provide us with considerable insight into Greek culture and values. For example, what do the facts that Herodotus chooses to relate about Miltiades reveal about the role played by participation in the Olympian and other panhellenic games in Greek politics? What role did visions and dreams play in Herodotus' account? Finally, what cracks in Athenian unity intruded almost immediately into the picture of heroic action?

The Athenian victory at Marathon was a setback for the Persians, but not an overwhelming defeat. They immediately set off by sea for Athens, hoping to seize the undefended city, while the Athenians raced at top speed by land to reach the city first. The Greeks arrived to see the Persian fleet approaching the city, but it turned and unexpectedly withdrew. Possibly the Persians realized that the Athenian forces had arrived in time; possibly they had received word that the Spartans were on their way to offer assistance. Whatever the reason, they abandoned their attempt to conquer Greece and returned home. When the Spartans did arrive, they were too late for the battle, but they visited the battle site and inspected the Persian equipment. Then, congratulating the Athenians on a job well done, they returned home.

Today the burial mound of the Greeks who fell at Marathon remains as a monument to the Greek victory. It is some 45 meters in diameter and stands at the spot where most casualties occurred, over the cremated remains of the Athenian dead. Many Persian arrowheads have been discovered in the soil of the mound.[6]

Another mound, containing the burials of the Plataeans and the slaves, has been excavated nearby,[7] but the Persian burials have never been found. Another contemporary memorial, a painting portraying three scenes of the battle, is described by Pausanias.[8] We, of course, recall the victory in our Marathon races.[9]

THE SECOND PERSIAN WAR

When the Persians sailed back home again after their defeat at Marathon, the relief at Athens must have been immense. Nevertheless, some recognized that the respite might be only

Figure 9.1   The burial mound at Marathon.
Photo by N. Demand.

temporary. Miltiades was the hero of the hour. At the height of his popularity, he proposed sending out a fleet to punish the Cycladic states that had gone over to the Persians, thus also securing the possible route of a Persian return attack (Hdt. 6.132–136). The fleet was sent out and had some successes before it turned against the island of Paros. Herodotus' sources were hostile to Miltiades, and the historian follows them in portraying Miltiades' attack and seige of Paros as motivated by personal interests. Moreover, he reports that during the seige, the commander committed an act of impiety that was responsible for the failure of the attack. A priestess, instigated by the god Apollo, tempted Miltiades into entering the precinct of Demeter Thesmophoros, a sacred area restricted to women. As he jumped over the precinct wall, Miltiades injured his leg. The wound caused him to withdraw the forces under his command from the seige, and by the time he reached Athens he was near death from infection. He was tried and found guilty of "deceiving the People," a form of treason for which the penalty was death by being hurled into a pit. The Assembly, however, allowed him to pay only a fine, although a huge one of 50 talents. He died soon after, probably of gangrene, and his son paid the fine.

The danger of one man gaining excessive power through too much success was exemplified by the fate of Miltiades. It is thus not surprising that the political instrument of ostracism was first used at this time. By this "negative popularity poll," which Aristotle explicitly included among the reforms of Kleisthenes, any person receiving a majority in an ostracism vote of at least 6,000 was required to go into exile for ten years. Ostracism was not a punishment, but a safety valve against excessive popularity. The ostracised man retained control of his property and its revenues and was permitted to maintain contact with his family from outside the borders of Attica. In the period after Marathon, three advocates of accommodation with Persia were ostracised, leading members of the Peisistratid and Alkmaeonid families. During this time another route to political preeminence was also closed with the change from direct election of the archons to a mixture of election and allotment, with a lottery used to select from 500 candidates elected by the deme assemblies. This safeguard was not effective for long, however, for it left open the way for holders of the remaining high elective office, the generalship, to amass political power.

The Greeks gained some respite from fears of a renewed Persian attack when the Persians became involved in a revolt in Egypt in 486. Darius died late in that year, and Xerxes, his son and successor, crushed the Egyptian revolt and imposed a harsh regime on the country. However, he made no move toward Greece. It was not until 483 that the signs again turned menacing for the Greeks: Xerxes began the work of digging a canal through the neck of the Athos peninsula, the site of the earlier disastrous loss of Mardonius' fleet.[10] Recent investigations (a combination of geophysical survey and analysis of sediments from bore holes drilled along the supposed course of the canal) have determined that the canal was indeed dug, and that its features conformed to those in Herodotus' description.[11]

In the meantime, bickering with neighboring Aegina occupied the Athenians. At this point, a new figure came to the fore at Athens, Themistocles, a strong supporter of naval power who had already advocated fortification of the Piraeus (port of Athens). He now persuaded the Assembly to use a rich deposit of silver newly discovered at the mines at Laurion for the construction of a fleet, ostensibly for the war against Aegina, rather than, as was their custom, to distribute it to the people (Hdt. 7.144). They agreed, and turned to building the fleet that was to be the key to their victory over the Persians in the second Persian War.

Xerxes Takes on the War

According to Herodotus, Xerxes did not inherit his father's zeal for war against the Greeks. This lack of enthusiasm on Xerxes' part gave the historian another opportunity to portray fate driving the Persians on in their misguided efforts to add the Greeks to their empire. The story, while it is enhanced by folktale elements that are not historical, is important in providing an insight into Herodotus' conception of the moral universe in which great wars occurred.[12]

Herodotus described Xerxes' preparations for the expedition in great detail, stressing the magnitude of the undertaking. In addition to the digging of the canal at Athos, the bridging of the Hellespont in particular provided the historian with an opportunity to portray the

Source Analysis

erodotus 7.5–19: How does this account compare with Herodotus' earlier account of Darius' decision to send out the first expeditions against Greece? Note especially the role of Artabanos, who plays the part of a type-character frequently found in Herodotus, the Tragic Warner. How might recognition of such type-characters be used in the assessment of the historicity of Herodotus' account? What does the story reveal about Herodotus' beliefs about the role of divinity in causation, and about the relationship between the gods and men?

hubris of the Persian king in the face of natural obstacles. The king had a pair of bridges constructed at Abydos, utilizing the principles of both suspension and pontoon construction and making use of 674 warships. When the first pair of bridges was destroyed by a storm, the angry king, in a dramatic act of hubris, ordered the engineer to be executed and the Hellespont to be punished by lashing.[13] The scale of the undertaking, from the digging of the canal at Athos and the bridging of the Hellespont, to the marshalling and provisioning of the vast expeditionary force, was remarkable. While Herodotus' estimate of 5,283,220 for the total number of the force is exaggerated, both Simonides "300 myriad" (3,000,000) and Aeschylus ("the entire strength of Asia's sons") attest to the Greek belief in the huge size of the expedition and to the vast areas of empire from which it was drawn.[14] As the combined sea and land expedition made its way across northern Greece, it drank rivers dry and consumed the entire food supply of small cities in a single meal, As Herodotus portrays it, it was a monumental and spectacular effort, with contingents from the far reaches of the Empire marching in their native garb and equipped with their native weapons.[15]

As Herodotus saw it, Xerxes did not embark on this monumental undertaking without warning from the gods. First came the advice of Xerxes' elderly uncle Artabanos, tested by dreams,[16] then an eclipse,[17] and finally two portents—a mare gave birth to a hare; and a mule, against nature, gave birth, and its offspring possessed both male and female sex organs.[18] But Xerxes was fated to overreach, and he ignored the warnings.

The Battles of Thermopylae and Artemisium

As had been the case with the battle of Marathon, few of the Greek cities chose to oppose the Persians, and in the subsequent march of Xerxes against Greece, many capitulated (**medized**). Some, such as Thebes, did so because of their exposed position along the Persian route of march; others, such as Argos, did so because of rivalry with their Greek neighbors. Moreover, in most cities there were Persian sympathizers who posed a threat of treachery from within, as had happened at Eretria.

The expedition of Xerxes, unlike those of Darius, was a combined action by both land and sea. The first land battle of the war, Thermopylae, was again one of the famous battles of history, although for quite different reasons than Marathon. As Xerxes' army approached, the Greeks of the mainland debated their chances for defense. There was a narrows at Tempe in Thessaly at which they might hope to stop the much larger force, but in the end it was determined to be less defensible than the narrow pass between the mountains and the sea at Thermopylae. Led by the Spartans under their general Leonides, the Greeks took up their stand at this point. For a time they succeeded in holding off the attacking Persians, but eventually a path over the mountain was betrayed to the enemy. With full recognition of the hopelessness of their position, the Spartans sent away the other Greeks and prepared to stand and fight to the last man. While the battle of Marathon had been a great, even legendary, victory for the Athenians, demonstrating the strength of free men fighting for their homeland, the battle of Thermopylae became part of the Spartan mystique. It embodied the traditional virtue of the Spartan warrior: to come home with his shield—or on it.

The heroic sacrificial stand of the Spartans at Thermopylae cannot, however, be considered in isolation from the contemporaneous victory that the Greeks won against the Persian fleet in the sea battle at nearby Artemisium. The Persian fleet, which was following along in support of the land army, had its first engagement with the Greeks in the narrow straits just off the coast at Thermopylae. Herodotus attributes the Greek decision to meet them there to Themistocles. The historian's anti-Themistoclean sources reported that the Euboeans bribed him to delay the Persian advance by a sea battle so that they could evacuate their homes, and that Themistocles used the money to bribe the commanders to stay –and kept some of it himself, which "nobody knew."[19]

The Persian fleet at first avoided battle; it was late in the day, and they feared that the Greeks, if they were defeated, would slip away in the coming darkness. To prevent this, they split their forces, sending 200 ships around Euboea to block any Greek attempt to retreat south. The first engagement, begun by the Greeks, was inconclusive. Then in the night a great storm arose; as Herodotus says, the god was protecting the Greeks, for the main body of the Persian fleet suffered great losses in the storm, and the 200 ships sent around Euboea were also lost. On the next day, emboldened by the arrival of reinforcements from Athens and by word of the Persian losses, the Greeks attacked and destroyed a small contingent of Persian ships. This so annoyed the Persians that they decided to launch a full-scale battle.

The ensuing encounter was nearly equal. Despits its losses, the Persian fleet was still larger than the Greek fleet, but its very size caused it to fall into confusion in the narrow passage, losing many ships and men. Herodotus notes as a coincidence that the battle of Artemisium occurred on the same day as the battle of Thermopylae, one at the sea pass, the other at the land pass. Despite Herotodus' story of the role played by Themistoclean bribery in the Greek decision to fight at Artemisium, the coincidence must, however, have been deliberate on the part of the Greeks. Not only was it strategically sound to coordinate the land and sea forces, but Herodotus reports that the Greeks had made plans for each arm of their forces to notify the other of the results of the two engagements.

The Persian victory at Thermopylae opened the way for their unimpeded march south. Athens lay first in the Persian path, and the immediate issue for the Athenians became the fate of their city. Led by Themistocles' interpretation of the oracle of Delphi that they would find safety behind wooden walls, the Athenians, with a few exceptions (according to Herodotus, the treasurers of Athena's temple on the Acropolis, and a few of the poor), decided to commit themselves to the sea, evacuating the city and taking to the wooden walls of their ships.[20]

S o u r c e   A n a l y s i s

I n addition to the account of Herodotus (8.40–41, 51), an inscription found at Troezen and published in 1960 may be a fourth-century copy of the decree of evacuation, although its authenticity is in dispute. It is interesting to compare the differences in these two sources, notably, the identification of those left behind on the Acropolis, and the dating of the evacuation. If genuine, the inscription gives important details about the marshalling of forces in the rapid expansion of the Athenian fleet.

THE TROEZEN INSCRIPTION (Greek text in Russell Meiggs and Deavid Leais, eds. (1988), *A Selection of Greek Historical Inscriptions to the End of the Fifth Century B.C.*, no. 23; tr. N. Demand.)

Gods....

It was decreed by the Boule [Council] and the demos, Themistokles son of Neokles of Phrearrhioi, spoke: To entrust the city to Athena Guardian of Athens and to all the other gods to guard and to ward off the Barbarian in defense of the land [chora]. All the Athenians and the aliens living in Athens, the children and the women to be placed in Troezen ... [under the protection of] the Founder of our land [Theseus]. [The elderly and the] property to be placed in Salamis. The treasurers and the Priestesses to remain in the Akropolis [guarding the possessions] of the gods. All the other Athenians and the adult aliens to board the [readied] two hundred ships and to fight the Barbarian for the freedom of themselves and of the other Hellenes, with the Lakedaimonians and Corinthians and Aiginetans, and all others who are willing to take the risk. And the generals to appoint 200 trierarchs, one for each ship, beginning tomorrow morning from those possessing land and an oikos in Athens and legitimate children and not older than 50 years, and the ships to be assign to them by lot....

They are to enlist ten fighting men [for each] ship from those between 20 and 30 years of age, and four archers. The crews to be assigned to the ships by lot when they appoint the trierarchs. Both the others and the generals are to be listed on a white board [for public display], the Athenians from the lists of the lexiarchons [deme registers] and the aliens from the list of the Polemarch. And to write up the assignments in order in 200s up to the number 100, and in each recorded order the name of the trierarch and of the crew, so that they know in what order and in which trireme to embark. And when they have allotted all the ranks assigned to the triremes, and the 200 ships are full, the Boule and the generals to sacrifice to Zeus the All-Powerful and to Athena and Nike and Poseidon the Savior. When they have filled all the ships, one hundred of them to go to assist the Artemision at Euboia, and one hundred to lie in wait all around Salamis and the rest of Attic, to guard the country [chora].

[In order] that all Athenians with one mind ward off the Barbarian, those banished for ten years [ostracised] are to go to Salamis and remain until the demos makes a decision about them. [Text breaks off]

The Peloponnesians opposed making a stand in defense of Athens, favoring instead the narrow isthmus to the Peloponnesus, which they thought would adequately protect their own cities. To them, the Persian army was the most obvious threat, far more dangerous than the Persian fleet. Yet, as the Athenians argued, continued Persian control of the sea would make a military victory at the isthmus meaningless: Persian ships could carry their infantry beyond any blockade of the isthmus to a landing anywhere along the coast of the Peloponnesus. In the end, Themistocles won out by threatening that, should the Greeks decide to retreat to the isthmus, the Athenians would withdraw their forces, put their families on board their ships, and sail away to reestablish their city at Siris in Italy.

The Battle of Salamis

As a result of Themistocles' persuasion and threat, the Greeks decided to meet the Persian fleet in the narrow bay of Salamis, off the coast of the Piraeus. Again a ruse of Themistocles' played a central role in events; he sent a man posing as an informer to tell the Persians that the Greeks intended to slip away by night. Believing the "informer," the Persians manned their ships and sailed around all night, keeping watch. Meanwhile, the Greeks slept. In the morning the refreshed Greeks met the weary Persians in battle. The Greeks drew the Persians into the narrows by pretending to escape north, and as at Artemisium, the Persians found themselves unable to keep their formation in the restricted space. The battle turned into a rout, with the Persians in their confusion falling victim to the more skilled Greek crews.

Source Analysis

E ight years after the battle, the tragic poet Aeschylus presented an eye-witness account of the events in his play, *The Persians*. In this scene, a messenger describes the disaster to the Persian queen, Atossa (Aeschylus *Persians* 353–432, tr. N. Demand)

Some avenging spirit or evil daimon caused this utter evil, oh mistress.
A Greek man from the Athenian army, coming to your son Xerxes, spoke thus:
    "When black night reaches total darkness
The Greeks will not stay, but escape to the rowing benches of the ships,
each for himself, to save his life by secret flight."
    When Xerxes heard this, not perceiving the treachery of this
Greek man, or the hatred of the gods,
    Straightaway proclaimed to all the ship captains this word:
"When the sun ceases the burning of its rays,
And darkness seizes the airy temenos of the sky,
Arrange the close array of the ships in triple order,
Send some to circle all round the island of Ajax,
and others to guard the outlet and the roaring passage."
And if the Hellenes should flee evil fate,
discovering a hidden escape for the ships,
he threatened that all would lose their heads.
He spoke thus with confidant heart,
for he did not know what was going to come from the gods.
    And not rebelliously, but with an obedient mind
The crews finished their dinner, and each seaman
Turned the thong of his well-pulled oar round the pin.
And when night came on, every man who was master of an oar
Went to his ship, and every man who was master of arms,
And they sailed as they were ordered.
    And the whole night through the commanders kept the fleet sailing back and forth
But as night advanced, the Greek host did not sail out in secret.
But when day on its white horses first rendered the earth brilliant to see,
Then first the tumult from the Greeks arose
Raising a high-pitched echo from the island's rocks.
Fear seized the barbarians, their plans gone awry,
For not as in flight the Greek sang the holy paean now
But rising up to battle with confidant spirits.
The trumpet of war inflamed them.

And straightaway the dashing oars, dipping together,
Struck the brine of the deep on the command
And quickly all were clear to see:
The right wing first, well-arrayed, led in order,
And then the whole fleet sailed out.
And we could hear the battle cry:
"Oh, sons of Hellas, come, free your fatherland,
Free your children, your women, the dwelling-places
Of your gods, the graves of your ancestors.
Now the battle is for all."

The Greek victory at Salamis turned the tide of the war in their favor. Faced with the defeat of his fleet—and tricked again by Themistocles, who sent a false spy to report that the Greeks were intent on destroying the bridge at the Hellespont and trapping the Persian forces—the king decided to make good his own escape, leaving behind a part of the army under Mardonius to continue the war.

The Battle of Plataea

After wintering in Thessaly, Mardonius resumed the offensive, marching first to Athens, which he sacked again. The Peloponnesians were for the moment secure behind their defenses at the isthmus, although vulnerable to attack should the Persian fleet return from Samos, where it lay idle, while the Athenians remained in refugee camps on Salamis and on their ships just off the coast. There could be no peace or return to normal life as long as Mardonius remained. In Athens, voices of accommodation began to be raised, and at least two of those elected to the generalship in 479 were possible advocates of reconciliation. Soon Mardonius made his offer to Athens through King Alexander of Macedonia: amnesty, local autonomy, recovery of territory, and Persian aid in rebuilding the temples destroyed in the war. It was a tempting offer. The Athenians asked time to consider, and perhaps some in Athens were responsible for circulating a prophecy that the Dorians would one day be driven from the Peloponnesus by the Athenians and the Persians (Hdt. 8.141). In consternation, the Spartans sent representatives to Athens while King Alexander was still present, and both sides put their arguments to the Athenian demos. In the end Herodotus portrays the Athenians patriotically declaring their intention to resist and calling upon the Spartans to march north to meet the inevitable Persian attack. Modern opinion suggests that the Athenians would not, in fact, have been so quick to give up the last card they held and opt for the possibility of a suicide stand.[21]

When the Athenians rejected his terms, Mardonius marched south, reaching Attica and reoccuping the city. He repeated his offer, but the Athenians were in no mood to accept it; when a citizen proposed that it be put to a vote, he was lynched, together with his wife and children. The Athenians, however, sent an urgent message to the Spartans, telling them that they would be compelled to accept the offer unless the Spartans came to their assistance at once. The Spartans, who were once again celebrating a festival and felt secure behind the defenses at the Isthmus, delayed their reply for two weeks. Finally, they sent a force of 5,000 hoplites with 35,000 helots in attendance under the command of Pausanias, in secrecy by a roundabout route north, telling the Athenians only after the fact. The ruse was intended to prevent their local enemies, the Argives, from sending word to Mardonius, in whose pay they were. The effort was unsuccessful, however, for an Argive messenger succeeded in getting word to Mardonius. The Persian general once again sacked Athens and then headed north to Boeotia, where Thebes was friendly and the territory would favor the Persian cavalry. He took up a position and constructed a fortification near the Asopus River, which formed the boundary between Plataean and Theban territory. In this way he would fight with Thebes behind him. His strategy was to do as little as possible, waiting for dissension to develop among the Greek forces and trying to lure them into battle on terrain unfavorable to their hoplite forces.

Meanwhile, the Athenians sent a force of eight thousand to join the Spartans under Pausanias, and other Greek cities sent contingents as well. The Greek forces took up a position across the river from Mardonius, in the foothills of Mt. Kitheron, in territory that gave maximum scope to their hoplite strength. As the Persian cavalry harassed them, new contingents of men and supplies continued to flow to the Greeks. Finally, Mardonius occupied the pass over Kithaeron, cutting off further reinforcements and supplies, and for good measure, choked the spring that the Greeks depended on for water. The Greeks then decided to withdraw to a better position that would provide water and relief from the cavalry attacks, but the planned nighttime move somehow went amiss and was delayed until daybreak. With daylight Mardonius could see that the Greeks had deserted their position, and he decided to attack. He caught the Spartans and Tegeans as they marched and compelled them to give battle. Both sides fought furiously, but the Persians, lacking the heavy armor or the long spears of the Greeks, proved no match for the hoplite forces. When Mardonius himself fell, the battle was decided. The surviving Persians rushed back to their fortified camp pursued by the Greeks, who stormed the camp, seizing a vast treasure of gold and silver furnishings, inlaid couches, concubines, horses, camels, and hoards of coined money.

A tithe of the plunder from Plataea was dedicated to Apollo at Delphi; from it a golden tripod was made, supported by a bronze pillar in the form of intertwined serpents. The tripod was later melted down in one of the Sacred Wars of the fourth century, but the serpent column survived, although headless, to be transported by the Roman Emperor Constantine to his newly refounded capital of Constantinople. It can still be seen in the Hippodrome in Istanbul, and on it can be read the inscribed names of the 31 states that fought against the Persians at Salamis or Plataea.[22]

Figure 9.2   Serpent column listing the Greek states that fought against the Persians, Istanbul. Photo by N. Demand.

Victory at Mykale

After the Greek victory at Plataea, the remaining Persian forces under the Persian general Artabazus headed for the Hellespont, and mainland Greece was soon free of the invader. But the Persian fleet still lay at Samos, off the Ionian coast, and the Ionian Greeks were still subject to Persia. The Samians begged the Greek fleet, which was stationed at Delos, for help, and the Greeks came to their assistance. As they approached the island, the Persian fleet withdrew to the shelter of Cape Mykale, where their army was stationed. The Greeks landed, attacking and burning the Persian camp. Victory for the Greeks was decided by the desertion of the Ionians who had been serving the Persians, and by this victory the Ionian Greeks gained their freedom. In his account of this battle, Herodotus rounds out his story by returning to its beginning: "for the second time Ionia revolted from the Persians," but this time with success (Hdt.9.104).

The expansionist ambitions of the Persians may originally have extended even beyond the mainland of Greece. When the Athenians realized that they faced an invasion, they sent a delegation asking for assistance to the powerful tyrant of Syracuse in Sicily, Gelon, whose fleet was second only to their own. According to Herodotus, Gelon agreed to send forces on condition that he be made commander of the Greeks, an offer that was sharply rejected by the Athenian ambassadors (Hdt. 7.157–63). In fact, however, the Greeks of Sicily soon found themselves forced to fight by an invasion of the Carthaginians, which they defeated in the battle of Himera, assigned by tradition to the same day as the battle of Salamis (Hdt. 7.166). While Herodotus treats this as sheer coincidence, one of the other sources, the fourth-century historian Ephorus, saw the Carthaginian attack as carried out in co-operation with the Persians. Ephorus' interpretation has some credibility, since Carthage was a Phoenician city, and the Phoenicians were Persian subjects.[23]

After the battles of Salamis and Plataea turned the tide for Greek freedom, the Persians were never again to return as invaders of mainland Greece. Nevertheless, Persian material culture, especially as it was revealed by the treasures seized after the victory at Plataea, had a lasting effect on the Athenians (see Chapter 10), and the Persian presence as a wealthy superpower in the eastern Mediterranean continued to affect the actions and policies of the Greek cities until Alexander the Great defeated another Darius and took on the mantle of the Great King himself in the fourth century.

SUGGESTIONS FOR FURTHER READING

Philip de Souza (2003), *The Greek and Persian Wars 499–386 BC*, a concise account, with excellent illustrations and battle maps. Peter Green (1996), *The Year of Salamis 480–478*, 2nd ed., covers the whole war, despite the title. Thomas Harrison (2000), *Divinity and History: The Religion of Herodotus. Cambridge Ancient History*, IV, various sections. Rosalind Thomas (2000), *Herodotus in Context: Ethnography, Science, and the Art of Persuasion*, an excellent book that discusses ways in which Herodotus reflects the scientific and medical thinking of his day.

Historical Fiction
Steven Pressfield (1998), *Gates of Fire : An Epic Novel of the Battle of Thermopylae*. New York : Doubleday, a page-turner about Spartan life and the battle.

MAP STUDY

Susa, Sardis, Thrace, Miletus, Ephesus, Lade, Hellespont, Macedonia, Cyprus, Abydos, Thessaly, Tempe, Thasos, Athens, Piraeus, Troezen, Sparta, Salamis, Marathon, Artemisium, Thermopylae, Paros, Aegina, Siris (Italy), Himera, Mt. Athos, Asopus River, Eretria, Mt. Kitheron, Thebes, Plataea, Cape Mykale, Constantinople

ON THE WEB:

A basic site for background on Herodotus:
   http://www.isidore-of-seville.com/herodotus/5.html

Herodotus' map of the world as he knew it:

http://www.henry-davis.com/MAPS/Ancient%20Web%20Pages/109.html

ENDNOTES

[1]See Philip de Souza (2003), *The Greek and Persian Wars, 499–386 BC*, an excellent brief and concise account, with fine illustrations and battle diagrams. Peter Green (1996), *The Year of Salamis 480–478*, 2nd ed. Thomas Harrison (2000), *Divinity and History: The Religion of Herodotus*.

[2]Green (above, n. 1), 14–15.

[3]Green (above, n. 1), 10.

[4]Aristotle, *Constitution of Athens*, 22.

[5]*Ancient evidence*: Suidas, *Khoris Hippeis. Pasturing*: N. G. L. Hammond (1968), *Cambridge Ancient History* IV, 511. Embarking: W. W. How and J. Wells (1928), *A Commentary on Herodotus* I, 362. Green (above, n. 1) 34–35.

[6]Pausanias 1.29.4.

[7]At Vrana, reported by S. Marinatos (1970), *Athens Annals of Archaeology* 3:357ff.

[8]Pausanias 1.15.3.

[9]But see the sceptical account by Frank Frost (1979), "The Dubious Origins of the 'Marathon,'" with comment on the Pheidippides/Philippides issue by the journal's editor, Ernst Badian, in *American Journal of Ancient History* 4:159–165.

[10]Herodotus 7.22–24.

[11]B. S. J. Isserlin, R. E. Jones, V. Darastathis, S. P. Papamarinopoulos, G. E. Syrides, and J. Uren (2003), "The Canal of Xerxes: Summary of Investigations, 1991–2001," *Annual of the British School at Athens* 98:xviii (abstract).

[12]On this passage, see especially Harrison (above, n. 1), 132–137.

[13]Herodotus 7.33–36.

[14]Simonides, quoted by Herodotus 7.228; Aeschylus, *Persians* 12.

[15]Herodotus 7.61–80.

[16]Herodotus 7.10–18, 46–52. On this passage, see Harrison (above n. 1), 132–137.

[17]Herodotus 7.37.

[18]Herodotus 7.57.

[19]Herodotus 5.3–5.

[20]Discussion by N. G. L. Hammond (1988), in the *Cambridge Ancient History* IV: 558–563; Harrison (above, n. 1), 150–152.

[21]J. P. Barron (1988), in *Cambridge Ancient History* IV, 596.

[22]See *Cambridge Ancient History* IV, p. 618, fig. 51.

[23]The information from Ephorus is found in the universal history of Diodorus Siculus, 11.1.4. The war in the west is discussed by T. J. Dunbabin (1948), *The Western Greeks*, chap. 14.

10

ATHENS
THE DEVELOPMENT OF
EMPIRE AND DEMOCRACY

ATHENS DEVELOPS AN EMPIRE

In the half-century following the Persian Wars, Athens turned its naval strength into imperialistic naval power and the *isonomia* of the Kleisthenic reforms into democracy—changes that were closely interrelated. After the defeat of the Persians, the league of Greek states that had fought against the invasion chose the Athenians to lead a campaign of retribution and vengeance against Persia. Gradually, Athens transformed its leadership in this league into imperial control, while in Athens itself the commitment to sea power that league leadership involved led to the extension of significant political rights to the lowest class, the *thetes*, who supplied most of the rowers for the fleet, and thus to the development of Athenian democracy.

Despite the importance of these years, no full-scale treatment of them by a Greek historian survives. Our main source is an abbreviated account by the historian Thucydides, the *Pentecontaetia*, or "Fifty-Years," which forms part of the preliminaries to his history of the Peloponnesian War.

THUCYDIDES AND OTHER HISTORICAL SOURCES

Thucydides, who was born ca. 460, was about 25 years younger than Herodotus. He was a member of an aristocratic Athenian family that possessed a considerable fortune, including interests in the gold mines of Thrace. In 424, when the Athenians were at war with Sparta

213

during the Peloponnesian War, he was elected general and stationed in the Chalkidike. During his command in that area, he failed to arrive in time to prevent the surrender of the Athenian settlement of Amphipolis to the Spartans, and, as a result, he was sentenced to exile (Thuc. 4.103–106; 5.26). He spent the next twenty years in exile until he was recalled during the final siege of Athens, probably spending much of that time on his family's holdings in Thrace. His exile gave him the opportunity to consult with both sides in the war, but of course he was denied first-hand knowledge of events in Athens during this time.

Thucydides was a scant generation younger than Herodotus, yet in many ways he seems to have belonged to a wholly different age. Although Herodotus was also well versed in the intellectual issues of his day, Thucydides reflects the full flowering of contemporary rhetoric, philosophy, and medicine in the late fifth century. He is said to have studied with the orator Antiphon and to have been an associate of the philosopher Anaxagoras, and he spent his exile in the north in the same area in which Hippocratic doctors were practicing. While Herodotus had described an earlier war that had ended in Greek victory and that was perceived as a glorious episode in Athens' past, Thucydides' topic was a contemporary war that Athens was to lose, and one that he saw as corrupting the most fundamental values of the Athenian state. In keeping with the gravity of the situation, Thucydides' aim was entirely serious. It was not his intention to entertain his audience by intriguing tales or to create an encomium for Athens, as Herodotus had. Rather, he was intent on making an accurate determination of events and investigating the psychological factors that drove men and states to pursue power. He knew that men, including the Athenians, were not always noble, nor did they always clearly reveal their true motives. In fact, it was his portrayal of the corrosive effects of power on those who wield it that was perhaps his greatest achievement. He himself said that he had written his work "not to win the applause of the moment but to be a possession for all time."(Thuc. 1.22).

Other contemporary sources for this period include Aeschylus' tragic trilogy, the *Oresteia*, which employed a story set in the post-Trojan War period in an effort to reconcile violent opposition to a present-day reform; the account of Athenian political development by an unknown writer known as Pseudo-Aristotle; and the *Athenian Tribute Lists* (ATL), fragments of the records of the annual payments made by the Athenians to the goddess Athena, inscribed on stone. These payments were made from the tribute paid by member states to Athens, of which Athena received one-sixtieth; therefore they can be used to reconstruct the tribute payments in the various years for which they are preserved. As interpreted by specialists in epigraphy, they provide valuable information about the ups and downs of Athenian control.[1] Finally, the work of Plutarch is a frequently used later source;. it is easily accessible and entertaining, but not entirely reliable. Plutarch was a Greek who lived in the time of the Roman Empire (ca. 46–120 C.E.). He wrote biographies, not history, and he wrote for a Roman audience with the aim of improving his readers morally while entertaining them. His choice of genre and audience naturally shaped his treatment of the material. He included much that Thucydides, if he knew of it, must have considered unsuitable for serious history, but he does at times preserve sound information that does not appear elsewhere. In each case, the historian must consider Plutarch's possible source and his purpose in using it, and weigh its historical value accordingly.[2]

Athenian Recovery

At the end of the war, Athens, twice sacked by the Persians, lay in ruins. An immediate need was to provide shelter, but the rebuilding of the walls seemed to the Athenians to be even more vital to the defense of the *polis*. The Spartans, disturbed by the Athenian display of initiative and vigor in the war, opposed the reconstruction of the walls, suggesting instead that all the cities of Greece tear down their walls (Sparta itself had no walls). Not willing to follow this advice, but also unwilling to escalate the matter into a direct confrontation, the Athenians, under the leadership of Themistocles, resorted to clever scheming to achieve their purpose.

Source Analysis

hucydides 1.89–93. Thucydides' account of this scheme, and of Themistocles' continuing role in turning Athens into a sea power, comes close to the methods of Herodotus in telling an interesting story in order to make a point: how the Athenians attained the position that in time enabled them to develop their empire. Some scholars discount the story because it fits so well into the pattern of stories illustrating Themistoclean trickery, but that in itself is not cause for rejecting the evidence that Sparta and its allies were ambivalent and that neither side was willing to risk a direct confrontation.

The Delian League

After their final victory, the Greek states of the Hellenic league that had fought against the Persians did not immediately disband but determined to maintain their forces in the Aegean. Sparta continued as leader of the coalition, but difficulties soon arose. The Spartan leader Pausanias began to affect Persian ways and became increasingly distant and arrogant.[3] The other Greeks found his behavior intolerable and appealed to the Athenians to take over leadership.

With Athenian acceptance of the leadership of the Greeks, a new league was constituted, which is called the Delian League by modern historians because the site of its headquarters was on the island of Delos. Each state agreed to furnish ships and men, or provide a monetary contribution; all states were to be autonomous and to have equal votes in the meetings of the league, which were to be held in Delos. Athens, as by far the strongest sea power, was to be hegemon, with supreme command in military operations and executive authority in the other dealings of the league. The Athenian Aristides (known as "The Just") determined the initial payments of each state, and the Athenians were to serve as treasurers of the funds, which were to be kept on Delos. The league eventually included most of the *poleis* on the Aegean islands and along its northern and eastern coasts, as well as those on the shores of the Hellespont, Propontus, and Black Sea, and along the southern coast of Anatolia. Sparta and her Peloponnesian allies did not join, however, and the old Hellenic League continued to exist until 462, when Athens and Sparta openly broke off relations. The Delian League in its inception was, however, in no sense anti-Spartan.

The original purpose of the Delian League was, according to Thucydides (1.96), to avenge the sufferings that the Persians had inflicted on the Greeks by ravaging the king's lands. The purpose probably also included preventing the Greeks in Asia Minor from again falling under Persian domination, but this is not stated in our sources. Still another motivation not mentioned by Thucydides may seem obvious to the modern reader: fear of another Persian invasion. In fact, it was not until 468, when the Athenian general Cimon won a victory over the Persian fleet at the battle of the Eurymedon, that Greece could feel altogether relieved of the possibility that the Persians might return. Thucydides, however, may be accurately reflecting his perception of Greek self-confidence at the time in portraying them setting out to *punish* the Persians, rather than to protect against them.

Democratic Developments in Athens

Even before the first joint action of the league, in 487, the first of a series of moves was taken in Athens that were to lead to the development of full democracy. This first step was the introduction of the lottery in the selection of archons. Although the lottery was still limited to a group of 500 men chosen by election, and these were all members of the two highest property classes, the office lost much of its prestige as a result of this change.[4]

It was probably at about the same time that a politician named Pericles introduced pay for jury duty.[5] Since Athenian juries were large (their numbers ranged from 200 to over 1,000), and the jury-roll included 6,000 men, this was a move that appealed to large numbers of people. It meant that many men could now serve on juries without fearing financial loss. In fact, for the poor and the elderly, jury service became an important source of income. The various courts not only tried civil and criminal cases, which were often politically motivated, but also presided over the audit that every Athenian official was required to undergo at the end of his term of office, in which the entire conduct of his office was examined. Moreover, as the empire developed, the Athenian courts were given jurisdiction over the more serious cases of the allies, who were required to go to Athens for trials. Thus participation on juries brought a substantial increase in the political influence of the *demos*,[6] as is illustrated in the *Wasps* of Aristophanes.

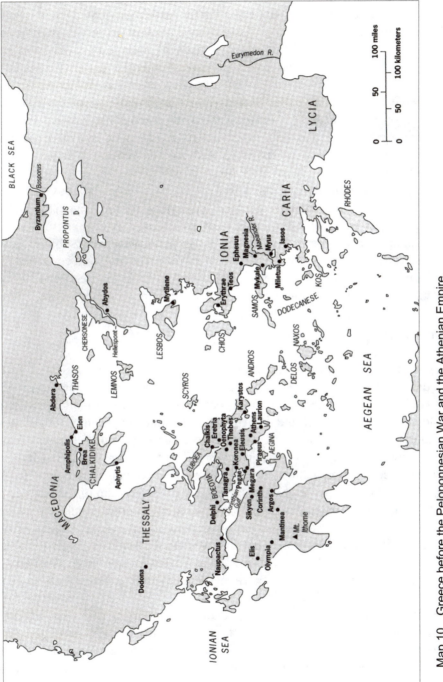

Map 10   Greece before the Peloponnesian War and the Athenian Empire.

How was the Athenian state financed? After the institution of the Delian League, tribute from those allies who elected to supply gold rather than ships (a growing number) provided a large share of the resources of the city. Income from the silver mines at Laurion, which were leased to private individuals, was another major source of income. Taxes and duties financed operations at the port of Piraeus. Finally, while there was no income tax, there was a system of civic contributions, called **liturgies**, that were imposed upon the wealthy. The major liturgies were the *trierarchy* (outfitting and being responsible for a warship for a year), and the *choregia* (oufitting and training a chorus for the dramatic festivals); other festival liturgies were the *gymnasiarchy* (preparing a team for competition in an athletic event), the *hestiasis* (providing a public feast), and the *architheoria* (leading a delegation to a foreign festival). The expenditures, especially for the *trierarchy*, were high, but many men outdid themselves in carrying out their assignments, competing for public acclaim and honor. On the other hand, it was possible for a man to avoid a liturgy by challenging another citizen whom he thought to be richer to perform the liturgy in his place, or to submit to an exchange of properties (we do not know how often this occurred). The most that could be required of a man was one festival liturgy in two years, and one *trierarchy* in three years, although some men voluntarily performed more liturgies and spent more on them than was required.

League Actions

The first military action of the Delian League occurred in 476, when league forces seized control of Eion, a fortress on the north Aegean coast at the mouth of the Strymon River that was still held by the Persians. In the same year, they took the island of Skyros, a pirate lair; they sold the pirates as slaves, and the Athenians occupied the island. Both of these actions were important in securing Greek control of the Aegean and its northern coast. A third action in the next few years was an expedition against Karystos, a Greek city in southern Euboea that had medized after the battle of Artemisium; the Karystians were compelled to join the league. All these actions were in keeping with the professed aim of the league.

Not every league member was happy with the required contributions to the league, however. In 470 the Naxians decided to withdraw from the league. The Athenians, probably with the approval of the other league members, viewed the secession as a violation of the permanent alliance to which they had all sworn, and the "revolt" was promptly crushed. Naxos was denied autonomy (a guarantee of the original league) and henceforth was to be subject to Athens.

One of the signal achievements of the league occurred in the next year, when the Greeks won a decisive victory over the Persian fleet at the battle of the Eurymedon River on the southern coast of Asia Minor. Two hundred Phoenician ships serving as the navy of the Persians were destroyed in the battle. This victory secured the Greek cities in Caria and Lycia for the league and effectively removed the threat that the Persians might attempt another invasion of Greece.

In 465 the island of Thasos, which was one of the most powerful members of the league, became disturbed by Athenian activities on the mainland opposite the island, the site of lucrative gold mines, which they saw as infringements on their rightful sphere of influence. Unsatisfied with the Athenian response to their concerns, they revolted. The Thasian fleet was quickly defeated, but a blockade of two years was required to put down the revolt. The city's walls were torn down and its fleet given to the Athenians. The Thasians relinquished all claims to the gold mines on the mainland, and the city became a tributary subject of Athens.

In all of these early league actions the league forces were led by Cimon, an Athenian aristocrat. Cimon played an important role in the direction of Athenian policy in the post-war period, pursuing a course of action that was both aggressively anti-Persian and pro-Spartan (even to naming one of his sons Lakedaimonios). In seeking good relations with Sparta, Cimon may simply have been avoiding the risk of military action on two fronts. Nonetheless, pro-Spartanism was a perennially popular attitude among Athenian aristocrats, often rooted in a hereditary relationship of *xenia* (guest-friendship) between aristocratic families in the two cities. Even in the later fifth century when Athens was at war with Sparta, the comic poet Aristophanes portrays the aristocratic son in the *Wasps* as dressing his father in Spartan shoes for an elite dinner party, reflecting the tendency of young Athenians of wealth to affect Spartan dress and hairstyles. In the fourth century, another Athenian aristocrat and general, Xenophon, had his sons educated in Sparta and took up residence there himself while he was in exile, and the philosopher Plato created his utopian state after the Spartan model. To such men, conservatives at heart, Spartan self-discipline and military prowess compared favorably with what they viewed as the undisciplined and licentious behavior of the Athenian *demos*.

In 464 Sparta suffered a severe earthquake. According to later sources, 20,000 died, including all the *ephebes* (men between the ages of 18 and 20), and all but five houses were destroyed.[7] The Messenian helots seized the opportunity to revolt, and Sparta was once again faced with a Messenian war. Help was sent by Aegina and Mantinea in Boeotia. By 462 the Messenian rebels had been confined to Mt. Ithome, and the Spartans sought the help of the Athenians, who were reputed to be expert in siege warfare.[8] Urged by the pro-Spartan Cimon, the Athenians sent 4,000 hoplites under his command.[9] But the Spartans suffered a change of heart when their traditional rivals, whom they viewed as both too enterprising and dangerously revolutionary, appeared in their own territory, and they sent the Athenians back home. The Athenian *demos*, angered by the ignominious end of an expedition that had been advocated by Cimon, ostracized him.

Reform of the Areopagus Council

With the conservative Cimon out of the way, his rivals were free to carry out reforms that increased the political power of their own base of support, the *demos*. In fact, in 462, even before Cimon's ostracism and while he was absent from the city on the expedition to Lakonia, Ephialtes had carried through the first in this series of revolutionary changes, stripping the ancient and conservative Council of the Areopagus of most of its powers.

Source Analysis

P S.-Aristotle, *The Athenian Constitution*[10]   The stages by which Athenian democracy developed are known to us primarily through a work called the *Athenian Constitution*, which was attributed to Aristotle; some scholars accept it as a genuine work of the philosopher, but it seems most probable that it was the work of one of his pupils who were assigned the task of collecting accounts of the constitutions of the various cities. This unknown pupil is usually referred to as "Pseudo-Aristotle" (Ps.-Aristotle).

The philosopher Aristotle's approach to the past was to see it as a continuous progress toward the present, and to view the institutions and ideas of his predecessors as early steps toward this goal. Ps.-Aristotle followed the same approach, portraying the early history of the Athenian democracy in terms of the ideological debates of his own day. Thus he saw the early fifth-century political scene in Athens in terms of a rivalry between an aristocratic faction (headed by Cimon), and a democratic faction (led by Ephialtes and Pericles). Although this schematization is too neat, and we cannot accept its ideological aspects as historical (the concept of democracy was not yet formulated when Ephialtes and Pericles opposed Cimon), the evolution in the Athenian constitution that Ps.-Aristotle recorded did take place, and he provides our only continuous account of it. Therefore we must follow him, bearing in mind that we cannot trust his account of the ideological motives that lay behind these changes. Can you identify any signs of the influence of ideological factors on this account?

PS.-ARISTOTLE, *CONSTITUTION OF ATHENS*: on the reform of the Areopagus Council: For about seventeen years after the Persian War, the constitution continued under the leadership of the Areopagus Council, although it declined a little. But with the demos increasing in numbers, its leader, Ephialtes, the son of Sophonides, who had a reputation for being uncorrupted and loyal to the constitution, attacked the Council. First he removed many of the members of the Council, bringing charges against them for their misadministration. Then when Konon was Archon, he abolished the extra powers through which the Areopagus was the guardian of the constitution, giving some to the Council of Five Hundred, and some to the demos and the courts.

The reformed Areopagus Council retained only its ancient religious functions, of which the most important was its role in trying murder cases. In 458, four years after the reform, the poet Aeschylus presented a tragic trilogy, the *Oresteia*, which apparently sought to conciliate the opposition by celebrating the importance of the powers still remaining in the Areopagus Council. It dramatized the civilizing and beneficial role of the council as a formal homicide court that replaced the unending chain of violence entailed by the primitive system of blood vengeance with a system of law and justice.

Pericles Enters the Political Arena

Despite Aeschylus' appeal for the acceptance of the changes in the role of the Areopagus Council, Ephialtes was assassinated shortly after his reform was instituted. His role as the foremost spokesman of the *demos* was taken over by his associate, Pericles (who had earlier introduced jury pay, mentioned above). Pericles was well suited by birth and ability to play an important role in affairs of state. He was a member of a powerful and influential aristocratic family, the Alkmeonids, through his mother's line. Recall, however, that this family bore an ancestral curse to which its political enemies could still appeal. His father had been a general at the battle of Mykale and was prominent politically. Pericles himself was an intellectual and included among his close associates the philosopher Anaxagoras, the sculptor Phidias, and the Milesian *hetaira* (concubine) Aspasia. She became his mistress and was said to have made considerable contributions to his policies. Although this claim may have been only a political attack by his enemies, she does appear as an unusual woman in a number of ancient sources.[11]

Following Sparta's rejection of the relief force led by Cimon, the Athenians became openly hostile to Sparta. In a series of moves, they strengthened their own position and challenged Sparta and its allies. They formally dropped out of the old Hellenic League and allied themselves with Sparta's enemy, Argos. In 461/460, they assisted Megara in a revolt against the Lakedaimonian League that arose out of a border dispute between that city and Corinth. By this assistance, Athens gained the alliance of both Megara and Pegae, a port on the Corinthian Gulf, as well as the lasting enmity of Corinth. In order to protect Megara, the Athenians built the Long Walls connecting that city to its port, which they themselves garrisoned. Megara, strengthened by its long walls, served to block a possible Spartan invasion of Attica. Moreover, the alliance with Pegae on the Corinthian Gulf gave Athens easier access to Naupactus, which they had recently seized from the Ozolian Locrians as a base to control the Gulf. After the Messenian rebels against Sparta capitulated under terms that allowed them to leave the Peloponnesus, the Athenians resettled them at Naupactus.

From 460 to 445, with the exception of one five-year truce, the Athenians were engaged in open hostilities against Sparta and its allies, the Peloponnesian League, in what is often called the First Peloponnesian War. Early in the war Athens had built the Long Walls connecting Athens to its harbor at the Piraeus, protecting this vital access to the sea (perhaps completed in 457). In 459, in the midst of this war, Athens also undertook a major overseas involvement in Egypt, assisting the revolt of the Egyptians against their Persian rulers. They contributed a large fleet, 200 ships that had been on an expedition to Cyprus where Greeks still lived under Persian control.

In 457, the Spartans marched north to help Thebes revive its position of leadership in the Boeotian League, hoping to establish that city as a check on Athenian expansion northward. The Athenians met them at Tanagra in Boeotian territory as they returned. The Athenians suffered a defeat in the ensuing battle, but the Spartans nonetheless suffered such high losses that they withdrew from Boeotia. Shortly after, the Athenians gained control of Boeotia with a victory at the battle of Oenophyta. They held power in Boeotia for ten years, but their defeat in the battle of Coronea in 447 brought an end to their attempt to establish a land empire to complement their naval domain.

It was also in 457 that the process of democratization in Athens was taken a step further with the opening of the lottery for the archonship to the *zeugitai*, the next-to-lowest property class. The use of the lot continued to be extended to other offices, with the exception of those that were considered to require specific skills, such as the generalship, financial offices, and the office of architect. Payment for offices other than that of juror was gradually introduced, although we do not always know the exact dates. Payment for attending the Assembly came only in the fourth century.

In 454 the Egyptian venture ended in overwhelming failure. The sources do not agree, but the Athenians and their allies may have lost as many as 250 ships and 50,000 men.[12] The disaster threatened the Delian League's control of the Aegean, and therefore the security of the island of Delos and the league treasury that was kept there; the Athenians consequently transferred the treasury to Athens. This was an important move that gave them physical control over the assets of the league, but Thucydides does not mention it. As we shall see, the Athenians soon exploited this new advantage, for they utilized league funds for the building of the Parthenon and other Periclean building projects.[13] The transfer of league funds to Athens also provided historians with an important new source of evidence about the empire, the Athenian Tribute Lists, which make possible the reconstruction of the tribute payments from 453 (see above).

In 451, under Pericles' sponsorship, the restrictive Citizenship Law was passed, requiring that a man be of Athenian parentage on both sides to qualify as a citizen. Previously, the only requirement had been that the father be an Athenian citizen, and aristocratic families had often sought brides from other Greek *poleis*, and even from among non-Greeks, in order to establish ties that would be useful politically. The law was problematic, and especially so for its sponsor, for when both of Pericles' sons by his Athenian wife died in the plague, he made a special plea for an exception to the law so that his son by the Milesian Aspasia could be declared a citizen. As the century wore on and the effects of the Peloponnesian War were felt, the law fell into abeyance. It was restored in 403, however, and was strictly enforced during the fourth century.

The Peace of Callias

In about 450 peace was concluded with Persia. Late ancient sources report an official treaty, the Peace of Callias, which granted autonomy to the Greeks in Asia Minor, excluded Persian satraps from Aegean coastal areas, and barred Persian ships from Aegean waters. Many historians doubt the existence of a formal treaty, however. Thucydides does not mention it, and Plutarch dates the peace to the period after the victory of the Eurymedon and mentions that doubts about the genuineness of the treaty had been raised as early as the fourth century. But whether there was a formal treaty or an informal understanding, major hostilities between the Delian League and the Persians ceased about 450. We will refer to this situation as the Peace of Callias, without making any commitments as to its exact form.

The Peace of Callias removed the justification for the Delian League, and Athens' allies soon objected to its continuation and to the continuation of tribute payments. There was much unrest, and some members of the league defected. The Athenians agreed to concessions to gain a new 30-year peace treaty with the Peloponnesians in order to concentrate on these problems with their allies. In the end the Athenians prevailed because the instruments of empire were already strong. Tribute was continued, and new and more stringent regulations were imposed on its collection. Documents began to refer openly to the allies as "those whom Athens controls," and the Athenians introduced new forms of control. In effect, these changes transformed the Delian League into an Athenian Empire.

One of the new forms of control gave special protection in allied cities to Athenians and their sympathizers, who were naturally unpopular in cities that resented their ties to Athens. Trials involving allies and Athenian citizens were already required to be held in Athenian courts for this reason; but to further protect Athenian citizens, the Athenians ruled that any city in which an Athenian, or an Athenian *proxenos* (local person serving as a representative of Athens), was killed would be subject to a collective fine of five talents, an amount that was more than the annual tribute of many of the cities. Moreover, anyone who killed a *proxenos* was held liable to the same penalty as one who killed an Athenian.[14]

The Athenians also took steps to control silver currency with the Currency Decree, which required every league member to convert its silver coinage into Athenian coinage, and thereafter to use only Athenian coins, weights, and measures.[15] The tone was peremptory, and penalties were established for failure to comply, suggesting that the Athenians anticipated resistance. The decree served Athenian imperialistic interests in more than one way. It smoothed the workings of the administrative machinery of empire, facilitating the handling of tribute, assuring that distributions and collections, such as fines, would be uniform in every city, and providing a uniform basis for payments in support of Athenian administrators and military forces abroad. It also graphically impressed the fact of Athenian power upon cities that had long expressed their civic autonomy by the distinctive designs of their coinage.

Athens at this time also began a policy of establishing Athenian settlements, or **cleruchies**, in allied cities.[16] The cleruchies were made up of Athenian citizens of the *zeugitai* and *thete* classes who received allotments of land taken over from local landowners. Unlike the citizens in most Greek overseas settlements, however, the cleruchs retained their Athenian citizenship.[17] The establishment of cleruchies provided an Athenian presence to keep an eye on the local population, as well as a safety valve for the growing population of the poor in Athens. Pericles himself led a cleruchy to the Chersonese, and others are known to have been established in Euboea, Naxos, Andros, and Brea in Thrace. Still others are inferred from the ancient evidence, but not specifically attested.

The cleruchies were naturally resented by the allies upon whom they were imposed, even though the tribute of cities with cleruchies was lowered. Not surprisingly, they were popular with the Athenian *demos* that benefited from them. It was not a coincidence that in 451 Pericles' Citizenship Law limiting citizenship to the offspring of two Athenian citizens was passed, for participation in a cleruchy was restricted to citizens.

Source Analysis

T hucydides 1.89–117 provides a condensed account of the development of the Delian League from its beginnings until its transformation into an Athenian empire. It is helpful to trace this in the form of a list, noting the chronological order of Athens' actions, locating their sites on the map, and considering the justification that Thucydides gives for each. Such a format reveals clearly Athens' escalating oppression of its allies.

THE CHANGING FACE OF ATHENS AFTER THE PERSIAN WARS[18]

The Growth of Persian Influences

The dramatic victory of the Greeks over the Persians in the Persian Wars brought a great influx of wealth into Greece in the form of booty taken from the defeated enemy. Spectacular Persian treasures fell into the hands of the Greeks with the defeat of Mardonius at Plataea (see Chapter 9). The royal tent, "adorned with gold and silver" (Hdt. 9.80), was filled with an abundance of valuables: gold and silver furniture, silver-footed couches covered with ornately embroidered textiles, gold and silver cups and bowls, and chests overflowing with costly objects of gold, silver, and ivory. One-tenth of the spoils were dedicated to the god at Delphi; the rest were divided up among the troops. Similarly, rich Persian spoils were distributed among the Greek victors in subsequent campaigns, particularly after the battle of the Eurymedon.

These valuable Persian objects introduced the Athenian population not only to a new level of luxury, but also to new fashions. Despite the natural post-war reaction against Persia, in which the Greeks vowed to band together to punish the invader and to prevent future attacks, an attraction to Persia and all things Persian underlay many of the expressions of late fifth-century Athenian culture. According to Aristophanes, some in the older generation were ambivalent about the new styles. In the *Wasps*, Aristophanes portrays Philokleon's dismay over the stylish new Persian cloak that his son insists on his wearing—a *kaunakes*, or woolen cloak with tufts or tassels hanging from it, "woven in Ecbatana," and to be worn with Laconian slippers.[19] Other styles borrowed from the Persians were the sleeved *chiton*; the *kandys*, a cloak usually made of leather with unused sleeves (converted to usable in many Attic versions); and the *ependytes*, a short wool or linen tunic worn over the chiton.[20] Miller points out, however, that over time the use of Persian fashion as an indicator of elite status devolved, as the lower classes and women adopted the marks of Oriental culture, as illustrated by the wearing of the *kaunakes* by Philocleon in the *Wasps*. In response, many elite males began to prefer the severe styles of Sparta.

A similar process of devolution occurred in the adaptation of Persian drinking vessels. While most Athenians could not follow the elite Persian fashion of using luxurious gold and silver vessels, Attic potters imitated and adapted them in Attic black gloss pottery.[21] The users of these clay adaptations of Persian metalware were, of course, not the elite, but the aspiring "middle" class.

Persian influence also appeared in architecture. It has been suggested that the model for the round Tholos, built in Athens about 470–460, and nicknamed the *Skias* (Sunshade), was a large royal tent left behind by the retreating Persians.[22] Another important building that reflected Persian style was the Odeion, built around mid-century on the lower slopes of the Acropolis.[23] Although little has been recovered of this particular building, and even its shape is not known certainly, Plutarch reported the belief that it was built on the model of the King's tent,[24] and Vitruvius says that the building was roofed using the masts and spars of the ships of the Persian spoils.[25] The imperialistic significance of the Odeion is underscored by Margaret Miller:[26]

> In producing the Odeion, the Athenians deliberately adopted a building type developed in Iran to convey a specific message of imperial majesty for the Persian kings; and they modified it slightly to make it buildable using Greek construction methods. Resonating against its Persian models, it is a proud statement of empire.

The Periclean Building Program

Following the Peace of Callias, ca. 450, Pericles proposed the rebuilding of the temples that had been left in ruins after the war as a reminder of the hubris of the Persians. When his call for a panhellenic conference on the issue failed to win support among the other Greek cities, however, the Athenians proceeded alone with a building program that he devised. This not only signaled the new state of peace with Persia, it also gave the Athenians the opportunity to display their imperial might and cultural splendor to their subjects, when they came to participate in the Panathenaic Festival or to have their cases tried in Athenian courts. Again, this is an element of imperialism that we do not read about in the history of Thucydides. The main sources are the remains of the buildings themselves, fragments of building accounts, and the later account in Plutarch's *Pericles*.[27]

The Greater Panathenaic Festival, held every fourth year, which had been reorganized by Peisistratos as a civic celebration, was now transformed into a celebration of the empire of the Athenians. Each subject state was required to play the role of a colony by sending an official delegation to the festival with an offering of a cow and a *panoply* (a full set of armor). Tribute assessments for the next four years were announced during the festival.

The focus of the Panathenaic Festival was on the Acropolis, to which the procession made its way from the lower city, bearing a new robe for the cult statue of Athena. The focus of Pericles' building program was also on the Acropolis. A new temple to Athena, the Parthenon, and a new gate-way to the Acropolis, the Propylaea, were built there, as well as a temple to Athena Nike (Victory). In the last quarter of the century, the Erechtheion, an elaborate and complex building celebrating a number of very ancient traditional Attic cults, was built . A significant portion of the funds used in the building program appears to have come from the league treasury.[28]

WEBSITE 10.1   THE ACROPOLIS

An interactive web site with a plan of the Acropolis; identifies the buildings, including the older temples replaced in the Periclean program:

http://www.ancient-greece.org/images/maps/plans/acropolis-plan.swf

---

The Parthenon was the centerpiece of the Periclean plan. After the first Persian War a new temple to Athena (the Old Parthenon) had been started to the south of the Peisistratid temple of Athena, but it had progressed only as far as the foundation and the surrounding colonnade at the time of the second Persian attack. The Persians set fire to the scaffolding used in the building of this temple, calcining the column drums of the colonnade. Twenty-six of these drums were incorporated into the rebuilt wall of the Acropolis in the 470s as reminders of Persian aggression. In 447/446 work on a new Parthenon was begun, built upon the foundation of the earlier unfinished building and utilizing its salvageable materials. In the Periclean scheme, however, the plan of this new temple was changed to provide an impressive setting for a colossal chryselephantine (gold and ivory) statue of Athena by the sculptor Phidias. Accommodating the statue required changes in the traditional standard plan of the Doric temple, the most obvious of which was an increase in the width of the temple from the traditional six columns to eight. The added width, which necessitated the enlargement of the existing foundation, made possible a more striking interior setting for the statue, for which an unusual three-sided colonnade formed a frame.[29] In front of the statue a large pool reflected its image and added humidity to help preserve the ivory.

The Parthenon was highly decorated with sculptured reliefs expressing in a variety of ways the glory of Athena's city and the triumph of the Greeks over the barbarians. On the entablature the Doric triglyph and metope frieze portrayed mythological combats of Centaurs against Lapiths, Amazons against Greeks, gods against giants, and Greeks against Trojans, each celebrating the victory of civilized Greece over the barbarous east. The pedimental sculptures portrayed the birth of Athena on the east and the contest between Athena and Poseidon for the possession of Athens on the west.

On the cella walls within the exterior colonnade, a running frieze, typical of Ionic architecture, represented, according to many scholars, a human event, the Panathenaic procession. The Ionic running frieze was in itself an innovation in a Doric temple, but the more striking departure was the portrayal in the frieze of a human, rather than a divine or mythological, event,[30] if, indeed, that is the correct interpretation.

The Parthenon frieze has also been interpreted as an adaptation of a relief frieze on a Persian imperial building: the great audience hall of Darius at Persepolis (the *Apadana*). The *Apadana* reliefs portray the festival celebration of the Iranian New Year; in it a procession of

Figure 10.1 Parthenon
Photo by N. Demand.

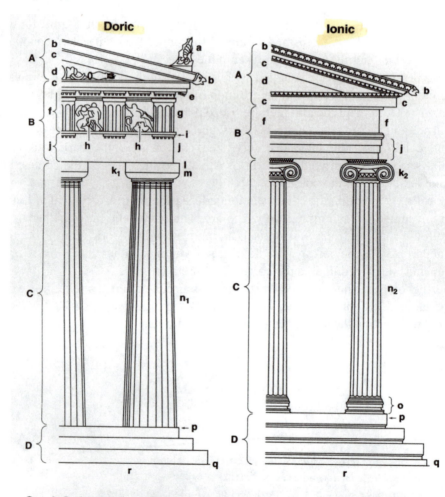

Doric

Ionic

Greek Orders of Architecture

A. Pediment
B. Entablature
C. Column
D. Crepidoma

a. Acroterion
b. Sima
c. Geison or Cornice
d. Tympanum
e. Mutule & Guttae
f. Frieze
g. Triglyphs
h. Metopes
i. Regulae & Guttae
j. Architrave or Epistyle

k_1. Capital (Doric)
k_2. Capital (Ionic) with Volutes
l. Abacus
m. Echinus
n_1. Shaft with flutes
   separated by sharp arrises
n_2. Shaft with flutes
   separated by blunt fillets
o. Bases
p. Stylobate
q. Euthynteria
r. Stereobate

Figure 10.2   Diagram of Greek architectural orders

WEBSITE 10.2   THE PARTHENON FRIEZE

This excellent web site is the English language version of the Greek Ministry of Culture site, which allows you to move through the entire frieze, with useful comments as you go (be sure to click on the little British flag at the right top of the page if you happen upon a Greek language version of the site).

http://www.ekt.gr/parthenonfrieze/index.jsp?lang=en

For an alternative interpretation of the Parthenon frieze, see:

http://academic.reed.edu/humanities/110Tech/ParthenonFriezeConnelly.html

delegates from the subject nations approach the King with gifts from one direction; from the other direction, Persian nobles, accompanied by a retinue of guards, horses, and chariots, bring their gifts of loyalty to the King. The message of the reliefs is one of imperial power and idealized social order. If the Parthenon frieze adopted the model of the Persian relief to depict the procession at the Greater Panathenaia. in which both the Athenians and their allies joined to honor the goddess, it sent, "a message of imperial aspiration articulated through a festival metaphor borrowed deliberately from the Persians and recast in the guise of an eminently Athenian celebration."[31]

The Athenians may have used the tents of the Persians captured at Plataea as building models, but how could they have known the contents of the *Apadana* frieze at Persepolis? Two probable ways in which the ideas could have been transmitted have been suggested. The first involves the presence of elite Greek visitors to Persia, of which there were many. The best candidate is Miltiades, who had left Athens as tyrant of the Chersonesos and returned home after the Ionian Revolt to become the hero of Marathon. He had spent enough time in the east to have become familiar with the imperial building program.[32] Embassies be-

WEBSITE 10.3   COMPARE THE APADANA FRIEZE TO THE PARTHANON FRIEZE

Study the Greek Minstry of Culture web site for the Parthenon frieze suggested above:

http://www.ekt.gr/parthenonfrieze/index.jsp?lang=en

Then consider this site on the Apadana frieze, which is sponsored by the Oriental Institute of the University of Chicago; look at a number of the pictures of the procession and compare them with the procession portrayed on the Parthenon frieze:

http://oi.uchicago.edu/OI/MUS/PA/IRAN/PAAI/PAAI_Apadana.html

Do you agree with the suggestion that the theme and message of the Parthenon frieze were borrowed from, or at least influenced by, the Apadana reliefs? Why, or why not?

tween the Greeks and the Persians were also frequent, as shown by the interception of the Persian Artaphernes at Eion on his way to Sparta in 425/424, carrying a letter that revealed that the Spartans had been negotiating with the Persian king.[33] Artaphernes was, of course, too late to have affected the creation of the Parthenon frieze, and he was dealing with the Spartans. But that Sparta was not exceptional in such behavior is shown by the embassy scene with the Persian ambassador at Athens in Aristophanes' *Acharnians*,[34] which suggests that the audience was all too familiar with Persian envoys. An even more likely means of transmission, however, was through the traveling sculptors who worked on the Persepolis building program, many of whom would have been attracted back to mainland Greece by the Periclean building project.[35]

In 437/436–432 the Peisistratid gateway to the Acropolis, the Propylaea, was reoriented and reconstructed on a monumental scale and plan. Since it replaced the defensive works that formerly guarded the entryway to the Acropolis, the new Propylaea graphically illustrated the new nature of Athenian power: with the Long Walls securing Athenian access to the sea, a formidable defensive system was no longer necessary to protect the Acropolis. The Periclean Propylaea was designed to impress those approaching the Acropolis, not to ward off attackers.

The Periclean building program celebrated the might and intellectual achievements of an imperial Athens, as well as its patron goddess Athena. Human activities were given a place beside the divine, symbolized not only by the Parthenon frieze, but also by the fact that the Parthenon was built as the home of a cult statue that was a work of art created by one of the most celebrated sculptors in the Greek world at the time.

The building program was not without its critics. Conservatives condemned it as a celebration of Athenian naval imperialism, focused on the defense of overseas possessions rather than of Attic farms and estates; as a creation of the *demos* rather than of aristocratic patronage; and as a project in which the wealth of the League was squandered on the workers of the *demos*. Some of these critics turned to the courts—a traditional forum of Athenian political attack. The sculptor Phidias was accused of embezzling gold intended for use on the great statue of Athena, and when this charge was defeated (he had made the gold portions of the statue removable, and they could be weighed and checked against the accounts), he was accused of portraying himself and Pericles on the shield held by Athena. According to Plutarch, Phidias was put into prison, where he fell sick and died; however, according to the third-century historian Philochorus, he fled to Elis where he made the great statue of Zeus at Olympia for the Eleans and was afterwards put to death by them.[36] The repeated motif of death at the hands of the state, in whichever form, is suspicious. The comic poets also attacked the building program; for example, Cratinus satirized Pericles as a new Zeus who went about wearing the Odeon on his head as a crown. Thucydides, the son of Melesias (not the historian Thucydides), who was the leading conservative after the death of Cimon, attacked the buildings as extravagant. But the building program was popular with the *demos*, for whom it provided employment. It is estimated that about 1000 men worked on the project from 447 to 432.[37] When the issue came to an ostracism vote, it was Thucydides, son of Melesias, and not Pericles, whom the people chose to ostracize.

Attic Drama and Politics

Performances in the theater—comedy and tragedy—were a powerful stimulant to the *demos'* consideration of the ethical and moral implications of human relationships, both on the individual and family level and in the wider public and political scene. But to best appreciate their role in Greek life, it is important to keep in mind the ways in which Greek theater differed from modern theater.

Both Greek comedy and tragedy developed out of earlier religious performances held during the annual festivals in honor of Dionysus, the god of wine and fertility, although each developed in its own direction and from different elements of these early performances. Tragedy grew out of a type of choral poetry called *dithyramb* from its characteristic meter; gradually solo parts developed until there were three actors and a chorus. The subjects of tragedy were serious and elevated, and the plays were intended to arouse pity and fear in the audience, leading, according to Aristotle, to the *kartharsis* (purging) of these emotions.[38] Comedy, in contrast, according to Aristotle,[39] developed out of phallic songs in honor of Dionysus, and the Dionysiac spirit of the new wine, fertility, and revelry was an essential element in its performances. It characters were ordinary, even uncouth, men who were often involved in ludicrous or even fantastic projects, and neither the gods nor human politicians escaped the barbs of personal invective and comic satire. The origins of the festival in fertility are reflected in the language of comedies, which overflows with double meanings and obscenity, much of which is lost (or suppressed) in translation. Comic choruses often have fantastic identities, sometimes as animals. In the *Clouds* the chorus is clouds, and in the *Wasps* it is jurors who are portrayed as wasps, ready to sting the defendants. Comedies follow a set form: a prologue sets the scene, and then the chorus enters, a spectacle in itself. The entry of the chorus is followed by a series of episodes, punctuated by choral passages. Some of the episodes have traditional formats. There will be an *agon* or contest, which often begins with a physical fight and ends with a verbal contest; and a *parabasis*, in which the chorus steps outside the framework of dramatic illusion, dropping the outer robes of their costumes, as well as their specific character, and addresses the audience on behalf of the playwright. The plays usually end with a celebration of the powers of life—a wedding or even a rejuvenation—and the exodus of the chorus.

Even the conditions of performance set Greek drama apart from the modern theater. There is little evidence on whether women were allowed to attend theatrical performances.[40] As actors, however, men played both male and female parts. Dramatic performances were not an everyday affair; they were held only during the annual festivals, when they were presented over the course of several consecutive days. They took place outdoors in daylight, and theater days were long. At festivals of tragedy, each contestant presented three plays followed by a satyr play; at the comic festivals, five contestants each presented one play. The spectators determined the winner of the prizes. There was little in the way of stage setting or props, but imagination set the scene for the audience. Actors were limited to three for speaking parts, and thus the same actor often played more than one role. The problems that multiple roles involved were overcome by the use of masks, which also served to make the characters more visible in the large theaters and to amplify the voices of the actors. The chorus was an integral part of the play, and to provide and train a chorus was an expensive civic duty, or liturgy, that fell to wealthy citizens.

Attic comedy and tragedy provide different perspectives into Athenian political events in the post-Persian War period. Comedy was often frank and open in its criticism of Athenian public figures, subjecting political leaders to the most personal attacks. Tragedy at times also openly addressed current political issues, although from a more elevated level, presenting contemporary events from a wider, more universal point of view. Thus Aeschylus' play *The Persians* presented the Persian defeat sympathetically, as a tragedy that afflicted a noble opponent; his *Oresteia* explored the reconciliation of ancient claims for blood vengeance with the new form of justice by a jury trial, while at the same time making a current political statement in defense of the controversial reform of the Areopagus Council. The tragic poet Phrynichus' portrayal of the fall of Miletus in 494 (now lost) so powerfully affected the Athenian public that the playwright was fined. At other times, however, the political allusions in tragedy are so subtle that to some they seem to exist only in the ingenuity of modern scholars.

Source Analysis
The *Wasps* of Aristophanes

T he political aspects of Attic comedy come out well in this play. We see the jury system as it operated to empower the *demos*—and, as Aristophanes thought, as corrupted by venal politicians it in order to exploit the *demos*. Aristophanes portrays the jury system in operation under Kleon, a demagogic successor of Pericles. Aristophanes had a personal grudge against Kleon, who had brought charges against him for an earlier comic attack, but Thucydides shared his objections to the leader. What criticisms of the jury system does Aristophanes make? Are they aimed at the jurymen, or at their exploiter?

Democracy and the Fleet in Athens

To a great extent, Athenian reliance upon sea power to maintain its empire determined the course of its political destiny. The nature of the *trireme*, the Greek warship in the fifth century, almost dictated an extension of political rights and powers to the lowest class, the *thetes*. Rowing was an arduous and often unpleasant occupation, and the nucleus of the crews was drawn from the poorer Athenians. Each ship was propelled by three banks of rowers, 170 men in all, and their cramped seating arrangements made exact co-ordination necessary at all times if the ship was not to founder in a tangle of oars. Effective crews thus had to be willing crews. The number of rowers was large: during wartime, Athens maintained a standing fleet of 100 triremes, each with a total crew of 200, which amounted to 20,000 men. Some would, however, have been supplied by the allies, but more and more, they chose to substitute monetary payments. Two hundred triremes were also kept in reserve, and often more than 100 ships were in commission. In addition, many *thetes* found a livelihood in building and repairing ships and in providing necessary materials and supplies. Thus, as the empire developed and the fleet grew in importance, so too did the political voice of the men of the lowest property class, who provided its crews and kept its ships in seafaring condition, while reforms increasingly limited the traditional political and social predominance of the wealthier Athenians.

> ### WEBSITE 10.4   THE TRIREME
>
> While there are many websites about the trireme, this undergraduate thesis from the University of Leicester in Great Britain by Rosemary Peck (2001): *Athenian Naval Finance in the Classical Period: The trierarchy, its place in Athenian society, and how much did a trieres cost?* provides extensive, easily accessed information:
> http://www-atm.physics.ox.ac.uk/rowing/trireme/thesis.html
>
> For a recent reconstruction of a trireme, see
> http://www.atm.ox.ac.uk/rowing/trireme/IMG_3246.jpg

In addition to its reliance for rowers on the lowest class of citizens, the *thetes*, Athenian democracy rested on the firm basis of the non-citizen substructure of society—women, slaves, and metics (resident aliens). Even at the height of the Athenian democracy in 431, it is estimated that, of the total population of about 315,500, 115,000, or approximately one-third, were slaves, and 28,500 were metics. Only 43,000, or 13.6 percent, were adult male citizens between the ages of 18 and 59. Those over the age of 30 eligible to hold office and hence to participate as full citizens would have been an even smaller percentage.[41] The non-citizen groups—slaves, women and metics—rarely appear in the pages of traditional history, but they formed the indispensable foundation that made the political activities of Greek male citizens possible.

SUGGESTIONS FOR FURTHER READING

The fundamental modern discussion of this period is R. Meiggs (1972), *The Athenian Empire*; on the building program, see Alison Burford (1963), "The Builders of the Parthenon," *Parthenos and Parthenon. Greece and Rome*, 10. 23–35, and other articles in the same volume. On Greek tragedy and comedy, P. E . Easterling (1997), *The Cambridge Companion to Greek Tragedy*; B. Zimmerman 1991, *Greek Tragedy: An Introduction*; Cedric Whitman (1964), *Aristophanes and the Comic Hero*.

ON THE WEB

Three useful web sites on the workings of the Athenian democracy:
DEMOS, with articles and sources:
   http://www.stoa.org/projects/demos/home?greekEncoding = UnicodeC
A good website on the Greek theater:
   http://www.cnr.edu/home/bmcmanus/tragedy_theater.html
An account of democracy and an account of the ancient critics of democracy by a noted Greek historian, Paul Cartledge:
   http://bbc.co.uk/history/ancient/greeks/greekdemocracy_05.shtml
   http://bbc.co.uk/history/ancient/greeks/greekcritics_02.shtml

MAP STUDY

Amphipolis, Chersonese, Delos, Hellespont, Propontus, Black Sea, Anatolia, Megara, Pegae, Corinth, Corinthian Gulf, Cyprus, Egypt, Naucratus, Boeotia, Thebes, Tanagra, Oenophyta, Coronea, Eurymedon River, Mytilene, Thasos, Naupactus, Mykale, Naxos, Persepolis.

ENDNOTES

[1]B. D. Meritt, H. T. Wade-Gery, M. F. McGregor (1939–1953), *The Athenian Tribute Lists*, 4 vols., contains the lists with translation and commentary.

[2]The best in-depth modern work on the empire is R. Meiggs (1972), *The Athenian Empire*.

[3]Thucydides. 1.95, 128–134. Pausanias was recalled to Sparta and tried for Medism, but was acquitted; nonetheless, he continued to raise suspicions and finally was driven to take sanctuary in a temple, where he was starved to death.

[4]This is questioned by E. Badian (1971), "Archons and Strategoi," *Antichthon* 5 1–34. Badian finds the number of 500 for those in the elected pool too large to have been practicable, given the probable number of men in the two upper classes, and suggests that 50 would have been a more reasonable number. He also analyzes the lists of known archons, both before and after the introduction of the lot, and finds no significant drop-off in the prestige of the archons; however, this seems less than conclusive, since too little is known about individuals in this period, with the exception of a very few outstanding figures, for us to compare relative importance of archons before and after the change.

[5]The date is uncertain. Plutarch's story that it was a countermove to Cimon's opening his orchards to the public suggests that it occurred while Cimon was still in Athens (before his ostracism). But Ps.-Aristotle's statement that Pericles only came to the fore after the death of Ephialtes suggests that the date should be later. P. J. Rhodes (1992), *Cambridge Ancient History* V, 76, therefore reads Plutarch as only implying that it happened during Cimon's lifetime, and dates it shortly after the reform of Ephialtes, the position that is taken here.

[6]See the oligarchic pamphlet called the *Constitution of Athens*, attributed to Xenophon 1.16–18; and the orator Antiphon 5.47, with the note in the Loeb edition of Antiphon, *Minor Attic Orators* I:192, which gives further references to inscriptions attesting to this requirement.

[7]Plutarch. *Cimon* 16.4–5; Diod.Sic. 11.63.1.

[8]Thucydides 1.100–103.

[9]The number is provided by Aristophanes, *Lysistrata* 1138–1144.

[10]Ps.-Arist. *Ath. Pol.* 25.1–2, tr. N. Demand. The work, which includes both a historical account of the development of the constitution and an account of its fourth-century workings, is available in full in A. W. H. Adkins and Peter White (1986), *The Greek Polis*; Penguin paperback edition, Aristotle, *The Athenian Constitution*, 1984, translated with commentary by P. J. Rhodes, who considers it to be the work of a pupil of Aristotle. A translation and commentary is also offered by J. M. Moore (1975), *Aristotle and Xenophon on Democracy and Oligarchy*, who holds that the author was Aristotle, as does J. J. Keaney (1992), *The Composition of Aristotle's Athenaion Politeia: Observation and Explanation*. But whoever its author may have been, a cautious approach is necessary in determining its historical value.

[11]Plutarch. *Per.* 24, 25.1, 32.1, 5. See Madeleine M. Henry (1995), *Prisoner of History: Aspasia of Miletus and her biographical tradition*.

[12]Diod. Sic. 11.77.1–5, in a highly rhetorical account, gives these figures, which agree roughly with Thucydides' account, in which an original Athenian fleet of 200 and a relief force of 50 ships were all lost, with most of their crews. The Athenian orator Isocrates (8.86) says that 200 ships and their crews were lost. Since Thucydides' account of the period following the disaster does not show the effects one might expect from such a great loss, some historians doubt these figures, preferring those of the Greek doctor Ktesias, a resident of Persia, who says that the 40 ships and their crews (6,000 Greeks) surrendered on condition that they be allowed to return home (Ktesias 32–34). To these we could add the 50 ships sent in relief, giving, conservatively, a total of about 100 ships lost, with a large part of the crews presumably surviving.

[13]The funding of the Parthenon is discussed in detail by T. Shear (1983), *Studies in the Early Projects of the Periklean Building Program*, 249–259. The use of League funds is questioned by L. Kallet-Marx (1989), "Did Tribute Fund the Parthenon?" *Classical Antiquity* 8: 252–266.

[14]See Meiggs (above, n. 2), 171–172.

[15]There is considerable debate about the date of this decree; a date in the 420s, once widely accepted, has regained support from the find of a large hoard of coinage in southern Asia Minor, which contains coins from the third quarter of the fifth century from cities that would have been affected by the Decree. In particular, it contains local coins from the small city of Aphytis, one of the sites at which a fragment of the Coinage Decree has also been found. See Meiggs (above, n. 2) 171–172, and the articles by M. J. Price, D. M. Lewis, and H. B. Mattingly in Ian Carradice (1987), *Coinage and Administration in the Athenian and Per-*

sian Empires. Until numismaticists have reached a clearer consensus on the hoard's implications for the dating of the Decree, we will continue to favor the earlier, mid-fifth century date.

[16]On the Athenian use of cleruchies, see Meiggs (above, n. 2), 121–123.

[17]It is not known if all cleruchs actually took up residence in their new allotment, as cleruchs later did, or whether some were absentee landlords, simply collecting "rent" from local residents. It seems likely, however, that the usual pattern was for cleruchs to actually become residents, and that absentee control was exceptional, for inscriptions attest the organization of cleruch communities with councils and archons (for example, IG i.2 40–42).

[18]Margaret Miller (1997), *Athens and Persia in the Fifth Century BC.*

[19]Aristophanes *Wasps* 1122–1174.

[20]On Persian influence on clothing, see Miller (above, n. 18), chap. 7.

[21]See Miller (above, n. 18), Chap. 6.

[22]D. B. Thompson (1956), "The Persian Spoils in Athens," pp. 281–291 in Saul S. Weinberg, ed. (1956), *The Aegean and the Near East: Studies Presented to Hetty Goldman on the Occasion of Her Seventy-fifth Birthday,* 283–283.

[23]For a thorough discussion of the Odeion and this question, see Miller (above, n. 18), chap. 9. She considers it part of the Periclean building program, but that designation is usually used only for the Periclean buildings on the Acropolis: the Acropolis, Propylaea, Temple of Athena Nike, and Erechtheion. See Jeffrey Hurwit (2004), *The Acropolis in the Age of Pericles*; John Travlos (1971), *Pictorial Dictionary of Athens,* 387–391. The odeon in the *agora* indicated on many maps is a later building.

[24]Plutarch *Pericles* 13.9–11. See too Pausanias 1.20.4.

[25]Vitruvius 5.9.1.

[26]Miller (above, n. 18), 241.

[27]See Hurwit (above, n. 23), abbreviated edition of Jeffrey M. Hurwit (1999), *The Athenian Acropolis : History, Mythology, and Archaeology Fom the Neolithic Era to the Present.*

[28]See above, n. 13.

[29]Rhys Carpenter (1970), *The Architects of the Parthenon.*

[30]A recent interpretation of the frieze by Joan Breton Connelly (1996), "Parthenon and Parthenoi: A Mythological Interpretation of the Parthenon Frieze," *American Journal of Archaeology* 100: 53–80, suggests that it represents a mythical story from early Athenian history—the sacrifice of the daughters of the king Erechtheus in order to assure Athenian victory. According to this interpretation, the central scene shows the King, Queen Praxithea, and the three daughters preparing for the sacrifice, watched by an assembly of the gods. The cloth is interpreted not as the sacred *peplos* of Athena, but as the shrouds of the daughters. The suggestion, however, has not been widely accepted by scholars; see Jeffrey Hurwit (2004), *The Acropolis in the Age of Pericles,* 224–236.

[31]Margaret Cool Root (1985), "The Parthenon Frieze and the Apadana Reliefs at Persepolis: Reassessing a Programmatic Relationship." *American Journal of Archaeology* 89:103–120, 113.

[32]Root (above, n. 35), 117.

[33]Thucydides 4.50.

[34]Aristophanes, *Acharnians* 61–135.

[35]For references, see Root (above, n. 35), 118, nn. 69, 71.

[36]See A. Powell (1988). *Athens and Sparta,* 59–67 for a defense of Plutarch's reports about the building program.

[37]See Alison Burford (1963), "The Builders of the Parthenon," *Parthenos and Parthenon. Greece and Rome* Supplement Vol. 10: 23–35, 34.

[38]Aristotle, *Poetics* 1449b. 24–31, tr. N. Demand.

[39]Aristotle, *Poetics* 1449b. 1–6.

[40]On the skeptical side, S. Goldhill (1994), "Representing Democracy: Women at the Great Dionysia," in R. Osborne and S. Hornblower, eds., *Ritual, Finance, Politics: Athenian Democratic Accounts Presented to David Lewis, 347–369*; S. Goldhill (1997), "The Audience of Athenian Tragedy," in P. E. Easterling, ed., *The Cambridge Companion to Greek Tragedy*, 54–68. On the other hand, J. Henderson (1991), "Women and the Athenian Dramatic Festivals," *Transactions of the American Philological Association* 121:133–148, is more optimistic.

[41]These population figures are based on A. W. Gomme (1933), *The Population of Athens in the Fifth and Fourth Centuries B.C.*, Table 1. This careful review of the ancient evidence remains the fundamental work on the subject of the population of Athens. Gomme's figure of 43,000 for the adult male citizen population in 431 is supported by the more recent estimates made in 1982 by M. H. Hansen of at least 40,000 and possibly as many as 50,000 (M. H. Hansen (1982), *Journal of Ancient History* 7: 173–174. Given the nature of the evidence, however, any estimates can only be educated guesses.

11

STATUS AND GENDER IN THE GREEK WORLD

IDEOLOGY AND THE POLIS

"An ideology… is a system of intellectual beliefs and emotional judgments that make up a model of the world according to which raw experience is interpreted…. This symbolic system provides a framework according to which the social world is arranged and given meaning."[1]

S tructuralism, a method of understanding ideology that holds that all societies organize their conceptual worlds according to a system of opposed categories,[2] is very useful in understanding the world of the classical *polis*. In that world, the use of a system of value-laden polar opposites is very clear, reflected even in the structure of the language.[3] Major dichotomies included male/female, free/slave, citizen/non-citizen, Greek/barbarian, but there were countless others as well. In each case, one pole represented the good and the desirable, the other, an inferior condition. It is, of course, clear that this is a gross oversimplification, and that the world cannot easily be so sharply divided. In fact, the Greeks did have many problems fitting their experiences of life and the world into such a rigid system, which sometimes led them to fail to see aspects of their culture that seem obvious to an outside observer.

ATHENIAN CITIZENS

Citizen Men

One of the most basic category distinctions in Greek society was that of gender. Men (that is, free citizen men) ran the Greek world. They participated in the government of their community, attended the Assembly, voted on community issues, served on juries, appeared in court in their own right, held all the offices (with the exception of some purely religious priestesshoods), and were the owners of any family property.

When a child was born, its father had the right to accept and raise it, or to expose it, but not to kill it. Exposed infants might be picked up and raised by anyone who found them, either as free or as slave. The birth father, however, retained a right to the child who had been exposed if he ever wished to claim it. In Greek comedy in the fourth century, many plots hinged upon the discovery of the true free status of young women who had been exposed as infants with tokens that allowed their identification as freeborn after they had been raised as slaves.

There is continuing debate about the extent to which Greeks actually exposed newborns.[4] It is generally agreed that abnormal or sickly infants were routinely exposed, and some suspect that female infants were also likely candidates for exposure because the few statistics that we have often show boys outnumbering girls. However, it is known that daughters were often simply not counted among offspring, and so such "statistics" do not provide firm evidence for a sexual imbalance.

The motives for exposure are usually taken to have been a desire to limit the male heirs in a system of partible inheritance and/or a desire to limit the expense of dowries for daughters. However, the high infant and child mortality in Greece—probably at best only half of all infants born survived to adulthood—and the high risk of losing even adult sons and daughters to the hazards of war and childbearing, suggest that the best strategy for all but the poorest parents would have been to raise all the children born in order to ensure the survival of a son to carry on the *oikos* and care for the parents in old age. Even a daughter would do; in the event of the death of her father without male heirs, she became an *epikleros*, (heiress), and her nearest agnatic male relative—father's brother or his son—was obliged to marry her and produce a son as heir for the deceased.

A male infant, when accepted by the father, became a full-fledged member of the family. Gender, however, does not always correlate neatly with physiological sex, but must be learned from the culture in which the child is raised. For the Greeks, adult men were recognized as manly by their display of a set of values, among which were strength, fortitude, courage, and playing the active role in sexual relations. Boys were acculturated according to these values. Part of this acculturation involved homosexual relationships between adult men and sub-adult males in which the youths played the passive role. Since the chastity of girls and women was closely guarded and unavailable except within marriage, such male-to-male relationships were accepted and even valued as a means of acculturation for young upper-class males, as long as they were not too easily persuaded. Thus Greek "love affairs" tended to be between men and adolescent boys. Such relationships were, in fact, much valued among the elite, providing status to the youths who attracted lovers,[5] although at the same time they involved serious risks for the youths if they should be seen as too cooperative or as "selling" their favors.[6] Ambivalence arose from the dishonor accorded to adult males suspected of playing a passive (female) role in a sexual relationship; they ran the risk of being indicted if they attempted to hold public office, prosecute a political case, or speak in the Assembly or council.

The practice of male homosexuality was closely associated with the symposium, or male drinking party, and thus with the predominance of aristocratic values:[7]

> ...the symposium is an organization of all-male groups, aristocratic and egalitarian at the same time, which affirm their identity through ceremonialized drinking. Prolonged drinking is separate from the meal proper; there is wine mixed in a krater for equal distribution; the participants, adorned with wreaths, lie on couches. The symposium has private, political, and cultural dimensions: it is the place of *euphrosyne* [festivity], of music, poetry, and other forms of entertainment; it is bound up with sexuality, especially homosexuality; it guarantees the social control of the polis by the aristocrats.

WEBSITE 11.1 SCENES FROM THE LIVES OF MEN

These can be found by entering identifying labels in the Search Box in the Perseus website:

http://www.perseus.tufts.edu

When a boy reached the age of three, he was introduced to the men's world of wine at the Chous festival, the second day of the festival Anthesteria, the Festival of Flowers, held in February when the new wine was ready; he was given a small pitcher of wine (*chous*), and crowned with flowers:

> Yale 1913.142, baby crawling, miniature *chous*
> Philadelphia 75–10-1 *chous*, dog and grapes

Homosexual courtship of boys:

> Boston 10.193, homosexual courtship
> Hamburg 1900.164: cup, drawing of the tondo, showing a boy seated with lyre, and a youth
> Würzburg L 482: interior: youth and man holding a hare (a favorite gift for boys)
> Malibu 86.AE.290 youth with lyre and teacher; school scenes (men with hares)

An important aspect of a boy's life was athletic practice and participation:

> Toledo 1956.58 Side B: trainer with athletes
> Boston 01.8019, wrestlers and trainer
> Boston 01.8020 discus thrower and jumper
> Boston 10.178 athletic victor, youth with wreath to crown victor
> Tampa 86.24, Panathenaic, two riders

The young man entered the world of male social connections and politics through the symposium:

> Malibu 86.AE.682 symposium (males)
> Louvre G 135: Tondo: symposium, man reclining, woman playing flute
> Brussels R 351 symposium, love-making (man, woman)

Serious pursuits were a part of life as well:

Louvre G 402, youth sacrificing

And when the youth reached the age of adulthood (18), he was enrolled as an *ephebe*, and underwent a year of military training, followed by a year of light-armed military duty on the frontiers, after which he became a full-fledged hoplite soldier and citizen:

Palermo 2564, man arming for war, woman

Women of Citizen Status

Women in general were characterized as the opposite of men—weak, fearful, ignorant, passive. Although necessary for the reproduction of the family and for the orderly working of the household, they were not considered as in any way the equal of men. In Athens, about which we know most, the legal position of free women of citizen parentage was, in fact, that of perpetual minors.[8] They were legally prohibited from managing property or handling money beyond the amount necessary to take care of household expenses for a few days. In any economic or legal transaction, they had to be represented by a guardian: before marriage by a father, after marriage by a husband, and as a widow, by a male relative or a grown son. In their role as mothers, women of citizen parentage served as transmitters of citizen status, but to what extent they were considered to be citizens themselves is not clear.[9]

Anxiety about possible challenges to the legitimacy of heirs probably lies at the basis of many of these restrictions upon women in the Classical period. From puberty until she passed the age of childbearing, a woman was seen as a potential threat to the honor and status of the *oikos*. It was not that women were necessarily suspected of wishing to harm the *oikos*; they were simply believed to be weak and easily persuadable, and men knew that men from competing *oikoi* were always on the lookout for ways to damage their neighbors. The legitimacy of a child, even one born within a marriage, would be questioned if there were any shadow of scandal about the mother. Therefore, women of citizen status had to be continually guarded and watched; any sexual activity by married (or marriageable) citizen women with males other than their husbands was treated as a grievous offense. On the other hand, sexual relationships between non-citizen females and males were considered part of normal male behavior and not penalized, and any homosexual activities among citizen females seem to have been completely ignored. The poems of Sappho, who was of upper-class status but not an Athenian, suggest that such relationships were beneath the notice of male society.

After their birth and formal acceptance into the family by their father, girls of citizen parentage were carefully sheltered throughout childhood to preserve their honor. During the course of childhood, girls participated in various public religious ceremonies, as recounted by the women in Aristophanes' *Lysistrata*: "I bore the holy vessels at seven, then I pounded barley at the age of ten, and clad in yellow robes, soon after this, I was Little Bear to Brauronian Artemis; then neckleted with figs, grown tall and pretty, I was a Basket bearer."[10]

Unlike their brothers, who were considered to have reached adulthood only at the age of 20, when they had completed the ephebate, women were considered adult and ready for marriage as soon as they reached puberty, conventionally set at 14. The husband was usually about 30, in a position to take over his familial *oikos* or to establish one of his own. Marriage involved the transmission of family property and was, in effect, a business matter, to be arranged by men: the girl's father or guardian and the potential groom and his male relatives. Marriages between cousins were favored, and in such cases the girl may have seen her prospective husband before marriage at a family occasion such as a wedding or funeral, but otherwise girls had no opportunity to meet potential husbands. Even second marriages of fully adult women were arranged. Sometimes a man even chose his wife's next husband in his will, or arranged for her remarriage before divorcing her (as Pericles did, with his wife's agreement, when he divorced her to live with Aspasia). Theoretically, a bride had a veto over a proposed match if the prospective candidate was morally objectionable, but probably few sequestered girls of 14 were in a position to object on those grounds.

Dowry was an important consideration in the choice of marriage partners and very important in assuring the security of the woman.[11] The dowry was legally attached to the woman, but managed by her male guardian. When she married, her husband became her guardian, and the dowry thus was his to manage. He was required to use part of the proceeds to support her, and he was responsible for managing the property in a responsible manner. In the event of a divorce, he had to return the dowry to the woman's new guardian (her father or nearest male relative). If a woman with one or more sons was divorced, the dowry still followed her, going to her new guardian; her son or sons by the dissolved marriage had no more claim to it.[12] The need for the husband to return the dowry provided the wife some protection against hasty divorce and also allowed her new guardian to dower her in another marriage. In the event she was widowed without sons, the dowry returned with her to her family, who would probably remarry her. If she had a son, he became her guardian, and the dowry, as well as the duty of maintaining her in her old age, was his. Upon the death of a married woman, the dowry became part of her guardian/husband's estate and was eventually inherited by her sons on his death.

After marriage the woman's primary role was to produce an heir for the *oikos*. Everyone was anxious to discover if she would be able to conceive and bear a child successfully. Failure would in most cases mean divorce, and there would be difficulty in arranging a remarriage, for the Greeks put the responsibility for sterility solely upon the woman. Testing for fertility and treatment for sterility were the province of midwives, although by the fourth century some Hippocratic doctors were recording midwives' recipes and bringing these problems into their own practices.[13] Midwives handled normal births, with the assistance of female kin and neighbors. Doctors were sometimes called in if complications arose after delivery, but there was little they could do without antibiotics or blood transfusions. Deliveries using forceps were possible, and various hook devices for extracting a dead fetus were tried, but these were extremely dangerous for the woman. Caesarian sections, while they may have been attempted as a last resort, and appear in myth, are unknown in the Hippocratic texts.[14]

As in all premodern societies, maternal mortality rates were high; it was only in the 1930s, with the advent of antibiotics, that the relatively low mortality rates that the United States now enjoys were reached (although the United States is still far from the safest country in which to give birth, especially for its poorest residents). Puerperal fever and the complications of malaria and tuberculosis took many lives.[15] Pregnancy in the early teens also contributed to the dangers of childbearing, and the practice of close-kin marriages (first cousins were favored) must also have contributed to the number of birth defects and to the mortality rate of newborns. If both mother and child survived, the mother's status was much enhanced within her new family, especially if the child was a boy, but even a pregnancy resulting in the loss of the infant enhanced a woman's status by proving her fertility.

Source Analysis

L ysias 1, 6–31, tr. N. Demand.　This speech in defense against a charge of murder provides a great deal of information about attitudes toward childbearing, living arrangements, and relationships within a marriage and household, as well as the law dealing with adultery.　The defendant, Euphiletus, is on trial for murder, having killed an adulterer, Eratosthenes, who was (as he claims) "caught in the act."

> When I, men of Athens, decided to marry and brought a wife into the oikos, at that time I was disposed neither to harass her nor to let her do whatever she wanted; I watched as I was able, and attended to her as was reasonable.　But when a child was born to me, I trusted her and handed over my possession to her, thinking that she felt very much a part of the family.　And at first, oh men of Athens, she was the best of wives, skillful at housekeeping, and thrifty, arranging everything in order.　But when my mother died, her death was the cause of all the troubles that befell me.　For at the funeral my wife was seen by this man, and in time she was utterly ruined.　He found out the servant-girl who went to the agora for us, and sent messages to my wife through her, and thus brought about her corruption.

Euphiletus explains that his house has two stories, with the women's quarters above and the men's on the ground level. But when the child was born, they had exchanged spaces, so that the mother could feed and wash the baby more easily without running up and down the stairs. He never suspected that his wife might be entertaining another man downstairs during the night. One night, however, he came home unexpectedly and after dinner the baby started to cry (he now thinks the maid was purposely upsetting it). Unsuspecting, he told his wife to go and feed the baby to stop it from crying.

At first she refused, as though she was happy to see me after such a long time. But when I became angry and ordered her to go, she said, "So that you can make a try at the girl—once before when you were drunk you dragged her about." I laughed, and she, getting up and going out, closed the door, and, pretending to joke, she drew the bolt. And I, thinking nothing of it, went to sleep happy to have returned from the country. At dawn, she came and opened the door. I asked her why the door had creaked in the night, and she said that the child's lamp had gone out in the night, and she had kindled it again at the neighbor's. I was silent, thinking this was what had happened. But it seemed to me, oh men, that she had whitened her face, with her brother not dead 30 days. Nevertheless, I said nothing, but, getting up, I left the house in silence.

After that, oh men, for some time I was unaware of my troubles, until an old woman approached me, sent secretly by the woman with whom that man was having an affair, as I learned later. She was angry and, thinking that she was being wronged, because he no longer came to her so frequently, she kept a close watch on him until she discovered what was the cause. The old woman approached me near my house. "Euphilete," she said, "in no way think me meddlesome for coming to see you. For the man who is dishonoring you and your wife is our common enemy. If therefore you take the slave girl who goes to the agora and serves you, and torture her [slaves could give testimony only under torture], you will understand everything. It is Eratosthenes of Oë who is doing this, who has corrupted not only your wife, but many others besides, for this is his crafty way."

Euphiletus threatened the slave-girl with torture, and she told him the whole story—the man had approached her after the funeral and at last persuaded her to be his messenger, how the wife herself had at last been persuaded, how they arranged for the man's visits, and how the wife had gone to the women's festival of the Thesmophoria with the man's mother while her husband was in the country. They set a trap for the man so that the husband could see for himself. After four or five days Euphiletus came home from the country and had dinner with a close friend upstairs in his rooms; the friend left and Euphiletus went to bed.

Eratosthenes, oh men, came in, and the servant girl woke me at once and told me that he was in the house. Telling her to take care of the door and going out silently, I went round to one after the other of my friends. Some I found at home, while others were out-of-town. Taking as many as I could from those present, I went along. And taking torches from the nearest shop, we went in to the house, as the servant girl had opened the door. Pushing open the bedroom door, the first of us to enter saw him lying beside my wife; those who followed saw him standing naked on the bed. And I, oh men, struck him and knocked him down. Pulling his hands behind his back and tying them, I asked him why he had dared to enter my house. And he admitted that he had done wrong and entreated and begged me not to kill him, but to take money in compensation. And I said, "It is not I who kills you, but the laws of the polis, which you transgress and esteem of less value than your pleasure, choosing to commit this affront to my wife and children rather than to obey the law and live an honorable life." And thus, oh men, he incurred the penalty that the law dictates for those who do such things, not dragged in from the street or seeking sanctuary at my hearth, as these people [the prosecutors] say.

Later Euphiletus had the law pertaining to adulterers read out; the law itself is not included in the speech, but Euphiletus paraphrased it:

> The Court of the Areopagus . . . has expressly stated that he who catches his wife in adultery and exacts this penalty, is not guilty of murder. And so strongly did the Lawgiver think this to be just in the case of a married woman, that he enacted the same penalty in the case of concubines [*pallakides*], who are of less account.

The central issue in the case was whether Euphiletus actually caught the man in the act, or, as the prosecutors charge, dragged him in off the street and framed him. Note the care Euphiletus took in providing witnesses; these were necessary, yet his admitting to having gone out to look for them took away somewhat from the spontaneity of the act; in emphasizing that many were out of town, he sought to prevent the situation from appearing to have been arranged beforehand.

The place of a citizen wife was within the household, not in the public life of the city or in its social life. The wives of citizens did not join their husbands at the symposia that were the central focus of male social and political life. The women who did provide female companionship at symposia were *hetairai*; in fact, the very presence of a woman at a symposium was enough to mark her as a *hetaira*, or prostitute.[16] Even within the home, women did not share in meals that included men from outside the household. As we saw in the Source Analysis, Euphiletos entertained his male guest separately from his wife.

The fact that women were expected to live their lives within the *oikos* does not mean that they literally never went out of the house, or that they had no influence on the running of the *oikos*. It was the job of the housewife to care for the *oikos* and its possessions, and to oversee the working of wool and other tasks carried out by younger women and slaves. Women also nursed sick household members, including slaves, and assisted the midwife at childbirths of neighbors and friends. As the plays of Aristophanes show, women also slipped out of the house to borrow household items and to visit with female friends and relatives. Within the home, women, especially older women, often had considerable informal influence. Despite the pessimistic judgment that at most five percent of Greek women were literate,[17] in Xenophon's discussion of the running of an *oikos*, the young wife is expected to be able to read lists of household items,[18] and in some of the speeches preserved from the law courts, women are portrayed as well informed about the financial matters of the *oikos*, knowledgeable about wills, and able to consult family records to prove their point.[19] Some of the best evidence for literacy consists of portrayals on vases of women with book rolls; 32 scenes show women with book rolls, 13 in domestic scenes.[20]

The only role that citizen women could properly play in public outside the confines of the *oikos*, however, was in religious rituals and ceremonies. As Euphiletus' story illustrates, funerals were a particularly female domain. It was female relatives who prepared the body for burial, and they were also allowed to participate in the mourning and the funeral itself. In service to the gods, a few women, usually from elite families, served as priestesses or in other ritual roles, but all women had some cult duties. All girls were obliged to serve the goddess Artemis in coming-of-age ceremonies before marriage (the *Arkteia*), and after marriage women joined in the annual celebration of Demeter Thesmophorios, the **Thesmophoria** (to which Euphiletus' wife went with the mother of her lover!). At the Thesmophoria, women left their homes for three days and camped out together in a *polis* of women from which men were rigidly excluded. The women celebrated the fertility of the soil and their own bodies, and enjoyed a release from the pressures of their day-to-day life, but within the confines of religious ritual.[21]

Such was the norm for life as a citizen woman. The poorest citizen families were not able to live up to this ideal of female confinement to the *oikos*, however, for their women were often obliged to work outside the home to help support the family. Such women might sell food or small items in the *agora* or function outside the home in extensions of their household duties, as wet nurses, midwives (if they were past childbearing age), or wool workers. Such activities outside the home were, however, always a threat to their reputation and that of their families.[22]

In trying to reconstruct the world of Greek women, we are severely hampered by the nature of our sources, almost all of which were the work of upper-class males—not only the historical texts, but also such sources as epitaphs, vase-paintings, speeches in the law courts, and medical texts. They convey male views of women and male expectations of women, but not necessarily the realities of women's lives. In the Classical period, women do not speak to us in their own voices; to find them, we often need to look for clues in non-traditional ways. One important source of information about the lives of females of the citizen class is provided by portrayals on Greek vases, although, as always, from the male perspective.

We do not find many women active in the events of political history or in the works of historians in the city-states of the Classical period. When they do appear, one must immediately be suspicious. Why has the ancient writer introduced them? In some cases—as in Herodotus' story of Queen Artemesia of Halicarnassus, who fought with the forces of Xerxes and served as an advisor to the king[23]—the women are foreigners who actually did play a role in history. One nonetheless suspects an ulterior motive here; did Herodotus highlight her role as the bravest commander in the Persian fleet to disparage the courage of the Persians? For if a woman was the bravest, how brave could the men have been? Often the information given is intended as slander, meant to attack a man through his women. For example, our information about the relationship between Aspasia and Pericles comes not from Thucydides, but ultimately from gossip, criticism, and parody. In the *Menexenus*, a parody of a state funeral oration, Plato portrays her as writing Pericles' speeches, a claim aimed ob-

WEBSITE 11.2

Vases illustrating the lives of citizen women, from Perseus website: enter the identifying label in the Search Box to view the scenes:

http://www.perseus.tufts.edu

Life for a citizen girl centered on her marriage:
St. Petersburg St. 1791, preparations for a wedding
London E 774 wedding preparations, working wool

After marriage centered on the bride's new household; working of wool an important task, and the bearing of a child an eagerly anticipated event:
Yale 1913.146 woman in domestic interior
Louvre CA 587, women, spindle, hand loom
Boston 13.189 seated woman working wool
London E 219 mother, maid and baby
London E 190 seated woman reading, perhaps checking household accounts

Family obligations sometimes took the woman outside her home:
RISD 06.050 woman bringing funeral offerings

viously at demeaning the statesman himself.[24] She was said to have operated a brothel,[25] and Aristophanes blames the Peloponnesian War on Pericles' efforts to help some of her "girls" (compare this with the criticism of the activities of some American presidents' wives, such as Hillary Clinton and Eleanor Roosevelt).[26] Similarly, information about another notable woman, this time from a citizen family, comes down to us mainly in slander. This was Elpinike, the daughter of Miltiades, the victor of Marathon, and half sister of Cimon. She was said to have lived with her brother as a wife (not illegal in Athens since they had different mothers), and to have been the mistress of the famous painter Polygnotus, who was said to have rendered her likeness in a portrayal of Trojan women on a wall painting in a public building (the Painted Stoa).[27] It was claimed that she was active politically, negotiating with Pericles for Cimon's recall from exile, and earlier, in 463, pleading with Pericles, who was one of the ten public prosecutors, when Cimon was charged with treason.[28] The picture of Elpinike appears to be that of a woman of noble family who took an active part in the culture and politics of Athens; the veil of slander and innuendo through which she is seen reflects not so much the truth about her actions, but male disapproval of such activity. Other evidence for the disapproval of female involvement in male affairs appears in the Athenian law that allows a will to be set aside if it was made "under the influence of a woman." Thucydides' advice to the widows of the war dead in the Funeral Oration for the casualties of the first year of the Peloponnesian War is most typical of the male Greek (or at least Athenian) norm for women: "To a woman not to show more weakness than is natural to her sex is a great glory, and not to be talked about for good or for evil among men."[29]

Nevertheless, there are hints in the sources that by the late fifth century the traditional role of women was being questioned in at least some Athenian circles. The literary sources on Aspasia seem to reflect such a situation,[30] and a number of the plays of Euripides also raise similar questions about the role and treatment of women.[31] Plato, in the *Republic*, sketched an ideal state in which children would be raised communally, and women would share the work of the state. Even though he maintained that women were inferior to men,[32] he condemned the waste of their talents when they were allowed to live out their lives in the seclusion of the *oikos*. In Aristophanes' comedy *Ecclesiazusae*, women take over the *polis* and create a new order that bears a remarkable resemblance to the ideas expressed in Plato's *Republic*. Since the comedy was earlier than Plato's work, and it is unlikely that the philosopher borrowed his ideal family structure from a comedy, the explanation must be that both reflect an ongoing and widespread debate in Athens about traditional family roles. Nevertheless, Greek women did not achieve significantly more rights and freedoms until after the demise of the *polis* in the Hellenistic period. This, together with the fact that restrictions on women increased as the *polis* developed, suggests that the search for an explanation for the disparity between the roles allotted to males and females in Classical Greece might well focus on the *polis* itself.[33]

NON- CITIZEN, FREE RESIDENTS—METICS[34]

With a few, mostly late, exceptions, Athenians did not allow entry into the citizen group by free non-citizen residents, but gave them a special status as resident aliens, or **metics**. This group crossed the gender barrier, encompassing both men and women. It included Greeks from other *poleis* and non-Greeks—freed slaves and the descendents of metics. In fifth-cenury Athens, any non-Athenian who remained in the city for more than a short period of time (probably a month) was obliged to register as a metic, obtain an Athenian sponsor, and pay the metic tax. Metics lacked most rights: they could not vote in the Assembly, serve as jurors, hold civic offices, or marry Athenian citizens. They were also excluded from ownership of land, either for agricultural or residential purposes. Nevertheless, they were required to pay the metic tax and other taxes as well, and males were obligated to perform military service. These restrictions obviously limited the ways in which metics could earn a living, and most male metics worked as craftsmen or traders, where they worked beside, and competed on an equal basis with, poorer citizens and slaves.

The lives of female metics probably followed much the same pattern as those of citizen women, with their fate depending on the affluence of their families. Most, who were poor or without a family, probably worked as prostitutes (*pornai*) or *hetairai* (perhaps "high-class call-girl" would be the best translation).[35] At the extreme end of the spectrum, Aspasia, a metic *hetaira* from Miletus, lived as the privileged mistress of Pericles and was rumored to have influenced his political decisions (see above, and Chapter 10).

Despite the disadvantages and restrictions of metic status, the economic vitality of Athens continued to attract resident aliens in large numbers and although most were men and women of modest means, a few were able to achieve great wealth and political prominence. Among these, in addition to Aspasia, was Kephalos, the wealthy father of the orator Lysias, who appears in Plato's *Republic*. Kephalos was not a freedman, but a citizen of Syracuse. His son Lysias, having inherited his metic status, is well known as the author of many important speeches for the law courts written for Athenian citizens. The role played by metics in the life of the city grew over time, and it is best attested by their appearance as litigants in speeches from the courts.[36] Admittedly androcentric sources, these speeches often provide information about daily life almost inadvertently. Written by men hoping to appeal to an audience of citizen males, they reflect common (male) opinion. In one such speech, a Greek male's view of the various classes of women is made clear in the following much-quoted excerpt:[37]

> We keep *hetairai* [in this case, probably prostitutes] for the sake of pleasure, *pallakides* [concubines] for the daily care of our bodies, and *gynaikes* [wives] to have legitimate children and as trustworthy guardians of our household possession.

Against Neaira, attributed to the orator Demosthenes but probably by another author—was one case in which the marital status of a woman, Neaira, was challenged. It makes clear how uncertain the lines between freedom and slavery sometimes were, especially in the case of women.[38]

Source Analysis
The Uncertain Border Between Freedom and Slavery: [Demosthenes] 59, *Against Neaira*

Neaira started life as a slave in Corinth, either born to that status or abandoned and picked up to be raised as a slave. She was purchased as a small child by a brothel keeper, Nikarete, who prided herself on recognizing promise in small girls. Trained in the art of her profession, Neaira was one of a small group of girls whom Nikarete offered to customers as her daughters. When Neaira had passed her prime (probably by her early 20s), Nikarete sold her to be the joint property of two of her customers for 3,000 drachmas. This arrangement lasted for a year or so before both men decided that it was time for them to marry and that they could no longer keep Neaira. The pair could have sold her to a brothel, but at her advanced age, they would not have been likely to recoup her initial cost. Perhaps they also felt some affection and concern for her as well. At any rate, they offered her a bargain—she could buy her freedom for 2,000 drachmas, if she moved from Corinth and pledged never to live or work there again.

The price was far above anything Neaira could afford, but she immediately set about taking up a collection from her previous lovers. A number of the men sent money, and one, an Athenian named Phrynion, made up the considerable difference between the collection she had assembled and her price, and took her home with him to Athens. Theoretically, he was helping her to purchase her freedom, but in fact he treated her as his slave, taking her about to dinner parties and humiliating her by insisting she have sex with him in public. Finally, she packed her bags (unfortunately adding a few of Phrynion's things to her own), and left him to go to neighboring Megara. Business was not good there, however, due to warfare. Thus she was fortunate when she met another Athenian, Stephanos, son of Antidorides, who offered to take her home to live with him. At this point the picture becomes somewhat fuzzy, because three children suddenly enter the picture. Whether they were hers, or his by a former wife (as he claimed), is unclear. Since the information about the children—in fact, the whole story—comes from the speech given by Apollodoros in a case he brought against her as a way to revenge himself on Stephanos (of this more later), it is suspect.

The pair had lived together for several years, and the girl child, Phano, had grown up and been twice married and divorced, when a litigious Athenian, Apollodoros, a former metic who had bought citizenship for himself through generous contributions to the city, brought charges against Stephanos. Apollodoros claimed that Stephanos was passing Neaira off as his legitimate citizen wife, which was illegal since she was not a citizen, and, even worse, that he had given her daughter Phano in marriage as his own offspring and as the child of a legitimate marriage between citizens.

The real target of Apollodoros' attack was not Neaira or Phano, but Stephanos; however, the charges, if upheld, would have had serious consequences for her—a return to slavery—while the penalty for Stephanos, while far less serious, was not negligible—a fine of 1,000 drachmas. In arguing the case, Apollodoros brought many scandalous charges against Neaira, which offer a glimpse into the murky world of prostitution in Athens, and demonstrate how important it was for a male citizen to be sure about the citizen status of the mother of his children. The case also illustrates the propensity of Athenians of citizen status to use the courts as the means of personal or political attack.

Unfortunately, we do not hear Stephanos' defense, nor do we know the verdict in the case, but we will meet Apollodoros again in Chapter 13, where he will appear as a voracious initiator of legal suits against a number of other victims.

SLAVES AND SLAVERY[39]

As the story of Neaira makes clear, the most crucial distinction in Greek society was that between freedom and slavery. In most Greek cities, as in Athens, the legal status of a slave was as chattel, or property, as was the case with slaves in the United States before the Civil War (hence the term "chattel slavery"). In a few Greek cities, such as Sparta, slavery took a form closer to serfdom than to chattel slavery (see Chapter 6), but in this chapter, the discussion will be about the more common form of Greek slavery, chattel slavery, unless otherwise noted. Like any other sort of property, slaves could be bought, sold, and disposed of by will and testament. Their masters could do what they liked with them, short of killing them arbitrarily.[40] Slaves could not own property or enter into contracts, including marriage. Having no property, they could be punished only through their bodies, enduring beatings and other physical abuse. In contrast, the bodies of free persons were invulnerable; to strike them was to commit *hubris*, a serious crime.[41]

Of the many disabilities suffered by slaves, perhaps the oddest to modern eyes is the fact that they could testify in court only under torture. Challenges to torture a slave for his or her testimony are frequent in the speeches from the law courts, but no actual case of torture appears. Thus it is not known how many, if any, slaves were actually tortured, and some scholars believe that the use of torture to obtain evidence was only a legal fiction.[42] Virginia Hunter argues, however, that the reason that torture fails to appear in the speeches is that it occurred outside the court.[43] One case in which a challenge to torture was refused appears in *Against Neaira* (see Source Analysis). In her discussion of the speech, Debra Hamel suggests that the defendant, Stephanos, did not want the fate of Neaira and her (his, or their?) children to rest upon the uncertain outcome of the torture of four slaves, adding that another factor might have been that Stephanos had some affection for the slaves, two of whom had been in Neaira's service for a long time and must have been at least in their mid-forties.[44]

Even when freed, slaves could not entirely leave behind their servile state. Even as freedmen, former slaves still owed service to their former masters. They and their descendants lived in the city only as metics. In the fourth century, at a time when the city was in dire financial straits, a few wealthy male metics were able to buy citizenship for themselves by making exceedingly generous contributions to the city, as did Stephanos. The vast majority of freedmen, however, had no hope of acquiring citizenship, either for themselves or for their descendants.

Thus the prospects of Greek slaves differed radically from those of Roman slaves, whose offspring born after they were freed were legally both freeborn and Roman citizens.

Sources of Slaves

The main source for slaves was Greece's non-Greek neighbors, "barbarians" not of Greek speech or culture, who were obtained by purchase from slave traders. Athenian citizens were legally prevented from enslaving other Athenian citizens as a result of the reforms of Solon in the sixth century, although there were some exceptions: it was allowed to sell into slavery a daughter who committed adultery or a man who was ransomed and failed to repay his ransomer. As noted above, the status of an infant of citizen parentage that had been exposed was unknown, and a stranger who picked the child up could raise it as a slave, but the child could be redeemed later if its identify could be established. Some Greeks, however, did fall into slavery to other Greeks as a result of war or piracy, although opinion seems to have condemned this, and most such captives were probably ransomed. However, in the fifth century, during the Peloponnesian War when Athenian democracy was at its height, the Athenians on numerous occasions sold the entire population of women and children of a rebellious subject-city into slavery as an object lesson to their other subjects—a practice that is presented by Thucydides as a sign of the corruption of Athenian character by the city's increasing imperialism.

Occupations of Slaves

Most Athenian citizens probably owned at least one slave. In the comedies of Aristophanes, slaves appear routinely, attesting to their ubiquity in Athenian life. They are portrayed stereotypically as idle, lazy, impudent, thievish, the sometimes wily recipients of frequent beatings. Even small holders probably had at least one male slave who did odd jobs in the household, ran errands, and worked the land, often beside his owner.[45] Men of hoplite status also needed to keep at least one slave to carry their heavy shields and armor on military campaigns. Most households also probably had at least one female slave to fetch water and do household chores, but her most important job was probably weaving, for a Greek household needed large amounts of cloth for clothing and bedding. Moreover, the sexual use of female domestic slaves by the men of the household was common. With luck, such a woman might become a favorite and take on the role of concubine, perhaps for a young, still unmarried son of her master (men did not ordinarily marry until about the age of 30).

Some male slaves were trained as craftsmen and worked outside the home earning money for their masters. Such slaves often worked together with free men: records from the building of the Erechtheion in Athens show slaves and free men working side by side for the same wages.[46] Although slaves could not legally own property, masters might allow slaves who worked outside the *oikos* to save some of their earnings so that they could eventually purchase their freedom: skilled slaves were a good investment, and allowing the slave to profit from his work would have been good management. Another job for slaves who worked outside the *oikos* was running small shops. Some were trained in accounting and business practices and worked for wealthy owners as business agents and even as bankers.[47] One such slave, named Phormio, who appears in the speeches in law courts, worked in a bank owned by a very successful freedman; when his master died, he was also freed and inherited the bank—as well as the banker's widow, who became his wife (more on Phormio below).[48] Such skilled slaves probably had a good deal of personal freedom and were able to live reasonably comfortable lives; a few even became wealthy.

The *polis* also owned slaves, employing them as clerical workers and as policemen (the Scythian archers). Public slaves, the *Dokimasteis*, tested coins for their silver content,[49] and others served as custodians of weight and measures, kept public archives, and acted as clerks to the council.[50] Although the rowers in warships were usually free men, in emergencies, slaves were also used, and they often received their freedom in return for this service. As war fleets grew larger and larger in the late fifth and fourth centuries, exceeding the capacity of the cities to provide citizen crews, the use of slaves ultimately became essential.[51]

Probably the worst fate for an Athenian male slave was to be employed in the silver mines at Laurion in southern Attica. Mining was extremely dangerous work with a high mortality, and there was no opportunity for forming any sort of personal ties with the owner that might ameliorate the harsh conditions. Not surprisingly, during the Peloponnesian War some 20,000 slaves from the mines took advantage of the opportunity to escape to a haven established by the Spartans at Dekeleia in the Attic countryside, inflicting great economic damage on Athens (see Chapter 12).

Slave women also worked outside the home. Trained as singers, dancers, or flute-girls, they brought income for their masters.[52] A good example is found in the Hippocratic medical texts, in which the doctor/author describes an abortion that he brought about:[53]

> The slave girl of a kinswoman of mine was a skilled singer of much value, who used to go with men. It was important that she not become pregnant and thus lose her value, but she did conceive. The singer had heard the sort of things women say to each other—when a woman is about to become pregnant the seed not does come out, but stays within. Hearing this, she had observed and always taken care. At this time she perceived that the seed had not come out, and she told her mistress. The story came to me, and when I heard it, I told her to leap so that her heels touched her buttocks. And when she had done this seven times, there was a sound and the seed fell out on the ground.

It is noteworthy that the slave was owned and controlled by a woman, and that she reported the suspected pregnancy to her mistress and cooperated with the abortion procedure because she was interested in continuing with her professional life; her mistress may well have allowed her to keep a portion of her earnings. Both Greek comedy and the portrayals on vases confirm that the line between entertainer and prostitute was a blurred one. If such a woman succeeded in buying her freedom, she would then be a metic, but without family connections, she probably had to continue to use these same skills to make her own living.

Vase paintings offer good illustrations of common slave occupations.[54]

Figure 11.1   Leningrad Painter
Kalpis, 490–470 B.C., red-figured Attic pottery, H. M 0,23, Banca Intesa Collection
This Attic Vase depicts a workshop of potters and pot-painters, probably mixed slaves and
metics; a worker on the far right (almost out of sight) is a woman.

WEBSITE 11.3

Other vase paintings illustrating slave occupations from the Perseus collection; enter the identifying label in the Search Box:

http://www.perseus.tufts.edu

Female slaves:
    Toledo 1961.23: slave women fetching water from a fountain
    Munich 2421: two hetairai partying, music lesson (lyre)
    St. Petersburg 644: four hetairai partying
Male metics and slaves:
    London E 23: carpenter
    Louvre C 10918: cooking was assigned to men (but women ground the grain)
    London B 507: foundry scene, two men at a forge
    Harvard 1960.321 and 1958.19: potters' workshop
    Berlin F 2542: potter at work
    Boston 01.8073: cup painter in a potter's shop (fragment)
The male worlds of privilege and service intersected:
    Baltimore, Hopkins AIA B4: youth with moneybag, perhaps contemplating the
        purchase of a vase

Implications of Greek Slavery

Slavery was practiced in Greece in all periods from at least the Bronze Age, but it became increasingly common with the growth and development of the *polis*. In fact, many believe that it provided the essential basis for *polis* life. For a culture that prided itself on being free, it would seem that reliance upon a slave class would have been troubling. But such relationships appear from within the society as normal and natural; they are an intrinsic part of the worldview, or ideology, of the society.[55] The fact that most slaves were barbarians who spoke Greek badly would have made it easier to believe in their natural inferiority. Even the philosopher Aristotle in the fourth century assumed the inferiority of slaves, considering them mere instruments or tools. There are hints, however, that the "natural" inferiority of slaves was being questioned in the late fifth century. These doubts appear for the most part in the plays of Euripides,[56] but the fact that they are the expressions of characters in plays, and not necessarily of Euripides himself must be kept in mind. It might be, however, that such radical ideas were growing more common, which might have led Aristotle to defend slavery on the grounds that it was natural: "Some men are by nature free, and others slaves, and that for these latter slavery is both expedient and right."[57]

The concept of slavery was given a political and metaphorical extension in Athens. Those people and countries were free who lived under the rule of law, while those who lived subject to the personal dictate of an absolute ruler were viewed as slaves of that ruler. The immediate example of the latter for Classical Greece was the king of Persia. In the United States in the early twenty-first century, freedom has again become a potent political slogan, identified with a form of western democracy, and opposed to eastern tyranny.

SUGGESTIONS FOR FURTHER READING

On women and the family, see Sue Blundell (1998), *Women in Classical Athens*; Mark Golden and Peter Toohey, eds. (2003), *Sex and Difference in Ancient Greece and Rome*. On childbirth, N. Demand (1994), *Birth, Death and Motherhood in Classical Greece*. On metics, D. Whitehead (1977), *The Ideology of the Athenian Metic*. On Greek slavery, N. R. E. Fisher (1993), *Slavery in Classical Greece*.

ENDNOTES

[1] Peter Hunt (1998), *Slaves, Warfare, and Ideology in the Greek Historians*, 20.

[2] Hunt (above, n. 1), 5.

[3] See Hunt (above, n. 1), 129–130. The language is structured in antitheses, with the pair of particles: *men ... de*, "on the one hand, x, on the other hand, y". Thucydides' own style is highly antithetical.

[4] D. Engels (1980), "The Problem of Female Infanticide in the Graeco-Roman World," *Classical Philology* 75:112–120; Mark Golden (1981), "Demography and the Exposure of Girls at Athens," *Phoenix* 35:316–331; W. V. Harris (1982), "The Theoretical Possibility of Extensive Infanticide in the Graeco-Roman World," *Classical Quarterly* 32:114–116; D. Engels (1984), "The Use of Historical Demography in Ancient History," *Classical Philology* 34:386–393.

[5] See Plato's *Symposium*. Modern discussions include Kenneth Dover (1989), *Greek Homosexuality*; Merrill Cole (2003), *The Other Orpheus : A Poetics of Modern Homosexuality*; Paul W. Ludwig (2002), *Eros and Polis : Desire and Community in Greek Political Theory*; and James Davidson (1998), *Courtesans and Fishcakes: The Consuming Passions of Classical Athens*.

[6] See Aeschines 1, *Ag. Timarchos*. Gifts, usually of pet animals (hares, horses), were acceptable in homosexual courtships, but not the exchange of money; however, the line could be a thin one. On the ambiguity of Athenian attitudes toward homosexual relations between men and boys, see David Cohen (2003), "Law, Society and Homosexuality in Classical Athens," pp. 151–166 in *Sex and Difference in Ancient Greece and Rome*, ed. Mark Golden and Peter Touhey, originally published in *Past and Present* (1987), 117:3–21.

[7] Walter Burkert (1991), "Oriental Symposia: Contrasts and Parallels," pp. 7–24 in W. J. Slater, ed., *Dining in Classical Context*, quotation from p. 7. See also O. Murray (1990), *Sympotica. A Symposium on the Symposion*. Plato's *Symposium* presents a picture of a symposium on the serious side, without musicians and women.

[8] In Sparta, due to its unique system, women enjoyed somewhat more freedom, as was discussed in Chapter 6. Nonetheless, Greek observers credited this female freedom with the ultimate collapse of the Spartan state.

[9]For example, Cynthia Patterson (1986), "Hai Attikai: The Other Athenians," *Helios* 13:49–67, holds that they were citizens, but not in the same sense that men were. They could not vote or hold office, were restricted in their rights to hold property and carry out legal transactions, and were not registered on the citizen rolls of their deme. Whether they were citizens in some essential way is a modern question; what was at issue in Classical Athens was whether their marital status qualified them to transmit citizenship to male offspring. This issue of *Helios* also has other interesting articles about women in ancient Greece.

[10]Aristophanes, *Lysistrata* 641–646, tr. Jack Lindsay. On the Arkteia at Brauron, see C. Sourvinou-Inwood (1988), *Studies in Girls' Transitions*. The poet Alkmaion's Fragment 1, *Partheneia*, was probably composed for such a ceremony.

[11]On dowry, which varied in matters of detail in different *poleis*, see David M. Schaps (1979), *Economic Rights of Women in Ancient Greece*. The text describes the Athenian situation.

[12]Schaps (above, n. 11), Appendix IV.

[13]These can be found in two Hippocratic gynecological treatises, *Diseases of Women* and *Nature of Women*. The Greek text with a French translation can be found in Littré's edition of Hippocrates (1839).

[14]Folklore attributes Julius Caesar's birth to a "caesarian"; this is doubted by some since his mother survived. For an early history of caesarian section see www.nlm.nih.gov/exhibition/cesarean/cesarean_2.html; on the problems of pregnancy and childbirth more generally, see N. Demand (1984), *Birth, Death and Motherhood in Classical Greece*, chap. 4.

[15]See Demand (above, n. 14).

[16]An argument used against Neaira, [Dem.] 59, *Against Neaira*.

[17]William V. Harris (1989), *Ancient Literacy*, 106–107.

[18]Xen. *Oec.* 9.10.

[19]Lys. 32.11–18; Dem. 41. Aesch. 1.170 refers to wealthy young men whose property is managed by their widowed mothers.

[20]See S. Cole (1981), "Could Greek Women Read and Write?" pp. 219–244 in *Reflections of Women in Antiquity*, ed. Helene P. Foley, esp. 223–224.

[21]See Aristophanes, *Thesmophoriazusae*. Froma I. Zeitlin (1982),"Cultic Models of the Female: Rites of Dionysus and Demeter," *Arethusa* 15: 129–157.

[22] See Dem. 57, esp. 30–31, 35.

[23]Herodotus 7.99; 8.68–69, 87–88, 93, 101, 103, 107.

[24]Plato, *Menexenus* 236A, 249D, which may not be a genuine work of Plato's. Other evidence about Aspasia comes from Plutarch, *Pericles*, who relates some of the gossip and comic attacks of the day. Aeschines the Socratic philosopher, who wrote a dialogue, the *Aspasia* (incompletely preserved) in which Aspasia criticizes the manners and training of the women of her time. Xenophon, who mentions her favorably in *Oecon* 52.14. For a modern study, see Madeleine Mary Henry (1995), *Prisoner of History : Aspasia of Miletus and Her Biographical Tradition*.

[25]By the comic poet Hermippus, cited by Plutarch *Pericles*, 31.

[26]Aristophanes *Acharnians* 524ff.; Plutarch *Pericles* 25, 30.

[27]Plutarch *Cimon* 4. Similarly, Phidias was said to have portrayed likenesses of himself and Pericles on the shield of the great statue of Athena in the Parthenon; Plutarch *Pericles* 31.

[28]Plutarch *Pericles* 10.

[29]Thucydides 2.45, tr. Jowett.

[30]See Henry (above, n. 24).

[31]See esp. Euripides, *Medea*.

[32]Plato *Rep.* 455d, *Laws* 781b, *Tim.* 42b.

[33]On this, see Demand (above, n. 14).

[34]David Whitehead (1977), *The Ideology of the Athenian Metic*.

[35]See Hans Herter (2003), "The Sociology of Prostitution in Antiquity in the Context of Pagan and Christian Writings," pp. 57–113 in *Sex and Difference in Ancient Greece and Rome*, ed. Mark Golden and Peter Touhey.

[36]The speeches of Isaeus dealing with inheritance, and the private orations of Demosthenes, or those attributed to Demosthenes, such as *Against Neaira*, are especially useful. These can be found in English translation in the Loeb Library series.

[37]Demosthenes 59.122 (*Against Neaira*).

[38]See Debra Hamel (2003), *Trying Neaira: The True Story of a Courtesan's Scandalous Life in Ancient Greece*; Konstantinos A. Kapparis (1999), [Demosthenes] 59: *Against Neaira* [D.59].

[39]See N. R. E. Fisher (1993), *Slavery in Classical Greece*.

[40]Dem. 21, *Ag. Meidias* 46–49 [in Loeb, Demosthenes Vol. III]. The prohibition may not have been widely obeyed. Plato's *Euthyphro* portrays the seer Euthyphro, who is about to indict his own father for causing the death of a slave, whom he has bound and cast into a ditch while going in search of advice on what would be the pious thing to do—Plato questions whether a man who would punish his own father for the death of a mere slave truly knows the nature of piety.

[41]Excessive violence against a slave was also considered hubris, but the offender was unlikely to be prosecuted. See Plato's *Euthyphro* (above, n. 40), and Fisher (above, n. 39) 62–64.

[42]M. Gargarin (1996), "The Torture of Slaves in Athenian Law," *Classical Philology* 91: 1–18. His argument is based upon his conviction that torture was cruel, ineffective, and thus "irrational"; unfortunately, the post 9–11 era in the United States has proven that many authorities do trust in its effectiveness, however irrational that may seem.

[43]Virginia Hunter (1992), "Constructing the Body of the Citizen: Corporal Punishment in Classical Athens," *Echos du Monde Classique/Classical Views* 36:271–291, 283–284; also Hunter (1994), *Policing Athens: Social Control in the Attic Lawsuits, 420–320 B.C.*, chap. 3.

[44]Hamel (above, n. 38) 55–60.

[45]For a discussion of the evidence for the extent of slave owning, see V. D. Hanson (1992), "Thucydides and the Desertion of Attic Slaves during the Decelean War," *Classical Antiquity* 11: 210–228; Fisher (above, n. 39) chap. 4.

[46]John M. Camp II and W. B. Dinsmoor, Jr. (1984), *Ancient Athenian Building Methods.* American School of Classical Studies at Athens, 3. The pay was one drachma a day, which was three times the minimum subsistence rate of two obols paid to recipients of public welfare.

[47]Banks handled small-scale transactions: money-changing, the holding of deposits, loans. These were not prestigious activities in the eyes of elite Greeks.

[48]Dem. *For Phormio*, discussed by Fisher (above, n. 39), 77–78.

[49]R. S. Stroud (1974), "An Athenian Law on Silver Coinage," *Hesperia* 43: 157–188, esp. 11, 13–16.

[50]Fisher (above, n. 39), 57.

[51]This is convincingly argued by Hunt (above, n. 1) chap. 5, in spite of the popular opinion (expressed in the first edition of this book as well) that slaves were not used to man Athenian ships or to serve as fighters in the army.

[52]An interesting article about these women is C. Starr (1978), "An Evening with the Flute-girls," *La Parola del Passato* 183:401–410.

[53]Hipp. *Nat.Child* 13 (7.490.3–11, Littre), tr. N. Demand.

[54]See S. M. Veni (1988), "The Caputi Hydria and Working Women in Classical Athens," *Classical World* 81:265–272.

[55]On ideology, see Hunter (above, n. 43), 273–277; Hunt 1998 (above, n. 1).

[56]For example, Euripides *Ion* 855–857; see Fisher (above, n. 39) 90–92.

[57]Aristotle *Pol.* 1255a 2–3, tr. Jowett.

12

THE SOPHISTS, THUCYDIDES, AND THE PELOPONNESIAN WAR

THE INHERITANCE OF THE IONIAN ENLIGHTENMENT

A thens in the second half of the fifth century was heir to the spirit of humanism and rationalism that had first appeared in the Ionian Enlightenment. It was embodied in the Periclean building program, in which the temples of the Ionians, conceived on such a grand scale, were succeeded by buildings on a more human scale that celebrated and forwarded, at least in part, the interests of human beings. But it was even more visible in philosophy, in which the efforts to explain the origins of the physical cosmos by the Ionian thinkers were in a sense replaced by the work of the philosopher Socrates, who turned men's attention to questions of human values, and by the Greek doctors, who carried on the speculations of the Presocratics in a tradition of rational medicine that culminated in the work of the near-legendary Father of Medicine, Hippocrates of Cos. The followers of Hippocrates, the Hippocratic doctors, traveled throughout the Aegean with their message that human illness was caused not by demons and the anger of the gods, but by natural processes. It was an age in which many traditional values were reexamined, and new grounds for these values were sought within the context of human concerns and social interactions.

The Sophists

Perhaps most important, however, for defining both the spirit of the age and the tenor of the Athenian political scene were the professional teachers of rhetoric, the Sophists.[1] It was these men who offered the expensive education that provided the skills for addressing the Assembly or law court that were vital to the politically ambitious. Interest in public speaking was not a concern only for the wealthy, however. While for the most part it was the wealthy who patronized the Sophists, less affluent men used the courts to attack their enemies or to defend themselves, often hiring the services of speech writers. There is even a speech preserved in which a man defends his right to the state pension that was given to the disabled poor.[2]

The Sophists found a ready audience in many Greek *poleis*, but most eventually made their way to Athens, attracted by its growing wealth and lively intellectual scene. It is there that we meet them, especially in the dialogues of Plato. In addition to their teaching of rhetoric, the Sophists also offered a broad intellectual education, including such subjects as the general management of one's affairs, grammar, music, poetry, medicine, and natural philosophy. With their teaching they contributed in large measure to the creation of the intellectual ferment of the Athenian Enlightenment.

Among the first Sophists to visit Athens was Protagoras of Abdera (a Greek city in Thrace), who appears together with the Sophists Hippias and Prodicus in the Platonic dialogue *Protagoras*. He associated with the leading intellectuals and political leaders of the time, including Pericles, the tragedian Euripides, and Socrates. He was especially interested in methods of argumentation, but he also taught a humanism and relativism that reflected the best in Sophistic thought. His interest and expertise in politics is confirmed by Pericles' decision to invite him to draw up the laws for the new colony of Thurii in southern Italy in 444.

Another Sophist who appears in the *Protagoras* is Prodicus; he was especially interested in the philosophy of language, specializing in the analysis of minute distinctions between almost synonymous terms. Thucydides sometimes makes distinctions that are credited to Producus, such as those between complaint and accusation, fear and terror, courage and boldness, revolt and defection, hegemony and empire. Still another Sophist, Gorgias of Leontini in Sicily, who appears in the Platonic dialogue *Gorgias*, first visited Athens in 427 as an envoy from his native city. He was noted for his powerful poetic style, in which he played with rhymes, balanced numbers of syllables, and used terms that are parallel in form, sound, or meter. He wrote a tribute to the powers of speech in his *Helen*, and Thucydides made use of many of his stylistic devices in writing his history.

The practical nature of Sophistic training is reflected in a popular stylistic device that has strong moral overtones, the *antilogy*, a set of paired speeches that argued opposite sides of a given question. The ancient historian of philosophy, Diogenes Laertes, attributed the invention of the *antilogy* to Protagoras, but in fact, it was a legacy of the law courts and appeared in the works of the tragedian Sophocles even before the Sophists had become popular. The use of *antilogies* was well suited to the Sophists and became especially associated with them, for it embodied the claim of some of these men to be able to teach methods of arguing effectively on both sides of a question. An anonymous treatise called the *Double Arguments* provided model arguments of this type, and the *Tetralogy* of Antiphon offers speeches for both sides of controversies, such as who is responsible if a boy is accidentally killed running in the path of the javelin throwers in the gymnasium. Three of the speeches of Gorgias argue in defense of a weak, seemingly indefensible thesis: one defends Helen against the criticism that her elopement with Paris caused the Trojan War; another defends the Homeric hero Palamedes on a charge of treason; and still another argues, in a parody of the philosopher Parmenides, that nothing exists, and if it did, it could not be known, and if it were known, it could not be communicated. The use—and misuse—of such *antilogies* figures largely in the *Clouds* of Aristophanes, in which the character Strepsiades seeks to have his son taught how to make the weaker argument prevail so that he can evade his creditors.

Despite different approaches and specialties, the Sophists shared a basic core of ideas that placed the locus of human values firmly in human society. Protagoras sounded the keynote in his famous relativistic dictum: "Man is the measure of all things, of those which are, that they are; of those which are not, that they are not." Protagoras also denied that the existence of the gods could be known. While this was a statement of agnosticism, not of atheism, it nonetheless provided grounds for seeking the nature of virtues such as justice not in the will of the gods, but in human life and society.

Socrates

Socrates, who is probably the most famous of the fifth-century thinkers, wrote nothing. We know him only at second hand, from the works of Plato, Xenophon, and Aristophanes. Plato portrays him as a poor workingman (a stone mason) who nonetheless mingled with, and challenged, the elite of Athens. By asking deceptively simple questions—such as, What is justice? and What is piety?—of men who had a reputation as experts, he led them into contradictions that revealed that they did not, after all, have the knowledge that they claimed. He also called the *polis* itself to account twice, once by refusing to participate in the illegal arrest of a man, and again, by opposing the decision of the Assembly to illegally try en masse the generals who had abandoned the dead after the sea battle at Arginousai.

Both the "new thinking" of the Sophists and the challenges that Socrates put to self-important citizens who claimed expertise in moral values were extremely popular among the young, but many of their elders saw these activities as subversive, as a threat to traditional morality. Criticism reached such a pitch that Protagoras was condemned to death for impiety and forced to flee Athens for his life, although, according to Plutarch, the attack was politically motivated and aimed at his friend Pericles. We see a reflection of this opposition to the new ideas in the *Clouds* of Aristophanes, presented in 423, three years after the arrival in Athens of the famous sophist Gorgias. In this play, Socrates appears as a Sophist, and, in fact, he seems often to have been misconstrued as a Sophist by the public.

Source Analysis
The *Clouds* of Aristophanes

T his is the second version of the play; the first, which has not been preserved, failed to win the prize, and the poet was so stung by the rebuke of the *demos* that he rewrote the ending, apparently to better reflect public opinion about the Sophists. How do you think the original version ended?

The works of the Sophists themselves have survived only in fragments, and for the most part we know them only through their enemies, of whom Plato was by far the most effective in molding later opinion. The result has been a highly biased and negative picture, but a number of modern scholars have recently presented a fairer assessment of these men, whose contributions often anticipated modern views. One of the most persuasive of these modern scholars is Jacquiline de Romilly.[3] She argues that the immorality often attributed to the Sophists represented not so much their own teachings, as the popular reaction that carried their arguments far beyond what the Sophists themselves advocated. Thus in the *Clouds*, it is Strepsiades who plots to use the teachings of the Sophist "Socrates" for unethical purposes, not "Socrates" himself. In fact, de Romilly argues that the Sophists' "destruction of traditional values" was, in fact, a reconstruction of values resting not on questionable myths, but on a rational foundation, and that to provide this foundation, they adopted notions that are familiar from the classic liberalism of early modern Europe: contract and utility. Human beings cannot survive outside society, and they therefore contract to exchange the fulfillment of some of their immediate selfish desires for the long-term protections offered by a cooperative life in society. Utility provided the basis for the Sophistic arguments of probability that were much used in Athenian courts; for example, a defendant might argue, "Would I have been likely to have killed the victim, considering that I am a 100-pound arthritic and he was a 300-pound wrestler?" As a result, a realistic, or even pessimistic, conception of psychology emerged. We can see this exemplified in the great historian of the period, Thucydides, in whose work people, despite the altruistic appearance of their motives, are frequently revealed as pursuing their own interests, expressed in intricate webs of thesis and antithesis.

THE PELOPONNESIAN WAR

The development of Athens into an imperial power, enforcing its will upon its allies-turned-subjects and openly appropriating the funds of the league for the creation of monuments of imperial splendor, naturally provided a focal point for the fears and jealousies of the other Greek *poleis*. Sparta and Corinth felt especially threatened by the growing power of Athens and by Athenian infringements on their spheres of influence, and many of the other cities of the Peloponnesus followed their lead. Thus the scene was set for a major conflict between the *poleis* of the Peloponnesus, whose greatest strength lay in their hoplite infantry forces, and Athens, whose advantage lay in naval power.

Preliminaries to War

Even though the scene was set, actual war was slow to develop. Thucydides deals at some length with two events that he saw as important precursors of the war. In 434/433 the Athenians came into conflict with Corinth when they accepted an alliance with that city's settlement, Corcyra, joining the Corcyreans in a sea battle against their mother city. This breach with Corinth then caused the Athenians to reconsider the stability of their own situation in the Chalcidic peninsula to the north, where their principal ally, Potidaea, was another Corinthian foundation. The Athenians demanded that the Potidaeans provide evidence of their loyalty by pulling down their south-facing walls, which were not needed for protection against Macedonia; giving hostages; and rejecting the magistrates that the Corinthians annually sent to them. The Potidaeans refused these conditions and appealed to the Spartans for help. Bolstered by a Spartan promise of assistance if the Athenians should attack, the Potidaeans rose in revolt against the Athenians.

The second important precursor to war was the passage by Athens, probably in 433/432, of the Megarian Decree, whose terms forbid the neighboring city of Megara access to Athenian markets and to all the harbors of its empire. Ancient sources saw the decree as a cause of severe economic difficulties in Megara and as *the* cause of the war.[4] Even Thucydides attributed to the Spartans the repeated claim that the lifting of the decree would prevent war (Thuc. 1.139).

Thucydides, however, saw the true cause of the conflict not in any immediate and specific occasion for complaint, but in Sparta's deep underlying fear of the growing power of Athens (Thuc. 1. 23). This power was centered on the sea and on control of the sea. Begun as a military strategy—Themistocles' counsel to use the windfall from the silver mines to build a fleet—by the middle of the fifth century the navy had made Athens rich and increasingly powerful.[5] Tribute payments were used for direct military expenditures, such as the building and outfitting of ships and the payment of wages to rowers, and the provision of other military forces, as well as for financing the Periclean building program.[6] A stream of well-to-do visitors from the subject states came to Athens to pursue their cases in the Athenian courts. They spent money locally on temporary housing, food, and other necessities. Athenian juries, who were paid for their services, were needed to serve at their trials, contributing considerably to the incomes of ordinary people. Aristophanes' outline of the balance sheet of empire in the *Wasps* leaves little doubt that people were aware of the importance of the empire to the Athenian economy.

But payments of tribute and the spending of visitors would not suffice to maintain the empire if certain vital imports could not be maintained, and securing the provision of these imports goes far to explain Athenian actions during the war. The first necessity was grain. By the late fifth century the city was dependent upon imports of grain to feed its population, and many of these imports came from the Black Sea area. Thus control of key points along the route to the Black Sea—the north Aegean coast and the Hellespont—was vital for Athens. The second crucial import for Athens was timber for the building of ships, which Attica could not supply. The main source for the type of timber needed was in the north, in Thrace and Macedonia. That same area had vast resources of silver and gold. Earlier these had provided the financial basis for Peisistratus' successful bid for tyranny, and Thucydides was probably supported in his exile in the north by family interests in the mines. Athens thus had several important economic reasons to maintain control in the north Aegean. In 436 the city established the *polis* of Amphipolis, located at a vital point on the east-west route where it crossed the river Strymon. While the foundation cost them a long and bloody struggle with a hostile local population, they were finally able to secure control of this area. Throughout the course of the Peloponnesian War it is often possible to see such economic factors behind incidents that Thucydides presents in politico-military terms. For example, the fact that Sicily was a potential alternative source of grain helps to explain the major expedition that the Athenians mounted to that island in 416, ostensibly in support of a small ally in a local dispute.

The War under Pericles

The spark that ignited open warfare was provided by a series of relatively minor military clashes in 431 involving the small city of Plataea. Plataea had long been an Athenian ally, but it lay just within Boeotian territory, and the Thebans considered it within their sphere of influence and thus properly a member of the Boeotian League. In 431 the Thebans tried to seize the city. The Plataeans successfully drove out the attackers, but in the aftermath they violated the norms of Greek warfare by massacring 180 Thebans whom they had taken prisoner. Retaliation by Thebes was anticipated. The Plataeans appealed to Athens, and the Athenians responded by sending a garrison and evacuating the non-combatants. Sparta then joined in the conflict by virtue of its alliance with Thebes. Both sides prepared for full-scale war, seeking support from uncommitted states, and even from Persia.

Enthusiasm for war was high on both sides, especially among the young men. Raised on tales of Homeric heroes and the exploits of their fathers and grandfathers against the Persians, but with no experience of war themselves, they saw it as a great adventure. The general feeling among the Greeks was heavily in favor of the Spartans, who were viewed as the liberators of a Greece enslaved by Athenian power.

In Athens, Pericles devised a daring strategy that called for the Athenians to carry to its logical extreme the development of their sea power: they would make Athens an island, invulnerable to the land-based attacks of Sparta. He persuaded the people to do this by moving into the city, thus abandoning the countryside to devastation by the Spartans. The Long

Walls, which connected the city with the port at Piraeus, coupled with Athenian control of the sea, would assure that the needs of the city could be supplied by sea-borne imports. But Pericles also counseled moderation, warning against attempts to extend the empire, advising the Athenians that it would be enough for them to preserve what they had.

The first year of the war brought a Peloponnesian invasion that sorely tested the self-control of the Athenians cooped up in the city. But Pericles bolstered popular resolve by a number of positive actions: Athenian forces made raids on the coast of the Peloponnesus, laid waste to the territory of Megara, and expelled the inhabitants of the island of Aegina, replacing them with Athenians from the crowded city. In the northern Aegean, Pericles scored diplomatic advances by securing the alliance of the kings of Thrace and Macedonia (Thuc. 2.23–32). When morale continued to fall, he refused to call the Assembly, thus preventing the discouraged people from acting on the basis of their immediate frustrations. He also shared in their sacrifices, donating his country properties to the state, for he realized that the Spartan general might spare them in order to strike at his popularity and effectiveness as a leader.

In the winter following the first year of the war, a public funeral was held in Athens for the men who had fallen. It was at this low point in the mood of the Athenian people that Thucydides reports the famous funeral oration of Pericles that sums up the greatness of Athens.

Source Analysis

T hucydides 2.34–46, THE FUNERAL ORATION   Annual civic funerals with orations were traditional in Athens and provided an occasion for the display of patriotic sentiments. The speech that Pericles gave after the first year of the war, as reported by Thucydides, was an encomium on Athenian democracy delivered at a particular moment in Athenian history, yet it is often presented as a characterization of all democracy. However, as the war progressed. Athens failed to live up to this picture. To see this most clearly, it is helpful to note the key words and concepts that Thucydides used to express the values of Athenian democracy—free, open, tolerant, brave, intelligent, generous, hopeful—and to watch for their recurrence in later speeches. These key terms are expressed in antithetical form, in typical Sophistic style.

The speech, as all Greek political speeches, was addressed to the men. Pericles' sole piece of advice to the women is also noteworthy—and famous: "the greatest glory of a woman is to be least talked about by men, whether they are praising you or criticizing you."

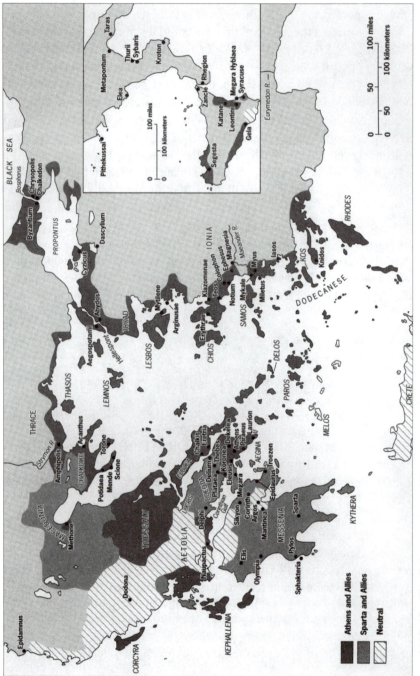

MAP 12   The Peloponnesian War

The Plague

The highly idealistic spirit of the Funeral Oration is juxtaposed antithetically in Thucydides' history with the first great disaster of the war. Crowded together in the city in accordance with Pericles' strategy, in the following summer, as the Spartans again invaded Attica, the Athenians fell victim to a virulent plague that was spreading throughout the eastern Mediterranean. The suffering of the victims and the number of deaths were overwhelming, and no preventive measures or remedies were of any avail. It has been estimated that a quarter, or perhaps even a third, of the population was lost. Moreover, the plague returned twice more, in 429 and in 427/426; it killed Pericles' two legitimate sons, and Pericles himself died during this time, probably as a result of the disease. Thucydides himself suffered from the plague but recovered, and his account thus has the advantages of personal experience (on the other hand, it might be less objective for that reason).[6]

Thucydides' account of the plague is a masterpiece that has often been used as a model for later accounts of plagues, from the Roman philosopher-poet Lucretius' retelling of the horrors of the Athenian plague to descriptions of the Black Death in early modern Europe. Thucydides' description, although based on personal observation and his own experience as a victim of the illness, was framed in terms of contemporary medical theory. His expressed intention was to provide as complete and accurate a description as possible, so that the illness could be recognized, should it ever recur in the future. Yet ironically, despite his very detailed description, modern scholars are unable to agree on the identification of the disease. Such investigations consider both the symptoms and the epidemiological pattern of the disease. For example, Thucydides' statement that the military rolls were full again by 415 (6.26), and his account of large losses among the troops, provide evidence that the illness struck adults more heavily than children.

Source Analysis

The Plague, Thucididyes 2.47–55. Thucydides' detailed description of the plague, following as it does immediately upon the idealism expressed in the Funeral Oration, creates an especially dramatic effect that can hardly have been accidental. What other devices does Thucydides use to enhance the drama of the situation? What elements seem to reflect contemporary Greek medical theory?

The Athenian plague was clearly not the bubonic plague of the Black Death in the fourteenth century C.E., for Thucydides does not report the characteristic symptom of the bubonic plague, the *bubo* (inflamed swelling of a lymph gland). Other identifications that have been suggested include measles, typhus, ergotism, and even influenza complicated by toxic shock syndrome. The case for typhus seems strongest both epidemiologically—the age groups affected are similar—and from the standpoint of the symptoms. Typhus is characterized by fever and a rash; it is known as a "doctors' disease" from its frequent incidence among caregivers; it confers immunity, and it often involves gangrene of the extremities. Patients during a typhus epidemic in the First World War were reported to have jumped into water tanks to alleviate extreme thirst, just as Thucydides describes Athenian victims doing. But the fit is not exact. The rash is impossible to identify on the basis of Thucydides' description (even modern medical texts resort to pictures to supplement verbal descriptions of rashes), and the mental confusion typical of typhus may not fit Thucydides' description. In the long run, however, all such attempts at identification may be futile. Diseases develop and change over time, and it may be, as has been argued, that the plague of fifth century Athens no longer exists today in a recognizable form.[7]

The social, political, and economic effects of the Athenian plague may be suggested by studies of the effects of the Black Death in Europe.[8] The loss of perhaps a third of the population, and the large number of sudden and untimely deaths, would have severely affected normal inheritance patterns. Distant relatives suddenly became heirs to unexpected fortunes, as Thucydides notes. Similarly, the normal pool of aristocratic candidates for political office was disrupted. Both of Pericles' sons by his Athenian wife, who would have been natural candidates for political leadership, died, and he made a special plea to set aside the citizenship law (which he himself had sponsored in 451) so that his son by the Milesian Aspasia could be declared a citizen. Then Pericles himself died, probably a victim of the disease or its aftereffects. Although the military rolls were full again by 415, the older generation that filled offices and provided experienced leadership was not so easily replaced.

The War from Pericles' Death to the Peace of Nicias

After the death of Pericles, the war entered a new phase, attributable at least in part to the long-term sociological and political effects of the plague. The shift of wealth to unexpected recipients, the loss of aristocratic youths being groomed as heirs to political power, and the "new morality" of selfish hedonism spurred by increased affluence and the patent uncertainty of life, changed the political scene at Athens drastically for the worse, at least in the eyes of the historian. Thucydides saw the new leaders as lacking in the statesmanlike qualities of Pericles, who had had the intelligence and foresight to formulate the most advantageous policy, and the strength to lead the people even when they failed to perceive their own long-term interests. The new political leaders did not so much lead the people as pander to their whims. They were, in fact, **demagogues** led by the people.

Of these demagogues, the most notorious according to our sources was Kleon. We have already seen Aristophanes' devastating portrayal of the man in the *Wasps*, and the depiction by Thucydides essentially agrees with this picture, although drawn in the more sober terms appropriate for history. For Thucydides, Kleon's actions embodied the disastrous direction that the Athenian conduct of the war took after the death of Pericles; thus we will focus on him in considering the course of the war up to the Peace of Nicias in 421, which followed the demagogue's death. But first a brief outline of the events of the period will provide a context for these events.

In 430 Potidaea surrendered at last, after a long and expensive siege by the Athenians. In the following year the Peloponnesians refrained from invading Attic, fearing a renewed outbreak of the plague; instead they began a siege of Plataea, Athens' Boeotian ally, that lasted for two years.

In the summer of 428, the island of Lesbos, whose largest *polis* was Mytilene, seized the opportunity to revolt from an Athens weakened by the effects of sustained war and by another attack of the plague. Lesbos was one of the most important subject-allies of Athens, and one of only three that still maintained a fleet rather than supplying payments in lieu of ships. The island's preparations for revolt, which included a synoikism (unification) of its cities with Mytilene, were disclosed to the Athenians by Mytilenian dissidents. The Athenians, in their weakened condition, were anxious to avoid war on yet another front, but their attempts to dissuade the rebels, who pinned their hopes on Spartan assistance, were unsuccessful. The Spartans, however, dragged their feet, and finally the Mytilenians were compelled to surrender.

The angry Athenian Assembly voted to punish the Mytilenians by executing the entire male population and enslaving the women and children. If we compare this punishment with those meted out to recalcitrant allies before the war, the drastic change in Athenian policy is evident. The Athenian condemnation included even the Athenian sympathizers who had informed them of the plot! By the following day, however, many had repented their hasty decision, and it was decided to debate the issue anew in the Assembly. Kleon argued against mercy (see Source Analysis), but he failed to persuade the Assembly, which revoked the sentence. After a dramatic race across the Aegean, the ship carrying the report of the changed decision of the Athenian Assembly arrived just in time to prevent the executions.

In 427 the Spartans succeeded in taking Plataea after a two-year siege when the Plataeans surrendered on the promise of a fair trial. The Spartan "trial," however, consisted of a single question: What had they done to benefit the Spartans? Those who had nothing to respond were summarily executed. In the same year vicious civil strife broke out in Corcyra, and Thucydides described the collapse of traditional values in that struggle in a set-piece intended to illustrate the moral degradation caused by the war.

In 425 the Athenians gained a significant edge over the Spartans, but at least as Thucydides portrays it, it came about by accident. One of Athenian generals, Demosthenes, happened to be sailing around the Peloponnesus as a passenger on an expedition headed for

Sicily, when he suddenly conceived the idea of fortifying Pylos, a site on the west coast of the Peloponnesus in Messenia, about 45 miles from Sparta. Demosthenes established an Athenian camp there. Again, as Thucydides portrays it, this was the result of serendipity: a storm temporarily stranded the expedition, and the soldiers, bored, spontaneously took to fortifying the spot as a means of keeping busy.

The Spartans, alarmed by this intrusion into their territory, immediately sent a hoplite force to the uninhabited offshore island of Sphakteria, which could serve as a base for an attack on the Athenians, but they were unable to dislodge the Athenians. Even worse, they lost control of Sphakteria, leaving their men on the island marooned and virtual hostages of the Athenians. Intent on getting their men back, the Spartans sued for peace. But the Athenians, following the advice of Kleon, refused the Spartan offers of peace. The Spartans then turned to drastic measures to supply the men on the island, offering freedom to any helot who could get food across to them. The Spartans' success in provisioning the men in this way raised concerns in Athens. Winter was approaching, and the Athenians realized that the weather would soon force them to abandon their naval blockade of the island. They would then lose the Spartan prisoners without gaining anything. Anger grew at Kleon for his advice to refuse the Spartan peace proposal. The demagogue then responded with an offer to go himself to bring the hostages back to Athens within twenty days, an apparently rash promise, but one that he was able to carry out successfully (see Source Analysis).

In 424 the Athenians departed from Periclean policy by attempting to extend their empire by land into Boeotia, an effort that had been unsuccessful earlier in the century (see Chapter 10). Their plan for a simultaneous attack on three fronts misfired when one of the generals mistook the day of attack. The Athenians did manage to fortify Delium, a Boeotian site on the coast, but the Thebans soon defeated them in battle, inflicting heavy losses and driving them out (Thuc. 4.89–101).

In the meantime, in the north Aegean, the Greek and local population had been in active revolt against Athens since 432, and recent Athenian successes had alarmed them, for they feared that Athens might now feel free to send a major force against them. In 424 they requested assistance from Sparta, and a number of factors contributed to the Spartan decision to send the general Brasidas to the area. The Spartans saw an expedition to the north as an opportunity to include in the force some of the more enterprising helots, who had been emboldened by the Spartan defeat at Sphakteria, thus removing a dangerous element from Lakonia. Moreover, some in Sparta, jealous of Brasidas' military successes and persuasive abilities, were happy to see him out of the way campaigning in the north.[9] Finally, the Spartans hoped that success in the north would gain territory that might be swapped for the prisoners from Sphakteria.

The Spartan decision to send Brasidas north cost Athens control over Amphipolis—a serious loss. Amphipolis commanded the crossing of the Strymon River, the main east-west route in the north, and the area was a vital source of the timber Athens needed for shipbuilding, as well as possessing lucrative silver and gold mines. At the time, Thucydides was serving as a general and stationed nearby at Thasos with a few ships. His failure to reach the city in time to put down the revolt before the arrival of Spartan support resulted in his exile, which gave him the opportunity to write his history (4.103-107).

In 423 Athens and Sparta concluded a one-year truce based on the status quo. Two days later, according to Thucydides, the city of Scione in Thrace revolted from Athens. In contrast to the Mytilenian affair, the fate of Scione is not presented as a dramatic set-piece by Thucydides, so its story must be pieced together from scattered references. Yet despite this understated, undramatic presentation, it too represented a significant step in the downward spiral of Athenian political morality. What was at issue was the timing of the revolt. While the Spartans claimed that the people of Scione had rebelled before the armistice, and thus that their claim to independence was part of the status quo protected by the treaty, the Athenians maintained that the revolt had occurred after the agreement (Thucydides accepted the Athenian claim.) On the motion of Kleon, a decree was passed to recapture Scione and put its inhabitants to death (Thuc. 4.122). A fleet was sent out, and the city was besieged. When the Athenians finally succeeded in reducing the city in 421, there were no second thoughts about harsh sentences; the men were put to death, and the women and children sold into slavery (Thuc. 5.32).

In 422 Kleon carried a resolution in the Assembly that Amphipolis should be retaken, and the Athenians, under his command, marched against the city. In the ensuing battle, Kleon fell, shot in the back by a light-armed Thracian peltast—an ignominious end that the historian emphasized. In contrast, Thucydides reports that the Spartan commander Brasidas fell nobly in the battle, having lived long enough to learn of the victory of his men. He was buried with public honors in the *agora* of Amphipolis, where the citizens accorded him worship as the true founder of the city, replacing Hagnon, the original Athenian founder (Thuc. 5.11).

Source Analysis

hucydides and Aristophanes on Kleon.   Both Thucydides and Aristophanes provide extended portraits of Kleon, and it is interesting to compare their treatments, bearing in mind the differing aims of the two authors and the different genres in which they worked.

THUC.3.36–50: THE MYTILENIAN DEBATE   This passage provides a graphic picture of Thucydides' opinions of the new direction in Athenian leadership. Note the key words and ideas in these speeches; consider Kleon's views on rhetoric and his interpretation of justice and right and compare with the views of Pericles expressed in the Funeral Oration.

THUC.4.27–41. THE PYLOS AFFAIR   Thucydides' account of the Pylos affair provides further insight into his attitudes toward Kleon as a political leader, as well as a good example of the way in which historians are able to turn apparent success into failure by the way they present facts. Note the role played by Demosthenes, who had originally been responsible for the fortification of Pylos. In particular, consider Thucydides' account of an earlier incident in which Demosthenes had fought during the war (3.96–98); how might this experience have affected the conduct of Kleon's expedition? Was the expedition as much of an accident as Thucydides suggests?

ARISTOPHANES *KNIGHTS*   Thucydides was not alone in seeing the demagogue as the undeserving victor in the Pylos situation. We have already met Kleon in the *Wasps* of Aristophanes, produced in 422. Two years earlier, in 424, the comic poet had made his most sustained attack on the demagogue in the *Knights*, which focuses specifically on the Pylos incident. In the *Knights*, how many references are there to Kleon's theft of Demosthenes' victory? Was Aristophanes' satire fair?

THUC. 5.6–11. KLEON AT AMPHIPOLIS   When Kleon appears for the last time in the pages of Thucydides' history, he is a general in his own right, fighting in the battle of Amphipolis in Thrace. Thucydides is merciless to the end in his treatment of the demagogue, portraying him as deserting his troops while they were still resisting the enemy, and fleeing for his life, only to be shot in the back by a barbarian. What devices does Thucydides use to influence his readers in this passage?

The Peace of Nicias, 421

The deaths of both Kleon and Brasidas during the battle of Amphipolis removed the two chief obstacles to a peace settlement, and both cities felt the need for a respite from war. The Spartans were anxious to regain the hostages taken at Pylos; moreover, their 30-year truce with Argos, which had been concluded in 451, was about to expire, threatening them with hostilities on a new front. In Athens, the loss of Amphipolis was added to the city's losses in the battle of Delium in Boeotia. Thus the two sides agreed on a truce, called the Peace of Nicias (the text is cited by Thucydides 5.18). Thucydides remarks that for six years and ten months they abstained from invasions of each others' territory, but that in no other way could it have been called a period of peace.

Among the many hostile actions carried out by both sides during the Peace of Nicias, Thucydides picked the suppression of the small island of Melos as a subject for a set-piece. While this was apparently a minor affair, by his presentation Thucydides elevated it to a position as the linch-pin of his history. As we saw in the last chapter, beginning with prewar punishments of Medizing Greeks (Greeks who had gone over to the side of the Persians), Athens had moved on to the compulsion of allies, becoming increasingly violent. Mytilene escaped total destruction by a hair. Scione was destroyed. Finally even Melos—a neutral city that simply asked to be left alone—fell victim to what can at this point only be called Athenian imperial greed.

Source Analysis

THE MELIAN DIALOGUE, THUC. 5.84–116   The dialogue form in which this incident is presented in itself serves to call attention to the significance of the passage. Thucydides nowhere else used this form, which was later employed in reporting philosophical discussions: the most familiar example can be found in Plato's Socratic dialogues. In the Melian Dialogue a philosophical topic—the nature of justice—makes the dialogue form especially relevant. Consider the values expressed in the arguments of each side, and compare them with those expressed in the Funeral Oration and the Mytilenian debate.

The Sicilian Expedition

The Sicilian expedition, which was the largest military expedition up to that time in western history, and which led to the greatest disaster Athens faced until its final defeat, began in a small way. The insignificant city of Segesta in Sicily, with which Athens was in alliance, hoped to gain some advantage for itself in its local squabbles with a neighbor by exploiting its powerful ally. Athens listened for a mixture of reasons; perhaps because expansion to Sicily, a rich grain-producing area, had long been a temptation for a city with a perennial need for grain; perhaps because its leaders were eager for personal glory; perhaps because the populace longed for the booty to be gained from a successful, and apparently easy, victory. Pericles, of course, had warned against expansion during the war, and Athenian involvement in Sicily now signaled a major break with his policies (although it could be argued that the city at this time was not technically at war). Thucydides presents both sides of the question in the form of a debate in the Assembly between two of the generals who were to lead the expedition: Nicias, a cautious and conservative older man known for his sponsorship of the Peace of Nicias, and Alkibiades, a wealthy and dashing young aristocrat who had been brought up in the household of Pericles as his ward, and who hoped for personal glory from the expedition. As Thucydides portrays Alkibiades, he is a charismatic but ambivalent character, and our other sources suggest that his enthusiastic but erratic political adventuring left other Athenians puzzled and undecided about him as well. Plato portrays him in the *Symposium* as a young, handsome, but spoiled admirer of Socrates who tries unsuccessfully to seduce the philosopher. Arguing against Alkibiades' persuasive rhetoric, the more cautious Nicias magnified the forces that he believed would be needed, but in response, the Assembly, swept by enthusiasm for the project, voted an even larger force—and even that, in the end, proved to be insufficient.

On the eve of the departure, near panic struck Athens when vandals attacked the shrines of the Herms throughout the city. These were cult statues of the god Hermes in the form of a pillar with the head of the god and an erect phallus, which stood at house gateways and crossroads to protect travelers. Rumors that the Eleusinian mysteries had been profaned in secret celebrations also circulated. Many were arrested. Alkibiades was among those accused of involvement, but his enemies did not dare to have him arrested while the army was still in Athens because of his popularity with the men. Better to arrest him en route and bring him back to Athens to stand trial when the army was no longer there to protest.

The departure was a glorious celebration, with almost the entire city turning out to bid farewell to the expedition. Thucydides called it the most costly and finest looking force that had ever been assembled by a single city.

As the fleet made its way to Sicily, however, the first blow fell. An arrest warrant was served to Alkibiades. At first he acceded, but later he managed to evade his captors and made his way to Sparta, where he bought sanctuary with advice that in the long run would prove very destructive for Athens. He counseled the Spartans to send reinforcements to Syracuse with an experienced general, and to fortify an outpost in Attica itself, at Dekeleia, which would offer a haven for runaway Athenian slaves from the silver mines at Laurion.

When the expedition approached Sicily, the remaining generals followed the strategy proposed by Alkibiades before his arrest, sailing around and trying to attract allies. They had little success, however. In the first engagement of the war, a battle in the harbor at Syracuse, they did achieve a victory, but Nicias, displaying his cautious nature, failed to follow it up. Instead, he ordered the fleet back to the Athenian camp at Katane, which gave the Syracusans the opportunity to prepare their defenses.

In 414 the Athenians attempted a siege of Syracuse, but their encircling wall was blocked by a Syracusan counter-wall. An extended and indecisive contest of wall-building ensued, in which the second Athenian commander, Lamachus, was killed. This left Nicias alone in command, and he was suffering from a debilitating kidney ailment. Athenian prospects deteriorated further when the reinforcements that Alkibiades had recommended that the Spartans send, arrived, accompanied by a talented general, Gyllipus. In mainland Greece the Spartans also followed Alkibiades' advice to fortify Dekeleia, providing a potential haven that tempted Athenian slaves to escape from the silver mines. During the war, as many as 20,000 slaves escaped from the mines, with many going to Dekeleia, creating a serious economic problem for the Athenians.[10]

Nicias sent a letter to the Assembly appealing for more forces and for relief from his command because of his illness. The Assembly refused to relieve him, but instead ordered a second, even larger expedition to sail to Sicily, under the command of the general Demosthenes.

On the day before Demosthenes arrived with the second expedition, the Syracusans won a major sea victory. When Demosthenes landed he saw that the only hope now lay with the capture of the Syracusan counter-wall. He ordered a daring night battle to accomplish this, but the attempt failed. Demosthenes then concluded that the most reasonable course of action was to withdraw Athenian troops from Sicily. Nicias, however, fearing condemnation by the Athenian Assembly, and misled by a wishful hope that the Syracusans would soon run out of money, refused to agree. Demosthenes honored Nicias' decision because he believed that Nicias had more information about affairs in Syracuse than he in fact had. And so the Athenians' best opportunity to escape was lost through fear on one side and misapprehension on the other.

When Demosthenes did finally succeed in persuading Nicias to withdraw, an eclipse of the moon occurred (August 27, 414). The soldiers saw it as an omen, as the soothsayers held, and urged the commanders to wait. Nicias himself, whom Thucydides describes as excessively given to divination, refused to even discuss leaving until the three-times-nine days that the soothsayers decreed had passed. But the soothsayers' advice proved fatal. On September 3, the Athenian fleet fought and lost a battle in the harbor, and the Syracusans began to blockade its entrance. On September 9 the Athenians suffered their final defeat at sea, when they were unable to break through the harbor blockade. At this point, the men were so demoralized that they refused to reboard the ships. They were trapped, and the only option left was to retreat by land.

But again the Athenian departure was postponed. With the Syacusan troops in drunken celebration, Gylippus realized that the only way to pursue the victory was to delay the Athenian march until his troops had recovered from the aftereffects of their celebrations. Accordingly, he sent a spy to the Athenians with a false warning that the roads were all watched and that they should wait. The Athenians fell for the ruse and waited for two days. As a result, when they finally set out in ignoble retreat, abandoning the sick and wounded and leaving the dead unburied, the Syracusans had recovered and were ready for them. The entire army was soon slaughtered or captured. Both generals were executed.

Source Analysis
Some Highlights of the Sicilian Expedition

T HUC.6.8–32. THE DEBATE IN THE ASSEMBLY BETWEEN ALKIBIADES AND NICIAS   This debate on the wisdom of the expedition to Sicily reveals not only the situation of Athens on the eve of the expedition, but also much about the character of these two men as seen by Thucydides. What characteristics of the two men does Thucydides reveal through the speeches that he attributes to them?

THUC.6.52–61. THE MUTILATION OF THE HERMS   Why does Thucydides tell the story of Aristogiton and Harmodus? Does the historian imply that Alkibiades was in fact involved in the mutilation?

THUC.6.30–32, 42–51. THE DEPARTURE OF THE EXPEDITION   What were the attitudes of the Athenians as the expedition set out? What responses did the expedition meet en route? What were the various plans put forward by the three generals? Do any forebodings of future difficulties appear in this passage?

THUC. 6.89–93. ALKIBIADES AT SPARTA   Are Alkibiades' justifications for offering assistance to the Spartans convincing?

THUC.7.10–18. NICIAS APPEALS TO THE ATHENIAN ASSEMBLY   How many of the problems faced by the Athenian forces had been anticipated by Nicias in his earlier speeches? On the other hand, to what extent had events borne out Alkibiades' predictions?

THUC. 7.55–72. THE LAST BATTLE IN THE HARBOR   Why does Thucydides provide so much detail about the participants in the battle? What changes had the Athenians made to their ships, and how had the Syracusans responded? What literary devices does Thucydides use to enhance the account of the battle?

THUC. 7.72–87. THE FLIGHT OF THE ATHENIAN FORCES   To what does Thucydides compare the retreating forces, and how does this effect the force of his description? Since he was not present, what sources might he have used for this passage?

The Ionian Phase of the War

After the Sicilian disaster, the Athenians displayed amazing resilience. They immediately set about building a new fleet, and by 412 they had achieved "something approaching parity" with the Peloponnesians, which Simon Hornblower calls "a staggering achievement."[11] Serious problems nevertheless loomed: the expenses of the expedition and the rebuilding of the fleet had depleted the reserves; the grain-supply route to the Black Sea was vulnerable; and Athens' allies in Asia Minor and the islands were restive (Thuc. 8.2). At the root, all of these were economic problems, and they provided an opportunity for Persia, with its vast supplies of gold, to intervene both with the Athenians and the Spartans. While the Persians had failed to defeat Greece militarily, Persian gold offered another, more fruitful means of attack.

After the Sicilian disaster, Athens' subjects vied with each other for Spartan assistance in revolt. The first to seek help was Euboea. It was quickly followed by Lesbos and Chios. Meanwhile, exiles from Megara and Cyzicus at the court of the Persian satrap Pharnabazus at Dascylium appealed to the Spartans for help in fomenting revolt in the Hellespont. In the tangle of intrigues that followed, Alkibiades was a key figure, playing all three sides—Sparta, the Persian satraps, and Athens—against each other in an attempt to further his own advantage.

Under the circumstances, Sparta faced a choice between concentrating its assistance on the Hellespont or in Ionia. It was Alkibiades, still in Sparta, who persuaded them to prefer the Chians' request and chose Ionia as the theater of war rather than the Hellespont. As often with Alkibiades' schemes, this may have been a mistake, for later events showed that the key to victory for the Peloponnesians lay not in Ionia, but in control of the Athenian supply route through the Hellespont.

In Ionia, the revolt of Chios was soon following by those of Erythrae, Klazomenae, and Miletus. Nevertheless, even in the midst of these reverses, Athens achieved some successes. In Samos the *demos* seized power from the oligarchic rulers with Athenian assistance, and the island became the base for the Athenian navy. The Athenians regained Lesbos and Klazomenae and seized a base on the island of Chios from which they could harass the Chians and provide a refuge for fugitives. Meanwhile, however, Knidos and Rhodes revolted.

THE OLIGARCHIC COUP OF 411: THE FOUR HUNDRED AND THE FIVE THOUSAND

Amid these problems with allies, there was also trouble at home in Athens. The class solidarity that had been promoted by the economic benefits of empire—pay and cleruchies for the rowers and hoplites and rich overseas landholdings for the wealthy—was increasingly undermined by their loss. The result was political instability and the growth of oligarchic schemes.

At this point, the machinations of Alkibiades once again came to the fore. In 411, safely ensconced with the fleet at Samos, where he had great popularity, he was one of the primary instigators of an oligarchic coup in Athens. Hoping to obtain his recall to Athens, he dangled the prospect of Persian gold before the leading Athenians in the fleet at Samos. He promised that if an oligarchic regime were to be established at Athens, he would use his influence with the satrap to secure Persian aid for Athens. In the end, he was unable to deliver the promised Persian assistance, but the oligarchic revolution he had instigated proceeded at Athens without him. The conspirators appealed to a fictitious Constitution of Dracon and promised to institute a body of 5,000 citizens, composed of those able to provide their own arms and serve in office without pay. As it turned out, however, the Five Thousand were never chosen, and a Council of Four Hundred instituted a reign of terror.

Envoys were sent from Athens to try to win over the fleet at Samos to the cause of the Four Hundred, but they failed in their attempt, and Alkibiades at this point switched his allegiance to the democrats. Thucydides credits him with doing the city a signal favor by persuading the sailors at Samos not to set out immediately for Athens to put down the Four Hundred by force, an action that would have caused a civil war and cost many lives. Instead, at Alkibiades' advice, they sent a message to Athens that the Four Hundred must go, but that there was no objection to the Five Thousand. This proved to be the turning point; the coup collapsed, and a mixed oligarchic-democratic regime of the Five Thousand was established. Thucydides called it the best government that the Athenians had ever had.

The War in the Hellespont

In 411 the Spartans at last transferred their theater of operations to the Hellespont. The Athenians followed, assembling their naval forces for an attack upon the Spartans at Cyzicus, which had revolted. Assisting the Athenian forces was Alkibiades, who played a major role in their victory and the recovery of Cyzicus. The Spartan commander was killed, and the Spartans offered peace terms, which the Athenians unwisely rejected under the influence of the demagogue Kleophon.[12] However, the victory enabled the Athenians to exact tribute from the area, relieving their immediate financial difficulties (at this time the Spartans had a ready supply of gold from Persia).

Soon after the Athenian victory at Cyzicus, Thucydides' history breaks off in mid-sentence. A recently discovered inscription from the island of Thasos suggests, however, that the historian lived at least until 397. This conclusion is based on the appearance in the inscription under the year 397 of the name of a local magistrate, Lichas son of Arkesilas. If this is the same man as the Lichas son of Arkesilas whose death Thucydides reports at 8.84.2, it demonstrates that the historian was alive and still writing seven years after the war; many scholars are skeptical about the identification, however.[13] But whether or not the historian lived on, he did not complete his history of the war,[14] and for the period after the victory at Cyzicus, our sources become much weaker. They include the biographer Plutarch; Xenophon, an Athenian aristocrat exiled by the Athenians in the fourth century for his pro-Spartan inclinations; and Diodorus Siculus, the author of a universal history in the time of Julius Caesar and Augustus. Xenophon undertook a continuation of Thucydides' history, but his work lacks the accuracy and impartiality of Thucydides' account. Diodorus Siculus is chiefly valuable for his use of the fourth-century Greek historian Ephorus, to which he added his own moralizing passages; while he put the material into annalistic form, he was often careless about chronology.

Following the victory at Cyzicus, the Athenians succeeded in capturing three sites on the Bosphorus: Khrysopolis, where they established a lucrative customs station, Khalkedon, and Byzantium. Alkibiades played a starring role in these successes, and in 407/406 the Athenians elected him general in absentia. He seized upon this show of good will to return to the city. Although he sailed back with great pageantry and display, he knew the fickle nature of the Athenian *demos* and cautiously waited to land until he saw relatives and friends among the crowd, who provided him with a safe escort into the city.

Alkibiades had no need to fear. The Athenian people welcomed back the charismatic figure as a savior in their time of need. He spoke in the Assembly in his own defense and was cleared of the charges of impiety in the mutilation of the Herms and even elected supreme general. Enhancing his public image, he undertook to lead the first procession by land to Eleusis since the war for the celebration of the Greater Eleusinian mysteries.[15] His credit and popularity had never been higher, but both he and the Athenian *demos* were volatile, and his days of glory were short-lived.

Before long Alkibiades sailed out again on naval operations off the Anatolian coast. The purpose of these operations is unclear, and during the expedition, a minor naval loss brought an end to Alkibiades' brief period of popularity in Athens. At Notium he left the main body of his fleet in charge of Antiochus, his pilot and drinking buddy, giving him orders not to risk battle, while he himself set out on a mission with a few ships. The sources do not agree on the facts of the situation. Was Alkibiades engaged in collecting necessary funds to pay the sailors? Or was this an indiscretion on his part? Was Antiochus a reliable choice? Did Antiochus disobey orders and offer battle, or was he caught in an ambush? Whatever the circumstances, a battle that ended in defeat took place at Notium in Alkibiades' absence. Athenian public opinion, always fickle, turned against him. Perhaps his difficulties went beyond the battle loss. According to Plutarch, his enemies brought other accusations against him, among them the charge that he had provided himself with a private fortress in the Chersonese as a possible refuge. At any rate, the *demos* did not re-elect him general in 406/405, and he prudently withdrew to his fortress in the Chersonese, fearing the wrath of the notoriously changeable Athenian people if he should return again. And it seems that the Athenians were indeed still in a quandary about his true aims, as we can see from Aristophanes' *Frogs*, produced in 405. In this play, when the characters Euripides and Aeschylus had to choose a poet to be resurrected as savior of the city, a decisive question was: "What should be done about Alkibiades?" Their advice, while comic, expresses the ambivalence felt about Alkibiades in Athens:[16]

> Euripides:
>
> I hate the citizen who's slow to help his city,
> But quick to harm it,
> Resourceful for himself, resourceless for the city.

> Aeschylus:
>
> It's best not to raise a lion cub in the city,
> But if it's raised, it's best to gratify its little ways.

The Battle of Arginusae, 406

The Athenians were to have one more great victory—and to turn it into a disgrace to the democracy—before their final defeat. This victory followed upon a great crisis. A new Spartan commander, Lysander, by cleverly appealing to the self-interest of the oligarchic leaders in a number of cities, was able to organize a fleet of 140 ships. He achieved immediate success in an engagement off Lesbos in which the newly elected Athenian general Conon lost 30 of the city's 70 ships, while the remaining ships were blockaded in the harbor of Mytilene. The situation for Athens was critical: gold and silver dedications in the temples were melted down, and freedom was even offered to slaves, and citizenship to metics, who were willing to join in the fight. In a month the Athenians managed to assemble a fleet of more than 150 ships, and they were able to defeat the Spartan forces in the naval battle of Arginusae.

After the victory at Arginusae, however, a storm arose, and the Athenian generals decided against staying to recover the dead from the 25 ships lost in the battle. This violation of religious custom enraged the people of Athens, and the generals, including the son of Pericles by Aspasia, were executed after being illegally tried *en masse*, rather than as individuals as the law required. Socrates, at the time a member of the Council, voted against the proposal for the illegal act, incurring the wrath of his fellow citizens. Later, however, many of the Athenians repented of their hasty and illegal action. As was too often the case, the Athenian *demos* acted first and thought afterwards.

The Final Defeat of Athens: The Battle of Aegospotami, 405

The Athenians lost the final and decisive battle in the Peloponnesian War almost entirely because of the negligence and internal dissension of their own leaders. They faced the enemy in the Hellespont, but the Spartans, in a strong position, refused to give battle. The Athenian position was weak, and their men had to go a long distance for supplies. Each day the Athenian fleet sailed out and tried to draw the Spartans into battle, and when this failed, they sailed back, disembarked, and the crews scattered in search of food and supplies. Alkibiades, whose refuge was nearby, saw the weakness in the Athenian position and advised them to move. According to Diodorus, he also offered the assistance of a large Thracian army under his command. The Athenian generals, however, refused his advice and his offer, in part out of jealousy and fear that he would reap the public relations rewards of any success they might have. Eventually, the Spartan commander Lysander observed the Athenian pattern of behavior and attacked when the men had scattered from their ships in search of supplies. The result was a massacre. Only 20 of the 180 Athenian ships managed to escape under the leadership of Conon; the rest were lost, and three to four thousand Athenians perished. Conon sent twelve of the surviving ships back to Athens while he himself took the other eight to seek protection from King Evagoras in Cyprus.

The victory at Aegospotami put Lysander in a commanding position, with nothing to stand in the way of a siege of Athens. Heading for Athens, he ordered that all overseas Athenians should be driven back home in order to put more pressure on the city's food supplies, and then began a siege. The Athenians held out for eight months while the demagogue Kleophon resisted acceptance of Spartan terms. Thucydides was recalled from exile during this time of crisis. Eventually, however, the Athenians, starving, were forced to capitulate.

The terms of the surrender were not as devastating as some of the Greek cities, notably Thebes, urged, for almost immediately the other Greek cities began to worry about the new balance of power. The Athenians thus did not receive the fate that they had meted out to others: their men were not slaughtered, nor were their women and children sold into slavery. Instead, they were made allies of Sparta, and were limited to 12 ships. The Long Walls to the Piraeus were torn down to the rejoicing sound of flutes, and a governing body consisting of 30 men (the Thirty Tyrants) was established by Sparta. The Thirty were appointed to draw up a new constitution, but instead they ruled arbitrarily, taking advantage of their power to purge the citizen body of their personal enemies. Again, Socrates stood against the acting government, refusing to participate in the illegal arrest of a citizen, Leon of Salamis. The harshness of the Thirty was so great that finally, in 403, the Athenians, aided by exiles who had found refuge in Thebes, succeeded in defeating and expelling them. Democracy was restored, and it was to last for three generations.

All was not well with the new democracy, however. While a political amnesty was declared in 403, in 399 the opponents of Socrates charged the philosopher with religious offenses—impiety, advocating foreign gods—and corrupting the youth. During the trial he defended himself by claiming to be a useful gadfly for the people of Athens, stinging them when they were headed in the wrong direction. The jury found him guilty by a vote of 280 to 220, but when, in accordance with Athenian practice, he was asked to propose a penalty, he suggested that he be given free meals in the Prytaneum for life because of his service to the *polis*. The jury, stung once too often by his provocations, voted for the death penalty by a much larger majority.

WEBSITE 12.1   SOCRATES

There are many web sites devoted to Socrates; some of the best are:

An Athenian Agora Guide Book, Socrates in the Agora, by Mabel Lang is an excellent illustrated booklet that can be downloaded free (or purchased for $3.00) from the Athenian Agora Excavations:

http://www.agathe.gr/publications.html

A university site that contains a short discussion of Socrates and a link to the text in English of the *Apology* can be found at:

http://www.wsu.edu:8080/~dee/GREECE/SOCRATES.HTM

Some questions to answer from this site:
   What activities of Socrates motivated opposition to him?
   Who among his companions might have contributed to this opposition?
   Explain *elenchus, dialectic.*

A longer discussion of Socrates by the noted historian of philosophy, W. K. C. Guthrie, can be found at:

http://socrates.clarke.edu/Guthrie.htm.

SUGGESTIONS FOR FURTHER READING

The best source for the events of the war is the account byThucydides himself, until his text breaks off in 411. Some interesting secondary works on Thucydides include W. Robert Connor (1984), *Thucydides*; Virginia Hunter (1973), *Thucydides: The Artful Reporter*; Lisa Kallett (2001), *Money and the Corrosion of Power in Thucydides: The Sicilian Expedition and Its Aftermath.* The standard commentary on the Greek text, A. W. Gomme, A. Andrewes, and K. J. Dover (1945–1981), *A Historical Commentary on Thucydides*, vols. 4, 5, contains historical as well as textual discussions.

MAP STUDY

Strymon River, Amphipolis, Athens, Sparta, Corinth, Corcyra, Potidaea, Amphipolis, Megara, Plataea, Aegina, Euboea, Thebes, Piraeus, Pylos, Messenia, Sphakteria, Delium, Thasos, Scione, Thrace, Melos, Segesta, Dekeleia, Syracuse, Katane, Eleusis, Notium, Arginusae, Bosphorus, Cyzicus, Dascylium, Aegospotami, Hellespont, Chrysopolis,

Chalkedon, Byzantium, Ionia, Lesbos, Mytilene, Chios, Erythrae, Klazomenae, Knidos, Rhodes

ENDNOTES

[1]The fragments of the Sophists, in Greek with German translations, are collected in the Diels-Kranz edition, *Fragmente der Vorsokratiker* (many editions and revisions; consult the latest). For English translations see R. K. Sprague (1972), *The Older Sophists*; and K. Freeman (1948), *Ancilla to the Pre-Socratic Philosophers*. Excellent discussions are to be found in J. de Romilly (1992), *The Great Sophists in Periclean Athens*; and W. K. C. Guthrie (1971), *The Sophists*.

[2]Lysias IV, *On the Invalid*.

[3]Jacquiline de Romilly (1988), *Thucydides and Athenian Imperialism*.

[4]Aristophanes *Acharnians* 515–539, 730–835; *Peace* 605–611, 615–618; Andocides III 8; Aeschines II 175; Ephorus, frag. 196 ap. Diod. Sic. xii. 38.1–41.1. For a full discussion, see G. E. M. de Ste.-Croix (1972), *The Origins of the Peloponnesian War*.

[5]On Thucydides' attention to economic issues, see Lisa Kallet-Marx (1993), *Money, Expense, and Naval Power in Thucydides' History*, 1–5.24; and Lisa Kallett (2001), *Money and the Corrosion of Power in Thucydides: The Sicilian Expedition and Its Aftermath*.

[6]L. Kallet-Marx (1989), "Did Tribute Fund the Parthenon?" *Classical Antiquity* 8:252–266, disagrees with the use of League funds for the building program.

[7] The probable burial site of plague victims was discovered in Athens in 1998 during excavations prior to construction of a subway station just outside Athens' ancient Kerameikos cemetery. See http://www.archaeology.org/online/news/kerameikos.html.

[8]A. J. Holladay and J. C. F. Poole (1979), "Thucydides and the Plague of Athens," *Classical Quarterly* 29:282–300, argue that the plague cannot be identified, but that Thucydides should be given credit for the first mention of contagion; in the course of their argument they provide a full bibliography for the various diseases. Nevertheless, new suggestions continue to be made. Toxic shock complicated by influenza by A. D. Langmuir, et al. (1985), "The Thucydides Syndrome," *New England Journal of Medicine*, 1027–1030; contra, D. M. Morens and R. J. Littman (1994), "Thucydides Syndrome" Reconsidered: New Thoughts on the 'Plague of Athens'," *American Journal of Epidemiology* 140:621–628. Marburg-Ebolu fevers: G. D. Scarrow (1988), "The Athenian Plague. A Possible Diagnosis," *Ancient History Bulletin* 11:4–8; also P. E. Olson, C. S. Hames, A. S. Benenson, and E. N. Genovese (1996), "The Thucydides Syndrome: Ebola Déjà Vu? (or Ebola Reemergent?)" *Emerging Infectious Diseases* 2: (Apr-June) 1–23. For discussion, see website: http://www.cdc.gov/ncidod/eid/vol2no2/olson.htm. On the intellectual effects of the plague, see J. Mikalson (1982), "Religion and the Plague in Athens 431–427 BC," *Greek, Roman and Byzantine Studies* 10:217ff. For another view of the issue of contagion, see J. Solomon (1985), "Thucydides and the Recognition of Contagion," *Maia* 37:121ff.

[9]For example, M. Meiss, (1951), *Painting in Florence and Sienna after the Black Death*.

[10]Thucydides 4.107.7 remarks that the leading men were jealous of him.

[11]See Kallet (above, n. 5).

[12]Thucydides 7.27–28. See Peter Hunt (1998), *Slaves, Warfare, and Ideology in the Greek Historians*, 111–115.

[13]Simon Hornblower (1983), *The Greek World, 479–323*, 143.

[14]But see A. Powell (1988), *Athens and Sparta*, for a defense of Athens' refusal.

[15]For example, S. Hornblower (1987), *Thucydides*, 151–153; P. J. Rhodes (1988), *Thucydides on Thucydides*, 2.1; P. Cartledge (1984), "A New Lease of Life for Lichas Son of Arkesilas?" *Liverpool Classical Monthly* 9, 7:98–102.

[16]However, some late-written passages have been identified in which Thucydides offered his opinion on the closing days of the war, Thuc. 2.65, 6.15.

[17]On Alkibiades' return, Xen. 1.4.8–20.

[18]See *Cambridge Ancient History* 2nd ed. V: 490–491.

[19]Aristophanes *Frogs* 1421–1432, tr. N. Demand.

13

GREECE IN THE FOURTH CENTURY

I n the century following the defeat of Athens in the Peloponnesian War, Sparta and Thebes—and eventually Athens as well—vied for power and leadership among the Greek cities. The balance of power shifted again and again, and as it shifted, political alliances changed as well, for as one power threatened to gain ascendancy, the others quickly realigned themselves in opposition. Warfare was almost constant, and Persia often entered in, usually from the sidelines, but sometimes playing a major role. Meanwhile, in Macedonia on the northern fringe of the Greek world, a new power was growing that was soon to engulf both the Greek cities and the Persian Empire.

No historian of the caliber of Herodotus or Thucydides dominated the historical scene in the fourth century. The principal sources for mainland Greece in the period following the Peloponnesian War are Xenophon's *Hellenica*, in which the pro-Spartan Athenian takes up the account of the Peloponnesian War where Thucydides' account breaks off, and the universal history of Diodorus Siculus, a writer of the Roman period who abridged the work of the fourth-century Greek historian Ephorus, which is otherwise mainly lost. The shortcomings in the historical accounts for the fourth century are to some extent made up by the evidence from inscriptions and by the abundant evidence of the Attic orators. The speeches include both political orations and arguments in private lawsuits; the latter, although often difficult to interpret, provide valuable information about social and economic life. In this chapter we will first consider briefly the main political events in mainland Greece during the period, and then turn to aspects of the economic and social scene in Athens and to developments in Macedonia.

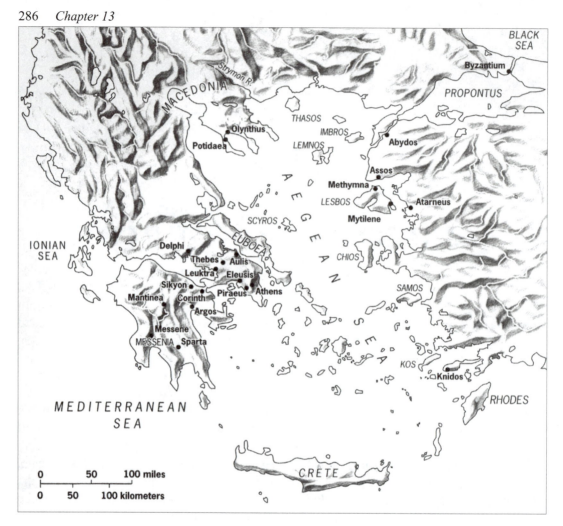

Map 13A   Greece in the fourth century

POLITICAL HISTORY IN GREECE IN THE FOURTH CENTURY

The Period of Spartan Hegemony

The fall of Athens left that city with great losses. Perhaps half the adult male citizens had died in the course of the war,[1] and a large number of women and children, unmentioned in our sources, must have also succumbed, especially in the famine brought on by the prolonged siege at the end of the war. The city's territory had been ravaged, its fleet wiped out, its empire gone, and its walls dismantled by the Peloponnesians to the rejoicing sound of flutes. With these losses, the city's economic base was shattered. Thebes, in contrast, was much enriched by years of plundering Attica, although angry with its ally Sparta for refusing to share the prizes of victory. Sparta itself emerged as the strongest power in Greece.

But the Spartans, despite their victory—in fact, because of it—had an unfulfilled "contract" with Persia hanging over their heads: the Persian gold that had made Spartan victory possible had been obtained at the price of a promise to turn over the Greek cities in Asia Minor to Persia. The Spartans had a choice: fulfill the contract or develop power capable of standing up to the Persians. And the latter choice, in effect, meant replacing Athens as an imperial power in the Aegean.[2]

The idea of a Spartan empire that could stand up to Persia was not an unreasonable one in some respects. The Spartans had unquestioned military strength and abilities, and they possessed an outstanding military and political strategist in Lysander, who had led them to victory over the Athenians at Notium and Aegospotami, conducted the successful siege of Athens, and been instrumental in establishing the rule of the Thirty in defeated Athens. Moreover, while in charge of Spartan operations in Asia Minor and the Aegean, Lysander had given Sparta a tangible basis for empire by the establishment in many east Greek cities of garrisons commanded by Spartan officials (*harmosts*) and governed by councils made up of ten local citizens sympathetic to Spartan interests (*decarchies*).

But in spite of all of their assets, the Spartans proved unequal to the demands of empire. Their economic base still rested on the continued exploitation of the helots, and to maintain them required a continual state of military alert at home, keeping them from carrying out extensive operations abroad. Moreover, the *agoge* that they had created to develop and maintain this state of readiness itself posed problems. While it successfully produced citizens who could function well within a tightly controlled hierarchical society, it did not prepare them to face the challenges of a life free from the oversight of their peers. Spartans had no experience in handling the temptations of wealth and individual power, nor were they accustomed to motivating men who had not been raised under the discipline of a similar system. Thucydides summed up the situation in the speech that the Athenian envoy made to the Spartans in the negotiations leading up to the Peloponnesian War, correctly predicting the troubles that empire would bring to Sparta:[3]

> If, destroying us, you were to rule, soon the goodwill you obtained from fear of us would change, if indeed you acted as you did towards the Medes when you were in command for a short time. For you have *nomima* [customs and institutions] that are incompatible with those of others, and, moreover, your citizens, going abroad, are neither obedient to your own *nomima*, nor follow the ones that other Greeks follow.

This prediction was amply borne out by events in the post-war period. The Spartan *harmosts* in the subject cities were often rapacious, and the Spartan system permitted no appeal from their decisions. *Decarchies* too often functioned as collective tyrannies above the law. Individual Spartans, forbidden the possession of gold, silver, and other luxuries at home, found them irresistible abroad. A striking illustration of this is provided by Gylippus, the Spartan commander who had led the Syracusans to victory over the Athenians in the Sicilian expedition. His conduct of the Sicilian campaign was outstanding, but in 404, when Lysander entrusted him with the task of carrying back to Sparta a treasure of captured gold and silver, he succumbed to the temptation to steal from it.[4]

It is somewhat ironic that Lysander, who was exceptional for a Spartan in his personal incorruptibility and creative ingenuity, was frustrated and eventually defeated by a second fundamental weakness of the Spartan system: its inability to control and make use of the talents of ambitious men in ways that served both their own and the state's interests. Lysander's success in establishing *decarchies*, garrisons, and *harmosts* in the east Greek cities appeared to jealous peers back home not as steps in the Spartan organization of new territory, but as steps in the building of Lysander's own personal clientele. Nor did he help his cause by his frank celebration of his own achievements, such as his dedication at Delphi of a grandiose monument with his own statue as centerpiece. He even accepted being worshipped as a god by the people of Samos, the first Greek to be so honored during his lifetime.[5] Disturbed by this un-Spartan behavior, the Spartans recalled him and repudiated the *decarchies* as his personal clients, although they kept the system of garrisons and *harmosts* intact. Deprived of his command and kept idle at home, prevented by law from holding his office of Navarch for a second time, and ineligible by birth for the hereditary kingship, Lysander saw no constitutional outlet for his ambitions. It was at this point that he apparently began to plot to alter the constitution to allow for an elective kingship. Success eluded him there as well, however; although he consulted (and bribed) a number of oracles, none supported him.

On the death of King Agis II in 397, Lysander saw still another opportunity. Agis' son, Leotychidas, who was next in the line of succession, was widely rumored to be the natural son of the Athenian Alkibiades, and many opposed his election to the hereditary kingship because of this. The brother of Agis, Agesilaos, was next in succession after Leotychidas. He was a mild-mannered man who had, moreover, been Lysander's boyhood lover. Lysander, believing that he might control Agesilaos and through him influence Spartan policy, encouraged him to put forward his claim.[6] The main obstacle was the fact that Agesilaos was lame; the kingship was a religious as well as a secular office, and physical defects were considered incompatible with service to the gods. In fact, an oracle was circulated that seemed to warn specifically against the accession of Agesilaos:[7]

> Beware, arrogant Sparta,
> lest, swift-footed, you sprout a lame kingship.
> For all too long unexpected troubles will possess you,
> And a confused wave of man-destroying war.

Lysander turned the apparently negative oracle to Agesilaos' advantage by pointing out that, correctly interpreted, it referred not to Agesilaos' physical lameness but to Leotychidas' suspect birth. If he was not the natural son of Agis but of Alkibiades, as there were grounds to suspect, he had no right to succeed, and his accession would result in a crippled kingship. Oracles were notorious for their ambiguity (remember the wooden walls that were to offer protection for the Athenians against the Persian invasion), and Lysander's symbolic interpretation convinced the Spartans. Agesilaos was accepted as king, but Lysander's hopes that he could control him were soon disappointed. Although Lysander was chosen to head the board of thirty advisers who accompanied the king on his expedition to Asia, the king consistently rejected his advice and refused his requests for favors for his friends in the east Greek cities. Sent back to Greece to serve in the Corinthian War, Lysander was killed in the first battle.

The Spartan system thus presented three major obstacles to effective control of empire: the necessity to maintain a strong military presence at home, the failure of the *agoge* to instill the society's values in its citizens, and a governmental structure that made no provisions for the effective use of outstanding individual talent and ambition. Nevertheless, the Spartans made the imperial choice. In 397, when the Persians demanded the promised submission of the east Greek cities and the cities appealed for assistance to Sparta, the first Spartan "imperial" activity was underway. In 396 King Agesilaos set out at the head of a Greek force, dramatically posing as the new Agamemnon in still another war of Greeks against the "Barbarian East." His intention was to depart with a Homeric flourish, offering sacrifice at Aulis, where Agamemnon had made the fateful sacrifice of his daughter in return for favorable winds as he set out for Troy. But Agesilaos failed to ask permission of the Boeotians, and they stepped in to prevent the sacrifice, alarmed by an expedition that they viewed as a dangerous display of power by Sparta. It was not a good omen for the expedition.

In the meantime, the Athenian general Conon, who had taken refuge in Cyprus after the disaster at Aegospotami, led a Persian fleet to victory over the Spartan fleet at Knidos. In response, the east Greek cities threw off their Spartan garrisons and declared themselves for Persia. So much for the Spartan contract and their hopes of "liberating" the east Greeks! At home, moreover, Thebes, Athens, Corinth, and Argos, frightened by the Spartan initiatives, put aside their animosities to unite in opposing Sparta. Facing war in Greece, the Spartans called Agesilaos home, forcing him to abort his planned Trojan War in order to fight a war against fellow Greeks in his own home territory.

This new conflict, the Corinthian War (395–387/386), was intended to confine Sparta to the Peloponnesus. The Persians, angry at Agesilaos' challenge to their role in Asia Minor, joined the anti-Sparta cause. The satrap Pharnabazus brought the Athenian Conon and his fleet to Greece to aid the enemies of Sparta and to ravage Spartan territory. When Pharnabazus returned to the east, he left the fleet behind with Conon in Athens and added money to the treasury of the *polis*, so that the Athenians could rebuild the Long Walls and fortify the port of Piraeus. Athens was thus restored to a position of potential equality with the other Greek states by Persian assistance.

Meanwhile, in Athens debate swirled around the issue of the democracy, while in the north of Greece, in Macedonia, a power was growing that was soon to sweep over them all, demonstrating the irrelevance of their petty disputes and of the *polis* itself as a political form. The few voices that were raised in alarm, such as that of the Athenian orator Demosthenes, were little heeded; in fact, the leading political thinkers were turning more and more to monarchical ideals. Plato's involvement with the tyrant Dionysius of Syracuse in Sicily provides a good example.

In Syracuse the incompetence of the democratic government in dealing with a Carthaginian military threat provided the opportunity for the establishment of a tyranny. Dionysius followed an almost classic pattern in his rise to tyranny. A young man of obscure birth, he first successfully argued in the Assembly for the deposition of the existing board of generals and was himself appointed as one of a new board. Then his demagoguery won him election as sole general with sovereign powers to meet the immediate Carthaginian threat. The final step to the tyranny was the provision of a bodyguard, voted to him when it was rumored that an attempt had been made on his life. The democracy was never formally overthrown, and as in Athens under the Peisistratids, the outward forms of democracy were maintained: the Assembly met, passed decrees, and elected magistrates.

As tyrant, Dionysius managed, in the course of four wars, to drive the Carthaginians into the northwestern corner of the island and to gain control himself over all the Greek cities in Sicily. He then extended his rule to southern Italy, creating a western Greek empire.

In 388, Dionysius invited the philosopher Plato to come to Syracuse to educate his son and successor, Dionysius the Younger. Plato had strong ideas about ideal government, which he expressed in his dialogue *The Republic*. Observing the activities of the Athenian democracy (which, not incidentally, had put his beloved teacher Socrates to death), Plato firmly believed that the *demos* was an unruly lot, incapable of governing properly. Just as one needs an expert to build a house or to train a horse, so, Plato argued, one needs an expert to govern a *polis*. But such an expert, entrusted with the highest office, must be educated to the highest level, and this level Plato described in *The Republic* as that of the Philosopher King. Beginning with the most fundamental principles of rational knowledge, which Plato saw in geometry, the student would progress to the most esoteric knowledge of Being-in-Itself. Plato was intrigued by the prospect of putting his ideas and ideals into practice by making a Philosopher King out of the heir to the tyranny of Syracuse, and he accepted Dionysius' invitation.

Unfortunately, the younger Dionysius was a poor candidate for such a rigorous educational program. While enthusiastic at first—the whole court for a time was immersed in the study of geometry—he soon tired of the effort required. Political intrigues by those opposed to any changes or reforms soon succeeded in making the situation intolerable for Plato, and at last Dionysius let him return to Athens, although the story has it that the tyrant arranged for his disposal en route, an effort that failed.

Plato's transformation of the Syracusan tyranny into a philosopher-kingship was not to be, but the attempt reflects the spirit of the age, with its growing impatience with the ineffectiveness of the *polis* and its increasing interest in monarchical forms of government. Plato's pupil Aristotle had better luck with a similar job; he was hired to educate the son of Philip II of Macedon, the boy who was to become Alexander the Great. Macedon, being by tradition a kingdom, was, however, perhaps a better basis, and Aristotle more practically minded than his teacher.

In the meantime, bolstered by their renewed defenses and restored fleet, the Athenians embarked once again on the imperialistic path. They seized the islands of Scyros, Imbros, and Lemnos and established cleruchies, in which they settled Athenian citizens who were allotted land to be worked for them by local inhabitants. Soon they won other allies along the route to the Black Sea, including Byzantium, where they re-established the 10 percent duty on ships sailing from the Black Sea. They imposed a tax of 5 percent on the maritime imports and exports of their allies, but they asked for no tribute as such. This renewal of Athenian imperialism frightened Sparta and Thebes, and they abandoned their mutual resentments to join in opposition to Athens. Peace was achieved only by the intervention of the Persian king, who oversaw a treaty called the King's Peace in 387/386.

The provisions of the King's Peace were generally favorable to Sparta. Spartan control of the mainland of Greece was supported, leagues were forbidden (including the Boeotian League, source of Thebes' power), and the Greek cities in Asia were given up to the Persians. In 382, however, another Spartan blunder turned the other Greeks against Sparta once again. In keeping with the provisions of the King's Peace, Sparta decided to put down the league that the city of Olynthus in northern Greece had gradually built up. Since leagues were outlawed by the terms of the King's Peace, Sparta was justified in sending a force to see to its dissolution. On their march north, however, the Spartans discovered a fortuitous combination of circumstances at Thebes—internal treachery and a **Kadmeia** (the Theban acropolis) that was undefended, having been given over to the women who were celebrating the festival of the Thesmophoria. The Spartans seized the opportunity and occupied the Kadmeia. The unexpected and unprovoked nature of the attack, the violation of a widely revered religious festival, and continuing Spartan occupation of the Kadmeia roused the feelings of the Greeks against Sparta.

In 378 still another example of Spartan high-handedness brought Athens into alliance with Thebes. A Spartan *harmost* in Thessaly, Sphodrias, set out by night to lead a surprise attack on the Piraeus. Sphodrias underestimated the distance, however, and dawn found his forces only in the vicinity of Eleusis; having lost the advantage of surprise, he turned back, abandoning the attack. Nevertheless, the incident frightened and angered the Athenians, and in 377, exactly a century after the formation of the Delian League, they formalized their relations with their allies in the Second Athenian Sea League.[8] The original members of the League were Thebes, Chios, Mytilene, Methymna, Rhodes, and Byzantium, but eventually it included some 60 to 70 members. In the new league, the Athenians tried to profit by their past experience; they allowed the allies a veto over Athenian actions, promising to establish no new garrisons or cleruchies and to levy no tribute. Within a year, Athens had regained supremacy of the sea.

The Battle of Leuktra and Theban Hegemony

The end of Spartan hegemony—the end, in fact, of Sparta as a major power in Greece—came in 371. Intent on breaking up the Boeotian League, the Spartans marched toward Thebes. They were met at Leuktra by the Theban army under the command of the general Epaminondas. Epaminondas had reorganized the Theban army to enable it to employ new tactics: a concentration of force on the left in depth (50-men deep, in contrast to the usual hoplite formation that was eight-to-twelve men deep); an oblique advance with the right wing holding back; the use of reserve forces, which gave the generals a role throughout the battle, not just at its onset; and the coordination of infantry and cavalry. Well trained in these innovative tactics, the Theban force of 6,000 won an overwhelming victory over a Spartan force of 10,000 hoplites, most of whom must have been *perioikoi*. Suddenly the renowned Spartan army was revealed to be no longer invincible, and Spartan power itself a discounted mirage.

The Athenians were ambivalent at this revelation of Spartan weakness. While they saw prospects of increasing their empire through alliance with Thebes, they also feared an overly powerful Thebes. The smaller Peloponnesian states had no such qualms, however, and they quickly seized the opportunity to escape from Spartan domination. Farther afield the effect of the revelation of Spartan weakness was an almost universal reaction against Spartan-supported oligarchies. The resulting democratic revolutions flooded Greece with exiles willing to sell their services as mercenaries to the highest bidder.

In the next campaigning season (370), Epaminondas followed up his victory at Leuktra by an invasion of the Peloponnesus. The city of Sparta escaped capture only because the river was swollen with winter rains and the bridge was well defended. The Spartans, driven to last resorts, offered freedom to 6,000 helots in return for military service; many of the helots deserted instead, as did many *perioikoi*. Epaminondas, however, did not take advantage of the situation to capture the city of Sparta; instead, he turned his forces toward the real heart of Spartan power, Messenia. He permanently freed the Messenians from Spartan control, recalled the Messenian exiles, and carried out a political unification, or synoikism, of Messenia, uniting the many small communities into the new city of Messene. At this point the Athenians, fearing the rising power of Thebes, switched their alliance to Sparta. They sent a force to assure that the Thebans left the Peloponnesus and did not attack Athens as they went.

Thebes, an oligarchy, controlled its new territories with *harmosts*, as had the Spartans, and as had been the case with the Spartan *harmosts*, the rule of the Theban *harmosts* soon led to discontent.[9] Two more Theban interventions were carried out to put down unrest and fighting in the Peloponnesus. In 362, in the course of one of these invasions, Epaminondas died fighting in a battle at Mantinea that was in all other respects a Theban victory. The general had been the moving spirit behind the Thebans' military and diplomatic achievements, and after his death they were never again to achieve similar successes. Thebes' brief moment as hegemon of Greece was over, but Spartan power was also broken forever. Perhaps Lysander's interpretation of the oracle had not been correct after all.

Athenian Hegemony

After the battle of Mantinea, Athens enjoyed a brief spell as the leading Greek state, once again the leader of a confederacy, the Second Athenian Sea League.[10] As Athenian power grew, however, the expenses of a growing fleet led it to place more and more demands upon its allies. Moreover, the original justification of the League, the threat of Spartan power, no longer existed. Discontent among the members of the League grew, and in 357 the Social War ("War of the Allies") broke out, led by Rhodes, Kos, Chios, and Byzantium, with assistance from the Carian dynast and Persian satrap Mausolos. In Macedonia in the north, Philip took advantage of the situation to capture Amphipolis. Peace came only in 355, when the Persian king, outraged by Athenian actions in Asia Minor, threatened the city with war. By the terms of the new peace, the independence of the rebellious states was recognized. Lesbos and other east Greek cities soon broke away as well, although a truncated Athenian League continued to exist.

THE ECONOMIC SCENE IN FOURTH-CENTURY ATHENS

By the second half of the fifth century, the economy of Athens had been increasingly monetized as state revenues were widely distributed in the form of cash in "democratic" payments (Assembly pay; payments to jurors and officials, payments for theater attendance, and payments to workers in building programs). The increased use of cash is evidenced archaeologically by the finds of coin hoards and inscriptions documenting the issues of coinage. This process accelerated in the fourth century, when it is attested by inscriptional evidence for cash-based economic activities in the recording of public mine and land leases and private loans,[11] and by the speeches in the law courts.

The traditional view of the Greek economy sees it as focused on land ownership, rather than, as in the modern world, successful investment for profit.[12] According to this view, economic decisions were "embedded" in the social and religious context of society. Wealth was transferred by marriage and by "gifts" between friends. In contrast, business and trade for profit were carried on by individuals of relatively low status, most of whom were not citizens but metics and even slaves. Wealth brought by trade did not automatically enhance their status, for status was determined by family connections and possession of land; as a result, traders were more likely to use gains from business to purchase land than to plough them back into the business.[13]

But, in contradiction to this traditional view, there is growing recognition of the fact that cash played an increasing role in the economic activities even of the elite from the late fifth century on, as evidenced by records of public and private land leasing and private loans, and payments made by those holding *liturgies*. Expenditure on equipping triremes and outfitting choruses could be extraordinarily high, depending upon the liturgist's interest in accruing glory for himself. It is significant that, of 15 wealthy estates recorded in the Attic orators, three had no land at all, but did have considerable assets in loans and commercial ventures, such as work gangs of skilled slaves.[14]

The traders who brought grain and other imports to the city were private merchants (*emporoi*); almost all of them were non-Athenians, and most were of metic status, men who derived most of their income from inter-regional trade.[15] A few traders were ship owners (*naukleroi*), but they were not big operators, few owning more than one vessel. Most traders, however, sailed on board the ships of others as *epibatoi* ("those on board," passengers). Most traders had to borrow money to finance their ventures. Maritime loans were usually provided by wealthy citizens or by metic bankers, who did not themselves engage in trade, although some loans are known to have been made by traders. Such maritime loans had the advantage of including an element of insurance: if the ship and its cargo were lost at sea, a not infrequent occurrence, the lender, not the borrower, bore the loss. Not surprisingly considering the risks for the lender, maritime loans carried a high rate of interest; the average interest on a loan for a voyage during the safest sailing season was 20 to 30 percent, but since such a voyage lasted perhaps two to three months, the annual rate amounted to 80 to 180% percent.[16]

Although most traders seem to have been relatively poor, some were able to become quite wealthy, and a few even gained Athenian citizenship through liberal contributions to the city. It is these exceptional men whom we meet in the speeches of the Greek orators, for they were the ones who could afford to purchase the services of an expert speech writer. The speeches are particularly rich sources of information about the daily life and economy of Athens, and especially in the increasingly important world of the metic and the metic/citizen.[17] It is true that in arguing their cases, these men must on occasion have bent the truth, if they did not lie outright; nonetheless, the basic structure, if not the specific details, of the trading activities and the transactions that they described must have been reasonably accurate in order to convince a contemporary jury.

The World of the Characters in *Against Neaira*

Looking at the background of the characters in *Against Neaira* (see Chapter 11), carries us into this marginal and often fractious world of freedmen, metics, and newly minted citizens and the socioeconomic changes it engendered. In this speech ([Dem.] 59, *Against Neaira*), Apollodoros was the instigator of a case nominally brought against the woman Neaira, but it was, in fact, an attack upon the man with whom she was living, Stephanos. This case was actually the culminating act, at least as the preserved speeches are concerned, in the career of Apollodoros, a rather litigious character who was also a speech writer and probably wrote a number of the speeches attributed to Demosthenes.

Apollodoros was the older son of the banker Pasion, a freedman (later a citizen) who had begun his career in banking as a slave working in the bank of two freedmen. Pasion's owners had freed him and given him the bank, which he had managed so successfully that he became quite wealthy and was even able to win Athenian citizenship by very generous contributions to the city. In addition to the bank, Pasion also owned a shield factory.

In ca. 370 Pasion leased the bank to Phormio, a slave (freed at some point) who worked in the bank, just as Pasion had once worked in the bank of his freedman masters. When Pasion died shortly afterwards, he appointed Phormio by will as one of the guardians of his minor son, Pasikles, and gave him his widow, Archippe, in marriage, with a dowry of two talents, an apartment building worth 1 talent, 4,000 drachms, her slave women and jewelry, and all her domestic belongings. Such arrangements by wealthy bankers were common; the arrangement of a marriage for a widow was a means of assuring her future, and was widely done by elite Athenians as well (see Chapter 11).

At the time of Pasion's death, Phormio's older son, Apollodoros, who had been enfranchised along with his father, moved out of the family house in the Piraeus and went to live in the country, where he lived the life of a wealthy Athenian citizen, having inherited more than 43 talents.[18] At this time, he became involved in a number of lawsuits, perhaps for the first time. In one of them (Dem. 52, *Against Callippos*), probably Apollodoros' first speech, he was prosecuted by Callippos, who was attempting to get money that Lukon, a man from Heraklea, had left on deposit at the bank before leaving on a voyage, and which Lukon had specified was to be given to a certain Cephisiades. When Lukon subsequently perished in a pirate attack, Callipos appeared at the bank trying to claim the money on the fallacious grounds that, as *proxenos* (official representative) of Heraklea in Athens, he was charged with taking care of the affairs of all Herakleans in the city. Apollodoros refused to give him the deposit, which he was subsequently able to deliver to its rightful owner, Cephisiades. Several months later, Callippos sued Apollodoros for the money. Another case brought by Apollodoros (Dem. 53, *Against Nikostratos*), developed out of his dispute with a friend and neighbor, Nikostratos, whom he had ransomed from pirates. Nikostratos not only did not repay the ransom, but secured a judgment against Apollodoros as a public debtor; he also arranged to have his brother vandalize Apollodoros' property and to assault and beat him. Apollodoros prosecuted the brother and secured a conviction, but the brother refused to pay the fine, and Apollodoros then launched this suit against him for the possession of two slaves in compensation for the fine.

In 368/367 Apollodoros served as *trierarch*, providing a ship for Athenian service with which he conveyed ambassadors to Sicily, where they were to try to effect an alliance with Dionysius of Syracuse. It was while Apollodoros was absent on this voyage that Phormio married his mother, Archippe, in accordance with her deceased husband's will, a marriage that Apollodoros bitterly resented because of Phormio's freedman status.

Apollodoros served as *trierarch* again in 365 and in 362. After the second of these trierachies, he prosecuted Timotheus, a wealthy Athenian general, for failing to assume his *trierarchy* on time, leaving Apollodoros to spend several extra months and incur additional costs before he was relieved of his command (Dem. 49, *Ag. Timotheus*).

Between 364 and 362 Pasikles came of age and the estate was divided between the two sons, with Apollodoros choosing the shield factory and Pasikles receiving the bank. At this point, Phormio's work as a guardian was finished, and he received a release from any further financial responsibilities for the sons.

In 361/360 Phormio was granted Athenian citizenship. He may still have been involved in banking, although his lease on Pasion's bank had expired; but he was certainly still engaged in sea trade. On the death of his mother, Archippe, in 360, Apollodoros sued Phormio, claiming a share in the estate, despite the release that Phormio had earlier received. Phormio agreed to arbitration and paid a substantial amount to Apollodoros in the settlement, again receiving a release. In 356 Apollodoros served as *trierarch* again, and in 352 as *choregos*.

Sometime in the late 350s, Apollodoros again attacked Phormio in court, seeking a share of the bank. In this case, he claimned that Phormio had embezzled the working capital of the bank while it had been leased to him; the case never came to court because Phormio brought a successful injunction against it (Dem. 36, *For Phormio*). In 342–340, blocked by the injunction against prosecuting Phormio again on the charge of embezzlement, Apollodoros instead attacked Stephanos, who had been one of the men who had testified for Phormio ([Dem.] 59, *Against Neaira*), accusing him of having given false evidence.

Stephanos had previously crossed Apollodoros in court. In 348 he attacked Apollodoros for proposing an illegal decree, and in 346 he charged Apollodoros with murder (both of these are attested only in *Against Neaira* and may not have been as they are presented there). In 343 to340 this feud between Apollodoros and Stephanos formed the context for *Against Neaira* (see Chapter 11). The real target in the prosecution of Neaira was, of course, not this woman, but Phormio. The case was further diverted from the actual combatants by being ostensibly brought by a kinsman of Apollodoros, Theomnestos; however, he very shortly handed it over to Apollodoros, who acted as a *synegoros* (unpaid fellow speaker). In his speeches in the case, Apollodoros was especially disrespectful to Phormio (his stepfather), accusing him of greed and ingratitude, taunting him for his "barbarian" origins, even suggesting that he was the real father of Pasikles (Dem. 35; 45 and 46, *Against Stephanos* I and II). We do not know the outcome of this case, but it is the last appearance of Apollodoros in the preserved speeches.

This tangled network of legal attacks and counterattacks demonstrates that a hard-working and talented slave could gain his freedom, and even become wealthy enough to buy his way into the citizen body, but that this still did not wipe out the taint of his slave origins. Ironically, Apollodoros was only one step farther up on the social ladder than his stepfather Phormio, yet he continually berated Phormio for his slave origins.

In addition to the picture this case presents of life in the shadowy world of metics and freedmen, it also provides insight into the role that rhetoric and the oratory of the courts played as sources of entertainment for the Athenian people, in addition to their more usually celebrated function as expressions of democracy. In the words of a modern Greek scholar:[19]

> ...those who aspired to political leadership and the honor and status that accompanied it repeatedly entered the legal arena, bringing suit against their political enemies whenever possible and defending themselves against suits brought by others whenever necessary. The ultimate judges of these public competitions were the common people, who seem to have relished the dramatic clash of individuals and ideologies. In this respect fourth-century oratory was the cultural heir of fifth-century drama and similarly appreciated by the citizens. Despite the disapproval of intellectuals like Plato, most Athenians legitimately considered their legal system a hallmark of their democracy and a vital presence in their culture.

The Increasing Use of Mercenaries[20]

While metics and newly minted citizens speculated and profited and attacked each other in the battleground of the courts, the small farmers who made up the majority of Athenian citizens suffered increasingly from the warfare that by the fourth century had become a year-round activity. The continuous threat of attack often kept them from carrying out the necessary tasks of the agricultural year, and when fighting did occur, olive trees and vines that took years to establish were often cut down and buildings were wrecked. Even when the fighting ceased, many small farmers lacked the capital necessary to bring their neglected or devastated land back into productivity. Selling out to wealthier men who could afford the costs of restoring the land, many small holders drifted into the cities, but there too there were few opportunities for making a living. Thus the poor filled the cities, the wealthy accumulated larger and larger estates, and the gulf between the rich and the poor grew. Constant civil strife brought exile and loss of property to large numbers of even the wealthiest, transforming men overnight from respectable landowners into wandering, homeless exiles. Tens of thousands of such homeless and destitute men roamed about Greece, often endangering the settled population. Their only hope of employment was to sell their services as mercenaries, a burgeoning job market since the ready supply of mercenaries in itself contributed to the discovery of new uses for their services.

Changes in the methods of warfare in the fourth century fostered the increased use of mercenaries who had the shrewdness to develop new fighting skills. Light-armed tactics became increasingly important, and these called for specialized skills in handling weapons that were traditionally associated with foreigners and looked down upon by the Greek hoplite. The non-professional farmer-citizen-hoplite lacked the time and opportunity, or the incentive, to develop these new skills, and as a result he became less important to the conduct of war, while mercenaries who had these skills became more desirable. The reforms of Epaminondas in Thebes extended this trend toward specialization to the higher ranks, for the greater role given to the general throughout the battle increased the need for specialized skills in commanders. While military and political power had previously been inseparable, with election to generalship being an intrinsic part of a political career (Pericles' political leadership was based upon his repeated election as general), maintaining the allegiance of a mercenary force called for a full-time commitment that was incompatible with traditional Greek political ambitions. As a result we see a growing split between the military and the political, with professional generals leading mercenary armies loyal primarily to their commanders, while civilian politicians exercised political power without military experience.

The politics of inter-*polis* warfare also contributed to the growth of mercenary service. In the struggle for a balance of power among the cities, allegiances became unclear as yesterday's enemy became today's ally. Goals were less evident. While the Persian Wars had clearly been a struggle for the survival of Greece in the face of the invasion of the Barbarians, the frequent wars of the fourth century often had little justification other than advancing the interests of prominent politicians or the profit of a few wealthy men. It is not surprising that ordinary citizens became increasingly reluctant to serve and preferred to provide wages to mercenary replacements.

The increased employment of mercenaries fed their use in a vicious circle. The expenses of mercenary pay became a real burden on economies already in crisis because of the effects of constant warfare. Unable to pay high enough wages, the cities attracted mercenaries by offering them the opportunity for loot and plunder, thus adding to the swelling supply of potential mercenaries.

PHILOSOPHY IN THE FOURTH CENTURY

After the death of Socrates, his pupil Plato memorialized his teacher in a group of works in which he portrayed the activities and ideas of his teacher. These works are in dialogue form, which we have seen used by the historian Thucydides in the Melian Dialogue. Among these dialogues is, of course, the *Apology*, which recounts the trial of Socrates. But they also include many lively scenes of Socrates at work as a gadfly, as well as portraits of the Sophists and philosophers who visited Athens in the late fifth century. The Sophists Protagoras and Gorgias are each accorded a dialogue, and the Presocratic Parmenides also has his dialogue. In these we can trace the development of cosmological questions introduced by the Presocratics. Did everything that exists (Being) rise from one primary substance, as Parmenides taught? If Being were only One, how would it change (what would it change into?); unlimited (what would limit it?); unmovable (to what "other" place would it move?). In sum, if Being were One, how did it then become many different things that we experience in the world? The pluralists gave an answer: Being was not one but four—fire, air, earth, water—or a multiplicity—seeds, atoms.

In his later dialogue, the *Timaeus*, Plato constructed a cosmogony of his own; however, his main interest lay in the organization of human affairs (politics). He devoted the *Republic* to the very Socratic question, What is justice? In it he presented the ideal life as one ordered by the overarching power of the state, and sought to construct an ideal state. It was ruled by Philosopher Kings, who had seen the absolute basis of all human values in the Ideas, a concept that is expressed in the allegory of the Cave:[21] those of us who are captive in the cave see only the shadow of reality, but those who have ascended to the outer world by a gradual process of education are at last able to see the true nature of reality: the Good Itself. Such men are truly Philosopher Kings, and by virtue of their knowledge of the Good Itself, are empowered to rule as absolute rulers. They are even allowed to practice deception for the good of their subjects. An important aspect of this is their creation of a social order based not on individual marriage, but on a community of women in which matings are secretly managed by the authorities for eugenic purposes. However, in his last work, the *Laws*, perhaps as a result of the near-disastrous failure of his attempt to turn the heir to the tyranny of Syracuse into a Philosopher King, Plato constructed a "real" Cretan city. He describes its institutions and legislation, which are based on those of Dorian states Sparta and Crete, as second-best, but the best possible in the situation in which men find themselves.

Plato's greatest pupil, Aristotle, was born in 384, the son of a doctor at the court of Amyntas II, king of Macedonia. He left Macedonia at the age of 17 to enter the Academy of Plato, where he remained until Plato's death, first as a student, later as a researcher. He then left Athens, spending three years in Assos, near Troy, at the court of the tyrant Hermias, where he conducted biological investigations into the marine life of the area, studies that formed the basis for later descriptions in his *History of Animals*. He then moved to Mitylene, where he spent five years and gained a reputation as an advocate of a united Greece against the power of Persia. The Macedonian king, Philip II, then invited him back to the Macedonian court to act as tutor to his son, Alexander, where he remained until Philip was assassinated and Alexander succeeded him as king.

Upon the death of Philip, Aristotle returned to Athens and set up his own school, the Lyceum. He did not follow Plato's metaphysical bent, but was more interested in scientific studies and in the organization of knowledge. He started a library, and students working under his direction produced works of research on botany, music, a history of philosophy, and a collection of the constitutions of 158 Greek states. Most of these works have not survived, but Aristotle's own work, which embraced works on logic, metaphysics, physics, biology, and ethics, proved to be enormously influential on the course of later Western thought.

PHILIP OF MACEDON

In 355, the same year in which Athens' second attempt at empire was cut back, Philip II of Macedon advanced south invited by Thebes and by the Delphic *Amphictiony*, (a coalition of states that controlled the shrine) to defend the shrine in a war provoked by the Phokian seizure of Apollo's treasury. Philip used the opportunity to take control of Thessaly and the gulf of Pagasai. At this point, the Athenians, temporarily aroused to concern by the growing threat from Macedonia,[22] blocked his advance further south at Thermopylae. Philip returned north, but as he went he attacked and besieged the city of Olynthus, on the

Map 13B   The rise of Macedonia under Philip

grounds that it had given refuge to two of his half-brothers, pretenders to the throne. In Athens, the orator Demosthenes tried to persuade the citizens to save Olynthus, but they sent only a small and inadequate force. When Olynthus fell Philip destroyed it, selling its citizens into slavery.

Macedonia Before Philip

Who was this intruder from the north? The Macedonian royal house laid claim to Greek heritage through mythological ancestors, professing to be the descendants of Temenos of Argos, one of the Dorian Heraklids, but whether the Macedonians were Greeks was a disputed question even in antiquity.[23] It is indisputable that the Macedonian government and way of life differed markedly from that of the *poleis* of central Greece and the Peloponnesus. In fact, in many ways the Macedonians resembled the Greeks of Homer's epics more than their Greek contemporaries. Many were pastoralists, their upper classes were chiefly occupied with hunting and fighting, and their kings were similar in many respects to Homeric kings.

The Macedonian kingship was not a constitutional office like the Spartan kingship, with well-defined powers and limitations. A Macedonian king's powers depended a great deal upon his personal strength—in effect, what he could get away with—yet it was in no way absolute.[24] Power was clan-based; thus from ca. 650 to ca. 310 the kingship was hereditary in the line of the Argeadae, but the principle of primogenture did not hold. A new king was expected to be an Argead, but beyond that there is too little evidence and too great a variety of situations for us to be able identify "normal" lines of succession. Often the succession was contested among a number of Argead candidates, resulting in a bloodbath, with the succession going to the survivor.

Although the Macedonian king had no formal council, he lived in the midst of a retinue of upper-class men—the Companions—from whom he variously chose his drinking companions in the symposium. Here he received advice and tested out his ideas, for Macedonian custom allowed men to speak freely to the king, and Macedonian drinking customs fostered this freedom, sometimes to disastrous ends. Nevertheless, he was under no obligation to follow the advice offered by the Companions.

Although Macedonia did not play a major role in Greek affairs before the reign of Philip II, some of its earlier kings were noteworthy. Alexander I (495–450) fought with the Persians *against* the Greeks in the Persian Wars; however, since he had also helped the Greeks with advice and the Athenians needed his timber for ships, he was rewarded by admission as a Hellene to the Olympic games with the honor of *proxenia* (official friendship) in Athens. He sought to emphasize his Greek status by Hellenizing the Macedonian court, to which he invited the poet Pindar. His successor, Perdikkas II (450–413), took part in the Peloponnesian War, now on one side, now on the other. Perdikkas' son Archelaus (413–399), who obtained the throne by the murder of his half-brother, continued the work of Hellenization, inviting noted Greek poets and artists to his court. Among these was Agathon, the tragic poet whose victory in a contest of poetry was honored in Plato's *Symposium*; the painter Zeuxis, whose skills were such that his grapes were said to deceive the birds; and Euripides, whose extant play the *Bacchae* was first performed at Archelaus' court and perhaps written there as well. After Archelaus was killed in a hunting accident (or was murdered), he was succeeded by Amyntas II.

Amyntas II had three sons. The youngest, Philip, spent three years in Thebes during his boyhood as a political hostage when his brother, Alexander II, was forced into an alliance with that city. Philip was in Thebes during the time when Epaminondas was reorganizing the Theban army, and he later used Epaminondas' tactics of the deep line and oblique advance.[25] Alexander II was succeeded by Amyntas' second son, Perdikkas III, who was killed in a humiliating defeat by an invading Illyrian force that cost the Macedonians not only their king but also 4,000 men.[26] The army was demoralized, and Perdikkas' son and presumed successor, Amyntas, was only a child. In the face of the crisis, the third son of Amyntas II, Philip, aged 23, stepped in as king.

Philip as King[27]

On his accession, Philip was faced with several immediate crises. The first and most pressing was the devastating defeat and demoralization of the army. A number of other claimants to the throne were at hand to advance their own causes by military force, one with the help of Thrace, another assisted by Athens. Meanwhile, neighboring tribes to the north took advantage of the situation to cross over the borders and plunder Macedonian territory.

Philip addressed himself first to the problems of the army. He instituted a regimen of intensive training, maneuvers, and reviews, and began a reorganization of his forces.[28]

Source Analysis

A rrian, *Anabasis* 7.9.2–4   In this later speech, in which Arrian portrays Alexander addressing the Macedonian troops, what benefits does he claim that they had received from Philip? While the context of this passage, a speech to the troops, suggests rhetorical exaggeration, the discipline that Philip imposed was also evident in his military successes.

Philip's most important military innovation was in the equipment and fighting style of the infantry phalanx. He adopted a line in depth of 16 men, whose main weapon was the *sarissa*, a longer than normal pike, up to 18 feet long, which gave his fighters the advantage of a longer reach.[29] He also increased the Macedonian cavalry, the army's strong suit.[30] Finally, he introduced the catapult into siege tactics, adding torsion to the simple catapult that had been used by Dionysius I of Syracuse in the battle of Motya in 397.[31] Another area in which money could buy power was the employment of mercenaries, which were available in plentiful supply, especially in the Greek states.

The money and resources that Philip was able to expend upon his newly reorganized and revived army was on a scale surpassed only by the Great King of Persia, and far more than that available to any of the Greek states, except the Phokians, who had seized and were spending the treasury at Delphi. Macedonia was rich in timber, and the silver and gold in the mines around Mt. Pangaeum became available when Philip took over the Krenides in 356. Moreover, as he expanded his territories, the dues upon landed property also grew, as did his resources of manpower. But he also spent lavishly. He invited the most prominent figures in the Greek world and high-ranking Persian refugees as well, to the court at Pella, where he entertained them in splendid Homeric fashion and showered them with guest-gifts. He also freely expended largess to secure allies, extending his kingdom by gifts as well as by conquest.

In the Macedonian kingship, royal marriages played a significant role. The royal house had long practiced polygamy for political purposes, and Philip continued the practice. Thus he married Audata the Illyrian,[32] who died after bearing him a daughter; Phila, of the Upper Macedonian royal house of Elimea; and two Thessalians, Nikesipolis of Pherae, who bore him another daughter; and Philinna of Larisa, who bore a son, Arrhidaios. Arrhidaios was probably Philip's first son, but he was disabled in some way, possibly mentally defective.[33] Philip's marriage in 357 to Olympias, niece of the king of Epirus, produced the first viable heir, Alexander. Subsequently Philip married the Thracian Medea, and finally, a Macedonian, Cleopatra, niece of his general Attalus, a marriage that proved problematic.

Despite his lavish expenditures, Philip did not ignore essential economic concerns. Seizing a much-needed opportunity to bolster Macedonian finances, he undertook to defend the Krenides, a group of Greek gold and silver mining settlements, when they appealed to him for assistance against the Thracians. Defeating the Thracians, Philip drew the mining communities together into one city (synoikism), and renamed it Philippoi. By introducing improved mining techniques, Philip was able to draw an annual revenue of more than 1,000 talents from the mines;[34] nonetheless, he spent so prodigiously that the treasury never ran an excess. Philippoi was the first eponymous Macedonian settlement to be established, and it set a precedent for future city foundations by Philip in Thessaly and Thrace, and by Alexander throughout the area of his conquests. At a time when the independent city-state was fast becoming obsolete, the Macedonian rulers turned the city into an instrument of the territorial state.

Philip and Athens

In 347 the Greeks invited Philip south to assist in the protracted Sacred War. The war was concluded in 346 with a formal peace agreement, the Peace of Philokrates, which gave Philip Phokis' seat in the Amphictyonic Council, in effect granting him Hellenic status. In fact, he was widely regarded as the Savior of Delphi and was accordingly allowed to join in celebrating Delphi's Pythian Games.

In the years following the Peace of Philokrates, in Athens the orator Demosthenes condemned Philip repeatedly. In 344 he persuaded the Assembly to rebuff an offer by Philip to renew the peace,[35] and after that he repeatedly castigated the Athenians for their laxity and pressed for a "military solution."

In 342 Philip set out on yet another campaign, moving against Thrace with the aim of subjecting it completely. This threatened the Greek cities in the Hellespont, and in Athens the orator Demosthenes once again harangued the Athenians on the dangers that Philip posed to their interests. Philip first besieged Perinthus, perhaps using the torsion catapult for the first time, but he met stubborn resistance and finally withdrew to besiege Byzantium. While he also failed to take that city, he did capture a grain fleet of 230 vessels, including 180 Athenian ships. This was a great blow to the Athenian economy and morale, and Demosthenes was finally able to rouse the Athenian *demos* to declare war. The Persians also joined in opposing the Macedonian king.

Before he marched south to meet the Athenian challenge, Philip moved against the Scythians in order to secure the northern frontier. In the Scythian campaign he suffered a serious injury, surviving an attack in which a spear passed through his thigh, killing his horse. As he recovered, plans went forward for the march into Greece, while in Athens, rumors of his demise circulated wildly. The way into Greece was opened when, in 338, the Amphictyonic Council invited him to take command of yet another Sacred War in defense of the Delphic shrine.[36] The Thebans abandoned their alliance with Philip to join Athens in opposing him. The two sides met at the battle of Chaeronea in Boeotia, in which Philip, with his young son Alexander at the head of the Macedonian cavalry on the left, won a crushing victory over the combined Greek forces led by Athens and Thebes. One thousand of the Greeks were killed, two thousand captured, and the rest fled, including Demosthenes, who had been serving as a hoplite.

With his decisive victory at Chaeronea, Philip effectively became master of Greece and ended the era of the independent *polis* in Greece. In Athens everyone expected to suffer the worst. Philip indeed punished Thebes severely for abandoning its Macedonian alliance, executing or confiscating the property of his leading opponents, establishing a garrison on the Kadmeia, and breaking up the Boeotian League, giving its cities their independence. But he showed surprising leniency toward Athens, in part out of reverence for Athenian culture, in part out of concern for the strength of the Athenian fleet and the possibility of a failed siege like those of Byzantium and Perinthus. He sent Alexander at the head of a procession to return the ashes of the Athenian dead, freed the Athenian prisoners, and left Athens in control of several of its island possessions. He established a new League, the League of Corinth, made up of all the Greek states, with himself as hegemon. The Greek cities were guaranteed freedom from outside attack, freedom in the conduct of their internal affairs, freedom of navigation, and freedom from tribute or garrisons (with the exception of Thebes). The affairs of the League were to be administered by a confederate council, or Synhedrion, in which all the Greek members were represented; it could enact decrees binding on the members, as well as pass judgment over them as a court.

These admirable concessions never got proper exercise, however, for Philip was now in an excellent position to carry out his plans for a panhellenic expedition against the Persians. The time was opportune. Since the beginning of the fourth century, Persia had suffered from problems in the succession and widespread revolts in the satrapies, and the Persian Empire and Persian military power may perhaps have reached their lowest point. The Athenian Isocrates had been advocating a common Greek war against Persia since the 380s, and in 346 had written an open letter to Philip suggesting that he lead such a crusade.[37] The projected expedition, by uniting the Greek cities in a common cause, would resolve the problem of constant warfare among the Greeks themselves.

In 337 the common council that established the League of Corinth declared war on Persia, and in the spring of 336 Philip sent an advance force to Asia Minor under the general Parmenio to lay the groundwork for the invasion. He also entered into his seventh marriage—to Cleopatra, the niece and ward of his general Attalus. Because Cleopatra, unlike his other wives, was a Macedonian, a son of this marriage could have especially threatened Alexander's claim to the throne. There were also other problems between father and son.[38] Thus there was much speculation when, on the eve of the expedition, Philip fell victim to an assassin's blow at the age of 46, during lavish ceremonies to celebrate both the marriage of Alexander's sister to the king of Epirus and the opening of the campaign against Persia. The new Trojan War was left to Philip's successor, Alexander.

SUGGESTIONS FOR FURTHER READING

On the period in general, see S. Hornblower (1983), *The Greek World 479–232*, chap. 13–16; or the fundamental work on this period in Macedonia, N. G. L. Hammond, G. T. Griffith, and F. W. Walbank (1972–1988), *A History of Macedonia* I–III. Useful works focusing on Philip include E. Borza (1990), *In the Shadow of Olympus: The Emergence of Macedon*, which provides the historical context for his reign. G. L. Cawkwell (1978), *Philip of Macedon*; and J. R. Ellis (1986), *Philip II and Macedonian Imperialism*. On the role of women in Macedonia, see Elisabeth Carney (2000), *Women and Monarchy in Macedonia*, and her many articles cited in the notes. On trials in Athens, a good brief introduction is Mabel Lang (1984), *Life, Death and Litigation in the Athenian Agora*, one of the Picture Book Series of the American School of Classical Studies in Athens. Also interesting is a longer work by Virginia Hunter (1994), *Policing Athens*. On mercenaries: Matthew Trundle (2004), *Greek Mercenaries: From the Late Archaic Period to Alexander*; G. T. Griffith (1935), *The Mercenaries of the Hellenistic World*.

MAP STUDY

Olynthus, Thebes, Aulis, Knidos, Scyrus, Imbros, Lemnos, Eleusis, Delphi, Messenia, Messene, Leuktra, Abydus, Mantinea, Thrace, Scythia, Chaeronea, Illyria, the Paionians, Epirus, the Krenides, Thasos, Philippoi, Perinthus

ENDNOTES

[1]This statement illustrates many of the problems inherent in population estimates. Reports of the war by Thucydides and Xenophon make it clear that casualties were sometimes severe (as in the plague, and the prolonged siege at the end of the war), but estimating the overall effect over the 30 years of the war is made impossible both by the paucity of the available numbers and by their frequent incommensurability. For ex-

ample, Thucydides 2.13 reports a speech by Pericles in which the Athenians are said to have had 13,000 hoplites in regular service in 431, plus 16,000 on the walls and garrisons, which included those above and below the age for regular service as well as metics. In apparent contrast, Xenophon (*Hell*. 4.2.17) reports that the city was able to put 6,000 hoplites in the field in 394. But it is not clear that these numbers are comparable. Those reported by Thucydides are given as total forces, while that given by Xenophon is of hoplites mustered for a particular battle, not necessarily the total hoplite force then available to the city.

[2] On the Spartan empire, see Paul Cartledge (1987), *Agesilaos and the Crisis of Sparta*, 86–87.

[3] Thucydides. 1.77.6, tr. N. Demand.

[4] Diod. 3.106.

[5] See Cartledge (above, n. 2), 82–84.

[6] On Lysander and Agesilaos, see Cartledge (above, n. 2).

[7] Pausanias 3.8.9, tr. N. Demand.

[8] On the Second Athenian Sea League, see J. Cargill (1981), *The Second Athenian League*.

[9] See above, n. 4.

[10] See Cargill (above, n. 8).

[11] Kirsty Shipton (2000), *Leasing and Lending: The Cash Economy in Fourth-century BC Athens*.

[12] As held by Moses Finley (1973), *The Ancient Economy*.

[13] See Finley (above, n. 12), and M. M. Austin and P. Vidal-Naquet (1977), *Economic and Social History of Ancient Greece*.

[14] Shipton (above, n. 11), 13.

[15] See C. M. Reed (2003), *Maritime Traders in the Ancient Greek World*.

[16] See Signe Isager and Mogens Herman Hansen (1975), *Aspects of Athenian Society in the Fourth Century B.C.*; Edward Cohen (1992), *Athenian Economy and Society: A Banking Perspective*; Reed (above n. 15).

[17] Speeches from private cases can be found in the Loeb editions of Lysias, Isaeus (who specialized in inheritance cases), and Demosthenes IV–VI, Private Orations. On the maritime cases in particular, see Isager and Hansen (above, n. 16). On loans and banking, see Cohen (above, n. 16).

[18] Debra Hamel (2003), *Trying Neaira: The True Story of a Courtesan's Scandalous Life in Ancient Greece*, 130.

[19] Victor Bers (2003), *Demosthenes, Speeches 50–59*, xxviii.

[20] Matthew Trundle (2004), *Greek Mercenaries*.

[21] Plato, *Republic*, Book VII 514–521.

[22] The main sources for Macedonian history as it affected the Greeks in the south are Athenian political pamphlets in the form of orations by Demosthenes, Aeschines, and Isocrates; the work of Diodorus Siculus (see chap. 13); and the *Parallel Lives* of Plutarch, a Greek author of the first/second century CE who wrote biographies for the moral edification of a Roman audience.

[23] See Ernst Badian (1982), "Greeks and Macedonians," pp. 33–51 in Beryl Barr-Sharar and E. N. Borza (1982), *Macedonia and Greece in Late Classical and Early Hellenistic Times*.

[24] On the constitutional and anti-constitutional positions taken by various historians, see Eugene Borza (1992), *In the Shadow of Olympus: The Emergence of Macedon*, 231–248; Elizabeth Carney (1995), "Women and *Basileia*: Legitimacy and Female Political Action in Macedonia," *The Classical Journal* 90:367–391. An anti-constitutional position seems the most persuasive and is the position adopted here.

[25] Ellis denies this because of Philip's youth; he was between 13 and 16 at the time; however, Philip was only 23 at his accession, and Alexander the Great was only 18 when he led the *hetairoi* cavalry to victory over the elite Theban Sacred Band at the battle of Chaeronea in 338. Even though the adolescent Philip had no assurance of ever becoming king when he was a hostage in Thebes, military matters could not have been far from the mind of a young male member of the Macedonian Argead clan.

[26]Diod. Sic. xvi.2

[27]See the collection of Eugene Borza's articles edited by Carol Thomas (1995), *Makedonika: Essays by Eugene N. Borza.*

[28]On the reorganization of the army, see N. G. L. Hammond and G. T. Griffith (1979), *A History of Macedonia* II, 405–449.

[29]Griffith, in Hammond and Griffith (above n. 28), 431.

[30]On the effectiveness of ancient cavalry, see I. G. Spence (1993), *The Cavalry of Classical Greece.*

[31]Griffith, in Hammond and Griffith (above, n. 28), 444–449; E. W. Marsden (1969), *Greek and Roman Artillery: Historical Development,* 5–17, 48–56.

[32]The order of some of these early marriages is uncertain; see Borza (above, n. 24) 206–208.

[33]See W. S. Greenwalt (1984), "The Search for Arrhideus," *Ancient World* 10: 69–77.

[34]In comparison, on their entrance into the Peloponnesian War the Athenians were collecting an annual tribute of 600 talents and had a reserve on the Acropolis of 6,000 talents laid aside for critical emergencies. They had spent 3,700 talents on the building program and the siege of Potidaea. In addition, Thucydides 2.13 notes that they had about 500 talents in the form of dedications in other shrines, and that the gold on the cult statue of Athena weighed 40 talents.

[35] Dem. vii.21, xviii.136.

[36]Philip had played a central role in the Sacred Wars of 355 and 347.

[37]Isoc. *Philippus.*

[38]The "Pixodaros affair," in which Alexander, feeling slighted when he learned of Philip's negotiations for a marriage alliance between his half-brother, Philip Arrhidaios, and the daughter of Pixodaros of Caria, a Persian vassal, had offered himself to Pixodaros as the bridegroom instead, angering Philip and bringing the wedding plans to an end. Plutarch, *Alex.* 9.3–12; Moralia 327c; Diod.Sic. 16.91–95. "Tragic-history" according to Griffith in Hammond and Griffith (above, n. 28), vol. II, 675.

14

ALEXANDER THE GREAT

After Philip's assassination in 336, members of the nobility in the palace at once proclaimed Alexander the successor, and within days he addressed a formal assembly of the people as king, promising to continue his father's policies. Nevertheless, the succession was problematic for a number of reasons. Rumors of the involvement of Alexander or his mother, Olympias, in the assassination were rampant, and other candidates stood in the wings, most notably, Amyntas, the son of Perdikkas, whom Philip had displaced as king when he was an infant, and who was now grown and a viable Argead candidate.

The actual assassin was killed immediately after the murder, and two of his alleged accomplices were ritually executed at Philip's funeral. Other potential rivals and foes were also quickly eliminated, as was common practice in Macedonian successions, given their frequent ambiguity. Philip's new father-in-law, Attalus, who had already alienated Alexander, could not be allowed to continue as a leader in the Asian campaign, and Alexander sent a friend to arrest or assassinate him. Attalus' senior general, Parmenio, demonstrated his loyalty to the new king by refusing to intervene, and although Attalus tried to bargain with Alexander for his life, the assassination was carried out before Alexander replied. Amyntas, who certainly posed a continuing risk, was also eliminated. Finally, it seems to have been Olympias who took on the task of eliminating Cleopatra, Philip's young widow, and her infant child. The child seems to have been a girl, but even a girl as an offspring of Philip could have served as a focus of dynastic manipulations through marriage. The sources—which are all Greek—condemn Olympias for her cruelty in this; however, if she was indeed responsible, she was acting in the traditional Macedonian pattern of eliminating possible risks to the throne. The only difference was her sex. Women, even royal Macedonian women, were not expected to indulge in bloody acts.[1] Alexander is reported to have been angry, but he had made no moves to protect the victims, nor did he punish the perpetrator.

As he struggled to consolidate his hold on the throne in Macedonia, Alexander faced external challenges from both the north and the south. The tribal peoples to the north, who sensed the prospect of freedom in the weakness of a successor, seized the opportunity to revolt, as did a number of Greek cities. Late in 336 Alexander made a quick march south into Greece to assert his right as hegemon of the Corinthian League and as leader of the panhellenic expedition. He then returned to Macedonia to deal with the northern tribes, for he could not afford to leave Macedonia insecure and vulnerable to attack as he marched into Asia. But while he was fighting in the north, rumors of his death began to circulate in Thebes, and the Thebans rose in revolt. Alexander responded with a lightning march south to deliver a lesson in terror to the Greeks by the destruction of the city. He spared only the house of Pindar (335 BCE)

THE SOURCES ON ALEXANDER

The sources on Alexander's life and campaigns are difficult at best; all our extant reports are late and second-hand, even though these are sometimes based on contemporary accounts that have been lost. All reports of the actual participants are now lost, except for those fragments that were quoted by, or incorporated into, the works of later writers. These eyewitness accounts included the work of Ptolemy, one of Alexander's generals and later founder of the Ptolemaic dynasty in Egypt; Aristobulus, one of the Greek philosophers, scientists, and technicians who accompanied the Asian expedition; Callisthenes, a relative of Aristotle by marriage, who wrote much of the official history of the campaign; Onesicritus, Alexander's helmsmen, a source mostly for descriptions of the natural curiosities of India; and Nearchus of Crete, who interlaced fact and romance in an account that disparaged Onesicritus. Another early source, although not a participant in the campaign, was Cleitarchus of Alexandria, who often preferred sensation and drama to the truth. The accounts of all these authors were colored and shaped by the purposes for which they were composed; one can hardly expect an official history of the campaign to be completely impartial, nor was impartiality and the recitation of unvarnished facts recognized as a particular virtue by ancient writers. There were morals to be pointed out, rhetorical flourishes to be displayed, personal grudges to be pursued, and a reading audience to be entertained. Our sources do all of these, often with abandon. Moreover, later writers who used this material often added their own rhetorical and even fantastic embellishments.

Of the extant, well-preserved sources, two stand out for their readability. The first is the account of Alexander's campaigns by Arrian, the *Anabasis*. Arrian was a native of Bithynia in Asia Minor who lived during the first two centuries of the Common Era. After a traditional Roman political career, culminating in the consulship and service as governor of Cappadocia, he retired to Athens, where he devoted himself to writing. His narrative gives the impression of being a sober evaluation, and he was long considered to be the most dependable and responsible source. In fact, N. G. L. Hammond has suggested that Arrian used direct discourse or attribution by name to present material from what he considered his most reliable sources, Ptolemy and Aristobolus, and indirect means, such as "the story goes," or "it is said," to indicate those that he considered less reliable.[2] But it seems that Arrian was sometimes taken in by the subtle bias of one of his major sources, Ptolemy. Ptolemy, one of Alexander's generals, moved quickly at the king's death to take over the satrapy of Egypt, going so far as to kidnap the body of Alexander and take it to Alexandria, where he eventually entombed it in great splendor. Traditionally, the task of burial was assigned to the heir and was an important element in securing his legitimacy as heir. Thus the burial was part of Ptolemy's propaganda program, aimed at impressing the common people. Similarly, the book that he wrote about the campaigns (and which Arrian used as a source) functioned as a part of this program, but aimed at an educated audience. It often magnified the general's own role in Alexander's campaign, most frequently by omitting the acts of others. Unlike many of the other sources, its bias was subtle and sophisticated; it apparently escaped the notice of Arrian and only recently has been recognized by modern scholars.[3]

Plutarch, the author of a brief biographical work, the *Life of Alexander*, was a Greek, a native of Chaeronea in Boeotia (46 to ca.120 C.E.) who spent his life mostly in service to his hometown and in scholarly writing. His work on Alexander formed part of a larger work, the *Parallel Lives*, in which he juxtaposed biographies of Greek and Roman personages to provide moral edification for his readers. His aim, to provide his readers with salutary role models while entertaining them, can, unlike Ptolemy's subtle bias, often be fairly easily detected.

Other important ancient sources for Alexander are the seventeenth book of the *Universal History* of Diodorus Siculus, a writer of the first century B.C.E., and the works of Strabo and Curtius, from the first century C.E. In each case, the particular information must be assessed for its reliability. This is often a job for the expert scholar, but other readers can be on the lookout for anecdotal material and for the clearly fabulous, and consider the possible motivations lying behind variant versions of a given incident.

THE EXPEDITION: ASIA MINOR AND THE SEA COAST

While Alexander settled affairs in Macedonia and Greece, Parmenio was in Asia Minor establishing a base for the invasion, having proven his loyalty by his acquiescence to the killing of Attalus. There were good reasons for continuing with the plans for an Asian expedition. Alexander had the momentum of Philip's expansion and an army primed to carry it on. The unstable situation in Greece still called out for a unifying cause. Finally, financial problems were also pressing Alexander toward action; Philip had left debts, and Alexander had added to them by the expenses of his own military campaigns. Appropriating the riches of the Persian Empire was a tempting solution, especially since this might be the last opportunity to take advantage of the weakness of Persian central authority, for the new Persian king, Darius III, was proving to be a competent ruler who might well revive the unity and strength of the Persian empire.

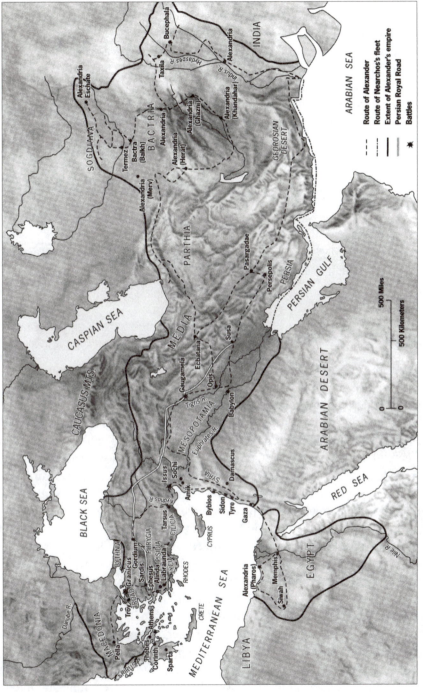

Map 14   The Route of Alexander

311

Leaving Antipater behind as regent in Macedonia and Greece, Alexander set out for the Hellespont in the early spring of 334, with an estimated 43,000 infantry, 6,100 cavalry,[4] and a 30-day supply of grain carried by the fleet.[5] This supply was sufficient to last until the harvest in May, when he would have reached Anatolia, where he could requisition food for his troops from the conquered.

Alexander's arrival on the continent of Asia was carried out with many symbolic acts that called attention to his heroic heritage.

Source Analysis

A rrian, *Anabasis* 1.11.3–12.1   That ceremonies did Alexander carry out? What do you think the significance of these ceremonies was to Alexander? To his army? Evaluating the source, can you identify the significance of Arrian's use of direct and indirect discourse?

The Persians chose to make their stand at the Granicus River,[6] forcing the Macedonians to cross the river to engage them. Although the water was probably no deeper than a meter in early spring, the riverbanks were very steep, in some places rising sharply three or four meters. This precluded a direct frontal assault in an extended line, for the phalanx would have been easy targets for slaughter in the river as they struggled up the banks. There were, however, places along the bank where gravel had accumulated so that access would be relatively easy, and Alexander sent some of his force ahead to utilize these spots, directing them to ride up in waves in a diagonal line rather than attempt a direct frontal assault on the banks. The vanguard met the enemy cavalry and suffered badly, but by absorbing the momentum of the Persian charge, they made room for Alexander to lead a counter charge. He plunged into the hand-to-hand fighting and, once recognized, became the focus of an attack led by the son-in-law of the Persian king (the king himself was not present). Alexander's helmet was shattered, and it was only the intervention of one of his Companions, Cleitus, that saved him from death. As a result, Alexander escaped without serious injury, and the Macedonian cavalry soon pushed the Persians back so that the remainder of the army was able to cross the river. They then advanced against the Persian mercenary infantry, which had been stationed far back in the foothills and had not yet taken part in the battle. The Persian infantry faced both the Macedonian phalanx and the cavalry, and although they inflicted heavy casualties on the Macedonians, they themselves were literally decimated, nine out of ten Persians falling in the fighting. The survivors, about two thousand, were taken prisoner. The Persian defeat was overwhelming, and the surviving Persian senior commander committed suicide. From this point on, the Persians recognized that they could not contest the Macedonian occupation of Asia Minor by land.

Alexander now established himself at Ephesus, a major port on the coast, in order to oversee the political organization of the newly acquired territory. At this time he also dismissed his fleet, since he was short on funds and the fleet was not large enough to achieve control of the sea. The problem of control of the sea was one that would determine Alexander's strategy throughout the first stage of the expedition. His plan was to use the Macedonian infantry to seize the ports, thereby gaining control of the Phoenician fleets based in them. These ships, which had provided the naval power of the Persians, would then serve as the Macedonian fleet. By this means, he would avoid direct confrontations at sea, where he was at a clear disadvantage, and he would continually add to his fleet while reducing the Persians' sea power. In accordance with this strategy, Alexander next headed for the port of Halicarnassus in Caria.

Alexander and Ada

The city of Halicarnassus resisted, and Alexander carried out his first major siege. He succeeded in taking the city, although some Persian holdouts who took refuge in the citadel were only defeated months later. Orontobates, the son-in-law of Pixodaros, led the Carian resistance. Not long in the past, Alexander had offered himself for this very position, son-in-law of Pixodaros (see chap. 13, n. 38).

Rule in Caria was contested, a factor that Alexander was able to use to his advantage. Pixodaros had usurped power from the legitimate ruler, his sister Ada, who, nonetheless, had been able to maintain herself for seven years in the stronghold of Alinda (from 341 to 334), thanks to strong local support. When Ada appealed to Alexander for reinstatement as the ruler of Caria, he granted her request by appointing her satrap of Caria, even allowing her to adopt him as a son. By these acts, he gained the allegiance of her political supporters and acquired a legitimate dynastic claim to Caria.

The appointment of Ada as ruler (satrap) of Caria was typical of Alexander's method of organizing the territory that he conquered. Adopting the Persian system of satrapies, he usually kept military control in the hands of Macedonians, but often gave control of civil affairs to natives who commanded local loyalties, as Ada obviously did, judging by her success in staving off Pixodaros and then Orontobates for seven years from the stronghold of Alinda. This policy of sharing rule with local figures stood in contrast to the traditional Greek view of the barbarians as the enemy, as well as to the reported advice of Aristotle that Alexander deal with the barbarians as a master over slaves. It demonstrates Alexander's independence from his former teacher and his pragmatic sense; if the Persian empire was truly to come under his control, it could not be held by force of arms alone. He expanded this policy of shared

Source Analysis

T he Literary Sources on Ada.   The story of Ada and Alexander is told by both Arrian and Plutarch. The differing approach of these two sources can be seen from a comparison of their respective treatments of this episode.

According to Plutarch: *Alexander.* 22, tr. N. Demand.

> Alexander was completely in control of his appetite, and he showed this in many other ways and by what he said to Ada, whom he made his mother and appointed ruler of Caria. For when she, indulging him, every day sent many tempting dishes, and finally the most skillful cooks of meat and pastries, he said that he would not accept them. For he had better cooks given to him by his tutor Leonidas—for breakfast, a night march, for dinner, a small breakfast. And this same Leonidas, he said, used to open his chests of bedding and cloaks, checking them to see whether his mother had put in anything luxurious or excessive.

Compare Arrian's version, Arr. *Anabasis* 1 23.7–8.

How would you summarize the approaches of these two sources on the basis of their treatments of this story?

Archaeological Evidence for Ada?

I n 1989 when workmen were laying the foundation for a house in Bodrum (ancient Halicarnassus), they came upon a sarcophagus with the bones of a woman who had died in mid-fourth century at about the age of forty. Gold ornaments from her clothing and a golden crown of a myrtle branch and flower design were found in the sarcophagus, as well as three rings, two bracelets, and two necklaces. Other burial goods included a black glazed wine pitcher and three wine cups. The richness of the burial, the excellent physical condition of the woman, and the dating of the remains, suggest that this was the burial of Ada, although no inscriptions have been found to confirm this. The Bodrum Underwater Archaeology Museum employed experts from Manchester University Museum and the university's medical art department to make a reconstruction of the queen, and they have provided a suitable setting for the exhibit of the burial in a replica of the *andron* (banquet hall) constructed by King Mausolos, the brother of Hidrieus and Ada who preceded them in rule, at the shrine of Zeus at Labraunda in 355 B.C.

WEBSITE 14.1   ARCHAEOLOGICAL EVIDENCE FOR ADA?

http://www.bodrum-museum.com/museum/depts/carian_princess.htm

administration as the campaign progressed, until it included the integration of Persians into the army itself. Alexander also adopted some of the dress and customs that his new subjects expected of their rulers. But many of Alexander's followers, especially the older men who had served Philip, did not share his vision of a bicultural future, and a current of opposition developed that at times threatened the campaign itself.

With affairs in Caria under control, the approach of winter required that Alexander find winter quarters for his army (334/333 BCE). He won popularity with many by sending the newly married men back home to Macedonia, with orders to enroll new recruits during their stay. Parmenio was sent to winter in Sardis with about a quarter of the army, and Alexander marched with the remainder along the warmer coast of southern Lycia and inland through Lycia and Pisidia, capturing or receiving the surrender of many towns. It was common practice to split up an army in winter, so that no single district was overburdened with their provisioning.

First Encounter with Darius

In the spring of 333 the army reassembled at Gordium, where Alexander visited a famous local landmark, the Wagon of Gordius, the mythical founder of the Phrygian dynasty. Tradition held that whoever was able to unfasten the knot on the yoke of this wagon (the famous Gordian Knot) would rule Asia. There are variant accounts of Alexander's actions. Arrian reports that most authors claimed that he cut the knot with his sword, while Aristobulus says that he removed the pole-pin that held the knot together, and so removed the yoke from the pole.[7] In both versions Alexander succeeded in a less than direct way to unfasten the knot, yet in both he still fulfilled the prophecy.

Alexander next marched southeast, passing through the Cilician Gates and encamping at Tarsus. Here he fell seriously ill with a fever after a swim in the icy river. The fever brought Alexander near death, and he was saved only when his doctor prescribed a strong purge. (This was a typical remedy in Greek medicine; Alexander's recovery from the "remedy" probably attests more to the strength of his constitution than to the efficacy of the treatment). This was one of a number of times when Alexander suffered serious illnesses or injuries during the campaign, episodes that were to culminate in his early death. In this case, the fever was probably a malarial relapse brought on by fatigue and chilling.[8]

Alexander made Cilicia his base for the next several months while he recovered. Meanwhile, the Persian king Darius was collecting his forces, which included a large number of

Greek mercenaries, and moving toward a confrontation. Alexander marched his forces south along the coast into the narrows between the mountains and the sea, hoping to meet Darius at a narrow site that would give the advantage to his smaller forces. But Darius was encamped east of the mountains at Sochi, in the Syrian plain of Amik. According to the sources, he delayed, at a loss for what to do. Some of his advisors urged him to stay put, since the plain gave his large army the advantage, but finally he decided to move forward. Perhaps delay was making supply of the army difficult; in contrast, Alexander was positioned on the sea, where his forces were easily supplied.

When Darius decided to move, he took an unexpected, circuitous route northward to a pass over the mountains and then down south again into the Cilician Plain, surprising the Macedonians at their rear. When he became aware of the situation, Alexander marched the bulk of his forces northward to meet Darius, probably leaving behind the allied infantry in case a second contingent of Persians should approach through the pass directly from Sochi and threaten to surround his forces. The Macedonians advanced until the two armies met at a relatively narrow spot along the coast, in November of 333, at the battle of Issus.[9] While the sources give obviously overstated numbers for the army of Darius, it is clear that Alexander's forces were, in fact, greatly outnumbered. However, the Persian line soon gave way before the Macedonian phalanx; Alexander's court historians, always on the alert to see the worst in the Persian king, suggested that Darius fled at the very start of the battle, but other sources report that he fought bravely.

The battle was brief, however, and Darius did soon flee, along with the rest of his army. They suffered terrible losses in the rout, reportedly losing 100,000 men, while the Macedonians lost only 500. A signal loss was that of the baggage train of the Persian king, which was captured with his treasury and the women of his court, including his wife and mother.

After the humiliation of his defeat, Darius quickly offered terms: if Alexander would restore his family, he would make peace and enter into an alliance. But Alexander was not ready to compromise. He countered with a list of all the grievances that the Greeks had against the Persians and a demand that Darius come to him as a suppliant, acknowledging him as King of all Asia, and that in the future Darius deal with him not as an equal, but as an overlord.[10] These terms were obviously unacceptable, and the war continued.

Alexander could not risk pursuing Darius into the interior as long as the Persians had control of the sea and could foment trouble with the restless Greeks at his back. He therefore remained on the coast to continue his plan of seizing the harbors used by the Persians. This was not to be easily accomplished, however. Although the cities of Byblos and Sidon surrendered, Tyre refused to submit, and it required a seven-month's siege[11] and all the ingenuity of Alexander and his engineers, to capture the island-city.

Alexander began his attack on Tyre by ordering the construction of a mole (raised earth bank) to provide access to the island for his soldiers. While his men worked, the defenders attacked them by sea. To protect their workers and to provide a base from which to fire down on the attackers, the Macedonians then built two towers covered with a screen of hides and positioned them on the completed portion of the mole. The defenders countered by outfitting and launching an incendiary ship against the mole, setting the towers on fire. People from the city joined in the defense, rowing in and setting alight all the engines not caught by the fire from the incendiary ship. After the destruction, however, Alexander rallied his forces to build a broader mole with more towers, and ordered the engineers to construct new machines, while he himself went off to collect more ships. The Phoenician naval commanders from Byblos and Sidon, learning that their cities had fallen to Alexander, brought their ships to join him, and commanders from Rhodes, Lycia, and Cyprus added their ships as well. Alarmed by the size of the new armada, the Tyrians refused to give battle, and Alexander set up a blockade of the city. When the mole was completed and the new engines ready, Alexander launched another attack. The city was stubbornly defended but finally fell. The mole permanently changed the island into a peninsula, and it remains so today.

Egypt and the East

From Phoenicia Alexander marched south toward Egypt, taking the city of Gaza in a bitterly defended siege in which he was wounded.[12] When Alexander entered Egypt he was welcomed as Pharaoh by a people who had been resentful of Persian rule. Two important events marked his stay in Egypt: the foundation of Alexandria in the spring of 331 and his visit to the oracle of Ammon at the oasis of Siwah (Libya).

Alexandria was the most successful of Alexander's many city foundations.[13] The location was strategically important; by connecting Pharos with the mainland, two good harbors were provided on a coast that had lacked harbors suitable for a large fleet. The military advantage this conferred gave the city a commercial advantage as well, and it later prospered. The foundation of the city as celebrated in the Roman period was April 7, 331. Alexander reportedly determined the general layout of the city, deciding the circuit of the walls, and the location of the *agora* and the main temples; he also selected the gods to whom the temples would be devoted—Greek gods as well as the Egyptian goddess Isis. Diodorus, who had visited the city, says that the streets were oriented so that the prevailing winds would cool the city and make it more healthful.[14] The original population was mixed, made up of Greek mercenaries, retired or disabled Macedonians, and local people from small nearby native settlements who would provide the labor force. Over time, however, the city attracted a large population from all areas of Greece and the Mediterranean.

Alexandria provided a model for many later Alexandrian city foundations, although none proved to be as successful. Plutarch attributed 70 foundations to him;[15] in fact, however, the exact number is not known. Some are mentioned by the ancient sources, others are identifiable by continuing tradition and later claims, and still others have been discovered only by scholarly detective work. Most, like Alexandria in Egypt, were named after him. Unlike Alexandria in Egypt, however, the later foundations were made in isolated areas, east of the Tigris, in a part of the world that had not yet been urbanized.[16] Many were founded on important trade routes or at their junctions; others at sites that provided protection against the intrusion of hostile tribes into conquered and pacified territory. Many have since disappeared or been changed radically, but five still remain as living cities: the original Alexandria in Egypt, Herat, Ghazni, Merv, and Termez. In addition to cities, Alexander also established numerous garrisons in strategic locations.

The second significant event that occurred during Alexander's stay in Egypt was his visit to the oracle of Ammon at Siwah in Libya. This oracle was already well known and respected in the Greek world, where the god was regarded as a manifestation of the Greek Zeus, and Siwah was a place of pilgrimage and homage for Greeks as well as Egyptians. In fact, there was a local branch of the cult not far from Alexander's home, at Aphytis in Chalkidike, whose coinage had long portrayed the horned head of Zeus Ammon. Alexander had long suspected that there was something exceptional about himself. Was it possible that he, like his ancestor Herakles, was the son of a god, in his case Zeus Ammon? This was the question that he was anxious to ask the oracle at Ammon.

The consultation was in private, and Alexander kept the details private. Thus none of our sources can speak with authority about the exact questions that Alexander posed to the oracle, nor about its precise answer. But all agree that the oracle's response confirmed Alexander's suspicions that he was the son of the god.

What did it mean, to be the son of Zeus Ammon? First of all, that he had a divine father did not mean that Alexander denied his human father, Philip; like Herakles, he had two "real" fathers, one human and one divine. Nor did it mean that Alexander himself was a god. For the Greeks, the offspring of mortals and divinities were heroes and mortal, not gods and immortal. There were, however, a few exceptional cases—heroes who, through extraordinary accomplishments had become gods, being translated directly to heaven without dying. This was the case with Herakles, and Herakles was considered by Alexander to be his direct ancestor.

Did Alexander at this point consider himself to be one of these exceptional cases? In Egypt, belief in the divinity of the ruler had been customary from the earliest period. When Alexander entered the country as a conqueror, the Egyptian people had naturally hailed him as Pharaoh and god. The pragmatic response for Alexander was not to try to revise thousands of years of Egyptian religious tradition, but to adapt to the expectations of his new subjects. The same problem was met by the Romans as they expanded into the east, where the common belief that the emperor as ruler was divine disturbed the Roman senators, who saw the emperor as a human being like themselves, albeit the first among equals. To what extent these two events—his recognition by the people of Egypt and his recognition by the oracle—merged in Alexander's mind to solidify his belief in his own divinity, we cannot know. However, it is clear that the nature of his "divinity" was a matter of serious debate among the Macedonians, and that Alexander's belief in his divine ancestry was a source of continuing irritation to some. Despite Herakles, and even despite a few harbingers of the elevation of important political figures to divinity that had already appeared in Greece (for example, Lysander had accepted worship from the people of Samos, Chapter 13), the Greeks did not traditionally attribute divinity to their rulers, and the idea was troubling to the more conservative men.[17]

When the political settlement of Egypt was concluded and Alexander's desire to visit the oracle satisfied, he turned back to the east and the unfinished business of Darius. The king, trying to forestall a military disaster, now offered even more generous terms to Alexander: 10,000 talents in return for his family; all the territory west of the Euphrates; the hand of his daughter in marriage; and future friendship and alliance. Many of Alexander's staff urged acceptance at this point, but the conqueror was unbending. He demanded again that Darius acknowledge his overlordship by coming to him as a suppliant. This uncompromising reply shows that Alexander was now firmly committed to rule as king over the entire Persian empire, an idea that had been gradually gaining force since the episode of the Gordian Knot. Requital for Persia's past wrongs was no longer enough.

On October 1, 331, Alexander met Darius in battle at Gaugamela, in Assyria near the Tigris River not far from Nineveh. Darius picked the battle spot, positioning his forces on a level plain that would offer the best scope for his strong point, the cavalry. In addition, he had two hundred scythed chariots, and he ordered the battle surface smoothed in order to assure their most effective use. In the clash of forces, however, the scythed chariots proved ineffective; the Macedonian light infantry attacked their horses, and those few that escaped were allowed to pass harmlessly through gaps opened in the Macedonian line. Alexander himself, at the head of a wedge-shaped formation, drove through a gap in the Persian line, continually widening it. Darius at the center came under increasing pressure, until finally he turned to escape—and Alexander followed. Alexander pressed his pursuit until evening, becoming separated from the rest of the army, but he failed to catch the king. The battle continued, however, and some of the sources seem intent on exonerating Alexander for his reckless abandonment of the field in the midst of the battle. Nevertheless, a general rout of the Persians followed, and the victory at Gaugamela was the decisive victory of empire. Darius, having fled the field in disgrace, now became a fugitive.

Rather than continuing his pursuit of the king at once, Alexander next turned his attention to gaining control of the various capitals of the Persian empire to which he now laid claim: Babylon, Susa, Pasargadae, Persepolis, and Ecbatana. In each of these he seized the royal treasury; the total was reckoned at 180,000 talents of gold, an amount equal to two hundred years of the income of Athens at the height of its power.[18] This treasure would radically alter the economy of the ancient world in the Hellenistic period as more and more of it was coined and passed into circulation.

Only at Persepolis, the capital associated with Darius I and Xerxes, was the army turned loose to loot, even though the city did not resist occupation. Until this time, the army had been restrained from looting, and the spoils were added to the treasury of the expedition. In Persepolis, however, the men were allowed their due share of the fruits of victory, and they fell avidly upon the riches in the homes of the Persian nobility, killing the men and seizing the women as slaves.

Alexander remained in the palace at Persepolis for some time, overseeing allocation of the treasury, distributing some of the riches to other centers, and setting some aside to travel with the army. Nothing was to remain in Persepolis; the city was to be downgraded and the new capital established at Babylon. Perhaps as a final show of disparagement, in the spring of 330, in a dramatic act that aroused great controversy even in antiquity, Alexander burned the great palace. The violent fire left marks that are still visible in the ruins today. Some sources maintain that Alexander's motive was symbolic retribution for the destructions caused by the Persian Wars, and that Alexander himself later regretted the act. Other sources provide a less savory picture, reporting that the conflagration was started at the suggestion of the Athenian courtesan Thais, the mistress of Ptolemy, during a drunken party.

The burning of Persepolis, whether on an impulse during a drunken party or as a sober act of policy, dramatically symbolized the end of the panhellenic campaign of retribution against the Persians.[19] Either the campaign was to be declared finished, or it had to take on a new goal. For Alexander, the answer was not in doubt. He had already declared himself Darius' successor as ruler of the Persian Empire, and his restless ambition framed even more ambitious plans for extending that empire. But he faced strong opposition from some of his generals, who were disturbed by his increasing adoption of Persian ways and felt strongly that the army should return to Macedonia. These men are sometimes characterized as the "Old Guard," men who had fought under Philip and were strongly imbued with the Macedonian ethos, in contrast to the younger men who had come to positions of authority under Alexander and shared his more pragmatic attitudes. It was surely significant that Parmenio, one of the most important of the "Old Guard," advised against the burning of Persepolis, for he soon became a key victim in one of a series of events that had the effect of eliminating the central figures of this Macedonian opposition.

Opposition Among the Macedonians

Parmenio's downfall came as a result of a plot that involved his son Philotas, and so has been named the "Philotas affair." Since Egypt, Philotas had been outspoken in his disapproval of Alexander's increasing adoption of the customs and dress of a Persian king and of his claims to be the son of Ammon. In 330 an otherwise unknown Macedonian called Dimnos told his lover that he was involved in a conspiracy to murder Alexander. The boy then told his brother, who reported it to Philotas. Philotas, however, failed to pass the information along, apparently not taking it seriously. The brother then revealed the plot to one of the Royal Pages, adolescent sons of Macedonian nobles who were enlisted for personal attendance on the king, and the page reported it to Alexander. Dimnos immediately, and conveniently, killed himself (or was killed). The charge against Philotas was that he had failed to warn Alexander of the conspiracy, which he did not deny. There was no evidence that he had played any positive role in a plot against Alexander. Nevertheless, the army judged him guilty and executed him. With the execution of Philotas, the question was naturally raised of the possible involvement of his father, Parmenio. Family ties were strong in Macedonia, and even if Parmenio had played no role in the "plot," he would still be expected to avenge his son's death. Alexander did not hesitate, but sent a letter to the generals under Parmenio's command, ordering them to kill the old general. Because of the obscurity of Dimnos and his compatriots, and Philotas' tenuous role in the action, some have seen the plot as a conspiracy against Philotas, perhaps even a complex scheme primarily intended to eliminate Parmenio.[20]

Others of a conservative tendency also fell at this time, and Alexander's friends came more to the forefront. The third Lycestian brother, Alexander, whose brothers had been executed as conspirators in the death of Philip, was executed now; and Ptolemy, who after Alexander's death eventually became Ptolemy I of Egypt, replaced a member of the king's bodyguard who had been a friend of Philotas. Aristotle's friend Hephaestion, who had played an active role against Philotas, also received his first important post, sharing the command of the Companion cavalry with Cleitus, who was soon to meet a fate similar to that of Philotas.

Meanwhile Darius had established himself in Ecbatana, the Median capital, still hoping to defend the Iranian heartland. As Alexander approached, Darius moved eastward. But the eastern satrapies were unwilling to continue to serve a king compromised by defeat, and opinions began to be expressed favoring the rule of Bessus, the strongest of the eastern satraps. A split developed in the Persian camp, and as Alexander gained on the fleeing king, Bessus imprisoned him, carrying him along in a wagon, bound in golden chains. When it became clear that Alexander would catch up with them, Bessus had Darius killed, preventing his being captured by Alexander and forced into the demeaning role of vassal.

On discovering the body of Darius, Alexander treated it with all the respect due to royalty, sending it back to Persepolis for a royal funeral and burial. He could now truly present himself as the King of Asia. The last Achaemenid king was dead, and Alexander was in possession of all the Persian capitals, the principal one of which, Persepolis, lay in ruins. Bessus, however, now claimed the throne as Darius' successor and undertook to continue the war against Alexander.

Alexander pursued Bessus, finally catching him in 330/329. Two stories are told of Bessus' death. According to one account, Alexander had him stand, stripped and wearing a spiked dog collar, beside the road as the army passed by, and then had him executed.[21] According to the other account, Alexander had him mutilated—his nose and ears cut off—before he was executed.[22] Both stories illustrate Alexander's adoption of Persian customs, in this case in the treatment of defeated foes. Which, if either, version is true is of less importance than the fact that rumors were circulating that expressed Macedonian opposition to Alexander's "Persianizing."

Other stories reporting opposition to Alexander among the Macedonians focused on his lack of *sophrosyne* (self-control). One relates an incident in 328, which ended with the death of Cleitus. Cleitus was the brother of Alexander's favorite nurse. He had saved Alexander's life in the first battle of the expedition, at Granicus, and he now shared with Hephaestion the command of the Companion cavalry. He seems to have been one of the more conservative men, however, and some sources report that he had just been appointed satrap of Bactria and Sogdiana, probably a form of "honorable exile." When the incident revealing Alexander's lack of self-control occurred, Cleitus and other friends of Alexander were drinking together with the king in one of the traditional Macedonian drinking parties, where the consumption of unmixed wine often reached heroic quantities. When several of the Companions flattered Alexander, likening him to various gods, Cleitus reproved them for showing disrespect to the gods, caustically remarking that Alexander's achievements were not so great nor had he achieved them unaided. Alexander grew angry, but Cleitus continued the taunting. As the king's anger mounted, Cleitus' friends desperately tried to get him away from the king. Finally, in a drunken rage, Alexander grabbed a pike and ran him through. All the sources report that the king was immediately struck by guilt at what he had done, and that he spent three days in remorseful seclusion, without food or water.

The second incident involved Callisthenes, a cousin and former pupil of Aristotle, whose job it was to write the official history of the campaign. Alexander was experimenting with having the Macedonians follow the Persian practice of doing obeisance to himself as king (the Greek term is *proskynesis*; the homage, which was secular and widely practiced among the Persians, was expressed in various ways, ranging from complete prostration before the ruler to bowing slightly and blowing a kiss). Callisthenes refused to do obeisance to Alexander, saying that this was an honor appropriate only to the gods. His arguments against obeisance pleased the more conservative Macedonians, who were uncomfortable with this new practice. But their disapproval greatly provoked Alexander. Callisthenes added to his problems by claiming that Alexander's fame did not rest on his own exploits, but on the history that he, Callisthenes, was writing. Alexander, however, bided his time, waiting for treasonous acts rather than mere words. Again, discovery of a plot provided the opportunity.

In 327 one of the Royal Pages anticipated Alexander in striking a wild boar during a hunt. As a punishment Alexander took away his horse and ordered that he be whipped in front of the other pages. Embittered by the insulting punishment, the boy persuaded several of his fellow pages to help him avenge the insult by killing Alexander as he slept. As it happened, however, Alexander did not go to bed that night but instead drank the night away, and the pages' plot came to nothing. The next day, however, one of the boys talked too much, and the plot was revealed. All of the conspirators were immediately arrested and confessed under torture, whereupon they were stoned to death by the army—the usual method of execution in such cases. Callisthenes was charged with having encouraged the pages in the attempt. Whether he was any more involved in this plot than Philotas had been in the plot that led to his death is unclear, however. According to some reports, Callisthenes was bound in chains and carried around with the army until he finally sickened and died; according to others, he was immediately racked, then put to death by hanging.

The Campaign Continues

Despite these problems in the Macedonian camp, the campaign went forward. Following the death of Darius and the execution of Bessus, Alexander faced no more counter-claimants to the Persian throne, but stubborn local resistance continued in the remote and mountainous areas of Sogdiana and Bactria (northern Iran, southern Russia, and Afghanistan). Three years of difficult guerrilla warfare were required to subdue these fiercely independent peoples. In the process, Alexander established a number of new cities, settling Macedonians and Greek mercenaries far from their homelands in the midst of an alien and hostile culture. While land and settlement were a customary reward for military service, many of these settlers were, not surprisingly, unwilling and unhappy residents in their new *poleis*.

India and Return

When he had succeeded in subduing the farthest eastern satrapies of the Persian Empire, Alexander might reasonably have turned back, having made good his claim to the Persian throne, in addition to fulfilling his original objective of retribution for the Persian Wars. But he was driven on by a desire to conquer India and to reach the end of the world at Ocean, which, like most Greeks, he believed to encircle and delimit the world.

Once he had crossed the Indus River, Alexander met serious opposition from the Indian king, Poros, and it was in India that he fought his fourth—and last—pitched battle. In it his forces confronted elephants in battle for the first time, although they had seen them earlier. Alexander had even acquired some for his own army, using them, however, for parade and display, rather than in battle, and not training his horses with them. Since untrained horses will not face elephants, the job of countering the elephant opposition was assigned to the infantry.

Despite Poros' decisive defeat, he fought bravely, not retreating from the battle until the end, when he was wounded. After much persuasion, he finally surrendered to Alexander, asking only to be treated as a king. Alexander rewarded his courage by returning his kingdom to him, and even adding to it; in return, Poros became a faithful ally to Alexander. The

Source Analysis

A rrian 5.12.2–7   Alexander versus Poros. Explain the methods Alexander used to meet the threat of the elephants to his troops.

Figure 14.1   Alexander attacking Poros; Alexander crowned by Victory.
The Frank Medallion, British Museum, BM1887-6-9-1.

victory was celebrated on coins, including large *decadrachms* (ten drachm pieces) portraying Alexander on horseback, armed with a sarissa and attacking Poros, who is mounted on an elephant, along with the driver. On the reverse, Alexander appears wielding the thunderbolt of Zeus and crowned by a small figure of Victory.[23]

After Alexander's defeat of Poros, the Indian ruler's enemies became Alexander's, and the fighting continued. Alexander's men, however, had finally reached the end of their campaigning zeal. They had been away from their homes for years (it was now 326), local replacements of their worn-out Macedonian clothing seemed even to challenge their Macedonian identity, and monsoon rains had been pouring down on them for over two months, rusting their equipment and generally making life miserable. To go on would mean more hardships, more river crossings, more battles, more elephants. They simply refused. Alexander tried to change their minds, even threatening to continue alone if necessary, but this threat was now followed by stubborn silence. Finally he called the army together and announced that they would turn back. At the news, the men wept and cheered and invoked blessings on Alexander. In the end, it was not the might of enemy forces but the exhaustion of his own men and their refusal to continue that brought Alexander's conquest of the world to an end.

While Alexander did agree to return, he did not take the fastest or easiest route back, choosing instead to use the journey for further exploration and conquest. The army set out down the Hydaspes and Indus rivers in a trip that lasted from November 326 to July 325, during which they again and again faced hostile tribes and perilous conditions.

Among the local peoples whom they encountered, the Mallians were especially ferocious. Anticipating Alexander's approach, the Mallians abandoned their cities and massed their forces for a single stand. When that failed, they took refuge in a heavily fortified settlement. Alexander's forces managed to break into the settlement, but as he took the foremost role in the fighting, he was gravely wounded, his lung pierced by an arrow. As he lay wounded, rumors circulated that he had died. To counter these, Alexander had himself carried before the army on a boat, weakly lifting his hand to greet them so that they would know that he still lived. And once again, he survived a life-threatening injury.

While Alexander convalesced, his good fortune continued, for the Mallians, apparently convinced of his invincibility, surrendered. New river boats were built in preparation for the trip down river. When Alexander had recovered sufficiently, the joint land and river expedition continued, although he sent Craterus with the elephants and most of the troops by an easier route. Perhaps the worst part of the entire expedition still lay ahead: the Gedrosian Desert. Alexander deliberately chose this dangerous and difficult route for the glory of achievement. It was, however, to have little glory for the many men and all the accompanying families who perished along the way.

Source Analysis

A rrian, *Anabasis* 6.24–26   Alexander has been criticized for the deaths of the camp followers. How would you defend him?

THE DEATH OF ALEXANDER

After the ordeal in the Gedrosian desert, Alexander, back in Persia, was met with numerous complaints of maladministration and even treasonous activities on the part of those he had left in charge during his long absence, many of whom had never expected to see him again. Severe punishments followed swiftly. Among those whom he executed were two of the three Macedonian generals who had executed Parmenio. In Alexander's absence they had plundered temples, disturbed tombs, and committed acts of injustice against the subject peoples. Not long after, the third of these generals was also executed for plundering the temple of Susa. Numerous other executions followed.[24]

Alexander next proceeded to Pasargadae, where he repaired and restored the plundered temple of Cyrus, founder of the Persian Empire. By his reverence to the tomb of the founder, Alexander expressed his own claim to be the legitimate ruler of the empire, heir not only of Darius but of Cyrus as well. He also went forward with the integration of the Persians into the Macedonian army and the administration of his conquests. Perhaps the most impressive of these acts of reconciliation and integration was the mass wedding he held at Susa for himself and other high-ranking Macedonians. Following the Macedonian tradition of royal polygamy, he married Statira,[25] Darius' eldest daughter, as well as Parysatis, the youngest daughter of Darius' predecessor. He had previously married Roxane, the daughter of the defeated ruler of Bactria. Any children born from these unions would be viable heirs to the kingship, able to claim both Argead and Achaemenid ancestry. Hephaestion, Alexander's closest friend, was married to a full sister of Statira; thus, as possible heir or regent, he too would have children who could claim Achaemenid ancestry. The Companions were also married to women from among the Persian ruling class. The weddings were conducted in Persian style. Alexander gave all the brides dowries and ordered that the other Macedonians who had already married Asian women be registered as well and receive gifts (Arrian reports that there were more than 10,000). He also paid all the debts that his men had incurred during the campaign and gave presents to those who had displayed conspicuous courage in battle.

But all did not go smoothly at these ceremonies. Many of the men were angry at being married to the women of a conquered people, and they also resented the reception into the army of 30,000 Persian youths whom Alexander had had raised in Macedonian fashion. These youths were dressed in Macedonian fashion and trained in the Macedonian style of warfare, and he rather tactlessly called them the "Successors." The Macedonians saw this as an effort by Alexander to reduce his dependence on them, and it also recalled to their minds the many other marks of accommodation to Persian ways that angered them: Alexander's own adoption of Persian dress and court ceremonies, the use of Persian wedding ceremonies in the mass marriages, and the recent introduction of Barbarians into the army itself, and even into the Companion cavalry.

The culmination of the discontent occurred shortly afterwards, in the summer of 324 at Opis. Alexander announced that he was discharging and sending home those Macedonians unfit for service because of age or disability, who would serve at home as a reserve and be replaced by fresh troops. This brought to the surface all the soldiers' past grievances, and they demanded that he discharge them all. Let him campaign in the future with his father Ammon! Furious, Alexander ordered his officers to arrest the most conspicuous agitators. Around 13 men were arrested and executed. He then harangued the stunned and silent men on their ingratitude to him and to his father, Philip, and told them all that they were free to return home. He himself went into seclusion for three days. This time, however, he did not relent. Emerging from his seclusion, he summoned the most capable of the Persian leaders and divided the commands of the army among them and made other plans to reorganize the army around his Asian forces. When word that they were being replaced reached the Macedonians, they were struck by remorse. They rushed to the palace and threw down their arms before the doors in supplication. Alexander then forgave them and ordered that a huge banquet of reconciliation be held. Nine thousand men shared in the feast at which Alexander prayed that harmony should prevail between the Macedonians and the Persians as partners in government.

In the autumn of 324 Alexander suffered a great blow when his closest friend, Hephaestion, fell ill and died. Alexander was consumed with grief, much like his hero

Achilles after the death of Patroclus. Hephaestion was buried at Babylon, and in the spring a funeral was held for him with splendid funeral games. Alexander ordered that heroic honors be paid to Hephaestion, even offering the satrap of Egypt pardon for past and future crimes if he would establish hero shrines for Hephaestion at Alexandria and Pharos. Alexander planned his friend's tomb himself, to be built at Babylon at a cost of ten thousand talents. It was to take the shape of a *ziggarat*, the traditional Mesopotamian pyramidal shrine platform. The walls of the tomb were to be decorated with elaborate friezes of gold, and the base decorated with gilded ship prows seized from the Persians. Diodorus Siculus, who provides the most complete description, states that the monument was completed, but no traces of such a building have been found.[26]

As Alexander recovered from his overwhelming grief, he laid plans for further exploration and conquest. Among these new adventures were an expedition to the Caspian Sea,[27] a voyage to conquer and colonize Arabia, and the construction of a giant harbor at Babylon large enough to anchor 1,000 warships.[28] Plans to conquer Carthage and to reach the Pillars of Herakles and Ocean in the west (Gibraltar) have also been attributed to him. Diodorus reports that notes about his future plans, including the western expedition, were found after his death (the *Hypomnemata*),[29] but when these were presented to the army, they rejected them as too ambitious.

As these plans for the future were being laid, Alexander fell ill once more. Again the illness came on after one of the prolonged drinking parties at the court. The fever progressed over the course of about ten days, despite efforts to alleviate it. At the end he lapsed into a coma, and on June 10, 323 he died. Rumors of poisoning circulated almost from the moment of his death, but both Arrian and Plutarch found them unpersuasive, as do most modern historians.[30]

Modern historians and others have suggested many possible causes of Alexander's death, including alcoholism[31] and even AIDS. It seems most likely, however, that he died of malaria,[32] aggravated by the heavy drinking of the Macedonian court, although typhoid has also been argued by the combined team of an ancient historian and a physician.

Source Analysis

Arrian, 7.27.1–3   What possible causes of Alexander's death are discussed by Arrian?

WEBSITE 14.2   THE DEBATE ABOUT THE CAUSE OF ALEXANDER'S DEATH

The argument that Alexander died of typhoid can be found at:
http://www.umm.edu/news/releases/bug.html

See also discussion from the New England Journal of Medicine:
http://web.archive.org/web/20001202125800/http://www.nejm.org/content/1998/
0339/0017/1248.asp

A collection of sites on the possible causes of Alexander's death (typhoid, poisoning, AIDS, West Nile virus, etc. but omitting the most likely cause, malaria) can be found at
http://www.isidore-of-seville.com/alexander/5.html

The Effects of Alexander's Conquests on Macedonia

Alexander died an untimely death at the age of 33, in the midst of plans for further exploration and conquest. His adaptation of the Persian system to the administration of conquered territory was still evolving, and he had made no arrangements for the succession. Arrhidaios, his disabled half-brother, was the only Argead successor, although Alexander's wife Roxane was pregnant.

The succession by long tradition belonged to the Argead clan, and none of the surviving generals immediately moved to claim it. Rather, they agreed that Roxane's unborn child, if it turned out to be a boy, should be king under their combined regency. The army, however, resented the idea of a half-barbarian king and pushed for the succession of Arrhidaios. When Roxane's child turned out to be a boy, a compromise was reached. He, as Alexander IV, and Arrhidaios, as Philip III, were to be joint rulers under a regency. The two were, of course, nothing more than puppets, to be eliminated when they were no longer useful.

The generals, however, sought very soon to carve out their own domains. First to act was Ptolemy, who laid claim to Egypt. To support his claim, he kidnapped the body of Alexander, which he took to Alexandria and installed in a magnificent tomb (yet to be found). Ptolemy fended off one early challenge to his control of Egypt, and from that time on his descendants ruled the rich territory until the Romans took over after the death of Cleopatra in 30 BCE. Struggles for control of the other conquests of Alexander went on intermittently for about 50 years. At the end of this period of chaos and warfare (the Wars of the Successors), the world conquered by Alexander had come to be divided into a number of kingdoms ruled by Macedonian dynastic rulers: Egypt, in the hands of the Ptolemies; Asia Minor and the Near East under the Seleucids; and Macedonia under the Antigonids, who also controlled Thessaly and some strongholds in Greece (see Chapter 15). But Macedon never regained its commanding role in the post-Alexandrian world.

Was Macedonian weakness in the period after Alexander brought about by years of manning Alexander's armies and peopling his new settlements? There is disagreement about this. A. B. Bosworth blames Alexander's conquests for the weakness of post-Alexandrian Macedonia.[33] During the period 334–331, he points out, over 30,000 men had been taken out of the country, and few of them ever returned—he calculates, at most, half. Those who failed to return included, in addition to battle casualties and the victims of accidents, disease, and the rigors of the march, the many men who were settled permanently in garrisons and city foundations at the far reaches of the empire. Bosworth concludes that the birthrate in Macedonia must have declined sharply as a result of these manpower losses, as is suggested by an abrupt reduction in potential recruits that shows up in the accounts of Macedonian military actions after 320. Bosworth thus gives an assessment of the cost of Alexander's conquests that is quite different from that of Arrian. In Bosworth's judgment, "He may have led his men to wealth and glory, but those who remained had little profit and lasting grief... the country was set on a path of decline that proved irreversible."[34]

In contrast, Richard Billows argues that Alexander's campaign losses and resettlements did not have a permanent effect upon the ability of the population of Macedonia to muster fighters.[35] Thus, he estimates that in 319 there were approximately 25,000 Macedonian troops in Asia and roughly the same number in Macedonia, in contrast to the 30,000 that he estimates Alexander had with him after the battle of Gaugamela. This optimistic view is based upon arguments from population estimates and demographic calculations relying on many unknowns and much supposition. For example, Billows puts the total Macedonian losses of Alexander's campaigns at 5,000 to 7,000 men, a casualty rate of some 12 to 20 percent.[36] He argues that such losses would be made up comparatively rapidly, since women and children were not casualties of war, many recruits had already started families before they left, many began new families on the campaign, and the citizenship was not a closed body. Yet Billows does not deny that Macedonian manpower declined, and that Macedonia sank to a level of relative unimportance in the post-Alexandrian world.[37] He attributes this decline, however, not to the campaigns of Alexander, but to the Gallic invasions of 280–277, which brought four years of devastation to the country. The Gauls killed not only men, but women and children as well. In the chaos, Philip's Greater Macedonia disintegrated. Many of the border areas that he had added broke away, and Illyrian and Thracian tribes again became a menace, as they had been in the days before Philip. Macedonia never fully recovered. Thus, in Billows's assessment, the campaigns of Alexander actually had little effect on the future of Macedonia, whether for good or ill. The villains were the Gauls.

SUGGESTIONS FOR FURTHER READING

J. Roisman (1995), *Alexander the Great: Ancient and Modern Perspectives*, offers a good introduction to the ancient sources and to key modern topics of discussion, as well as a useful annotated bibliography. The best full scholarly book on Alexander is A. B. Bosworth

(1988), *Conquest and Empire: The Reign of Alexander the Great*. A very interesting book on an important topic is D. W. Engels (1978), *Alexander the Great and the Logistics of the Macedonian Army*. A collection of articles by Eugene Borza can be found in Carol Thomas, ed. (1995), *Macedonika: Essays by Eugene Borza*.

MAP STUDY

Major battles: Granicus River, Halicarnassus, Tyre, Issus, Gaugamela, Hydaspes River
   Other significant locations: Ephesis, Alinda, Labraunda, Sardis, Lycia, Pisidia, Gordium, Syria, Byblos, Sidon, Rhodes, Cyprus, Tigris Tiver, Euphrates Rivers Gaza, Alexandria, Siwah, Libya, Herat, Ghazni, Merv, Termez, Babylon, Susa, Pasargadae, Persepolis, Ecbatana, Bactria, Sogdiana, Indus River, Gedrosian Desert, Opis, Caspian Sea
   On other maps (use map index to find these): Carthage

ON THE WEB

http://www.isidore-of-seville.com/alexander/5.html offers a collection of sites, including access to some old sites that are now difficult to access.

ENDNOTES

[1]See E. Carney (1993), "Olympias and the Image of the Royal Virago," *Phoenix* 47: 29–56.

[2]N. G. L. Hammond (1993), *Sources for Alexander the Great*, 189–191.

[3]See R. M. Errington (1969), "Bias in Ptolemy's History of Alexander," *Classical Quarterly* 19:233–242.

[4]These figures are derived from the various figures given in the different sources by P. A. Brunt (1976), *Arrian* I: lxix–lxxi. A. B. Bosworth (1988), *Conquest and Empire: The Reign of Alexander the Great*, 35, 259. Bosworth estimates a figure of about 50,000 at the beginning of the expedition, including the forces already in Asia Minor.

[5]D. W. Engels (1978), *Alexander the Great and the Logistics of the Macedonian Army*, deals with the interesting question of how the troops were provisioned.

[6]Arr. *Anabasis* 1.13–16.

[7]Arr. *Anabasis* 2.3.6–8; Plutarch, *Alex.* 18.4 also gives both explanations.

[8]Peter Green (1974), *Alexander of Macedon*, 220, diagnosed this episode of illness as bronchial pneumonia. The German scholar F. Schachermeyr (1973), *Alexander der Grosse: das Problem seiner Persönlichkeit und seines Wirkens*, 202, suggested inflammation of the lungs. It should, however, be considered in connection with the debate about Alexander's death.

[9]Arr. *Anabasis* 2.6–12. J. Roisman (1995), *Alexander the Great: Ancient and Modern Perspectives*, Part V is especially useful.

[10]Arr. *Anabasis* 2.14.

[11]From January through August 332.

[12]September to October 332.

[13]On Alexandria, see P. M. Fraser (1972), *Ptolemaic Alexandria*.

[14]Diod. Sic. 17.52.

[15]Plutarch, *Moralia* 328.

[16]See the study of the eastern foundations by Frank Holt (1988), *Alexander the Great and Bactria: The Formation of a Frontier in Central Asia.*

[17]For the sources and various interpretations of Alexander's claims of divinity, see Part VII in Roisman, (above, n. 9).

[18]Green (above, n. 8), 316.

[19]Arr. *Anabasis* 3.19.5.

[20]E. Badian (1960), "The Death of Parmenio," *Transactions and Proceedings of the American Philological Association* 91: 324–338; W. Heckel (1977), "The Conspiracy Against Philotas," *Phoenix* 31:9–21, finds this similar to the complicated plots of Agatha Christie. If the "plot" had been a ruse to ensnare Philotas, and Philotas *had* reported it to Alexander, the plotters would seem to have been in a serious position themselves. Both articles are reprinted in Roisman, (above, n. 9) part VI. Badian rethought his interpretation in 2000, E. Badian (2000),"Conspiracies," pp. 50–95 in A. B. Bosworth and E. J. Baynham, eds. (2000), *Alexander the Great in Fact and Fiction.*

[21]Arr. *Anabasis* 3.30.

[22]Arr. *Anabasis* 4.7.

[23]See Frank Holt (2003), *Alexander the Great and the Mystery of the Elephant Medallions.*

[24]Arr. *Anabasis* 7.4.

[25]Arrian calls her Barsine; he may have confused her with Barsine, the daughter of Artabazus, who was said to have been Alexander's mistress and the mother of his son Herakles; or Barsine may have been Statira's official name, a fact missed by the other ancient sources. See P. A. Brunt (1975), "Alexander, Barsine and Heracles," *Rivista di Filologia e di Istruzione Classica*, 22–34.

[26]Diod. Sic. 17. 115.1–4.

[27]Arr. *Anabasis* 7.16.1–4.

[28]Arr. *Anabasis* 7.19.3–6.

[29]Diod.Sic. 18.4. On these reported last plans, see P. A. Brunt (1983), *Arrian* II, Appendix 23; Bosworth (above, n. 4), chap. 8.

[30]But see A. B. Bosworth (1971), "The Death of Alexander the Great: Rumour and Propaganda," *Classical Quarterly* 21: 112–36.

[31]J. M. O'Brien (1992). *Alexander the Great: The Invisible Enemy.* While O'Brien provides a useful bibliography, his account should be approached with caution, since he makes no distinction between the sources, accepting whatever they report at face value.

[32]See D. Engels (1978), "A Note on Alexander's Death," *Classical Philology* 73: 224–228.

[33]A. B. Bosworth (1986), "Alexander and the Decline of Macedonia," *Journal of Hellenic Studies* 106: 1–12.

[34]A. B. Bosworth (above, n. 4), 2. For a debate about the interpretation of Alexander's campaign, see Ian Worthington (1999), "How 'Great' was Alexander?" *Ancient History Bulletin* 13.2:39–55; and the reply, Frank Holt (1999), "Alexander the Great Today: In the Interests of Historical Accuracy?" *Ancient History Bulletin* 13.3: 111–117.

[35]Richard A. Billows (1995), *Kings and Colonists: Aspects of Macedonian Imperialism*, chap. 7. See also E. Badian (1994). "Agis III: Revisions and Reflections," pp. 258–292 in I. Worthington, ed. (1994), *Ventures into Greek History*, esp. 261–268. N. G. L. Hammond (1989), "Casualties and Reinforcements of Citizen Soldiers in Greece and Macedon, *Journal of Hellenic Studies* 109:56–68. Bosworth defended his assessment in 2002, *The Legacy of Alexander: Politics, Warfare, and Propaganda under the Successors*, chap. 3.

[36]Billows (above, n. 35), 188.

[37]Billows (above, n. 35), 206.

15

THE HELLENISTIC WORLD

T he death of Alexander removed the charismatic figure that had held the great expedition together. His death occurred in the midst of plans for further exploration and conquest, and his adaptation of the Persian system to the administration of conquered territory was still evolving. He left the succession unclear; tradition reports that he gave his signet ring to Perdikkas and the rule to "whoever was strongest."

None of the surviving generals claimed the succession, which by long tradition belonged to the Argead clan. Roxane's child, Alexander IV, and Arrhidaios, as Philip III, were made joint rulers under a regency. The empire was divided among the major Macedonians: Ptolemy received Egypt, Antigonus western Asia Minor, Lysimachus Thrace, Antipater Macedonia (soon to be succeeded by his son Cassander), while Seleucus was given Babylonia. The elimination of the Argead heirs did not not take long. In 317 Olympias, the mother of Alexander, returned to Macedonia and imprisoned Philip Arrhidaios and his wife Eurydike; subsequently she had Philip stabbed and forced Eurydike to commit suicide. She also engineered the assassinations of more than a hundred of the followers of Cassander, who had inherited control of Macedonia from his father, but in 316 Cassander took revenge and killed her. Five years later Cassander killed the other dependent king, Alexander's son Alexander IV, as well as his mother Roxane, thus eliminating the Argead heirs of Alexander.

With legitimate heirs out of the way, the survivors threw themselves into a bloody struggle for Alexander's legacy, which went on intermittently for many years (Wars of the Successors). At the end, Alexander's empire was broken up into three major kingdoms ruled by Macedonian dynasties: the Antigonids who ruled in Macedonia and northern Greece; the Seleucids, who ruled from the Mediterranean to the borders of India; and the Ptolemies, who ruled Egypt and Libya. Syria/Palestine remained contested territory, shifting from Ptolemaic to Seleucid control and back again, and a fourth small kingdom later gained independence at Pergamon in Asia Minor, site of Alexander's treasury, under the rule of the **Attalid** dynasty.

After the Battle of Ipsus, 301 BCE

Antigonus the One-Eyed was the most aggressive and ambitious of the Successors[1] and the first to declare himself king. A coalition of the other generals formed to oppose him, defeating him in the Battle of Ipsus in central Anatolia, in which he fell. His defeat and death marked the end of the hope of maintaining Alexander's empire intact. In the settlement, Lysimachus was given all of Anatolia north of the Taurus Mountains, while Seleucus, who already held Babylonia and Iran, received Mesopotamia and the coastal regions of southern Anatolia and Syria. Ptolemy, who had never made it to the battle, remained in control of Egypt. The battle settled for a time the overall shape of the Hellenistic kingdoms.

Antigonid Macedonia. In 277 Antigonus II Gonatas, the grandson of Antigonus the One-Eyed, defeated an invasion of Gauls near Lysimacheia in Thrace. The Gauls, Celtic peoples whose original home had probably been in northwestern Europe, constituted a pervasive threat in the Hellenistic period.[2] They had been on the move for generations, steadily infringing on their southern neighbors. In 387 they sacked Rome, and in 279 some 300,000, accompanied by 2,000 wagons, entered Macedonia. A band reached Delphi but failed to capture the shrine as the result of a snowstorm, which the Greeks attributed to the intervention of Apollo. Antigonus' defeat of them at Lysimacheia won him control of Macedonia and most of the Greek states. This victory marked a turning point in Macedonian affairs, for Antigonus was able to hold on to power, and he established the Antigonid dynasty in Macedonia and Thessaly, a dynasty that ruled until the Roman conquest.

Antigonus' reign was, however, far from trouble free. Pyrrhus, the king of Epeiros (the home of Olympias, Alexander's mother) attacked him. A number of Greek cities headed by Athens waged war against him from 266 to 262 (the Chremonidean War), causing him to lose control of Macedonia for a short time. Antigonus prevailed, however, capturing Athens and retaking Macedonia. Then in 251 the Achaean League, under Aratos of Sikyon, gained power, and Antigonus lost Corinth for a time, although he succeeded in regaining it.

Despite all the warfare, Antigonus was a devotee of Stoic philosophy, who considered kingship as "noble servitude." He established a sophisticated court in Macedonia, to which he invited poets and scholars. Among them was Aratus of Soloi in Cilicia, who wrote a poem commemorating Antigonus' victory over the Gauls in 277, and an astronomical poem describing the constellations in which he identified Zeus as the all-knowing god of the Stoics. Another of the scholars at Antigonus' court was Hieronymos of Kardia, whose history (now lost) covered the period from the death of Alexander to the death of Pyrrhus in 272; parts of his work survive in the work of Diodorus Siculus, for whom he was the main source, and also in the works of Plutarch, Arrian, and Justin.

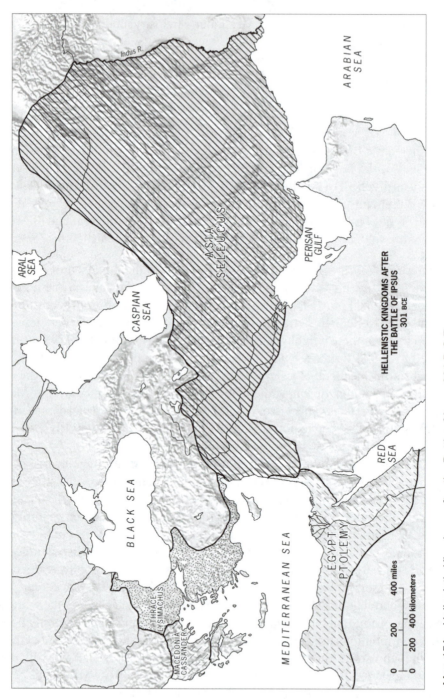

MACEDONIA
CASSANDER

THRACE
LYSIMACHUS

ARAL
SEA

CASPIAN
SEA

BLACK SEA

Indus R.

ASIA
SELEUCUS

PERISAN
GULF

ARABIAN
SEA

MEDITERRANEAN SEA

EGYPT
PTOLEMY

RED
SEA

HELLENISTIC KINGDOMS AFTER
THE BATTLE OF IPSUS
301 BCE

0   200   400 miles
0   200   400 kilometers

Map 15A   Hellenistic Kingdoms after the Battle of Ipsus 301 B.C.E.

334

Ptolemaic Egypt. Of the Hellenistic kingdoms, the most stable and long lasting was Ptolemaic Egypt. Alexander's general Ptolemy had been given Egypt in the initial distribution of territories, but he dramatically sealed the grant by kidnapping the body of Alexander, which he took to Alexandria and installed in a magnificent tomb (an archaeological prize yet to be found). Ptolemy and his descendants ruled the rich territory until the Romans took over after the death of Cleopatra in 30 BCE.

Almost all of the Ptolemaic rulers engaged in and supported intellectual and literary activities, as well as carrying on seemingly incessant warfare. The first Ptolemy (called Ptolemy I Soter) founded the Museum in Alexandria to provide an environment in which scholars could think, debate, and write while being supported by the state. He himself wrote an account of Alexander's campaigns that serves as an important source for modern historians. Ptolemy II Philadelphus, who may have founded the Library, was especially interested in science. Ptolemy Euergetes I wrote a literary account of his entry into Seleucia and Antioch in 245, and Ptolemy Philopator composed a tragedy and founded a temple and cult to Homer in Alexandria. Ptolemy Euergetes II wrote his memoirs and a work of Homeric criticism. Finally, Cleopatra VII composed literary works on various subjects and spoke a number of languages, including Egyptian; in this, she was unique among the Ptolemies.

On the domestic front, control of the powers of kingship was vital, and the Ptolemies sought to keep their bloodlines close to home. To this end, the most desirable matches were considered to be those with close relatives: marriages were concluded not simply between the traditional Greek cousins and second cousins, but between siblings, step- and half-siblings, and even between parents and their own offspring. Marriages were frequent, and multiple marriages and polygamy were common. Every domestic connection was in the interests of dynastic politics, not romantic love or personal attraction. Marriages with partners belonging to other Macedonian dynasties necessarily entailed diplomatic relationships, and need to be read in that way. For reasons unknown to modern science, all this close intermarriage does not seem to have resulted in large numbers of notably defective offspring or unusually high infant death rates, although infant death rates were high for all births throughout antiquity.

Because of their vast size, all of the Hellenistic kingdoms were bureaucratic in their organization, and the Ptolemaic dynasty was often singled out in the past for especially efficient management of its economy. However, Ptolemaic bureaucratic efficiency now appears to be somewhat of a mirage. The abundant Ptolemaic records that supported this view are now recognized not as evidence for rational planning, but as expressions of little more than wishful thinking. It is true that Egypt was a wealthy country and could provide abundant food supplies in most years, but the Ptolemies seldom managed it well, too often squandering their wealth in ostentatious display and mismanaging the Egyptian workers who produced that wealth. Official graft and corruption, and mistreatment and oppression of the Egyptian workforce, were widespread. Eventually, the Egyptian base upon which Ptolemaic rule rested spiraled down into widespread revolt, lawlessness, and chaos. Nonetheless, the dynasty outlasted its Hellenistic competitors and left lasting legacies of intellectual achievement.

In 285, two years before his death, Ptolemy I appointed his son as co-ruler, as Ptolemy II. He was called Philadelphos ("Sister-loving") because of his marriage to his full sister, Arsinoë II, a marriage that provided a model for later Ptolemaic brother-sister marriages. Arsinoë was co-ruler from about 275 until her death in 268, and her influence on Ptolemy II was internationally recognized. She was the first Ptolemaic queen to be portrayed on coins, and the first Ptolemaic ruler to enter an Egyptian temple as a "temple-sharing goddess." Theokritos celebrated her piety towards the god Adonis in his fifteenth *Idyll*.

Ptolemy II inherited an empire that extended over Libya, Rhodes, Palestine, Cyrenaica, much of the Aegean, and the Levant, together with the fleet that sustained it. The two imperatives of Ptolemaic foreign policy were to command the land route through the Levant and to control harbors in vital areas of the Mediterranean that would provide stopping points for rest and the replenishment of supplies for their fleets, in Cyprus, the Levant, and on some of the Aegean islands. Ptolemy II enlarged the fleet and completed a number of important projects, which collectively earned Alexandria the title "Mistress of the Sea." Among these projects, the most remarkable was the building of the great Pharos lighthouse between 285 and 280. More than 330 feet tall, it projected rays up to 70 miles out to sea, providing vital assistance to ships approaching the harbor.

Figure 15.1   Coin celebrating Arsinoe II, The John Max Wulfing Collection #397, twice life size. Courtesy of The John Max Wulfing Collection, Washington University, St. Louis.

> ## WEBSITE 15.1   EXCAVATIONS OF THE PHAROS
>
> The report of the discovery of an ancient monument once thought lost:
> UNESCO site: http://www.unesco.org/csi/pub/source/alex6.htm
> Nova site: http://www.pbs.org/wgbh/nova/sunken/
>
> In print, an article in *Archaeology*, March/April 1999.

It was probably during the reign of Ptolemy II that the great physician Herophilus worked at the Museum.[3] He followed the Hippocratic tradition of empirical observation and therapy based on humoral theory. The progress of Hippocratic medicine had been hindered, however, by its lack of knowledge of the anatomy of the human body.[4] Dissection of the bodies of the dead was forbidden by Greek religious norms, and even in Egypt, where the dead were mummified, the priests neither sought nor gained significant knowledge of the function of the body's operations in the process. The Ptolemies, however, saw the potential of such knowledge, and they permitted Herophilus to conduct autopsies, even providing the bodies of condemned criminals for the purpose. Some ancient reports also held that vivisection was practiced, but this is contested. As a result of his anatomical studies, Herophilus' achievements included the distinction of the parts of the eye; the discovery of the ovaries and fallopian tubes; the discovery of nerves and the distinction between sensory and motor nerves; the first reasonably accurate description of the liver; a basic description of the anatomy of the heart, its valves, and vascular system; the description of the paths of the cranial nerves; and the role of the brain as the center of the nervous system, rather than, as Aristotle and others had claimed, the heart.

Ptolemy III Euergetes I (246–221) inherited from Philadelphus a powerful empire with numerous territories, a large fleet, trade contacts, and vast financial resources. In his encouragement of trade, Euergetes also made important contributions to the advancement of knowledge by sponsoring investigations of coastal sites. During his reign, Timosthenes of Rhodes wrote a treatise on harbors, now lost. Euergetes also supported the geographer Eratosthenes, who served as a family tutor and director of the Library. Eratosthenes maintained that the world was round and estimated the circumference of the earth, writing *On the Measurement of the Earth,* and *Geographica,* which made vital contributions to the craft of map making.

Seleucid Asia.   Following the battle of Ipsus, the Seleucid kingdom, the largest of the Successor kingdoms, comprised for the most part the areas that had been part of the Persian Empire—a vast collection of sociopolitical and cultural entities. It was centered in the Fertile Crescent (Mesopotamia and north Syria) and western Iran; Anatolia and central Asia to the borders of India constituted its outer frontiers.[5] Just as the Persians had incorporated the ancient Assyrian and Babylonian political heritage into their imperial system in governing these areas, so the Seleucids in their turn incorporated Persian political institutions and practices into Macedonian rule.[6]

In 300 Seleucus founded the city of Antioch as one of his capitals to serve the limits of his kingdom as it then existed. Antioch is a typical example of what has been called "the mass production of new Hellenistic cities" under Alexander and his successors.[7] Nothing remains for excavation because of centuries of over-building, but according to ancient reports it was built on a gridiron plan, oriented to the sun and the prevailing winds according to the principles of city-planning laid down by the Milesian Hippodamus. Seleucus built two granaries, an aquaduct and sewer system, an *agora* with a temple of Zeus Bottios, and probably a theater. There were almost certainly other temples, as well as buildings of an administrative or military nature. The city was liberally adorned with statues, including figures representing Tyche (Fortune), the protector of the city and provider of success, fertility, and prosperity; Athena; and the eagle of Zeus that had showed the site of the city to its founders. The foundation ceremonies included the dedication of a statue in honor of Seleucus' horse, bearing the inscription "On this Seleucus fled Antigonus, and was saved; and returning and conquering him [Antigonus], he destroyed him."[8]

In 292 Seleucus made his son Antiochus co-ruler. It was perhaps at this time that he also handed on his second wife, Stratonike, to his son. This was an act memorialized in an anecdote that lauded the skill of the Hellenistic doctor Erasistratus. In the story, Erasistratus diagnosed a puzzling illness of Antiochus as love-sickness for his step-mother, leading the magnanimous Seleucus to give Stratonike to his son.[9] Antiochus with his new bride was sent to govern the eastern satrapies, where he brought order and stability, controlling the satraps, establishing or refounding cities, and issuing royal coinage.

During the last years of his reign, Seleucus extended his ambitions to Asia Minor. Pergamon, a city in northwestern Asia Minor where the treasury of Alexander was kept, was at that time part of the domain of Lysimachus. Lysimachus had, however, become increasingly unpopular in the area, in part because of his murder of his son Agathocles.[10] In 283 the keeper of the treasury at Pergamon, Philetairos, revolted against Lysimachus, offering his allegiance to Seleucus, and in 281 Seleucus defeated Lysimachos at Corupedium in Lydia and won control of Asia Minor. He soon overextended his reach, however, making a claim to Lysimachus' territories in Thrace and Macedonia. This quickly led to his assassination by Ptolemy Thunderbolt (son of Ptolemy I of Egypt), who himself coveted those territories and soon took them over.

The assassination of Seleucus did not cause a crisis of succession since he had made his son Antiochus co-ruler in 292. Thus Philetairos of Pergamon affirmed his continuing loyalty by delivering the king's ashes to Antiochus as the legitimate successor. Antiochus, however, granted Philetairos no wider authority as a reward for this show of fealty, and Philetairos was ambitious for more. As master of Pergamon, he used the wealth of the treasury liberally to ensure the support of neighboring cities, while biding his time.

One of Antiochus' major achievements was the defeat and settlement of the Gauls in Asia Minor (Galatia), a victory that earned him the title "Soter" (Savior). Despite his loss of

Pergamon in 262 (see below), he did much to consolidate his kingdom. He personally partic-ipated in the foundation ceremonies in the rebuilding of temples in Babylon and Borsippa, in accordance with the expectations of a Babylonian king. He established or re-established a large number of cities,[11] among them the ancient city of Sardis in Lydia, Antioch Margiana, originally one of Alexander's foundations, and Antioch-Persis, originally established by Seleucus.

At Ai Khanoum in Baktria, first established by Alexander, Antiochus carried out the ur-banization that is best known because of its excellent preservation when excavated.[13] Unfortunately, under the Taliban and subsequently, the remains have been thoroughly looted and destroyed. It was also the site of the discovery in 1966 of a copy of the Delphic Maxims, carried there by a Greek traveller, Klearchos, some time in the first half of the third century BCE.[14] This find demonstrates the dedication to Greek culture of these far-flung Seleucid cities, which went beyond the superficial aspects of architectural fashion to efforts to transmit a Greek way of life.

WEBSITE 15.2   AI KHANOUM

The site: http://www.utexas.edu/courses/citylife/ai_khanoum.html
This site provides two plans and a number of pictures, but no text. It can be supple-mented by a chapter from a guidebook to Afghanistan, which does not mention Antiochus, but contains excellent descriptions:
> http://www.zharov.com/dupree/chapter29.html

Delphic Maxims:
> http://www.csad.ox.ac.uk/CSAD/Images/200/Image277.html

Current conditions, looted and destroyed:
> http://www.flonnet.com/fl1906/19060660.htm
> http://www.iwpr.net/index.pl?archive/rca/rca_200110_77_4_eng.txt

---

In 262 Philetairos' successor in Pergamon—his nephew and adopted son Eumenes I (263–241)—defeated Antiochus when he attempted to strengthen Seleucid control in Asia Minor. Eumenes underscored Pergamon's independence by placing his own image on its coins instead of that of Seleucus, but it was his successor, his cousin and adopted son Attalus I (241–197), who was the first ruler of Pergamon to take the royal title, which he did after a victory over the Gauls. Attalus celebrated that victory by the dedication at the sanctuary on the citadel of Pergamon of a group of sculptures representing the defeated Gauls. In a larger sense, these also symbolized the victory of Hellenism over the barbari-ans. Among them were the well-known figures of a dying Gaul and of a Gaulic warrior killing himself and his wife.

WEBSITE 15.3   THE CELEBRATION OF VICTORY OVER THE GAULS BY ATTALUS I

http://www.mlahanas.de/Greeks/Arts/Pergamon.htm—a general site on Pergamon
http://harpy.uccs.edu/greek/sculpt/deadbarb.jpg—the Dying Gaul

Antiochus I was succeeded by his second son, Antiochus II (261–246). His reign is obscure because of the lack of sources, but it seems to have been marked by setbacks and losses. He tried but failed to extend Seleucid control to southern Syria, Phoenicia, and Palestine, and saw the continued independence of the kingdom of Pergamon and the further expansion of Ptolemy II of Egypt.

Antiochus II was succeeded by his eldest son, Seleucus II (246–225). In the early 230s of his reign, the satrap of Baktria, Diodotus, revolted and took the title of king. The causes of the revolt are not clear,[15] but the archaeological discoveries at Ai Khanoum demonstrate that the area was fully integrated into the greater Hellenistic world, and that Baktria under Diodotus (256?-235) and his successor, Diodotus II (235–225), remained prosperous. Nevertheless, the Seleucid realms were shrinking.

THE KINGDOMS AFTER ROME ENTERED THE PICTURE, CA. 200

An increasing factor in the Hellenistic period was the growth and expansion of the Republic of Rome. Rome had been slow to develop among its Italian neighbors, taking little or no part until the eighth century in the active network of interconnections that had linked the Etruscans with the Sardinians, Cypriots, and Greeks, and that had produced some of the earliest city-states in the area (see Chapter 4).

The earliest signs of what would become the city of Rome appear in about 750 BCE when archaeological evidence attests that a few settlers occupied huts on the Palatine hill. By 600 these settlers and others on nearby hills had joined together to form the city-state of Rome, but during most of the ensuing century they were ruled by Etruscan kings. About 509 they overthrew their last Etruscan king and began the gradual development of their own state. In 387 Rome was sacked by the Gauls, but it recovered and went on to conquer its Etruscan neighbors, one by one. By 265 all of Italy south of the Po River was under Roman control, and Rome turned against its remaining great rival, Phoenician Carthage. Beginning a series of wars that ended in 140, Rome finally totally destroyed the Phoenician city. During this time, and as part of their rivalry with the Carthaginians, the Romans became involved in the affairs of the Hellenistic kings.

Philip V of Macedon and Troubles with Rome.   In 221 the seventeen-year-old Philip succeeded to the Macedonian kingship as Philip V (221–179). In 215 Philip entered into an

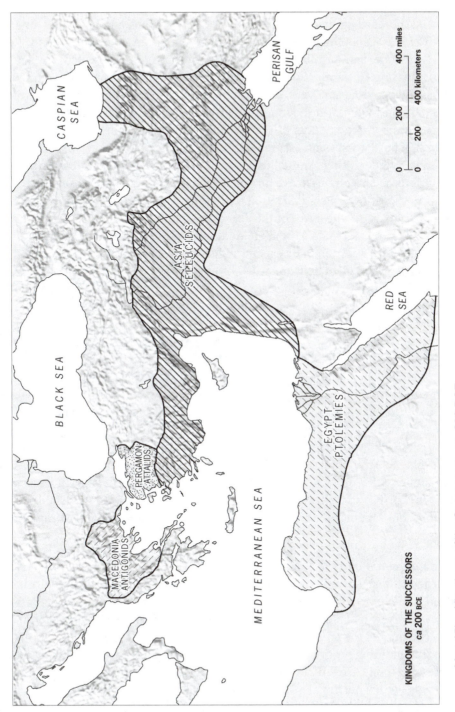

Map 15b Kingdoms of the Successors, ca. 200 BCE

alliance with the Carthaginians, which provoked the Romans and led to the First Macedonian War (215–204), and then into a war against a coalition of Rome, Egypt, Pergamon, Rhodes, Byzantium, and Aetolia (201–197). In both wars he was defeated. His last defeat, at Cynoscephalae in 197, was the first victory of Romans over Greeks in a major pitched battle. Philip was forced to accept very unfavorable terms: the evacuation of his forces from Greece, a thousand-talent war indemnity, the freedom of the Greek cities, and the establishment of garrisons in the "Fetters of Greece," the Greek cities of Demetrias, Chalcis, and Acrocorinth, whose possession assured control of Greece.

In 192 the Seleucid king Antiochus III invaded Greece, and the Roman Republic responded in force. The Romans drove him back to Asia Minor, where he suffered a major defeat at the Battle of Magnesia in 189, in which the cavalry of the kingdom of Pergamon assisted the Romans. By the terms of the Peace of Apamea (188 B.C.E.), Antiochus III gave up possession of most of Asia Minor. He died within a year of this defeat.

Philip V died in 179, soon after executing his younger son, Demetrius, for treason. The charge had been trumped up by Demetrius' brother Perseus, and Philip almost immediately recognized his mistake, but the kingdom nevertheless fell to Perseus. Perseus had difficulties with the Romans, not least because they had favored his executed brother Demetrius, who had gained popularity in Rome when he spent time there in his youth as a diplomatic hostage. Perseus' active campaigning against Macedonia's neighbors and his suspected intrigues with Eumenes of Pergamon roused Roman fears, and his marriage to Laodice, daughter of the Seleucid king Seleucus IV, added to Roman suspicions of his ambition in a culture in which diplomacy and the crafting of alliances was often a matter of dynastic marriages. Finally, in June 168 Roman forces under Aemilius Paullus met Perseus and the Macedonians at Pydna, on the coast of Macedonia, and slaughtered the Macedonian forces almost to a man. Perseus escaped to the island of Samothrace after burning the court records, and it was there that the Romans seized him. They took him off to exhibit in Paullus' triumph at Rome, along with a dazzling display of Macedonian wealth. Perseus, the last Antigonid king, died in captivity in Rome a few years later. The monarchy was abolished and Macedonia split into four separate states; in time they were also dissolved, and Macedon became a Roman province.

Attalid Pergamon and the Seleucids.   Meanwhile in Pergamon, the reign of Eumenes II (197–158), eldest son and successor of Attalus I, saw the peak of that city-kingdom's power and achievement. After the city's assistance to Rome in the defeat of Antiochus III, Pergamon received much of western Asia Minor by the terms of the Peace of Apameia. Eumenes II enlarged the city to include all of the southern slope of the acropolis, instituting a massive building program that turned the city into an architectural showplace that is still impressive today. He built a spectacular terraced, fan-shaped theater; the monumental Altar of Zeus, with a portrayal of the battle between the Giants and the Gods (now reconstructed and on exhibit in the Berlin Museum); and royal libraries, all of which were enclosed within new defensive walls (see web site below). Eumenes and his successors supported the arts and learning in Pergamon, and the city became a center for noted philosophers and artists.

Eumenes supported Rome in its defeat of Philip V of Macedonia. Unfortunately for Pergamon, this rendered its strength unnecessary and even suspect, and Rome began to withdraw its support, declaring the rebellious Gauls free, and favoring Eumenes' brother and co-ruler, Attalus II. Attalus II succeeded to the throne on the death of his brother in 158 and ruled until 138. During his reign, many scholars expelled from Alexandria in 146 found refuge in Pergamon, adding to its fame as an intellectual center. He is especially remembered for his gift to Athens of the famous stoa in the Athenian Agora that bears his name.

The Seleucid Antiochus III was succeeded by Seleucus IV. His younger brother, Antiochus IV Epiphanes, usurped the throne in 175 with the backing of Eumenes II of Pergamon, perhaps with the connivance of Rome. His reign marked a high point of luxury and magnificence for the Seleucid capital city of Antioch, at the time when Seleucid power was declining because of the shadow of Rome left by the defeat of Antiochus at Apamea. In fact, enlarging and adorning the capital of Antioch was part of his campaign to bolster and enhance Seleucid power by unifying the people with a renewed focus upon Hellenic religion and the ruler cult. To this end, he produced magnificent processions and spectacles, and even introduced Roman gladiatorial shows to Antioch. He also enhanced the city, adding many

Figure 15.2   The Stoa of Attalus in Athens, rebuilt by the American School of Classical Studies at Athens. Photo by Jayne Warner.

WEBSITE 15.4   THE CIVIC PROJECTS OF THE KINGS OF PERGAMON

The projects with which the Attalids embellished their city began with the statues of Attalos I, commemorating the defeat of the Gauls. The style of these works, Asian Baroque, differs from the Classical Attic norm, which portrayed the human body in its perfect form and in attitudes of calm self-control.

What do these projects reveal about the way in which the kings of Pergamon regarded themselves? about their resources? about their cultural identify and aspirations?

Eumenos II: the rebuilt city and the Pergamon Altar
        http://www.utexas.edu/courses/citylife/pergamon

---

new buildings, statues, and monuments. Most notably, he enlarged the city with the foundation of an entire new district, called Epiphania, which had its own *agora* and *bouleterion* (council-house). Antiochus also gave gifts to cities throughout his realm, as well as to numerous cities in Greece. He financed much of this expenditure by confiscating the property of non-Greek temples that were being used as bases by the opposition. Prominent among these was the Temple at Jerusalem, which he plundered, carrying off the sacred vessels to Antioch and rededicating the Temple to Zeus Olympius. Opposition to Seleucia in Judaea under the nationalists led by Judas Maccabaeus continued well past the death of Antiochus. Finally, in 164, under the child-king Antiochus V, negotiations led to concessions and the Temple was re-dedicated, an event celebrated by the Jewish festival of Hanukkah.[16] While the resolution of the Jewish revolt did not result in the independence of Judaea, many other small states broke away from the Seleucid domains in this period, including Babylonia and Commagene.

The last Attalid ruler of Pergamon was Attalus III (138–133), son of Eumenes II. The literary sources on his rule, which are mostly anecdotal and represent a hostile tradition, report that he was unpopular and neglected public affairs in order to devote himself to scientific study, especially botany and pharmacology. The sources may have been influenced, however, by his final act. At his death (of natural causes) in 133, he bequeathed the kingdom of Pergamon to Rome. While the Seleucid kingdom lived on for another century, it continued to decline, and in 64, Seleucid Syria became a province of the Roman Republic.

Egypt: A Time of Troubles, 217–130.   Egypt also fell into increasing decline from the late third century. Ptolemy III Euergetes was succeeded by Ptolemy IV Philopator I (222–205/204), who came to the throne at roughly the same time as Philip V of Macedonia and the Seleucid ruler Antiochus III the Great. This timing was unfortunate for Egypt, since these two energetic rulers demonstrated great interest in Ptolemaic possessions at a time when the Egyptian government had became increasingly corrupt, and Philopator took little interest in governmental affairs.

Trouble arose, ironically, because of an Egyptian victory. When Antiochus III invaded Egypt in the Fourth Syrian War (219–217), Philopator faced a serious dilemma. His lackadaisical attitude toward the job of ruling his country had led to the neglect of his mercenary forces, which were in no condition to meet the challenge of an invasion. Consequently, Philopator was forced to call upon native Egyptians and to recruit mercenaries from Libyia, Cyrene, Gaul, and Thrace. The new mercenaries performed well, and by the peace terms after the battle of Raphia (217), Philopator regained Coele-Syria and Phoenicia. However, the victory awakened the Egyptian troops to their own military potential, and a period of insurrection began. From 206, Thebes was lost to central control for over 20 years while in Alexandria, government was largely in the hands of court officials. In 205 two of these officials, Sosibios and Agathokles, murdered Philopator in a palace coup and managed to keep his death a secret for several months.

When Philopator was finally succeeded by his five-year-old son, Ptolemy V Epiphanes (205–180), Sosibios and Agathokles tried to hold on to power by arranging the murder of the queen mother, Arsinoë III. Both officials died soon afterwards, however; Agathokles was lynched by the people of Alexandria, with whom Arsinoë was popular.

Under Ptolemy V most of Egypt's possessions in the Aegean and Asia Minor were lost to the Seleucids and Macedonia. However, when the young king came of age in 197, he was crowned at Memphis in traditional Egyptian fashion, and a period of cooperation between native and Ptolemaic factions followed.

Egypt: Dynastic Strife, 180–118, and the Affairs of Ptolemy Physcon ("Fatty").   After the death of Ptolemy V in 180, Egypt was torn by dynastic strife that was marked by many lurid episodes, internal dynastic quarrels, expulsions and returns of rulers, as well as occasional coalitions among members of the royal house. Ptolemy V had two sons and a daughter. Upon his death, his elder son succeeded to the throne as a child, as Ptolemy Philometor, with his mother Cleopatra I ruling as regent. After the death of Cleopatra in 176, Ptolemy married his sister, Cleopatra II, and from 169 to 164 he ruled with Cleopatra and his younger brother, Ptolemy VIII Euegetes I (Physcon, "Fatty"). During this time, Antiochus invaded Egypt twice, in 169 and 168; the second time he was even crowned king and left only when Rome intervened.

In 164 Philomator was driven out by Physcon and fled to Rome, where he appealed for assistance in regaining his throne. In 163 the brothers finally reached an agreement, which involved a partition of the kingdom, Physcon receiving Cyrene, and Philomator receiving Alexandria. In 156 Philomator tried to have Physcon executed, while Physcon threatened to leave Cyrene to Rome in his will. In 154 Philomator captured Physcon off-limits in Cyprus and returned him to Cyrene. In 145 Philomator I intervened in Syria and was offered, but refused, the Seleucid throne. Shortly after this, he was wounded in battle and died from his wounds.

With the death of Philometor, Physcon seized his opportunity and returned to Alexandria from Cyrene. He married Philometor's widow, Cleopatra II, and proposed a joint rule of the two with Ptolemy VII, Cleopatra's son—a short-lived arrangement, for Physcon had Ptolemy VII assassinated at the wedding feast. In 144 Physcon was enthroned in Memphis; he celebrated this event by conducting mass purges of those who had opposed him, including the Jews and the intellectuals in the Museum. Prominent among the scholars who were expelled were Aristarchus, then chief librarian, and Apollodorus the geographer. The scholarly refugees from the Museum scattered to other intellectual centers, and from that time Pergamon, Rhodes, Athens, Berytus (Beirut), and Antioch surpassed Alexandria in intellectual accomplishments.

In 143 Physcon seduced and then married his niece Cleopatra III, Cleopatra II's daughter by Philometor. This did nothing to reduce family tensions, but the ill-assorted group continued together until 132/131 when riots broke out in support of Cleopatra II and the mob set fire to the palace. Physcon, Cleopatra III, and their children fled to Cyprus, while Cleopatra II had her twelve-year old son, Ptolemy Memphitis, acclaimed as king by the mob. Unfortunately, the boy at the time was either with Physcon in Cyprus or in Cyrene, and Physcon was able to get hold of him. He had the boy killed and dismembered, sending the pieces of the body in a box to Cleopatra II as a birthday present.[17] Not surprisingly, a civil war followed. It involved much intrigue as Cleopatra II, blockaded in Alexandria, offered the throne of Egypt to Demetrius II Nicator, the Seleucid husband of her daughter Cleopatra Thea. Demetrius advanced as far as the Egyptian border, but was stopped by Physcon's troops, and Cleopatra prudently followed him back to Syria. Demetrius was, however, faced with rebellion in Syria, where he was ultimately murdered. A year later (124) Cleopatra II was back in Alexandria, reconciled with both Physcon and Cleopatra III.

On the positive side, in 118 the trio made a vigorous attempt at re-establishing order and reviving the economy. They issued a royal amnesty forgiving all misdeeds except murder committed during the troubles, remitted debts to the crown, and declared a number of benefits and grants. Physcon died in 116, aged about 65, bequeathing his power to Cleopatra III and whichever of her sons she might prefer. Egypt then entered a fresh period of divisive royal intrigue, which would have tempted the Romans to intervene had they not themselves been engulfed in unending wars and internal strife at home, culminating in civil war between Caesar and Pompey.

The Ptolemaic dynasty finally was brought to an end by Roman intervention during the reign of Cleopatra VII (51–30), the most famous of all Ptolemies. She was the daughter of Ptolemy XII Auletes ("Fluteplayer"), under whom Ptolemaic affairs reached a low point with the loss of all of Egypt's foreign possessions. At the death of Auletes in 51, Cleopatra, at the age of 17, came to the throne as co-ruler with her 10-year-old brother (and husband) Ptolemy XIII. She was a strong and wily ruler and an accomplished woman, fluent in several languages; he is said to have been the only Ptolemy who learned the Egyptian language. She worked to exploit the political situation in Rome during the Civil War to Egypt's advantage, although ultimately she failed. Her affair with Julius Caesar in the 40s scandalized Rome and led to the birth of a son, Ptolemy XV, known as Caesarion. After Caesar's assassination, she returned to Egypt. She later became the mistress of Mark Anthony and ultimately his wife, according to Egyptian tradition. Under her influence, Anthony restored possession of Cyprus and Cilicia to Egypt. The pair defied Rome, aiming, it seems, to establish an empire in the east; in the end, however, they were unsuccessful. Octavian defeated Anthony at the battle of Actium in 31, and Cleopatra and Anthony fled to Alexandria. Ten months later, when Octavian captured Alexandria, Anthony committed suicide, as did Cleopatra shortly afterwards, according to legend by the bite of an asp. With the fall to Rome of the last Hellenistic kingdom, the focus of history shifted inexorably to Rome.

HELLENISTIC CULTURE

The official language of the kingdoms was that of their Macedonian rulers, Greek, but in a simplified form called **Koine** ("common," the language of the Greek New Testament). The use of local languages continued, however. Thus, in the Seleucid kingdom scribal languages such as Aramaic remained in use for official records,[18] while in Ptolemaic Egypt both Demotic (a somewhat formalized version of the Egyptian language) was used as well as Greek.[19] This was necessary since local people as well as Macedonians played a role in government service.

Hellenistic Kingship. Politically, the Hellenistic world was vastly different from the old world of the *polis*. Kingship was the rule everywhere. The descendants of Alexander's generals ruled autocratically over native populations in giant states, replacing the face-to-face interactions of a self-ruled *polis* by remote rulers. Kingship was kept firmly within family lines; kings were succeeded by their sons, or when sons were lacking, by near relatives adopted as sons, although violent struggles often arose over succession.

The Hellenistic kings saw kingship much as Alexander had, and this was essentially a Homeric view. A king needed to be accomplished in war and adventure, generous in the display and use of great wealth, and reverent toward the gods. Moreover, he himself was in some sense a sharer in a hierarchy of divinity that passed from the immortal Olympian gods, to numerous localized spirits associated with particular sacred places—heroes of semi-divine status (the offspring of gods and women) and men who had provided special benefits to the community, such as the founders of cities. In a word, a king must be "rich, generous, warlike, and godlike."[20] But as Samuel points out, these royal characteristics did not include "an idea of ordered government, of administration, of attention to and regulation of detail, of the monarch as the directing head of a complex bureaucracy."[21]

That a king in some sense shared in divinity was not an entirely new idea in Greek tradition; outstanding men had been given divine honors before. The reformer Lykourgos of Sparta (if he existed) was only a man, but he was worshiped as a god; founders of city-states were regularly worshipped as heroes after their deaths. Some Greek kings in the Classical period, such as the kings of Sparta and Macedonia, claimed descent from the gods. Alexander had focused upon and enlarged this idea, proclaiming himself the son of Zeus Ammon and even demanding *proskynesis*, although he soon discovered that the Macedonians were not entirely comfortable with the idea and he drew back (see Chapter 14). The Hellenistic rulers, however, gradually developed this idea even further, instituting official ruler cults. This was easiest in Egypt, where the Pharaoh had always been viewed as a god, and the utility of fulfilling the expectations of their large Egyptian population probably contributed to the Ptolemaic kings' increasing use of deification after Ptolemy II Philadelphus proclaimed his late father, Ptolemy I Soter, a god, and subsequently set him up beside his wife, Berenike, as Savior Gods. The Seleucids followed suit: Antiochus I deified his dead father, Seleucus I, and dedicated a temple and a precinct to him at Seleuceia in Pieria. Antiochus III instituted a dynastic cult throughout his empire, with high priests of the living king in all the provinces, including a priesthood for his wife, Laodice.[22] The Antigonids were the least enthusiastic about the use of the ruler cult; their kings were deified only after their deaths. In contrast to these dynastic cults, which the kings themselves instituted, Hellenistic rulers and their families were also the objects of municipal cults offered by cities that they had benefited. Thus Antigonus Monophthalmus was honored as a god by Scepsis in 311, and together with his son Demetrius, at Athens and in the Cyclades a few years later; Lysimachus in 287/286 received a statue, an altar, and an annual procession from Priene in return for military aid against its neighbor Magnesia.

Did the people really believe that these human rulers were gods? We cannot fairly answer that question today, or perhaps even understand it, coming as we do from strongly monotheistic religious traditions. It may help in understanding to focus on the idea that in Greek polytheistic thought divinity was not an absolute condition; rather, the Greeks saw various grades of divinity. In their view, displaying attributes of divinity was quite different from being an immortal god. Since, on the human side of the spectrum, the exploits of some people, especially kings, far surpassed anything a common person could achieve, people revered them for their unusual achievements, which they might well consider in some sense divine. Mikalson suggests that the introduction of a divine cult of rulers by Greek cities may be seen "as a recognition in these cities that these supremely powerful kings were now providing to their Greek subjects what Greeks traditionally asked of their gods: peace, protection against foreign enemies, food, economic prosperity, and personal safety… critical elements in their lives that were no longer in their own control."[23] On the other hand, as Alexander discovered, some people objected strongly to the claim of divine kingship, especially among the elite, who were often quite aware of the human failings of their kings. Nevertheless, even skeptics could recognize and exploit the utility of a ruler cult in inspiring obedience among the masses of people.

Homeric kings were also great warriors. Keeping this in mind makes it easier to understand the seemingly endless wars in which the Hellenistic kings engaged. Much of this bellicose activity involved kings fighting for the sake of bolstering their kingly prestige. There were, however, also good strategic reasons why a Hellenistic king might covet a particular piece of territory. Many vital resources had to be obtained from a distance. Timber, necessary for the construction of ships and monumental buildings, was lacking in Egypt but available in abundance in Macedonia and Lebanon. Lebanon also offered the necessities of elite display: purple dyed cloth, intricately carved ivory, and the gold and spices that came via the Levant from India and beyond. Cyprus had an abundance of copper, as well as skilled metal workers. In order to access these foreign sources, a king had to maintain a fleet, or at least provide harbors for the merchant ships of others. Thus coastal areas with harbors suitable for a fleet were much contested pieces of real estate, as were interim naval bases that would enable these fleets to operate freely at a distance wherever the need arose. Such considerations lie behind a number of wars, especially the ongoing contests between the Ptolemies and the Seleucids for control of the Syria-Palestine coasts, which also offered access to trade routes by land to India and the east.

Homeric kings were also noted as generous hosts, and this was a tradition that the Macedonian kings had long followed by their royal patronage of the arts. Alexander I invited the poet Pindar to his court, and Archelaus (413–399) played host to Euripides, whose play, *Bacchae* was first performed at the Macedonian court and was perhaps written there as well. Archelaus also played host to Agathon, the tragic poet, and to the painter Zeuxis. The father of Philip II employed Aristotle's father as a doctor at his court, and Philip chose his son Aristotle as a tutor for the young Alexander. Aristotle's Lyceum was itself a "Mouseion"—a temple of the Muses—and it provided a model for the Ptolemy's establishment of the Museum in Alexandria. The Attalids of Pergamon were especially given to architectural expressions of the grandeur and achievements of their city, monuments that are still impressive today even in ruins.

Homer also provided models for the "unofficial" power that women often exercised in Hellenistic royal households. Penelope managed, even without official powers, to juggle her suitors for years in order to maintain Odysseus' rights as the master of the *oikos* and those of their young son as his heir [*Od.* 2. 85–110]. Unlike Athenian women, she appeared in the presence of men, coming from her room to chastise the suitors for their rowdiness. Her son Telemachus, however, demonstrated the limits of a woman's actions, bluntly telling her that it was no longer necessary for her to run the household since he was now an adult, and sending her back to her room (*Od.* 1.328–344). But when Telemachus visited Menelaus of Sparta in search of information about his father, a woman, Helen, played a central role in the interview. She came and sat beside her husband and questioned Telemachus "about everything" (*Od.* 4.120–147); she then prepared a soothing drink for the visitors and told them about events at Troy (*Od.* 4.219–264). In Phaiakia, the princess Nausicaa advised the disheveled Odysseus, whom she found on the beach, to approach her mother, Arete, in supplication (*Od* 6.305–315). When Odysseus came before the royal couple, he followed Nausicaa's advice and addressed Arete (*Od.* 7.140–152), and it was Arete who urged him to tell his story (*Od.* 7.231–239).

Similarly, Macedonian royal women were allowed—or took—a considerable informal role in public affairs, especially in the turmoil of the wars of the Successors. Some, surpassing the activities of Homeric royal women, even fought in battle. Duris of Samos reported that the first war between two women was fought between Olympias, the mother of Alexander, and Eurydike, the granddaughter of Philip's first wife, the Illyrian Audata.[24] Audata's daughter Cyannane raised an army and went to meet the Macedonian army of Craterus and Antipater in Asia to force the marriage of her daughter Eurydike to Arrhidaios; she was murdered in the attempt by Alcetas, the brother of the regent Perdikkas, but the army rebelled and forced the marriage of the two.[25] Eurydike was trained by her mother in warfare and followed her example in stirring up and influencing the army,[26] but she eventually fell victim to Olympias, who was responsible for both her death, a forced suicide, and the death of Arrhidaios.[27] Olympias also conducted a bloody purge, killing a hundred prominent Macedonians.[28]

In the later, more settled Antigonid period (277–168 B.C.E.) there was a dramatic decline in the political and military influence of royal women in Macedonia.[29] In contrast to this decline in Macedonia, however, women gained in prominence over time in the Ptolemaic and Seleucid kingdoms, perhaps because these kingdoms emphasized dynastic succession and made more use of dynastic marriage alliances than did the Antigonids.[30] For the most part, however, Hellenistic royal women held little real power. They were prominent in the sense that they served as pawns in the game of political marriages and as vehicles of dynastic propaganda; cities were named after them and cult worship was held for them. These were honorific acts, however, carried out in the interests of male-centered dynasties. Only a few exceptional royal women acting in exceptional situations were later able to manipulate the machinery of male power as the early Macedonian women did, and even fewer were powerful in their own right. In the later Ptolemaic dynasty, however, some queens did play independent roles in dynastic struggles, such as Cleopatra II, and, most famously, Cleopatra VII, who manipulated even Rome in her affairs with Julius Caesar and Mark Anthony.

Wealth and Insecurity: Religion and Philosophy.   Although the vast majority of people still led agrarian lives, for many enterprising individuals, the Hellenistic period was one of expanding possibilities, and the lives of many ordinary people were vastly improved. There was much greater freedom of movement than in the Classical period, even though some—perhaps most—of it was forced by economic circumstances. The kings commanded vast wealth and required large staffs to fill administrative jobs, as well as large numbers of mercenaries to fill their armies, and this opened opportunities for those willing to move. Men were also in demand as settlers for the many new city foundations, especially in the far reaches of the kingdoms. Divorced from ancestral ties to *polis* communities, many who resettled found opportunities for landholding and civic participation that they had never experienced before. Women—at least, women of wealth—also shared in the extension of opportunities for economic and political activity, some even holding minor offices in return for their willingness to use their wealth for civic purposes.[31] However, as was the case with royal women, most of this was in the service of husband and family, and marriages and divorces were still arranged by men for economic and political aims, with women having little or no say in their fate.

The rapidly changing Hellenistic world led not only to new economic and political opportunities for many individuals; it also was an unsettling environment in which to live. The search for security and a sense of control over one's life became a crucial concern. This led in many directions, from the establishment of ruler cults by the various cities, to an increased interest in mystical and savior cults and new philosophical systems.

Mystical and savior cults, especially those of healer gods, were especially popular. Some were devoted to non-Greek divinities, for the polytheistic Greeks had no problems with adding new helpers to their pantheon. The best-known example is Sarapis, an amalgamation of the Egyptian god of the underworld, Osiris, and the Apis bull. Both Osiris and the Apis bull had long associations with the Pharaohs, and the Ptolemaic kings were quick to adopt Sarapis as a guarantor of their own power, building a Sarapeion (Temple of Sarapis) in Alexandria in his honor. Sarapis was accompanied by Isis, the sister-wife of Osiris, goddess of the Nile flood, and thus of fertility, who was a special protector of women, especially in childbirth. Both Sarapis and Isis were healing gods who treated the sick by incubation; the worshipers would sleep overnight in the temple, and while they slept, the god would either heal them directly or provide a prescription in a dream. The worship of Sarapis and Isis spread throughout the Hellenistic world and later into the world of Rome.

The Greek healing god Asclepius, son of Apollo and a mortal woman, accompanied by his dog and his snake, had a long life as a popular healing god, although his worship seems not to have gone back much before the late fifth century. He was introduced into Athens from Epidauros in 420 by the tragedian Sophocles, perhaps as a result of the Athenian plague. From the fourth century his worship spread to many areas of the Mediterranean, with major shrines established in Kos, Pergamon, and Epidauros, all devoted to incubation healing. He has been seen as a chief competitor of the Christian Jesus.

Another divinity that gained great popularity in the Hellenistic period was Tyche (Chance), a god who reflects well the irrational and uncontrollable aspects of life in the Hellenistic world. Tyche was by nature ambivalent; she could be either favorable or unfavorable. However, a pervasive optimism underlying Hellenistic life led to the view that Chance was, on the whole, likely to be favorable. (A similar irrational optimism afflicts the long lines of obviously needy people who wait to buy lottery tickets in the United States, as well as the more affluent speculators in the boom of the moment, whether dot.com or real estate.)

These new divinities, who were primarily helpers seen as meeting the needs of the individuals who called upon them, did not, however, displace traditional *polis* religion. Dedications continued at traditional local shrines of the various *poleis* and at the great panhellenic shrines. Life in the *polis* was a continuous round of cult festivals, celebrated as in the Classical period, with dramatic performances and with musical, athletic, and other contests.

Finally, for a segment of the population, philosophy also offered ways to cope with the uncertainties of life. The best known and most influential of the schools of philosophy was Stoicism, a system of thought developed by Zeno of Citium and brought to Athens in 313. It was named for the meeting place used by Zeno in Athens, the Stoa Poecile (Painted Porch). The Stoics were radical empiricists, and their philosophy was totally materialistic: the world is made up of material objects and their interactions, which operate according to laws that have no exceptions. It is these laws that men call Fate or Providence. At the same time, human action is free and morally responsible. Because humans are morally responsible, however, they cannot withdraw from the world, but must participate in order to make the best of their situation. The emphasis thus falls upon controlling what one can control (one's internal state), while accepting the uncontrollable blows inflicted by the external world with equanimity. The Antigonid king Antigonus II Gonatas was devoted to Stoicism, and it later became especially popular among, and useful to, the Roman elite, who served their country loyally as they faced, and often were the victims of, the irrational actions of their rulers.

Another popular school of philosophy was Epicurianism, invented by Epicurus (341–270), a native of Samos who eventually settled in Athens. According to Epicurus, the cosmos consists of material atoms swirling about according to no overriding purpose. Gods exist, but they do not interact with, or concern themselves with, the lives of men. Since one cannot control one's destiny, the best course is to make life as pleasurable as possible, although this is tempered by the realization that many so-called pleasures in reality end up causing pain. The ideal thus becomes not a life of riotous parties, but a quiet and private existence, as pain-free as possible.

WEBSITE 15.5

For a full discussion of Stocism and Epicurianism, see the website of the Stanford Encyclopedia of Philosophy:

http://plato.stanford.edu/entries/stoicism/#Oth
http://plato.stanford.edu/entries/epicurus/#Oth

The Polis in the Hellenistic World.   Despite the replacement of the *polis* by the territorial kingdom as the basic political form, cities continued to play a vital role in the Hellenistic kingdoms. They served rulers as capitals and provided the framework of administration, as well as continuing to be the centers of culture and of an expanding commerce. The foundation of new Greek cities was a major activity of the kings, and one that had roots going far back in Greek and Macedonian history, from the overseas settlements of the Greeks in the eighth century, to the foundation of Philippoi by Philip and the many Alexandrias founded by Alexander. The new foundations allowed the kings to consolidate their control over large

territories of non-Greek-speaking peoples, but they also provided important political benefits for their inhabitants. They opened up the possibility of land ownership and civic participation for large numbers of Greeks and Macedonians. Moreover, cities could enhance the
lives of their inhabitants by bargaining with Hellenistic kings for their "freedom"—from
various taxes and other burdens—and by lavishing honors and accolades upon the kings that
often took the form of civic improvements that made life better for the citizens. It was a sym-
biotic relation; kings and cities both needed, and profited from, the other.[32]

SUGGESTIONS FOR FURTHER READING

Two recent authoritative treatments of Hellenistic history are Peter Green (1990), *Alexander
to Actium: The Historical Evolution of the Hellenistic Age*; and Graham Shipley (2000), *The
Greek World after Alexander 323–30 BC*. On specific topics, see P. M. Fraser (1972), *Ptolemaic Alexandria*; Susan Sherwin-White and Amélie Kuhrt (1993), *From Samarkhand to
Sardis: A New Approach to the Seleucid Empire*; Frank L. Holt (1999), *Thundering Zeus :
The Making of Hellenistic Bactria*; and Carol Bakhos (2005), *Ancient Judaism in its Hellenistic Context*. On women in the Hellenistic period, see Elizabeth Carney (2000), *Women
and Monarchy in Macedonia*; and Sarah Pomeroy (1984/1992), *Women in Hellenistic
Egypt: From Alexander to Cleopatra*.

MAP STUDY

Alexandria, Pergamon, Seleucia on the Tigris, Antioch.
The extent of the various kingdoms after the battle of Ipsus in 301 and in 200.
Detailed maps reprinted from William Shepherd (either 1911 or 1923–1926 edition), *Historical Atlas*, can be found on the website: http://www.lib.utexas.edu/maps/historical/shep-
herd_1911/shepherd-c-018-019.jpg

ENDNOTES

[1]See Richard Billows (1990), *Antigonos the One-Eyed and the Creation of the Hellenistic State*.

[2]Graham Shipley (2000), *The Greek World after Alexander 323–30 BC*. 52–54.

[3]Estimated dates 300–250. Whether the physician Erasistratus, who also is reported to have performed
dissections of human cadavers and made important contributions to knowledge about the body, worked in
Alexandria is a contested question.

[4]See P. M. Fraser (1972), *Ptolemaic Alexandria*, 338–376.

[5]Modern Turkey, Syria, Lebanon, Iraq, Kuwait, Iran, Afghanistan, and large portions of the former Soviet Union: Armenia, Tadzhikistan, Uzbekistan, and Turkmenistan.

[6]Susan Sherwin-White and Amélie Kuhrt (1993), *From Samarkhand to Sardis: A New Approach to the
Seleucid Empire*, 1.

[7]R. E. Wycherley (1976), *How the Greeks Built Cities*, 35.

[8]Glanville Downey (1961), *A History of Antioch in Syria : From Seleucus to the Arab Conquest*, 77.

[9]Plutarch *Demetrius*, 38; Appian, *Syrian Wars*, 59–61.

[10]Sherwin-White and Kuhrt (above, n. 6), 31.

[11]See Sherwin-White and Kuhrt (above, n. 6) 20–21, 142–187.

[12] Sherwin-White and Kuhrt (above, n. 6) 180–184.

[13]Frank L. Holt (1999), *Thundering Zeus : The Making of Hellenistic Bactria*, 41–44.

[14]Holt (above, n. 13) 37–47, Appendix D, Inscription #4; L. Robert, *Comptes rendus de l'Académe des Inscriptions et Belles-Lettres* (1968), 422–457, #2.

[15]Sherwin-White and Kuhrt (above, n. 6) 107–111. See also Holt, (above, n. 13), 52–66.

[16]I *Macc.* 1–2. See Carole Bakhos (2005), *Ancient Judaism in its Hellenistic Context.*

[17]Diodorus Siculus 34.14.

[18]Shipley (above, n. 2), 295.

[19]Shipley (above, n. 2), 197–201.

[20]Adapted from Alan E. Samuel (1989), *The Shifting Sands of History: Interpretations of Ptolemaic Egypt*, 68, 75.

[21]Samuel (above, n. 20), 81.

[22]See Sherwin-White and Kuhrt (above, n. 6), 202–210, with translations of the decrees establishing the cults.

[23]Jon D. Mikalson (2005), *Ancient Greek Religion*, 203.

[24]Reported by Athenaeus 560. Diodorus Siculus 19.11.2 reports that, during Eurydike's struggles with Olympias, the Macedonian general Polyperchon met Euydike's army with the expectation of deciding the campaign in a single battle, but Eurydike's forces changed their allegiance out of respect for Olympias.

[25]Arr. F Gr H 156, F 9.22–23; Polyaen. 8.60. Elizabeth Carney (2000), *Women and Monarchy in Macedonia*, 129–131.

[26]Diodorus Siculus 18.39.1–4; Carney (above, n. 25), 40–46, 132–133.

[27]Diodorus Siculus 19.11.5–7; Carney (above, n. 25), 136–137.

[28]Diodorus Siculus 19.11.7; Carney (above, n. 25), 122.

[29]Carney (above, n. 25), 180.

[30]Carney (above, n. 25), 203.

[31]See Sarah Pomeroy (1984/1992), *Women in Hellenistic Egypt: From Alexander to Cleopatra.* Carney (above, n. 25).

[32]See Billows (above, n. 1), 70–73.

GLOSSARY

acropolis: the defensible hill that formed the nucleus of a Greek city; when the Athenian acropolis is referred to, it is often capitalized.

Aer: the basic substance of the cosmos according to the philosopher Anaximenes.

agoge: a rigorous system of training and education for Spartan boys that sought to develop courage and collective identity while weakening family ties.

agon: generally, a contest; applied to the formalized contests of an Attic comedy, which often begin with a physical fight and end with a verbal contest.

agora: the civic center of a polis; buying and selling took place, but the agora was far more than a market.

Agroikoi: three archons, probably of farmer or less than noble status, of the board appointed to resolve the anarchy after the reforms of Solon.

Alkmeonides: The Athenian clan considered to be accursed as a result of the killing of suppliants by Kylon in the seventh century. Some prominent Athenians were Aklmeonides: Kleisthenes, Perikles, Alkibiades.

Amazons: literally, *a-mazon*, "without-a-breast"; legendary female warriors and rulers in their own barbarian society in Scythia, they cauterized one breast in order to be able to fight more effectively with a bow; as non-Greek and non-male, they served an ideological function for the Athenians, representing the Barbarian "other."

Amphictiony,: a coalition of states supporting a common shrine, for example, at Delphi.

Antigonids: the ruling familiy in Macedonia in the Hellenistic period.

antilogy: a set of paired speeches that argue opposite sides of a given thesis; it was a favorite form of Sophistic teaching.

Apeiron: in the world system of the philosopher Anaximander, the Boundless or Unlimited, out of which everything arises and into which everything passes away.

apoikia: a permanent Greek settlement based on the possession of an agricultural hinterland, or *chora*, often translated as "colony."

Archon: An Athenian official.

Archon Eponymous: the Athenian archon whose name was used as a designation of the year.

Areopagus Council: Athenian aristocratic council consisting of men who had served as archons; membership was for life, and the power of the council was apparently great but vague before the reforms of Ephialtes in the early fifth century; after the reforms, it retained mainly its ancient religious prerogatives, notably the trial of homicide cases.

Aristotle: philosopher, pupil of Plato, teacher of Alexander the Great; founded the school and research institution called the Lycaeum in which the constitutions of the Greek cities were collected; historical source on a number of subjects.

astu: the urban center of a polis.

Athenian Tribute Lists (ATL): fragmentary lists inscribed on stone covering several years and listing the portions of the tribute of the members of the Delian League that were paid to the goddess Athena; the ATL allows historians to reconstruct the payments of tribute.

Attalids: the ruling family in Pergamon in the Hellenistic period.

Bacchiads: the closed group of aristocrats that ruled Corinth up to the middle of the seventh century; it consisted of 200 members of a single clan who intermarried only among themselves.

basileus (pl. *basileis*): Greek word for king; during the Mycenaean period it was probably applied to a minor local official.

Building BG: a monumental building at Lerna in the EH II period.

chora: the agricultural territory of a polis, often containing dependent villages.

cleruchy: a settlement of Athenian citizens established in an allied city; the *cleruchs* kept their Athenian citizenship and were assigned plots of land that were worked for them by the local owners; because the cleruchs were usually of the lowest property class, this helped to relieve Athens of some of its poorer population and also provided an element of control over the allied population.

Companions: a group of Macedonian nobles, originally cavalrymen, who acted as companions of the king; they received estates in return for their loyalty and service.

Cyclopean masonry: Mycenaean building technique using huge blocks that seemed to later Greeks so big that only the Cyclops could have lifted them.

dactylic hexameter: the special meter for Greek epic, consisting of six feet, each with a pattern of short and long syllables in the form, long, short, short (the dactyle), or its equivalent (two shorts substituted for a long or visa versa).

damos: Dorian form of *demos*, people (citizen men in assembly).

decarchies: boards of ten local citizens set up by Lysander in a number of cities in Asia Minor after the Peloponnesian War; they served to govern their own poleis under Spartan control.

Delphic Amphictyony: the league of states set up to control and administer the shrine of Apollo at Delphi.

demagogue: a "leader of the people"; a pejorative term applied to the Athenian democratic leaders who held power after the death of Pericles.

Demiourgoi: two Athenian archons of craftsman status on the board appointed to resolve the anarchy after the reforms of Solon.

demiourgoi: craftsmen.

demes: villages that were the basis of Kleisthenes' tribal reform; membership in a *deme* became the official basis of Athenian citizenship.

demos: Greek word meaning "people"; probably originally the assemblied army, it was applied to the collective of male citizens in a polis.

diolkos: the stone dragway for ships across the Isthmus of Corinth built by the tyrant Periander in the early sixth century.

Dorian Invation: Greek tradition held that Greeks who spoke in the Dorian dialect were driven out of Greece and returned as invaders at the end of the Bronze Age, but contemporary scholarship suggests that they either filtered in after the collapse of the Mycenaean palaces, or were the underclass of the palace economy, left behind after the collapse.

Doric order: the simplest of the three orders of classical Greek architecture, it is characterized by fluted, heavy columns with simple cushion-shaped capitals and by a metope-and-triglyph frieze.

dromos: the long entryway that led into a tholos tomb.

Emporoi: trade centers.

Enneakrounos: the ornamental fountain house built by the tyrant Peisistratos in the Athenian agora as part of his water supply system.

entablature: in Greek temple architecture, the horizontal superstructure supported by the columns, including the frieze.

ephebes: a Greek term for men between the ages of 18 and 20, a period of military training prior to being admitted to adult citizen status

Ephetai: in Athens, a special court to try criminal cases.

ephor: one of the five annually elected Spartan officials who acted as a check on the kings.

epibatos: a trader who sailed with his merchandise on a ship owned by another; a passenger.

epikleros: literally, "with the estate"; a daughter who was the sole surviving offspring and thus inherited her father's *oikos*; her nearest agnatic male relative, her father's brother or brother's son, was obliged to marry her or arrange a marriage for her in order to produce a son who would be the effective heir of the deceased and carry on the *oikos*.

Erechtheion: a temple on the Athenian acropolis that was part of the Periklean Building Program, featuring a mixture of archaic cults and architectural styles.

Ethnos (plural, **ethne**): a loosely-structured group of people living as a tribe, not as a *polis*.

eunomia: orderly conduct of government, having good laws.

Eupatrids: "sons of good fathers"; the term was applied to the old aristocratic families in Athens who originally ruled over the state.

Faience: a vitreus paste made from ground sand.

frieze: in Greek temple architecture, a horizontal band on the entablature, decorated by running figures in the Ionic order and by metopes and triglyphs in the Doric order.

genos: the Greek term for clan.

Gerousia: Spartan board of 30 elders consisting of the two kings and 28 men over 60 who were elected for life; it put proposals before the Assembly for vote without debate.

Great Rhetra: the Spartan constitution, traditionally attributed to the semi-legendary Lykurgus.

Greater Panathenaia: the enhanced celebration of the *Panathenaia* (the annual festival of Athena) that took place every fourth year; traditionally attributed to the tyrant Peisistratos.

Greek Renaissance: the eighth century, the period when Homer recalled the Bronze Age Mycenaean world; also called the Orientalizing Revolution because contacts with the east led to adoption of eastern orientalizing motifs in vase painting.

guest-friendship (xenia): a relationship of mutual hospitality and privilege between two men in different poleis or between two states.

harmost: a Spartan governor of a dependent poleis, a role instituted by Lysander; the term was also used by the Thebans.

hebontes: Spartan male citizens between 20 and 30 who played a quasi-parental role in socializing their young charges in the *agoge*.

hektemoroi: in Athens before the reforms of Solon, men who were "sixth-parters," working the land of others for a one-sixth rent; when they failed to pay, they fell into slavery.

Helen: mythical character, wife of King Menelaus of Sparta; her seduction by Paris, son of Priam of Troy, was the cause of the Trojan War.

Heliaea: the Athenian assembly when it met as a court of appeal; instituted by the reforms of Solon.

helot: in Sparta, an agricultural worker tied to the land allotment of a Spartan citizen; helots and their families produced food for the Spartans and accompanied them into battle as servers.

Heroön: a tomb where honor was paid, and sacrifices offered, to a deceased mortal considered to be a hero (between a mortal and a god).

hetairoi: literally, companions or friends; in the Archaic period, the small circle of aristocratic friends who provided each other with political support; in the Classical period, its meaning became broader and it could be used to refer to political supporters of any social class; thus Kleisthenes was said to take the *demos* as his *hetairoi.*

hetaira: a female companion; it usually refers to a woman who entertained men in both a social and sexual sense.

Hippeis: the second of the property classes of the reforms of Solon; they were men whose property yielded 300 to 500 bushels, which made them able to support horses; they were eligible for the lesser offices and possibly for the archonship.

homoioi: Equals, or Similars; status term applied to Spartan male citizens.

hoplites: Greek infantrymen who fought in a line formation using a round shield called a *hoplon*; they had to supply their own armor and weapons, and hence being a hoplite involved having a certain economic status, probably *Zeugitae.*

Horns of Consecration: Minoan symbol, stylized horns of an ox.

Horos (plural **horoi**): border marker; one of Solon's reforms was to remove the *horoi*, freeing the land in Attica; although in the fourth century *horoi* marked mortgaged land, their exact legal function in Solon's time is not understood.

House of Tiles: a monumental building at Lerna, constructed over Building BG in the EH II period; it is named after its tile roof; functions of display, storage, and public convenience were apparent, and it perhaps paralleled the proto-palaces on Crete.

Hypomeiones: a Spartan status term, Inferiors; perhaps men who failed to be elected to a mess, or failed to keep up their required mess contributions.

Ionian League: a league that was established by twelve Ionian cities founded during the Ionian Migration at the end of the Mycenaean period; its members celebrated their ethnic identity in the festival of the Panionia.

Ionian Migration: the legendary migration of Ionian Greeks from mainland Greece to Anatolia at the end of the Bronze Age, under the leadership of Athens.

Ionic order: one of the three orders of classical Greek architecture, characterized by fluted columns with ornamental scrolls on the capitals and by a running frieze.

isonomia: equality under law; the term applied to the constitution of Kleisthenes.

Kadmeia: the acropolis of Thebes.

Keftiu: Egyptian word, "People of the Islands," probably refering to the Minoans.

Koine: the simplified form of Greek that was widely used in the Hellenistic kingdoms; also areas with similar material culture.

Kouloures: monumental circular walled underground pits, placed in front of the principal façade of a Minoan palace, probably for the storage of grain.

Krypteia: in Sparta, a Secret Service that consisted of young men up to age 30; they exercised control by terror over the helots, killing those who showed dangerous leadership potential.

kylix: a Greek drinking cup.

laconic: terseness of speech; the style adopted by the Spartans (from "Lakonia," with a Latinized transliteration of the Greek).

Lakedaimonia: see Lakonia.

Lakonia: the territory of Sparta.

Lapiths: a legendary Thessalian people of the heroic age, conquerors of the centaurs.

lawagetas: a Mycenaean official lower in rank than the wanax; in later Greek the term meant "Leader of the War-host."

Leuktra, battle of: battle in 371 B.C.E. in which the Thebans under Epaminondas defeated the Spartans, signalling the end of Spartan military supremacy in Greece.

Linear A: Minoan syllabic script; has not been deciphered yet.

Linear B: Mycenaean syllabic script; deciphered as early Greek; used for palace records.

liturgy: civic expenses assigned to wealthy Athenians, including the provision of choruses for dramatic festivals and the outfitting of triremes; the person assigned a liturgy could enter a suit objecting that he was less capable of affording the expense than another specific citizen and challenging him to either accept the liturgy or exchange properties; the suit was called an *antidosis*, a giving-in-exchange.

Logos: measure, proportion, reason; the principle of the cosmos according to the philosopher Heraclitus.

lustral basin: a pool or other container for water used for ritual cleansing.

Lykurgus: Spartan reformer to whom the constitution (the Great Rhetra) and institutions of Sparta are attributed.

magazine: long, narrow storage room characteristic of Bronze Age palaces.

medize: to take the side of the Medes (Persians).

megaron: a typical building form of the Mycenaeans, consisting of a rectangular room or rooms with a porch and entrance on the short side and a central hearth.

Menelaus: Mycenaean king, husband of Helen, whose abduction by Paris of Troy caused the Trojan War.

mess, or **sysitia**: the fundamental institution of adult Spartan male life; men were elected to a mess at the end of the agoge and lived, fought, and ate together until the age of 30, after which they could establish individual households, but they continued to eat and fight together; continued membership in a mess was conditional upon making contributions to the common meals and was a prerequisite for full Spartan citizenship.

metope: the square area between the triglyphs in a Doric frieze.

metic: a legal resident alien; metics were subject to registration and the metic tax, were obliged to serve in the military, and were required to have a citizen sponsor; metics were not allowed to own land or house and, except in unusual circumstances, neither they nor their descendants could become citizens.

miasma: ritual pollution from the shedding of blood; it afflicted not only those who killed another person, intentionally or otherwise, but also women after the shedding of blood in childbirth. If not ritually cleansed, miasma could bring bring afflictions upon the individual, his/her entire community, and even subsequent generations.

Minyans: name given to first Greek-speakers in Greece, traditionally dated to about 2000 BCE.

Neodamodes: in Sparta, a helot who had been freed for service as a hoplite.

naukleros: a trader who owned his own ships.

Navarchy: supreme command of a fleet, office held by Lysander in Sparta.

Neolithic Revolution: shift from hunting and gathering to agriculture (plant and animal husbandry); occurred in Greece in about the seventh millennium B.C.E.

niello technique: painting in metal, a technique employed on objects in the Shaft Graves at Mycenae; niello, a compound of silver, copper, lead, and sulphur, was used to create figures in the metal; the technique appears earlier in Byblos and probably came to Greece from Syria.

nomothetes: a lawgiver; in Athens, a member of a committee charged with revision of legislation.

nuraghe: Sardinian conical Bronze Age defensible stone tower, with single or multiple towers, often surrounded by a village.

obai: a political division in Sparta mentioned in the Great Rhetra.

obsidian: a volcanic glass that can take a very sharp edge and was used as a cutting tool (still used today in some surgery); its source in the Greek Neolithic was mainly on the island of Melos.

Odeon: a building on the slope of the Athenian Acropolis in which musical performanaces took place; it was part of the Periclean building program.

oikos: household, family; it encompassed the property of the household as well, including buildings, equipment, animals, and slaves.

oikistes: the founder of a Greek colony who led the colonization; he became the leading citizen of the new polis and received heroic honors after his death.

oka: a Mycenaean term for military units.

Oracle of Apollo at Delphi: one of the most important Greek oracles; it offered advice to states more often than to individuals, and is credited with involvement in political decisions such as the constitution of Sparta (Great Rhetra) and the colonization of Cyrene.

ostracism: a ten-year period of exile decided by a special vote of the Athenian Assembly as a precaution against the return of tyranny; the ostracised man retained his citizenship and his property.

Owls: the coinage bearing the image of the owl of Athena introduced by the tyrant Hippias; it remained the basic Athenian coin until the second century B.C.E. and was widely used throughout the Greek world.

paidonomos: Spartan official in charge of all males between the ages of seven and thirty.

parabasis: stepping aside; in a Greek comedy, the formal section in which the chorus steps outside the framework of dramatic illusion and addresses the audience directly on behalf of the playwright.

pediment: the triangular gable on a building; on temples the pediment usually bore sculptural decorations.

Peloponnesian War: Greek war between Athens and its allies and Sparta and its allies, 431–404 B.C.E.

Pentecontaetia: the "Fifty Years," the name applied to the condensed account of Thucydides of the period between the Persian and the Peloponnesian wars.

Pentecosiomedimi: the highest of the property classes in Solon's reforms; men whose property yielded 500 bushels who were eligible to serve as archons and treasurers.

perioikoi: in Sparta, "dwellers-round-about;" Dorian inhabitants of outlying villages, allied to Sparta and self-governing in local matters, but without citizen rights in Sparta; they served in the Spartan army and probably worked as craftsmen and traders as well as farmers.

Pheidon: tyrant of Argos, early seventh century, defeated Spartans in the battle of Hysiae.

phratry: a political division in Athens, perhaps a fictive "brotherhood"; acceptance by the phratry of his father was the mark of legitimacy for an Athenian male.

pillar-and-door partitions: an architectural feature of the Minoan palaces, in which walls were made up of a series of pillars with inset doors that could be opened or closed as the weather dictated.

pithoi: large clay storage jars for agricultural products such as grain, oil, wine, and olives.

Plato: Athenian philosopher, pupil of Socrates; his written works took the form of dialogues; although his primary aim was philosophical and not historical, his dialogues are often used as historical sources, especially the *Republic* and *Laws*.

polemarch: in Athens, one of the ten archons, who originally served as the commander-in-chief of the army; after the reforms of Kleisthenes there were ten generals, one elected from each tribe.

Polis (plural **poleis**): Greek city-state; it was autonomous and controlled a territory, usually consisting of an urban center and countryside (*chora*) with dependent villages. It developed to the point of recognition in the eighth century B.C.E.

Propylaea: the monumental gateway to the Athenian acropolis, part of the Periclean building program.

proskynesis: the oriental practice of doing obeisance to the king; the act may range from prostration before the ruler to blowing him a kiss; introduced into Greek life by Alexander.

pornai: prostitutes.

proxenos: an "official friend" of a state; a local person who served as a representative of Athens in his own polis; a practice especially adopted by the Athenians to control the empire; the office (the *proxenia*) was awarded by the Athenians as an honor to the Macedonian king Alexander I.

prytany: the rotating body of 50 members from the Council of 500 that served as the executive each month of the Attic year.

Ptolemies: the ruling family in Hellenistic Egypt.

rhetra: a Spartan law; see also Great Rhetra.

satrap: the governor of a Persian satrapy, or province.

Sea Peoples: invaders of Egypt who came in search of land to settle around 1200; the Egyptian pharoah Ramses III claimed to thave driven them back in 1186. Among them only the Philistines have been identified; some were probably Mycenaean refugees.

Second Intermediate Period: a period in Egyptian history (ca. 1785–1550 B.C.) when the Hyksos (foreign princes, probably from the Levant) invaded and took over control.

Seisachtheia: in Athens, the "Shaking-off-of-Burdens" enacted by the reforms of Solon; it removed the *horoi* (see "*horoi*"), freed those enslaved for debt, and abolished debt slavery in the future.

Seleucids: the ruling family in Hellenistic Asia, primarily the areas that had belonged to the Persian Empire.

shaft graves: burials in large rectangular shafts in the ground; at Mycenae a group of especially rich shaft grave burials dated to 1600–1500 with grave goods showing the influence of a wide range of different cultures from Anatolia to Central Europe; they were surrounded by two circles of stones in the Mycenaean period.

Social War: a war between allies

Sophist: a traveling teacher of rhetoric who offered instruction for a fee in a number of different subjects in addition to public speaking, including grammar, music, poetry, and philosophy.

sophrosyne: self-control.

Stoa: a building with an open colonnade on one side.

symmachia: military alliance.

symposium: a male dinner and drinking party; symposia served as the central focus of elite male social and political life.

synoikism: the unification, political or physical, of Greek settlements; in the case of Attica, the unification was a political union of towns attributed to the mythical hero Theseus, but probably occurring during the Dark Age.

Systitia: Spartan common men's messes.

thalassocracy: control over the seas.

Thesmophoria: the annual festival of the goddess Demeter; the most widely celebrated Greek religious festival, it assured the fertility of the grain and of women by various rituals that lasted for several days (varying according to the polis); it was restricted to women.

thesmothetes: Six of the ten archons in Athens who acted as recorders of judicial decisions and as court officials.

Thetes: the lowest of the property classes instituted by the reforms of Solon; men with property that yielded less than 200 bushels, including those without land; they were eligible to attend the Assembly. This class gained significant political rights by the development of democracy in the fifth century.

tholos tomb: a beehive-shaped tomb constructed on the principle of a corbelled arch found in mainland Greece; they first appeared in Messenia around 1500.

triglyph: in a Doric frieze, the element between the metopes that is divided into three parts by two vertical grooves.

Trireme: a Greek warship with three banks of rowers, basic to fifth-centure fleets.

trittys: a third of a tribe; Kleisthenes divided Attica into 30 trittyes, one third in each region, and constructed the tribes by taking one trittys from each region.

type site: an archaeological site that is used as representative of a group of sites that are similar in date, culture.

Tyrtaeus: archaic Greek poet who worked at Sparta at the time of the Second Messenian War; perhaps a Spartan.

wanax: Greek word for "lord"; in the Mycenaean period it referred to the ruler; in Homer and later Greek it was ususlly applied only to the gods, but it was used for the sons of the basileus on Cyprus (Plural *wanakes*).

Wappenmünzen: "heraldic coins"; they were the earliest Athenian coins, probably instituted by Peisistratus for the payment of mercenaries and long-term contracts in the building program.

Zeugitae: the third of the property classes instituted by the reforms of Solon; they were men whose property yielded 200 to 300 bushels; the word perhaps refers to their ability to maintain a yoke of oxen., or to their hoplite status; they were eligible for minor offices.

ziggurat: the traditional Mesopotamian pyramidal platform of a shrine.

Zoroastrianism: the dualistic religion of Persia initiated by Zoroaster, in which the god of Justice and Truth, Ahura Mazda, fought against the god of Evil and the Lie, Ahriman; the religion emphasized the purity and value of fire.

MAP EXERCISES

The blank outline maps that follow may be used for map exercises or as practice maps for qiuzzes.

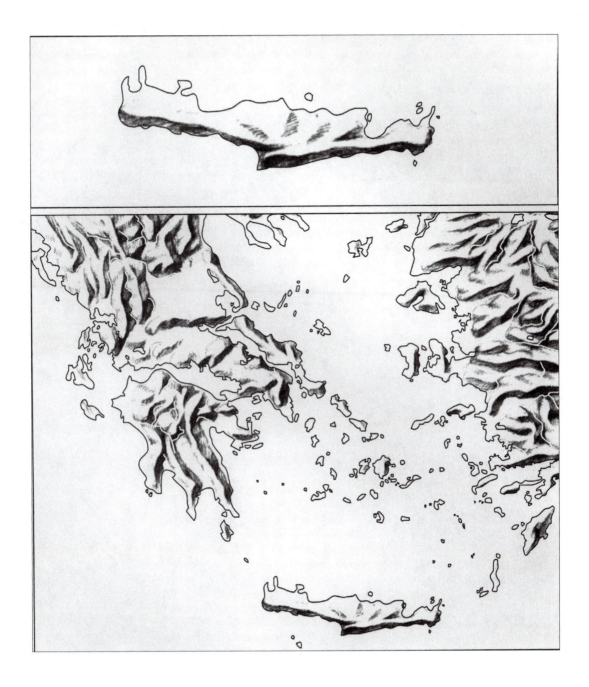

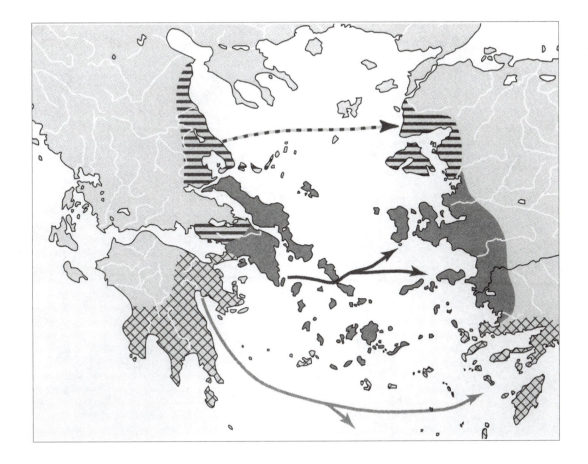

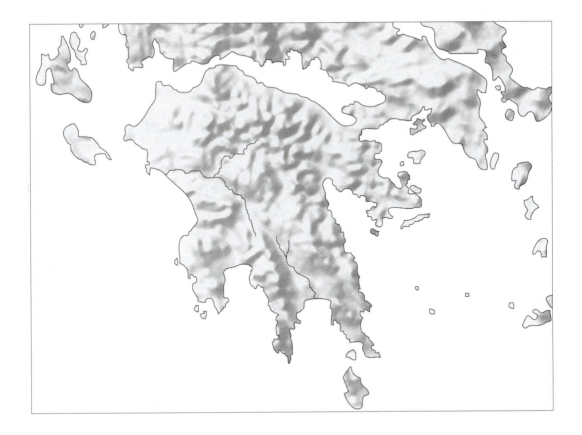

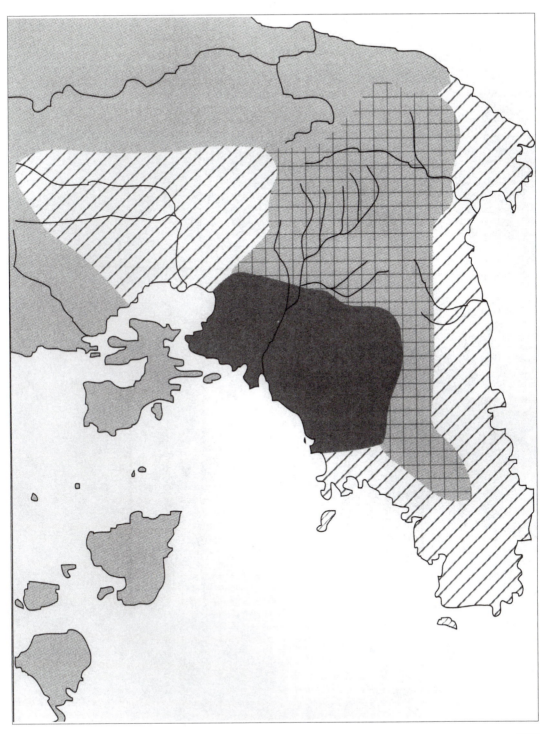

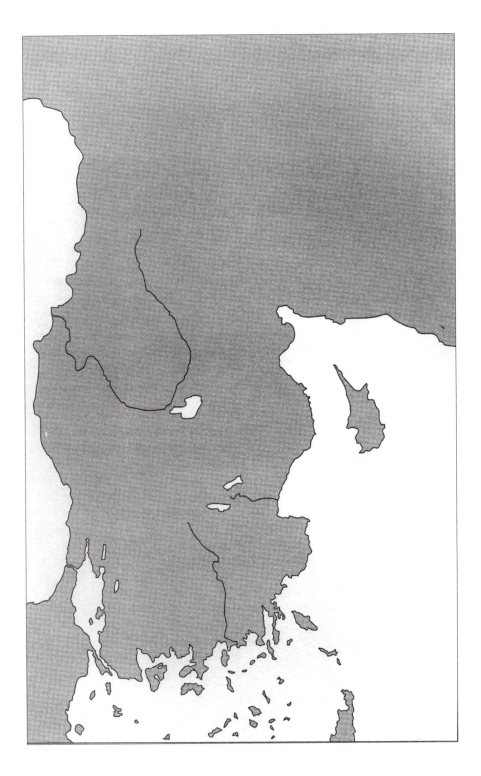

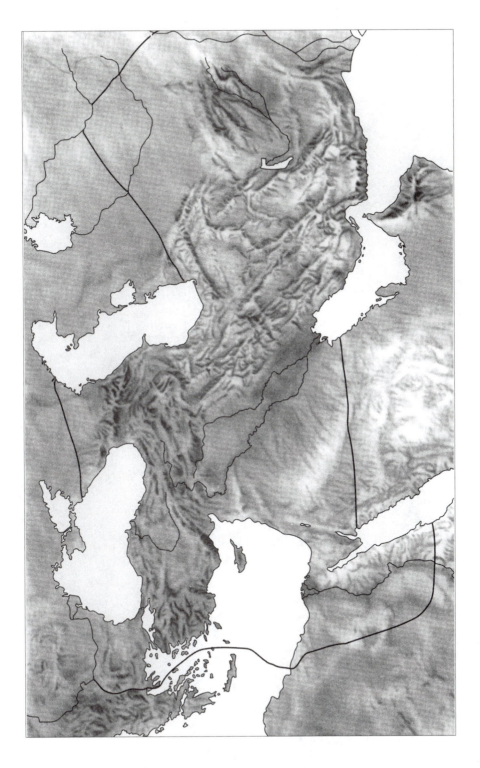

383

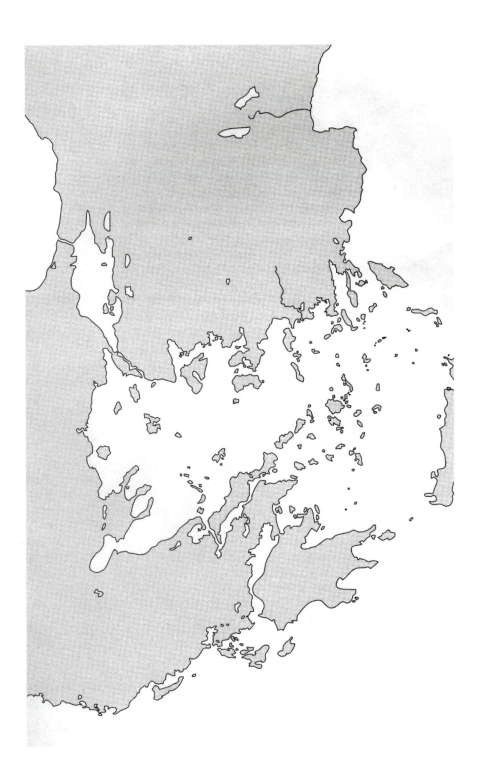

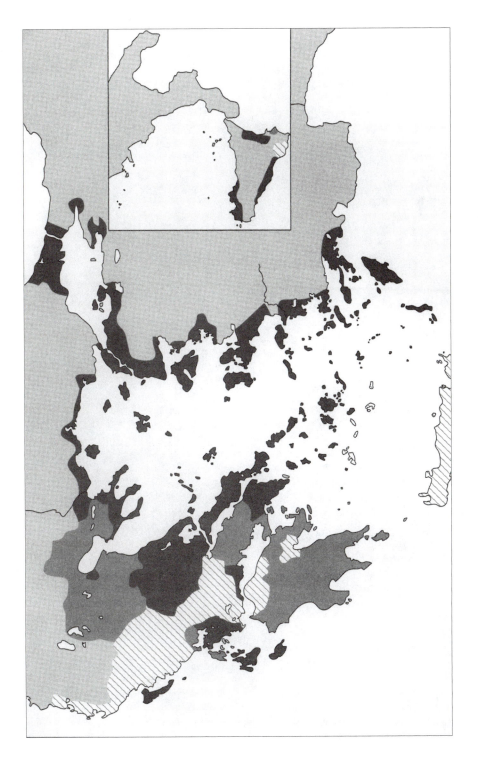

389

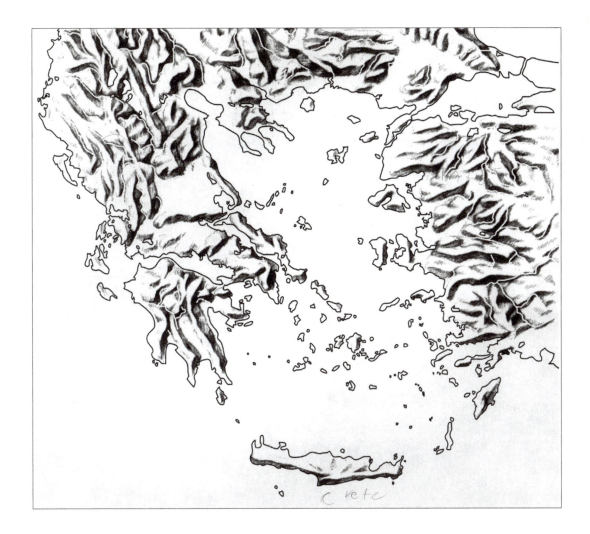

Crete

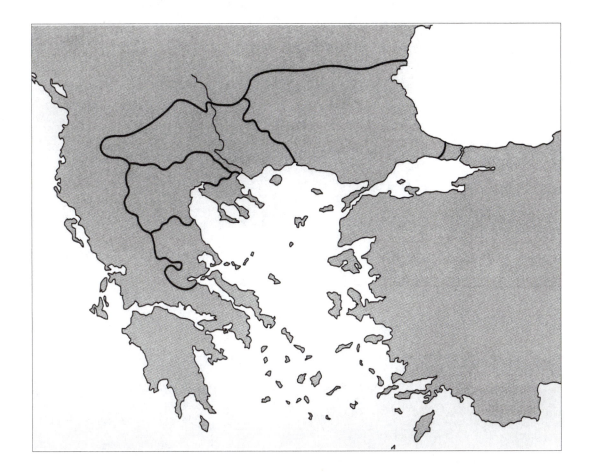

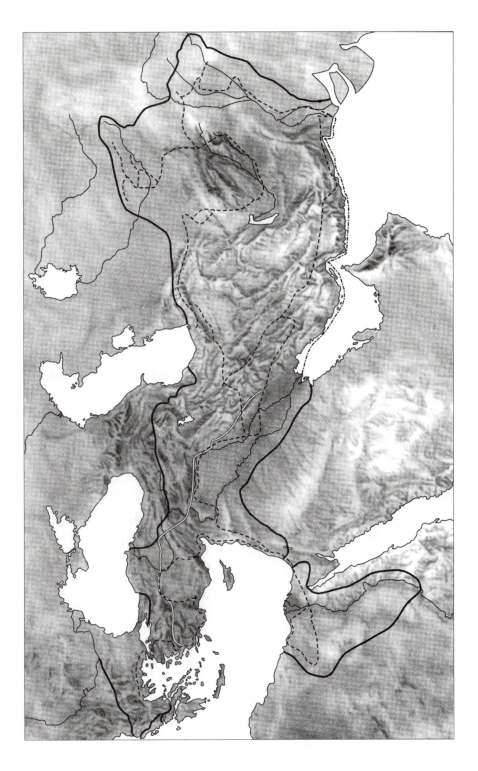

395

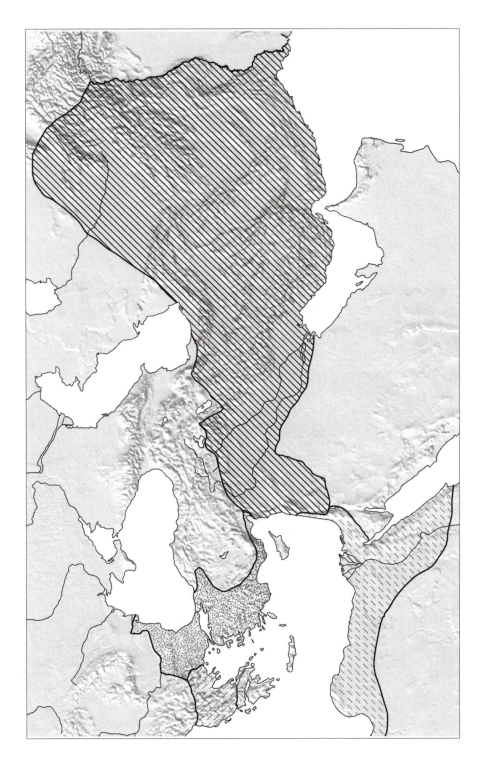

397

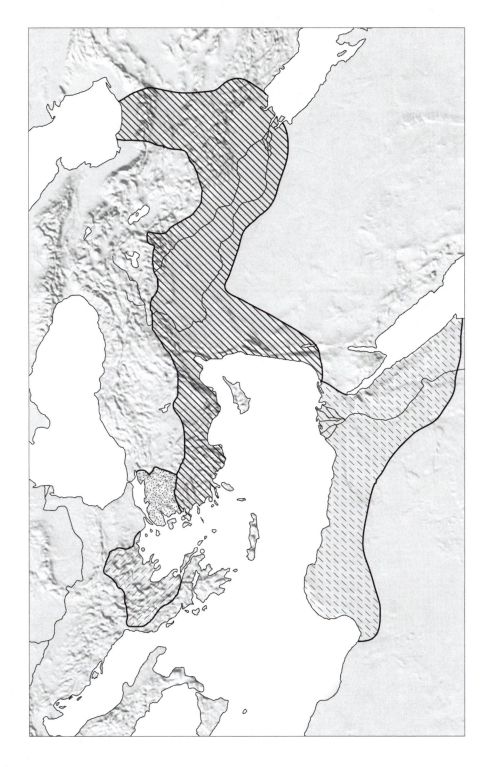

399

INDEX